Laurel's Kitchen

Recipes

Laurel Robertson
Carol Flinders &
Brian Ruppenthal

LAUREL'S KITCHEN RECIPES

Ten Speed Press, Berkeley, California

Some of the material in the chapter on bread appeared in a different form in The Laurel's Kitchen Bread Book (Random House, 1984).

TEN SPEED PRESS
P.O. Box 7123
Berkeley, California 94707

Library of Congress Cataloging in Publication Data
Robertson, Laurel.
Laurel's kitchen recipes / by Laurel Robertson, Carol Flinders & Brian Ruppenthal
p. cm.
An abridged ed. of: The new Laurel's kitchen. c1986.
Includes index.
ISBN 0-89815-537-1
1. Vegetarian cookery. 2. Nutrition. I. Flinders, Carol.
II. Ruppenthal, Brian. III. Robertson, Laurel.
New Laurel's kitchen. IV. Title.
TX837.R62 1993 641.5'636 93-1018

PRINTED IN CANADA

3 4 5 6 7 8 9 10 99 98 97 96

CAUTIONARY NOTE *The recipes, instructions, and nutritional information contained in this book are in no way intended as a substitute for medical counseling. Please do not attempt self-treatment of a medical problem without consulting a physician.*

For our teacher, Eknath Easwaran, who understood the appeal in the eyes of a glossy black calf on its way to the slaughterhouse many years ago and inspired us, and thousands of others like us, to give the gift of life.

Introduction

Since *Laurel's Kitchen* made its first appearance some sixteen years ago, it keeps turning up in places we'd never have predicted. A Carmelite nun wrote last year from her convent in Santa Clara, for instance, to tell us about the small miracle it had worked in her life. The role of head cook rotates among all the nuns in her small community, she explained, and she knew that the weeks when she was in charge of feeding everyone had long been regarded as only just this side of Lent itself in terms of austerity. With *Laurel's Kitchen* in hand, though, she had learned to prepare meals that everyone loved. In rich gratitude – for it had meant so much to her to be able to please her sisters and nourish them well – she wrote to invite us to her Jubilee, the anniversary of her fiftieth year as a Carmelite, and to tell us she was sure we had the blessing of the mother founder of Carmel, Teresa of Avila, who taught that God can be found not just on one's knees in prayer but in the kitchen, too, among the pots and pans.

We liked that a lot.

Gratifying in a different way was the book's appearance in June, 1989, in the magazine *Mother Jones*. In an eloquently written article called "The Great Boomer Bust," journalist Katy Butler outlined a discovery that an entire generation has had to absorb in the past several years: the realization that people who are now in their sixties and seventies are enjoying considerably higher standards of living, for the most part, than their children or grandchildren ever will. Soberly, she charted the "disguised but deepening depression" that the national economy has undergone over the past twenty-some years and the far-reaching consequences of our failure to come to grips with it.

Looking hard at her own life, at diminishing financial expectations and unrealistic spending patterns – looking, too, at her friends' lives, at the indebtedness they were incurring and their frenetic efforts to conceal this even from themselves – she had come to see that in the wild scramble to spend, and to lay hands on more money to spend, time itself had become as scarce as money – and that her home was little more than a launching pad and her neighborhood a collection of strangers. She began to suspect that her restlessness for a life she would never have was cheating her of the life she did have. Thoughtful now, and genuinely alert to alternatives, she sat over lentil soup with her brother, a perpetual student who had made his own peace with scarcity, and listened closely when he said, "If it's by choice, and it's not overwhelming, having no money can be a way of entering more deeply into your life."

Shortly afterwards, Ms. Butler began to downsize. She quit her full-time job as a reporter and took up free-lance work. She had her name removed from catalog subscription lists and started using her library card. She sold her ancient, temperamental luxury automobile and bought a lower-maintenance used car – boring to drive, but it got better gas mileage. In addition, she bought a copy – also used – of *Laurel's Kitchen* . . .

We won't fuss over how she could have gotten along without the book up until then; we loved that she could just say "and I bought *Laurel's Kitchen*," as though her readers would understand implicitly what that gesture meant. In case they didn't, though, she goes on to make it abundantly and lyrically clear. Enough of paraphrase – let the author speak for herself:

> I began facing the life I had, not the life I dreamed of having or thought I had the right to have. I turned off lights. I started to cut the link between consumption and pleasure, between consumption and self-worth. And that paved the way for some unexpected things. I recycled – because it saved money on garbage pickup – and ate less meat and more beans. I walked downtown instead of getting into the car. Having less money forced me to get to know my neighbors, and a network of borrowing emerged. My nextdoor neighbor Mack, a salesman, lost his job and borrowed my computer to type résumés; when my husband's car broke down, Mack lent us his . . . One weekend last fall, my husband and I came home from a walk and saw four of our neighbors standing outside Mack's house around a pyramid of lawn sod.

"Found it at the dump," said George, the young contractor who lives down the block. He picked up a roll of sod, laid it out in Mack's front yard, and jumped up and down to set it.

. . ."There's plenty left," said George. "Dig up your yard, and we'll do it too." They all carried their tools around the geraniums that serve as a hedge between our houses . . . soon our weed patch was covered with a quilt of green, its nap running every which way. Jan knelt down with clippers and snipped along the edge of our walk as though cutting out the armhole of a dress. . . I squeezed lemons into a jug of iced water, and we sat around on the fresh new grass in the afternoon sunlight with no sense that anything needed to be repaid. I shut my eyes and felt no need to compare our block, held in its growing net of mutual favors and borrowings, with anything else I'd ever known.

Nearly thirty-six million Americans are living below the poverty line – two million more in 1991 than in 1990. Since 1985, the number of hungry people in the United States has increased by half. One child out of five lives in a home where there is not enough to eat and no medical care. The bubble of the eighties has burst – even those who can still afford to eat at the marvelously innovative bistros that were the talk of the last decade are finding that it isn't as much fun now, because to get in the door you often have to step around whole families who are laying out their bedrolls for the night. We are a democratic nation, and as the chasm opens out wider and wider between those who are making it and those who are not, I know very few people – even among those who are on the safe side – who feel comfortable with the situation. Perhaps it's because everyone has friends now, a brother or sister, a daughter or a nephew, who have lost their footing and slipped through the safety nets we'd thought firmly in place.

The occasion for this particular edition of *Laurel's Kitchen* should be clear by now. I am glad that Katy Butler was able to get a secondhand copy of the book for reduced price, but I know, too, that there aren't nearly enough used copies available for the number of people who need it today. In recognition, then, of the severity of our times, we are issuing this distillation – this affordable digest – of the original. The complete work is still available, and in 1996 we hope to issue a new twentieth anniversary edition, but for now, here it is: *Laurel's Kitchen* for the trenches, for the *re*-trenches – for digging out and for discovering in the process that a simpler life, one that respects the needs of a whole planet full of

other lives, has its own incalculably rich rewards. More and more now the words of that old Shaker song seem to say it perfectly:

> 'Tis a gift to be simple, 'tis a gift to be free,
> 'Tis a gift to come round where you want to be –
> And when we come round to the place just right,
> We will be in the garden of love and delight.

A garden, or maybe just a well-functioning neighborhood, where people keep an eye out for one another, and bring a casserole around when someone's sick, or see that her kids get to school. A neighborhood that stretches on out into a city and a region and a nation whose first and last concern is kindness to one another.

. . . See you there.

Table of Contents

Introduction

Questions and Answers

Recipes & Menus

The New Laurel's Kitchen Food Guide

Every day include
4 servings

Whole Grains

Whole-grain bread (1 slice) or
cooked grain – like rice –
or noodles (½ cup)

High-Carbohydrate Vegetables

Artichokes, potatoes, sweet
potatoes (1 medium);
beets, carrots, parsnips, winter
squash, turnips (1 cup);
corn (1 ear or ½ cup)

and
2 servings

Low-Calorie Vegetables

A tomato; green beans, cabbage,
cauliflower, leeks, cucumber, eggplant,
mushrooms, peppers (1 cup);
lettuce (2 cups)

and
1 serving

Super-Vegetables

Dark leafy greens (¾ cup cooked);
edible-pod peas, brussels sprouts,
broccoli, asparagus, okra,
bok choy (1 cup).

Legumes

Cooked dry beans, lentils,
split peas (½ cup)

and
1 serving

Dairy Foods

Milk or yogurt (1 cup);
cheese (3 oz.);
cottage cheese (½ cup)

Nuts & Seeds

Fruit

Eggs

add
ample
servings
to fill out
calorie
needs

Welcome to Laurel's Kitchen

The people who worked together to make the first *Laurel's Kitchen* weren't born vegetarian, and we came from many ethnic backgrounds. Our first vegetarian meals together were a world of discovery – Sultana's spanakopita, Carol's cannelloni, Leela's maloshyam, Sarah's chillaquillas – wonderful dishes we had never tasted before. We were sure that if others could have a collection of these recipes they'd find switching to meatless meals as easy and satisfying as we had: that was the beginning of *Laurel's Kitchen*. The first handbound printing of 5,000 copies sold out in a month, and, more than a million copies later, the book is often called "the bible of vegetarianism."

We have been eating deliciously together for two decades now, and the children who came along during that time are growing up, straight and strong, tall and smart: no meat, and not a dud in the lot. The proof *is* in the pudding! It gives a person confidence.

The recipes in this book are drawn from our daily cooking – a dozen families and many good friends. If you already eat along vegetarian, whole-foods lines, these dishes will fit gracefully into your repertoire; they should be especially helpful if you are trying for lower-fat meals. If whole-foods cookery is new to you, the following pages will ease your period of transition. There are some happy surprises, some new ideas, but all in all, this is satisfying everyday home cooking, straightforward to prepare, good to eat.

If you check our food guide on the facing page, you will see how easy it is to get all the nutrients you need no matter what your eating pattern is. Well – almost! We are talking about a variety of fresh, whole, natural foods, eaten temperately. For health, it isn't only meat that gets phased out: stripped foods like white rice and white flour have no place; refined sugar in its myriad forms is reserved for special occasions; greasy, salty items (especially the ones sold in plastic bags) get the boot. Such a diet promotes health both for the eater and for the planet: fresh, natural foods do not waste petroleum in travel or energy in processing, nor does their packaging waste space in the landfill.

❢

Beyond that, though, even when the food is nutritious, and even when the needs of the planet are taken into account, people are not just bodies that run better on higher-octane gas and worse on cheap stuff. Cooking with full attention and care benefits the cook, very much. And meals that are prepared with informed concern for our needs, served to us with love in a serene setting and in joyful company, nourish best. Children raised on such fare have a special security; adults face their days with special confidence. This book is about food and nutrition, but let's not forget that these intangibles are at least as important as protein and fiber.

Menus

No one feels limited to standard menus anymore, so we cooks have a lot more scope for creativity. Eaters too: around our place, you are nearly as likely to find someone's breakfast plate piled up with last night's broccoli as with cereal and toast. In the next few pages, we have gathered some combinations that seem good to us, keeping the Food Guide requirements in mind, and aiming to give ideas and inspiration as much as set menus.

BREAKFAST

Breakfast, of course, is a somewhat personal matter, but these are some of our favorites:

*Hot whole-grain cereal with
    low-fat milk, toasted
    sunflower seeds, and stewed
    prunes
Grapefruit*

*Homemade Granola with sliced
    fresh figs and
    buttermilk*

*Spoonbread
Black-eyed Peas Virginia Style
Fresh peaches*

*Cheese Blintzes
Applesauce*

*Boston Brown Bread
    with ricotta cheese
Boston Baked Beans
Pears*

*Masala Dosas
Yogurt
Mangoes*

*Whole Wheat Toast
Hot chocolate
Tangerines*

LUNCH

After a while, favorite meal patterns emerge – for us, nowhere more than at lunch. Basically, there are two:

Sandwiches accompanied by raw vegetables or fruit

Soup, salad, or a pot of beans with fresh bread, muffins, or polenta.

DINNER

A casserole or "hearty dish," flanked by a vegetable unless the casserole is already laced with them

A medley of steamed or stir-fried vegetables, served over or alongside rice, bulgur wheat, pasta, or potato (see page 224)

Soup with muffins, bread, rolls, or breadsticks

Two or more vegetables cooked separately, along with something hefty: the "vegetable plate" pattern.

Dinner too has its patterns, without anyone getting tired of the variations. Ours are always accompanied by a salad, with fresh fruit for dessert.

On the next few pages are a few sets of menus for lunch and dinner. Following our Food Guide, each day includes at least three servings of vegetables, one of which is a "super-veggie." Assuming that you've dispatched two servings of some kind of whole-grain food at breakfast – a bowl of cereal, for example, with a slice of toast – these lunch and dinner pairs illustrate ways of filling out the rest of the Food Guide plan.

The dishes in parentheses are optional: you can omit them or substitute something simpler. For instance, whole-grain rolls may be easy on baking day, but you could certainly serve brown rice, muffins, or noodles instead. Don't feel constrained by these menus – they are illustrations, meant to inspire and set your imagination free.

QUICK & EASY
(add salad & fruit)

Broccoli spears
Poppyseed Noodles

Sarah's Curried Rice
Steamed greens

Lazy Pirogi
Whole wheat noodles
Sugarsnap peas

Chinese Vegetables
Brown rice

Green soup in a cup
Persian Rice Salad

COMPANY
Eggplant Parmesan
Greek Cauliflower
Spinach and Mushroom Salad
French Bread
Apple Spice Ring with Yogurt Cheese Topping

Lasagna al Forno
Mixed green salad with Lemon-Parsley Dressing
Breadsticks
Yogurt Cheese Pie

Astonishing Salad
Cabbage Rolls Normande
Artichokes
Buttermilk Rolls
Strawberries and peaches and Anise Seed Cookies

SIMPLE FOR A CROWD
Sarah's Curried Rice
Raita
(Green vegetable &/or salad)
Melon slices

Minestrone
Bread or rolls
(Baked apples, yogurt)

SUMMER

Summertime, and the livin' really is easy: fruits and vegetables are at their best now. Think about meal-in-a-bowl salads made with perfect lettuce, or stir-fries of the newest arrivals in the garden: fresh tomatoes, corn, zucchini, eggplant, green beans, peas, tender chard, oh, my . . .

LUNCH FROM THE
GARDEN
Creamy Green Soup
Tomato-Pepper Salad
Oat Crackers

SOUTH INDIAN DINNER
Cauliflower Eggplant Curry
(Aviyal)
Brown rice
Coriander Chutney
Payasam

SOUP & SALAD LUNCH
Fresh Corn and Tomato Soup
California Tossed Salad
Whole-grain bread
Blackberries and yogurt

CHINESE DINNER
Sweet and Sour Tofu over
brown rice
Chinese Asparagus
Stir-fried Bok Choy
Plums

SIMPLE LUNCH
Sandwich of almond butter,
sprouts, and tomato with
Dijon mustard on whole-
grain bread
Apricots

GARDEN DINNER
Broiled half tomatoes
Baked Zucchini
Potatoes Tarragon
Spinach and Mushroom Salad

AUTUMN

With the fall, temperatures drop and appetites quicken. Many of the summer vegetables – eggplants for instance – stretch on into October. Local apples come in, streaked with red, then ripe yellow pears and golden pumpkins.

LUNCH
Ceci Salad
Breadsticks
Fresh figs

DINNER
(Early Autumn Fruit Soup)
Mushrooms Petaluma over
whole-wheat noodles
Slaw Chez Nous

SUNDAY LUNCH
Sebastopol Pizza
Green salad, Curry Dressing

DINNER
Eggplant Parmesan
Chard with Lemon Butter
Green Salad
(Whole-grain dinner rolls)

LUNCH
Soy Pâté sandwich on
whole-grain bread with
mustard and sprouts
Carrot Soup

SOUP & SALAD DINNER
Creamy Cauliflower Soup
Shades of Green Salad
Cracked-Wheat Rolls

LUNCH
Black Bean Soup
Light Rye Rolls
with Jack and Dill Spread
Fresh pears

DINNER
Bulgur Pilaf
Mustard greens
(with Wickedly Good
Sauce)
Carrot Salad
Baked Apples

WINTER

Hearty appetites need food to match: substantial soups, assertive root vegetables, squash and potatoes and broccoli and kale. Variety is limited during the cold months, but your presentation doesn't have to be.

LUNCH
Sarah's Curried Rice
Spinach sautéed with ginger
    and garlic
(Raita)
Orange slices

DINNER
Lentil Nut Loaf
Steamed collards
(Red Onion Raita)
Sandy's Gingered Squash
Baked Pears

HOT LUNCH
Lynne's Spiced Pumpkin Soup
Boston Brown Bread with
    ricotta
Apples

DINNER
Poppy Seed Noodles
Glazed carrots
Broccoli spears
Green Salad with Lemon-
    Parsley Dressing

SOUP & SALAD LUNCH
Catalina Potato Soup
Green salad, Avocado Dressing
Whole-grain crackers

DINNER
Tempeh à l'Orange over bulgur
    wheat
Savoy cabbage sauté
Green salad with Bright Minty
    Dressing

SPRING

Just when you think you'll come undone at the sight of one more coleslaw or rutabaga, a break in the weather brings a welcome change in fare. Now you can think fresh and young again: tender asparagus, crisp green spinach, new potatoes and peas, tiny whole beets and baby carrots. Fruits, of course, are citrus and winter-storage apples until the first strawberries appear.

BAKE-DAY LUNCH
Pine Nut Pinwheels
Asparagus Soup
Orange and grapefruit slices

DINNER
Artichokes Tellicherry
Whole-grain pasta with
    Stroganoff Sauce
Spinach Salad

LUNCH
Mock Rarebit on whole-grain
    toast
Russian Salad

DINNER
Spinach Crepes
Green salad with
    Orange-Parsley Dressing
Fresh raspberries and yogurt

MIDDLE EAST LUNCH
Pita Bread stuffed with Neat
    Balls, shredded lettuce, red
    cabbbage, grated carrots
Xergis

DINNER
Asparagus spears
Green Rice Casserole
(Sesame-glazed Parsnips)
Butter lettuce salad
Fresh strawberries

HOLIDAY FEASTS AND ETHNIC DINNERS

FOURTH OF JULY
Vegetable platter with French
    Onion Tofu Mayonnaise
Finocchio Salad
Boston Baked Beans
(Corn on the cob)
(French Bread)
Watermelon
(Blueberry Cheese Pie)

ITALIAN DINNER
Antipasto
Cannelloni
(Peas with mushrooms and
    fresh basil)
(Breadsticks)
Fresh fruit with Marsala

CHRISTMAS DINNER
Relish tray
Cranberry Squash
Brussels Sprouts with
    Chestnuts
Wild Rice
Pineapple-orange ambrosia
Herb Puffs
Figgy Pudding

PASSOVER DINNER
Spinach and Barley
    Dumplings in broth
(Cabbage Rolls Normande)
Potato Carrot Kugel
Dilled Cucumber
Yogurt Salad
Braised Beet Greens
Yogurt Cheese Pie

THANKSGIVING DINNER
Tomato Aspic on lettuce
    leaves
(with Mock Sour Cream)
Creamed Spinach
Large mushroom caps filled
    with Stuffing
Mashed potatoes with Good
    Gravy
Cranberry sauce or relish
Buttermilk Rolls
Mock Mince Pie

GREEK DINNER
Spanakopita
(Green Beans Hellenika)
Greek Salad
Melon and figs

A note to beginners

There are a lot of recipes in this book, but they aren't difficult, and the tips tucked in here and there will be helpful to you if you are not yet utterly at home in the kitchen. The chapter introductions are a gold mine of useful information.

Many of our recipes begin with suggestions about how to serve or vary them. Each recipe gives the number of normal servings, or the amount the recipe makes.

The first time you prepare a dish, read the recipe through carefully to the very end to make sure of the directions and the timing. (This is a step experienced chefs would never omit, but one that beginners sometimes don't think of.) Our instructions are step-by-step and all the ingredients are listed; we never ask for sophisticated techniques. If you follow the directions, you'll do fine!

When you start to work, gather up all ingredients the recipe calls for, so that they are near at hand. In a list of ingredients you may come across one that's already prepared – if a recipe calls for 3 cups broccoli florets, for example, cut the broccoli into small

GOOD & EASY

Porridge
Pancakes
Stewed Apples
Cinnamuffins

Sandwiches
Smoothie
Sprouts
Greek Salad
Coleslaw
Carrot Salad
Persian Rice Salad

Golden Noodle Soup
Creamy Green Soup

Corn Chowder
French Bakes
Steamed vegetables
Chinese Vegetables
Greek Cauliflower
Corn on the cob
Baked Zucchini
Quick Vegetable Relish
Mock Sour Cream
Lemon Butter

Poppyseed Noodles
Potato Poppers
Polenta
Bulgur wheat
Green Rice Casserole
Rice Lentil Polou
Stuffing

Baked Apples
Diane's Apple Crisp
Vanilla Pudding
Oatmeal School Cookies
Peanut Butter Bars

pieces and measure them before you begin following the main instructions.

Just because you are a beginner doesn't mean you can't develop some fancy specialties, particularly things you really like to eat.

Choosing a recipe

So many considerations come into play when you plan a meal: first, probably, what have we got on hand? If you've just come back from the garden with a fragrant armload of summer bounty, the meal will build itself easily around that. If it's late winter, and you're getting kind of tired of broccoli and kale, maybe your energy will go into trying to make the *rest* of the dinner fun and interesting. Can we afford to splurge on wild rice? Is there time to bake Apple Crisp?

Whatever else you are thinking about, though, in the back of your mind you remember the needs of the eaters – and this is what gives home cooks a special glow that no restaurant chef can match. You don't load your family with fatty food or sweets just to stoke your ego on their praise. You make sure they get their nutrients, even if it takes sleight of hand. You keep a watchful eye on the budget. And there are other kinds of needs . . . Michael has been having finals all week. Melanie's lost her skateboard. The dog chewed up Francisco's new boot, and Shanti's tennis elbow is acting up. Everyone needs a break. What would be fun to do?

In our family, we might make pizza, if there is time, or bake Gingerbread for dessert. In summer when the tomatoes are at their best, we'd have a Mexican Feast with tortillas, Refritos, Salsa, and all the trimmings. Once in spring, dinner might be spinach salad followed by a mountain of strawberries for shortcake. To celebrate a graduation, many hands together make Cannelloni. And so it goes, at your house and at ours, each one unique because the people in it are very, very special.

For everyday cooking, these are the recipes we choose over and over again:

RECIPES WE RELY ON DAY TO DAY

Basic Bread
Better-Butter
Yogurt
Porridge
Breakfast Beans
Old-Fashioned Pancakes

Bean spreads
Green salads
Carrot Salad
Coleslaw

Golden Noodle Soup
Vegetable Soup
Minestrone
the Green Soups
Corn Chowder
Kale Potato Soup

Broccoli spears
Steamed greens
Chard Cheese Pie
Tomato Kale
Baked potatoes
Baked squash
Creamed greens
Chinese Vegetables

Homemade Ketchup
Mock Sour Cream
Tomato Sauces
Lemon Butter
Lasagna al Forno

Plain brown rice
Spoonbread
Polenta

Spanish Rice
Green Rice Casserole
Spaghetti
Tennessee Corn Pone
Stuffing
Refritos

Baked Apples
Vanilla Pudding
Banana Bread
Gingerbread

FAVORITES

Buttermilk Bread
French Bread
Better-Butter
Oatmeal Pancakes
Sebastopol Pizza

Garbanzo Spread
Astonishing Salad
Sweet Potato Salad
Fruity Beety

Fresh Corn and Tomato Soup
Favorite Green Soups
Black Bean Soup

Quick Vegetable Relish
Chinese Asparagus
Green Beans Hellenika
Corn on the cob
Crumby Greens
Parsnip Patties
French Bakes
Creamed Spinach
Zucchini Provençal
Sandy's Gingered Squash

Ratatouille
Cauliflower Eggplant Curry
Lasagna al Forno
Crepes
Spanakopita
Pizza
Stuffed Chard Leaves
Chillaquillas
Fiesta
Uppuma
Spanish Rice
Sarah's Curried Rice
Pilaf Avgolemono

Diane's Apple Crisp
Oatmeal School Cookies
Mock Mince Pie

CERTIFIED KID-PLEASERS

Pancakes
Smoothie
Tofu Bars

Golden Noodle Soup
Potato Cheese Soup
Green Potatoes for Six
French Bakes
Green soups

Lasagna al Forno
Crepes
Cheese Blintzes
Potato Poppers
Rice Lentil Polou

Apple Crisp
Peanut Butter Bars

Questions & Answers

Why eat whole foods?

Percent loss:

34%	Protein
97	Fiber

VITAMINS

39	Vitamin E
57	Folacin
77	Riboflavin*
83	Niacin*
66	Vitamin B-6
55	Pantothenic acid
90	Thiamin*

MINERALS

67	Calcium
44	Iron*
77	Magnesium
79	Potassium
62	Zinc

Whole grains are natural sources of these nutrients. Only the four marked with ★ are replaced commercially after whole wheat is refined to make white flour.

There are lots of ways to eat that provide all the nutrients human beings need for good health. People have tried many of them through time, and until the industrial revolution came along, most patterns worked well enough, so long as the eater got enough food.

When refined grains became the norm, though, vitamin and mineral deficiencies were suddenly common, along with bowel problems and bad teeth. When the West was won, and there was meat for all, both fat and oil got to be cheap too – cooking oil and cattlefeed are produced from the same seed – so their use increased, as did cancer, diabetes, and heart disease. When commercial agriculture and food processing replaced small farms and home cooking, many chemicals entered the food supply. Scientists are only now beginning to count the costs: human and animal diseases, depleted topsoil, polluted water.

We can turn this around: let's eat a variety of whole foods, in moderation – organically grown, whenever possible.

Variety provides interest for cooks and eaters alike; it also helps insure that your nutritional bases are covered. No one food can do it all – not even kale!

Whole foods provide the full range of vitamins, minerals, and fiber, "packaged" in a way that our physiology has evolved to use best. The newspapers are daily coming out with scary reports about some chemical or some lost nutrient that no one suspected could cause trouble. But if you aren't eating processed, refined foods, none of that affects you because the chemicals aren't in your food, and the nutrients are.

Moderation is good advice "in all things" – surely in every aspect of eating. We would like to slip in a special plea for moderating zeal. If we benefit from eating better, our health and happiness will glow. No need to try to convert others. No need to feel guilty if we backslide occasionally.

Is it important to buy organic food?

Vegetarians who prepare most of their meals at home from unprocessed basics – whole grains, beans, and fresh vegetables and fruits – and who avoid imported and out-of-season produce, have relatively few worries about chemical additives, adulterants, and pollutants in their food. Purchasing organically grown foods, when that is practical, improves your situation even further; you will avoid many chemical residues, and you'll be immune to scares like the EDB and ALAR alarms in recent years.

The situation with organics is changing rapidly. Even in California, just a few years ago organically grown produce was scarce, and if you found some, either it was pretty awful, or much too expensive, or both. Now, many grocers offer organic fruits and vegetables, grains and beans. Even large supermarkets often have a section devoted to organic produce. The federal government has begun to recognize organic agriculture as a viable option, and is working to establish uniform standards for what can and can't be called "organic." The momentum behind this depends a lot on how you and I spend our food dollars in the next few years, but we can hope for a better picture, which will be especially important for our children.

Safer food is definitely a consideration, but many people who choose organic food point to other advantages, too. Organic farming is sustainable: farmers must carefully build up their topsoil and protect it with soil-building plants like clover between cash crops. Commercial farms that rely on chemical fertilizers often let unprotected topsoil wash or blow away – a problem of national concern. Organic farmers and their employees don't get sick or die from exposure to pesticides and herbicides; nor do these chemicals drain off to pollute the neighboring water supply. Wild birds and other creatures are safer, too, when their food and water are

1. *White bread, rolls, crackers*
2. *Doughnuts, cookies, cakes*
3. *Alcoholic beverages*
4. *Whole milk*
5. *Hamburgers, cheeseburgers, etc.*
6. *Beef steaks, roasts*
7. *Soft drinks*
8. *Hot dogs, ham, lunch meat*
9. *Eggs*
10. *French fries, potato chips*

G. Block et al. 1985, American Journal
of Epidemiology 122:13–40

not contaminated. It is not only we and our families but our world, too, that benefits when we support organic farming.

What if you can't prepare all your food at home, from basics? One welcome development in natural-foods stores is a dazzling array of wholesome fast foods and convenience foods that honestly taste good. Often, they're prepared from organic whole grains, are low- or no-fat, and have no chemical additives at all. (The prices, though, so far, are for those who have more money than time.)

As time goes on, supermarkets and restaurants offer better options too. *The Nutrition Action Healthletter*, published by the Center for Science in the Public Interest (1501-16th Street, NW, Washington, DC 20036), fills its pages with reliable, up-to-date news about what choices are most healthful in the mainstream.

An aside on the subject of contaminants in our food: though pesticide residues and certain approved additives do affect our health, what we do in the kitchen can have even more influence. Being careful with fat, for example, protects against cancer better than avoiding every chemical additive. Food poisoning causes many deaths each year, and a lot of days in bed with what we think is "flu." At home, we can prevent this by not leaving perishable food at room temperature (between 40° and 140°F), and by keeping surfaces, dishcloths, and chopping boards clean. Such a simple measure as being sure to wash hands before cooking (and eating) effectively helps keep colds and flu from spreading.

How will this impact my health?

DIET	HEART DISEASE	DIABETES	CANCERS	HYPERTENSION
Have plenty of: *Green leafy* *vegetables* *Whole grains*	*Soluble fiver from fruits, vegetables, and legumes lowers blood cholesterol naturally.[1]*	*Water soluble fiber lowers blood cholesterol,[1,7] and helps even out and control blood sugar levels.*	*Fiber, especially insoluble, "cleans" intestine which reduces toxin production by microbes.[12,13]*	*Vegetables, fruits, legumes have potassium and other minerals that help lower blood pressure.[17]*
Avoid excess of: *Food in general* *Fat as percent of calories* *Protein as percent of calories*	*Slim body lessens burden on heart; lowers blood fats (including cholesterol).[2]*	*Reduced body weight, reduced fat intake, improve sensitivity to insulin.[2,8]*	*High fat intake promotes cancer formation and growth.[13]*	*Reduced weight helps control blood pressure.[17] Reduced protein intake lessens burden on kidney.[18]*

LIFESTYLE

	HEART DISEASE	DIABETES	CANCERS	HYPERTENSION
Mental equilibrium *Even-mindedness* *Good concentration* *Postive outlook*	*"Type A Behavior" and "Hurry Sickness" are major risk factors for heart disease.[3]*	*Lack of mental equilibrium leads to loss of blood sugar control.[9] Improved mental control keeps stress from raising blood sugar level.*	*"Anger-prone personality" is linked to cancer incidence, fear of breast cancer is linked to breast cancer incidence.[14]*	*Agressiveness, competitiveness, greed, depression linked to hypertension, perhaps causally.[3,19]*
Exercise *Aerobic* *Stretching*	*Aerobic exercise increases "good" chol. in blood (HDL); reduces "bad" (LDL).[4] Yoga asanas lower muscular tension.[5]*	*Moderate, regular exercise helps to control blood sugar levels.[10]*	*Regular exercise probably helps against bowel cancer by lowering transit time.[15]*	*Moderate and regular exercise can help reduce blood pressure.[17,20]*
Service *Love people, serve them* *Find joy in giving* *Be devoted to a higher cause*	*Antidote to Type A risk factors.[6]*	*Antidote to mental disequilibrium.[11]*	*Antidote to fear and anger which can be cancer promoters.[14,16]*	*Antidote to competitiveness, etc.[21]*

Notes for this page, and the following pages, are on page 39.

Can I live with low fat?

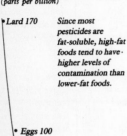
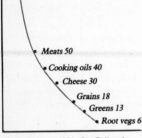
There are some objective reasons that people go for foods with lots of fat and oil. For one thing, flavor essences are mostly fat-soluble compounds, so these foods are tasty. Fat digests slowly, so fatty foods give a satisfying full feeling that lasts a long time. In the kitchen, cooking with fat is fast and easy. (If you were used to sautéing onions in plenty of oil, and have switched to using only a teaspoon – or none – you know what we mean.)

Alas, there's an enormous weight of scientific evidence now that a lower-fat diet is a healthier one. How low does it need to be? A wide range of opinion opens here, from the U.S. Dietary Guidelines at 30% of calories as fat, to some successful therapeutic diets at 10%. But most of us probably can just start working on "lower" because Americans (including vegetarians) average more than 40% from fat, and it takes plenty of ingenuity to coax the tastebuds gradually down the fat ladder from there. Yet, if we work gradually and persistently – not pushing so hard that there's rebellion – improvement is assured. Here are some things anyone can do to make the percentages better, cooking and eating:

🍃 Make the most of whole grains, beans, vegetables, and fruits. They are naturally very low in fat, and their fiber content gives a satified feeling. Reduce or eliminate meat, processed foods, and fried foods.

🍃 If you use milk products, choose lower-fat or skim; substitute them for higher-fat ones in cooking.

🍃 When planning a meal, if you don't want to cut out a "heavy" favorite, balance it with leaner dishes, thinking of the whole meal, the whole day, rather than trying to figure food by food.

🍃 If a food you eat every day is a concern, sometimes it is better to substitute something completely different instead of trying to Use Less. For example, skimping on the Better-Butter for our breakfast toast seemed an impossible deprivation (toast with lots of butter gets 50% of its calories from fat; with only a little, 30%; with none, about 12%). But switching to hot cereal with fruit and yogurt (less than 10%) proved to be just as enjoyable. What you spread on your bread can really make the fat mount up, whether it is at breakfast or other times.

🍃 Sandwiches with mayonnaise, cheese, or nut butters make a

meal that can be rich indeed. Look for alternatives in our Lunch section, page 111.

🍃 Explore ways to flavor food without fat: parsley and lemon, fresh basil, exotic vinegars, lemon or orange peel, yogurt, shoyu, flavorful mustards, spices. There are many suggestions in Sauces and Such, page 229.

🍃 Commercial salad dressings can be a mire of fat or weird chemicals. Try our alternatives, pages 129-132.

How can I control the fat in daily meals?

Most of us seem to have an individual approach to breakfast and lunch; once you get a couple of menus that work, these meals don't require day-to-day adjustments.

Dinner is another matter, especially if you cook for others. Who has time or inclination to add up how much fat is in each ingredient as supper takes shape? We offer here a rule-of-thumb approach that has worked very well for us. Rough, yes, but it has helped us keep our dinners averaging less than 25% calories-as-fat without complicated mathematics.

When planning dinner, the cook allows 2 teaspoons of oil or the equivalent per person. (See the margin for "fat equivalents.") If you're serving four, you have 8 teaspoons to divvy up for sautéing your onion, making salad dressing, and whatever else involves added fat. Any high-fat food like those in the margin should be measured as part of the fat allotment. It doesn't take long to learn which combinations work and which are entirely out: if you have muffins, for example, you don't put cheese on the broccoli. It works like that.

FAT EQUIVALENTS

1 tablespoon oil
 (= 3 teaspoons)
has as much fat as:

1 tablespoon butter,
 mayonnaise, or
 Better-Butter
2 tablespoons nut butter
3 tablespoons nuts
3 tablespoons sunflower seeds
3 tablespoons sesame seeds
⅓ cup sesame meal
⅓ cup grated cheddar
½ cup grated mozzarella
2 large eggs
¼ cup cream
1½ cups whole milk
3 cups low-fat milk
 ("2 percent" milk gets
 30 percent of its calories
 from fat)
½ cup dried shredded
 coconut
⅓ avocado

How can I calculate my fat intake?

TO CALCULATE *the percentage of fat calories in your diet, add up the calories and grams of fat in 1 day's food (use tables at back), then convert grams of fat to calories by multiplying by 9. Fat calories divided by total calories, multiplied by 100, gives the percentage of calories as fat. For example:*

1 day = 2250 calories,
72 grams of fat

72 g × 9 cal/g = 648 calories from fat

648 ÷ 2250 = .288
= approx. 29% calories as fat

We aim for 25% of dietary calories as fat, which is quite within reach for a whole-foods vegetarian. Half the battle is won by avoiding fast foods and convenience foods and limiting the fat you add at the table. Even so, we suggest that you check your diet at least once to see where your calories are coming from.

FAT INTAKE FOR VARIOUS PERCENTAGE TARGETS

Check your fat intake and caloric level to see what percentage of calories come from fat

OR *Pick a percentage target for your calorie level and see how much fat per day it allows*

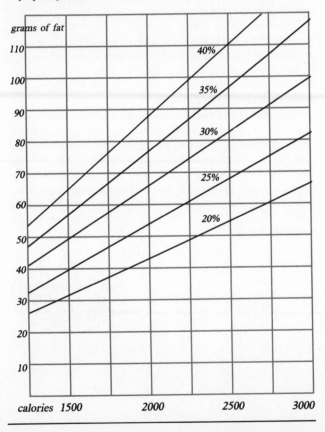

For complete nutrient tables of foods used in this book, and the recipes themselves, see The New Laurel's Kitchen.

What about protein?

Protein was one of the very first elements of food that nutritionists discovered and studied. They were dazzled by its importance, and so a long time went by before they figured out that we simply don't have to eat as much of it as they had thought. In fact, protein is required for so many functions in our physical workings, that our bodies carefully recycle the precious stuff in every way possible. Most Americans, including vegetarians, eat far more protein than they need to, without thinking about it at all.

True protein deficiency does occur, but even when you're talking famine, the deficiency is usually calories. The reason for this is that the body has to meet its energy needs first; if there is carbohydrate handy, great, but if not, the next choice for fuel is protein; in very low-calorie diets over a period of time, the body will burn its own muscle tissue, but even there the problem is that calories are needed for energy. Every real food has protein, and a diet that meets your calorie needs from whole, natural grains and vegetables will have enough protein.

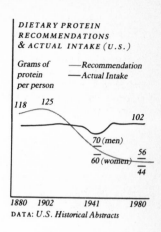

DIETARY PROTEIN
RECOMMENDATIONS
& ACTUAL INTAKE (U.S.)

Grams of — Recommendation
protein — Actual Intake
per person

118   125

102

70 (men)

56

60 (women)

44

1880   1902   1941   1980

DATA: *U.S. Historical Abstracts*

But are plant proteins complete?

It isn't that they aren't complete, it is just that they may contain proportionately less of one or two essential amino acids (EAAs) than the "ideal" pattern. Another way to look at it would be that they have "extra" amounts of the other EAAs. You can get complete protein from these foods; it just takes a little bit more of them. When overall protein needs are met, adults require only 20% of their protein to be "complete" – which is to say, to have the ideal proportion of essential amino acids. The adult requirement for essential amino acids is covered by just 11 grams of "completed" protein a day[22] – a little more than is supplied by 1 glass of milk. Any one of the foods listed in the margin meets the essential amino acid requirement without any other source of protein.

Each meets the essential amino acid requirement without any other source of protein:

2 ⅔ cups wheat
3 cups cooked rice
5 ¾ slices Basic Bread
3 cups diced potato
⅓ cup Soy Spread
½ cup wheat germ
2 ¼ cups rice with ⅓ cup cooked peas
3 cups spinach

Can you get too much protein?

The RDA for protein is double what nutrition scientists have established that most people really need. This is to provide a "safe margin." Most Americans eat twice the RDA, including most vegetarians. Can a person get too much protein? Recently we have been hearing more "yes" answers to this question.

When you take in more protein than you require, the body breaks down the excess to provide calories for energy, if needed, or else converts it to fat. In the process, the nitrogen – the element that makes protein special – becomes waste in the form of urea, and has to be eliminated. Urea is toxic, so the body dilutes it by adding more water and calcium to the urine. Thus, an increased urine flow washes calcium out of the body and also places stress on the kidneys. Eating too much protein is known to be harmful to people with compromised kidneys and is implicated in loss of calcium from bones – osteoporosis.[23]

The connection between excess dietary protein and osteoporosis was first studied two decades ago, and researchers continue to investigate it today. It is not uncommon for Americans to eat 90 or more grams of protein per day, and at that amount, even the RDA of 1200 mg of calcium cannot maintain positive balance: more calcium is spilled in the urine than the body retains.

Vegetarians will be somewhat relieved to hear that the sulfur-containing amino acids, which are especially abundant in meat and eggs are the outstanding culprits in this calcium-wasting pattern. Vegetable proteins, including soy protein, give more leeway for enjoying protein foods while still retaining the calcium you need for strong bones.[24]

Please turn to page 37 for more on this topic.

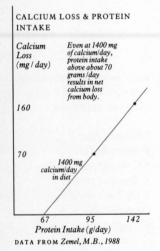

CALCIUM LOSS & PROTEIN INTAKE

Calcium Loss (mg / day)

Even at 1400 mg of calcium/day, protein intake above about 70 grams /day results in net calcium loss from body.

160

70

1400 mg calcium/day in diet

67   95   142

Protein Intake (g/day)

DATA FROM Zemel, M.B., 1988

How do I decide what not to eat?

It is relatively simple to stop eating meat. Beyond that first step, though, the task of bringing our food choices into line with our personal convictions and what we know about the food supply is not simple at all. It turns out, for example, that the excessive use of meat in our country has made animal by-products so cheap that they turn up everywhere – as additives in processed foods, where they have at least to be identified in labeling – and in all kinds of other unpredictable places, too: bandages, photographic film, perfume, floor wax, Freon, detergents, medicines, asphalt, you name it. We try to be knowledgeable in our purchasing and avoid dubious products, but we remind ourselves, too, that as more people stop eating meat, animal by-products will stop being so cheap and ubiquitous.

A tougher question – because after all, we don't eat floor wax or asphalt, and we can easily *refrain* from eating processed foods – relates to milk, cheese, and eggs. These are nourishing foods, and tasty; including them gives us cooks a lot of options for making meals appealing and varied, and can make all the difference to someone who, for reasons of appetite or digestion, can't face big servings of greens every day. At the same time, no one who reads needs to be told that in much of the country factory farming makes life miserable for cows and chickens. Health questions arise, too, when newspapers report that antibiotic and hormone residues have been found in samples of dairy products.

Moved by these concerns, many of our friends have decided to stop eating milk and eggs. Others continue to use them, but look for sources of pure milk from small dairies where the cows are treated well, and for eggs laid by free-ranging hens. These products are unusual today, but they can be found, and the future is theirs.

Our own circle of vegetarian friends includes vegans, lacto-vegetarians, and ovo-lacto-vegetarians, as well as people who wheeze when they eat wheat, and sneeze when they eat peanut butter, and part of *being* one another's friends, it seems to us, is the willingness to honor one another's choices and needs. In the long run, the kindness and consideration with which we treat each other may be at least as important as our food choices in bringing about a world without violence.

In any event, our food choices can express compassion and

connectedness in a great many ways. Buying organic foods, for example, protects the health of agricultural workers. It builds topsoil, helps clean up the water supply, and saves wildlife. Buying local produce in season reduces the exploitation of farmers in the Third World, boosts your local economy, and conserves petroleum. Cooking whole natural foods bought in bulk makes you healthier, saves energy, and keeps some packaging out of the landfill. Growing your own accomplishes all of these and supplies more tangible delights as well. For that matter, you may have room in your backyard for a few chickens . . .

೩

These topics are discussed at greater length throughout this book. For more, take a look at the list of books below.

Berry, Wendell. *What Are People For?*, *Home Economics*, *The Unsettling of America*, *The Gift of Good Land*. If you haven't read anything by Wendell Berry, you have a great treat in store.

Gussow, Joan. *Chicken Little, Tomato Sauce, & Agriculture*. The Bootstrap Press, 1991. A clear and prophetic look at the state and direction of our food system in its widest aspects.

Hart, John. *Farming on the Edge: Saving Family Farms in Marin County, California*. University of California Press, 1991. The story of how one county in California protects its open spaces against the pressures that come from being next door to a big city.

Longacre, Doris Janzen. *Living More with Less*. Herald Press, 1980. Anecdotes and experiences of Mennonites trying to live well and thriftily in today's world. Inspiring and informing.

Robbins, John. *Diet for a New America*. Stillpoint Publishing, 1987.

Rifkin, Jeremy. *Beyond Beef: The Rise and Fall of the Cattle Culture*. Dutton, 1992. His discussion of the many uses of animal by-products is on pages 274-275.

Teitel, Martin. *Rainforest in Your Kitchen*. Island Press, 1992. A practical introduction to the problem of diminishing biodiversity and ways you can affect it with your purchases. Those who would like more depth, please read Cary Fowler and Pat Mooney's *Shattering: Food, Politics, and Genetic Diversity*. University of Arizona Press, 1990.

A very good source of information for vegetarians and especially vegans, is the Vegetarian Resource Group, P.O. Box 1463, Baltimore, MD 21203. Their *Vegetarian Journal* is full of interesting and reliable information.

New vegetarians, and anyone wanting an endless source of new recipes and thoughtful articles will want to subscribe to *Vegetarian Times*. Write to them at P.O. Box 446 Mt Morris, IL 61054.

Whether or not you choose to include milk and eggs, *Laurel's Kitchen* is a good book for you. Most of our recipes do not use dairy, and nearly all of the ones that do can be made successfully with soymilk. When this really won't do – when a particular recipe does depend on milk, cheese, or eggs for its character – we have placed this symbol near its title. Soymilk, even the flavored kinds, is fine in quick breads: substitute it in equal measure for milk, and substitute a quarter cup for each egg. For sauces, we suggest unflavored soymilk or vegetable broth. If you are economizing, read the label when you buy soymilk. The "lite" variety is half soymilk, half water, plus sugar and gums to add body, but it sells for the same price as regular full-strength soymilk. If you would like to make your own good-tasting soymilk, see page 105.

VITAMIN B-12

1.0	Milk, whole, *1 cup*
4.0	Soymilk (our recipe, fortified), *1 cup*
1.2	Cottage cheese, *½ cup*
1.0	Skim milk, *1 cup*
1.0	Egg, *1 large*
.5	Buttermilk, *1 cup*
.3	Yogurt, low-fat, *1 cup*
0	Swiss chard, *1 cup cooked*
0	Kale, *1 cup cooked*
0	Broccoli, *1 cup cooked*
0	Collard greens, *1 cup cooked*

RIBOFLAVIN

0.41	Whole milk
.54	Skim milk
.44	Buttermilk
.44	Yogurt
.38	Collard greens
.31	Broccoli
.31	Cottage cheese
.20	Kale
.16	Swiss Chard
.15	Egg
.07	Soymilk

PROTEIN

8.5	Whole milk
16.5	Cottage cheese
11.0	Skim milk
8.8	Buttermilk
8.3	Yogurt
7.5	Soymilk
6.8	Collard greens
6.5	Egg
5.0	Kale
4.8	Broccoli
2.6	Swiss chard

CALCIUM

290	Whole milk
390	Skim milk
360	Collard greens
350	Soymilk
300	Buttermilk
290	Yogurt
210	Kale
140	Broccoli
115	Cottage cheese
110	Swiss chard
27	Egg

What does a vegan need to know?

A well-planned all-plant (vegan) diet can be a healthful one, though, like any limited diet, it requires some extra care. Specific problem areas are calcium and riboflavin, which most people get from milk; and vitamin B-12, which is not supplied by any plant food. Simply getting enough food to supply the needed nutrients and calories can be a problem for the young and the very old, because of the bulkiness of vegan fare. We recommend against a vegan pregnancy.

VITAMIN B - 12

Vitamin B-12 is necessary to prevent spinal cord deterioration, which proceeds unnoticeably and slowly, but can lead to irreversible damage. Please do not court a B-12 deficiency! Preventing it is as simple as a vitamin tablet that contains at least 2 micrograms a day. Since the body stores B-12, and the tablets often come in larger doses, you could take one per week, if you want. Some kinds of nutritional yeast are cultured with B-12-producing bacteria, and these too are reliable sources, but check the label to make sure.

BENEFITS & DIFFICULTIES OF A VEGAN DIET

BENEFITS

Low-fat, especially saturated fat; no cholesterol
Usually low in calories, and so good for weight loss
Eliminates the possible pesticide, hormone, and antibiotic residues sometimes present in milk and eggs

DIFFICULTIES

Hard to eat enough greens to get adequate calcium and riboflavin
Must take B-12 supplements
Hard for those on the nutritional edge to get enough calories to maintain weight

---

CALCIUM

There is increasing evidence that when protein intake is reduced to RDA levels, the body can adjust to lower levels of calcium and still keep strong bones. Still, for safety, we recommend keeping your calcium levels up to RDA. Without milk, this translates to several servings of broccoli or dark leafy greens a day, or taking a supplement. Teenagers and young adults, who are building bone mass for the rest of their lives, should be doubly sure to have plenty of calcium and plenty of exercise. (More below.)

RIBOFLAVIN

Riboflavin can be found in the same places as calcium, and also in nutritional yeast. (Please note, this important B vitamin is easily lost when exposed to light and leaches out into cooking water.)

Don't I need lots of calcium for bones?

Our bones grow and get stronger through our teens and even into our forties. Getting plenty of exercise and dietary calcium during that time builds bone mass, and, later on, the same prescription slows down its loss. Low-fat milk and yogurt are good sources of calcium, and green vegetables and legumes. Being sure that you do not take in too much protein guards against loss of calcium. Make a real effort to avoid going far over the RDA for protein.

Phosporic acid (in soft drinks), excess salt, and alcohol consumption all lead to loss of calcium, so keep these to a minimum.[25]

DIETARY FACTORS ASSOCIATED WITH CALCIUM LOSS FROM BONES:

LACK OF
Calcium (sources: milk or greens)
Magnesium (beans, grains, greens)
Fluoride (from water)
Vitamin D (from milk; or sunshine)

EXCESS OF
protein (stay near the RDA)
Phosphoric acid (from soft drinks)
Sodium (from salty foods)
Alcohol

LIFESTYLE FACTORS ASSOCIATED WITH CALCIUM LOSS FROM BONES
smoking
sedentary habits
lack of sunshine

Osteoporosis leads to over 700,000 bone fractures every year in the U.S. in women 45 years or older.

Hip fractures are the second leading cause of death in people 47 to 74 years of age.

R. Daview and S. Saha 1985, American Family Physician 32:107–114

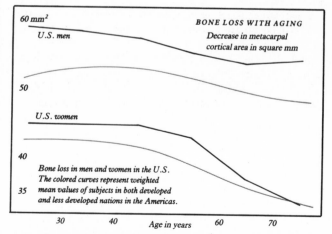

BONE LOSS WITH AGING
Decrease in metacarpal cortical area in square mm

60 mm²
U.S. men
50
U.S. women
40
35

Bone loss in men and women in the U.S. The colored curves represent weighted mean values of subjects in both developed and less developed nations in the Americas.

30   40   Age in years   60   70

REDRAWN FROM *Garn et al. 1969, "Population similarities in the onset and rate of adult endosteal bone loss," Clinical Orthopedics 65:51–60*

Know an easy way to check nutrients?

Nutrient tables for all the foods used in this book, and recipes, too, can be found in The New Laurel's Kitchen. *(Ten Speed, 1986)*

Sometimes when people want to improve their diets, they think they have to look up all the ingredients of all the foods they eat, to make sure they get the recommended amounts for each vitamin and mineral. But the vitamins and minerals work together in our bodies – and in our foods they come together in packets. One researcher, Jean Pennington,[26] studied these interactions, and came up with seven "index" nutrients: if you are getting enough of these seven, and enough calories from a variety of whole foods, you can be confident that you are filling your need for all the nutrients for which an R D A is established.

If I don't eat meat, where do I get iron?

SOURCES OF IRON

4.8	spinach,	*¾ cup cooked*
4.4	blackstrap molasses,	*1 tbs*
4.1	pumpkin seeds,	*2 tbs*
3.5	split peas, green,	*1 c cooked*
3.4	lentils,	*½ c cooked*
3.3	kidney beans,	*½ c cooked*
3.0	chard,	*¾ c cooked*
3.0	peas, edible pod,	*1 c raw*
2.9	bulgur wheat,	*1 c cooked*
2.9	pinto beans,	*½ c cooked*
2.6	garbanzo beans,	*½ c cooked*
2.5	navy beans, dry,	*½ c cooked*
2.5	soybeans, dry,	*½ c cooked*
2.5	peas, fresh,	*1 c cooked*
2.5	potato, cooked, with skin	
2.4	sesame meal,	*¼ c*
2.3	prune juice,	*6 oz*

As you can see from the list in the margin, there are plenty of sources of iron besides beef! You will hear that the kind of iron in vegetables is "less easily absorbed" than the kind in meat. Yet iron deficiency is less prevalent in vegetarians than in omnivores.[27] While iron is essential for red blood cells, it is also a highly toxic mineral in excess. Recent reports suggest that excess iron may play a dramatic role in promoting heart disease.[28] Perhaps one reason that vegetarians have such low heart disease risk is that the body will not absorb iron beyond what it needs from vegetarian sources.

Still, for many women especially, getting enough iron from food is a challenge. To maximize your iron intake, use iron pots for some of your cooking: they contribute usable iron to the food cooked in them. When you are eating food that is rich in iron, or if you are taking an iron tablet, you can make sure that you absorb it best by having fruit or some other source of vitamin C along with it. Tea inhibits iron absorption by 60%, coffee by 40%, so avoid having these beverages when you eat your "iron food."[29]

NOTES: PAGES 27 – 38

[1] *American Medical Association, 1992: Role of water-soluble dietary fiber in the management of elevated blood cholesterol in healthy subjects.* Am J Cardiol 69:433-439.

Anderson, J.W., et al., 1992: Prospective, randomized, controlled comparison of the effects of low-fat and low-fat plus high-fiber diets on serum lipid concentrations. Am J Clin Nutr 56:887-894.

[2] *Pi-Sunyer, F.X., 1991: Health implications of obesity.* Am J Clin Nutr 53:1595S-1603S.

[3] *Dembroski, J.E., et al., 1989: Components of hostility as predictors of sudden death and myocardial infarction in the Multiple Risk Factor Intervention Trial.* Psychosom Med 51:514-522.

Friedman, M., D. Ulmer, 1984: Treating Type-A Behavior and Your Heart. New York: Knopf.

[4] *Stein, R.A., et al., 1990: Effects of different exercise training intensities on lipoprotein cholesterol fractions in healthy, middle-aged men.* Am Heart J 119(2, part 1):277-283.

Suter, E., et al., 1989: Effects of long-term, moderate exercise on body composition and serum lipid profiles: a controlled study in middle-aged Swiss men and women. Intern J Vitam Nutr Res 59(4):423.

[5] *Ogar, D., 1991: Is yoga good exercise?* The University of California, Berkeley, Wellness Letter, March, 1991, p. 8.

Ornish, D.M., et al., 1979: Effects of a vegetarian diet and selected yoga techniques in the treatment of coronary heart disease. Clinical Research 27:720.

[6] *Friedman, M., D. Ulmer, 1984: op. cit. (ref. 3).*

[7] *Gabel, L.L., et al., 1992: Dietary prevention and treatment of disease.* Amer Fam Phys 46 (suppl): 41S-48S.

Anderson, J.W., et al., 1991: Metabolic effects of high-carbohydrate, high-fiber diets for insulin-dependent diabetic individuals. Am J Clin Nutr 54:936-941.

[8] *Anderson, J.W., et al., 1991: op. cit. (ref. 7).*

Pi-Sunyer, F.X., 1991: op. cit. (ref. 2).

Krall, L.P., R.S. Beaser, 1989: Joslin Diabetes Manual, 12th ed. Philadelphia: Lea & Febiger, p. 82.

[9] *Lehman, C.D., et al., 1991: Impact of environmental stress on the expression of insulin-dependent diabetes mellitus.* Behavioral Neuroscience 5:241.

Anon., 1991: Less stress, more control. Importance of relaxation for people with type I diabetes. Diabetes Forecast, July, 1991, p. 75.

[10] *Dinsmoor, R.S., 1992: Exercise and adult-onset diabetes.* Harvard Health Letter, Nov. '92, pp. 6-7.

[11] *Simono, R.B., 1991: Anxiety reduction and stress management through physical fitness.* In Diamant, L., ed., 1991: Psychology of Sports, Exercise, and Fitness: Social and Personal Issues. New York: Hemisphere Publishing Corp.

Hatfield, B., 1991: Exercise and mental health: the mechanism of exercise-induced psychological states. In Diamant, L., ed., 1991: op. cit. (above).

[12] *Bingham, C.A., 1988: Meat, starch, and nonstarch polysaccharides and large bowel cancer.* Am J Clin Nutr 48:762-767.

Jacobs, L.R., 1988: Role of dietary factors in cell replication and colon cancer. Am J Clin Nutr 48(3):775-779.

National Research Council, 1983: Diet, Nutrition, and Cancer. Washington: National Academy Press.

[13] *Carroll, K.K., 1991: Dietary fats and cancer.* Am J Clin Nutr (4 suppl):1064-1067S.

Doll, R., 1990: An overview of the epidemiologic evidence linking diet and cancer. Proceed Nutr Soc 49:119-131.

[14] *Melnechuk, T., 1988: Emotions, Brain, Immunity, and Health: A Review.* See section entitled "Attitudes and cancer initiation." In Clynes, M., J. Panksepp, eds., 1988: Emotions and Psychopathology. New York: Plenum Press.

[15] *Koffler, K.H., et al., 1992: Strength training accelerates gastrointestinal transit in middle-aged and older men.* Med Sci Sport 24:415-419.

[16] *Orth-Gomer, K., J.V. Johnson, 1987: Social network interaction and mortality. A six-year follow-up study of a random sample of the Swedish population.* J Chronic Dis 40(10):949-957.

[17] *Chesney, M.A., et al., 1987: Nonpharmacologic approaches to the treatment of hypertension.* Circulation 76 (suppl) :I,104-108.

[18] *Kopple, J.D., 1988: Nutrition, diet and the kidney, in: Shils, M.E., V.R. Young,* Modern Nutrition in Health and Disease, 7th ed. Philadelphia: Lea & Febiger, pp. 1239, 1242.

[19] *Chesney, M.A., et al., 1987: op. cit. (ref. 17).*

[20] *Yeater, R.A., I.H. Ullrich, 1992: Hypertension and exercise: where do we stand?* Postgrad Med 91(5):429-436.

[21] *Krantz, D.S., et al., 1987: Psychosocial factors in hypertension.* Circulation 76(suppl) :I,84-88.

[22] *Food and Nutrition Board, National Research Council, 1980: Recommended Dietary Allowances, 9th ed.* Washington: National Academy of Sciences, p. 43.

[23] *Kerstetter, J.E., L.H. Allen, 1990: Dietary protein increases urinary calcium.* J Nutr 120: 134-136.

Hunt, I.F., et al., 1989: Bone mineral content in postmenopausal women: comparison of omnivores and vegetarians. Am J Clin Nutr 50: 517-523.

Zemel, M.B., 1988: Calcium utilization: Effect of varying level and source of dietary protein. Am J Clin Nutr 48: 880-883.

Linkswiler, H.M., et al., 1981: Protein-induced Hypercalciuria. Fed Proc 40: 2429-2433.

[24] *Zemel, M.B., 1988: op. cit. (ref. 23).*

[25] *Kline, D.A., 1991: Diet and diseases of lifestyle.* In: Kline, D.A., 1991: Nutrition for Women. San Marcos, California: Nutrition Dimension.

[26] *J.A.T. Pennington, 1976: Dietary Nutrient Guide.* Westport, Conn.: AVI.

[27] *Helman, A.D., I. Darnton-Hill, 1987: Vitamin and iron status in new vegetarians.* Am J Clin Nutr 45: 785-789.

Latta, D., M. Liebman, 1984: Iron and zinc status of vegetarian and nonvegetarian males. Nutr Rep Int 30: 141-149.

Anderson, B.M., R.S. Gibson, J.H. Sabry, 1981: The iron and zinc status of long-term vegetarian women. Am J Clin Nutr 34: 1042-1048.

[28] *Salonen, J.I., et al., 1992: High stored iron levels are associated with excess risk of myocardial infarction in eastern Finnish men.* Circulation 86(3):803-811.

Sullivan, J.L., 1982: Stored iron and ischemic heart disease: emperical support for a new paradigm. Circulation 86(3):1036-1037.

[29] *Morck, T.A., S.R. Lynch, J.D. Cook, 1983: Inhibition of food iron absorption by coffee.* Am J Clin Nutr. 37: 416-420.

The New Laurel's Kitchen Food Guide

Every day include
4 servings {

Whole Grains

Whole-grain bread (1 slice) or
cooked grain – like rice –
or noodles (½ cup)

High-Carbohydrate Vegetables

Artichokes, potatoes, sweet
potatoes (1 medium);
beets, carrots, parsnips, winter
squash, turnips (1 cup);
corn (1 ear or ½ cup)

and
2 servings

Low-Calorie Vegetables

A tomato; green beans, cabbage,
cauliflower, leeks, cucumber, eggplant,
mushrooms, peppers (1 cup);
lettuce (2 cups)

Super-Vegetables

and
1 serving {

Dark leafy greens (¾ cup cooked);
edible-pod peas, brussels sprouts,
broccoli, asparagus, okra,
bok choy (1 cup).

Legumes

Cooked dry beans, lentils,
split peas (½ cup)

and
1 serving

Dairy Foods

Milk or yogurt (1 cup);
cheese (3 oz.);
cottage cheese (½ cup)

Nuts & Seeds

Fruit

Eggs

add
ample
servings
to fill out
calorie
needs

Introduction to Recipes

The New Laurel's Kitchen Food Guide

Our plan for a meatless diet is based on one simple but rather recently proven truth in the field of nutrition: all known nutrients are adequately supplied by a varied diet of whole foods which meets your energy needs. To put it in dinner-plate terms, if you get enough calories from a reasonable variety of unrefined grains, vegetables, and fruits, it is difficult to get too much fat and almost impossible to get too little protein, vitamins, or minerals.

Grains

Whole-grain cereals and breads are basic to a meatless diet. Grains have been staple foods since ancient times, and for good reason: their nutritional contribution is balanced and reliable. They contain starch and protein roughly in proportion to our calorie and protein needs, along with the vitamins and minerals the body needs to metabolize that starch and protein. The fiber whole grains contain is well appreciated now, even by meat-eaters. New vegetarians may be surprised to find themselves with a sudden liking for the heartiness of whole grains and legumes – it's a natural, because that slice of whole-wheat bread supplies many nutrients they used to get from meat.

Our Food Guide calls for a minimum of four servings of whole-grain foods per day. This can be bread, cooked breakfast cereal, noodles, brown rice, kasha, polenta, pizza, or pasta. The required serving is small – one slice of bread or half a cup of cooked grain – so this is an easy task. It's fine to eat more, but we recommend that you not eat less, because the nutrients supplied by grains (especially vitamin B-6 and zinc) aren't easy to get in other foods.

Vegetables

The vegetable groups include the whole glorious range of edible roots, shoots, stems, leaves, florets, and fruits that nature provides. Ideally, they are the freshest food in our diet.

SUPER-VEGETABLES

Asparagus
Beet Greens
Broccoli
Brussels Sprouts
Bok Choy
Chard
Collards
Dandelion Greens
Kale
Mustard Greens
Okra
Peas (edible-pod)
Spinach
Turnip Greens

From a nutrient standpoint, not all vegetables are created equal. They fall roughly into three groups: high-protein leafy greens, high-starch root vegetables, and low-calorie vegetables. For nutritional contribution, the greens reign supreme. This group is such a nutritional powerhouse that even the so-called "most perfect food," milk, can't match them for key nutrients like folacin and magnesium. They are surprisingly rich sources of protein, too: one middle-sized stalk of broccoli, for instance, provides 5 grams of good-quality protein.

In this group are many of the foods that have shown specific ability to protect against chronic diseases, cancers especially, and heart disease and diabetes. But these foods are not just healthy; they are delicious. They are so useful in the kitchen that our recipe section goes overboard on ways to bring out their best: the delicacy of spinach, the spicy heartiness of kale, and the sheer fresh exuberance of broccoli, snap peas, and asparagus.

HIGH-CARBOHYDRATE VEGETABLES

Winter squashes and root vegetables – potatoes, yams, beets, carrots, parsnips – provide more than just calories. Most have a respectable amount of vitamin C, and the orange ones are loaded with carotene, which our bodies convert to vitamin A: the deeper the color, the richer the provitamin A content.

Potatoes may even still be consigned unfairly to the "forbidden" category because of the persistent notion that they are fattening. At around 100 calories, though, the average baked potato is a caloric bargain, full of nutrients, and with no more calories than a medium apple. The challenge is to learn to like them just as well with less grease, and this is not impossible! Baked winter squash and yams are delicious perfectly plain, once you get used to the idea.

This family contains the most widely used vegetables in this country: lettuce, celery, tomatoes, green peppers. While they don't have a remarkable nutrient profile, they are relatively dense in nutrients, because their calorie content is so low: you get a lot per calorie. They also contain various sorts of dietary fiber, each with its own beneficial effects.

Legumes

The legume family includes all the beans, peas, and other pod-growing pulses. Foods in this group are rich in protein and have a kind of dietary fiber that helps regulate blood sugar and cholesterol. They are rich in folacin and good sources of several minerals.

We are impressed with the versatility of beans in our kitchen, but it has taken some years of experimentation to settle on just what their place is in our own food scheme. Their gas-producing potential is undeniable, but so are their dazzling nutrient profiles and delicious flavors. Our current feeling is that you don't have to eat beans every day, and if you pile them on, you may be getting more protein than you need. Today we serve beans in many guises, and we enjoy them for all their good qualities, but we are likely to eat smaller quantities at a time. Look for some very helpful suggestions on pages 292-299.

Nuts & Seeds

Nuts and seeds add a whole range of flavors and textures to a meatless diet, and they can make a significant nutritional contribution too. In general, this group is a good source of magnesium and especially of trace minerals such as zinc. Unfortunately, nuts and seeds contain too much fat to be sprinkled liberally throughout the day's menu. Chestnuts, with only 15 % of their calories from fat, are a welcome exception.

Fruit

Fresh fruit in season has to be one of the greatest pleasures of the table. It's also the easiest and best of snacks – best because it provides a quick boost without the subsequent letdown you get from fruit juices, let alone candy and refined sweets. Fruit, of course, is a good source of vitamin C, and many fruits supply provitamin A and magnesium. The soluble fiber in fruit helps lower blood cholesterol.

Fruit is good food, but here, too, moderation is necessary: don't let vast amounts of it crowd out other necessary foods like grains and vegetables.

Dairy Foods

Most vegetarians include dairy foods – milk products and cheese – in their diets. This makes it very easy to keep the diet balanced, because milk is a rich source of nutrients, including some otherwise hard-to-get vitamins (riboflavin, vitamin B-12) and minerals (calcium and magnesium). The protein in milk is abundant and complete in all the essential amino acids. A rich source of these nutrients can make the difference between good and poor health for certain groups, especially older people, children, and pregnant women. We recommend dairy products for people in these groups.

Around the world, people who live on traditional cereal-based cuisines include some form of supplementary animal food. To us, this seems to be the best role for dairy products in our diet too. New vegetarians often feel more comfortable eating familiar foods like macaroni and cheese, than more adventurous things like adzuki beans and pilaf. In time, though, they may find that their use of dairy products declines. Large quantities of dairy foods can make the diet higher than it should be in protein and saturated fats, and often lower in fiber and iron. In addition, animal foods in general, and fatty ones like butter and cheese in particular, have greater concentrations of chemical residues than most other vegetarian choices.

Eggs

Eggs perform magic in the kitchen that no other ingredient can quite match. Still, they aren't an ideal food, and we have to offer some caveats. To start with, the cholesterol content of the yolks is a serious consideration for many people, and maybe no one should eat more than about four a week on that account. If you use eggs, try to buy them from someone who has free-ranging hens, or at least from a supplier whose hens are given unadulterated foods. Hormones and antibiotics are administered daily to commercially reared chickens and show up in their eggs. These are not beneficial to humans who eat the eggs. The modern henhouse is far from humane, and for this reason, also, we urge those who wish to include eggs in their diet to look for a supplier who keeps free-ranging hens.

Exercise

The third step of our Food Guide says to fill out your caloric needs with a variety of whole foods. But what are your caloric needs? Basically, you need to get enough energy from foods to maintain your body's basic functions (your basal metabolism), plus whatever more is needed for daily activities.

When you exercise, you need more calories. This is helpful nutritionally because the more food you eat, the easier it is to get all your vitamins and minerals. In addition, weight-bearing exercise (anything except swimming and cycling) strengthens bones. Exercise also builds muscle, and that is helpful for controlling weight both ways: thin people add healthy pounds, and the rest of us burn fat off faster. How it happens is excellently explained in Covert Bailey's *The New Fit or Fat* (Houghton Mifflin, 1991).

Aerobic exercise could almost be called another kind of vitamin, so necessary it is for keeping our bodies healthy. Aerobics strengthen our heart and lungs, and make our cardiovascular system more efficient, so we can get nutrients quickly to where they are needed and promptly remove all kinds of waste products. When we exercise regularly, all this continues during the day and night, not just while we jog or dance.

A plea on behalf of children: let them be active too!

Without getting into its other drawbacks, television watching can be bad for kids' bodies. Two well-researched problems are

[30] *Anon, 1992: Body fatness and TV viewing. Nutrition Research Newsletter, January 1992*

Gortmaker, Steven L., William H. Dietz, Jr., and Lilian W.Y. Cheung ,1990: Inactivity, diet, and the fattening of America. Journal of the American Dietetic Association 90:1247 ff

Anon, 1992: TV lowers metabolsim, increases weight gain. The Brown University Child and Adolescent Behavior Letter 8:6 (Oct 1992)

[31] *Wong, Nathan D., et al,1992: Television viewing and pediatric hypercholesterolemia. Pediatrics 90 (1 part 1): 75-79*

Much more can be said about television and its effects. Jerry Mander's Four Arguments for the Elimination of Television *(Morrow, 1977) says it well. We also heartily recommend Mander's* In the Absence of the Sacred *(Sierra Club Books, 1991).*

childhood obesity and elevated blood cholesterol levels in children. The connection with obesity seems straightforward: kids watching TV aren't out playing active games. But physical activity may be more than merely minimized when the TV is on. In one recent study of young girls watching a television program, average metabolic rates dropped 14% below what they would have been if the girls had simply been doing nothing.[30]

Obese children have a rough time as youngsters, and later on, too. But there may be even more serious consequences of too much TV. University of California researchers looking for ways to prevent heart disease studied the activities of 1081 boys and girls. They found that if you want to predict who will have elevated blood cholesterol levels, there is a better way than looking at whose families had a history of either premature coronary disease or high cholesterol: look at their TV habits. Kids who watch two hours or more per day were twice as likely to have elevated blood cholesterol levels as those who watched less than two; in the four-hours-or-more group, the risk was five times as great.[31] This is a book about food, but no amount of broccoli can bring health to a child under these circumstances. Kids need to run and play!

The recipes in this book are not restaurant-style cuisine, too rich for every day. They present delicious, healthful, satisfying home cooking from ordinary ingredients imaginatively prepared. These are the recipes we cook from regularly. We hope you will find them as useful as we do, both as they are, and as springboards for your own creativity.

Bread

Breadmaking has held a special place in our lives for a long time, but it was when we took to vegetarian ways that the hearty brown stuff became the cornerstone of our diets—friendly and familiar as breakfast toast, sandwiches for lunch, after-school snack, and sometimes rolls or muffins at dinner. In some mysterious way it filled the gap that opened up when meat left the scene.

In the decade since *Laurel's Kitchen* first appeared, we've learned quite a lot about how to make our brown Staff of Life lighter and tastier. To tell the complete story would take a book— and did: *The Laurel's Kitchen Bread Book* (Random House, 1984) gives the full story on whole-grain breadmaking, ingredients, techniques, fancies, and all. Naturally, we recommend it with unreserved enthusiasm. In this chapter, we hope to tantalize you with some wonderful loaves; there is enough here to give you an excellent start as a breadmaker. Once you know how rewarding it is, there'll be no stopping you.

We have talked at length elsewhere about what a splendid food whole grains are. Good wheat bread may well be the whole grain *par excellence*. Where fiber is concerned, the fermentation of the dough in breadmaking softens rough bran without lessening its effectiveness. Fermentation also releases minerals that otherwise can be bound up in the grain by phytic acid. All the nutrients of the whole grain are present, of course, including the two dozen that are not replaced in "enriched" white flour.

Fresh bread is so irresistible that it displaces a lot of less nourishing food, especially at snack time. Whole-grain bread is a good choice for dieters because it's low in calories but still nourishes, fills, and satisfies. (This is true even if you butter it, though as San Francisco gourmet Harvey Steiman opined while happily munching our homemade slices, "Bread that isn't good enough to eat without butter isn't worth eating.")

Besides the good food, though, something wonderful happens to your kitchen and your life when breadmaking becomes a regular activity. The fragrance and suspense of it, the sharing of its warm goodness at the end, the very fact that you care enough to take the time—all these remind us that home is a fine place to be. Though perhaps a small thing, breadmaking is one counter-

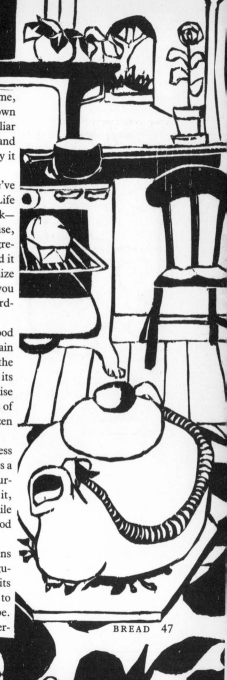

weight to the forces pulling family and friends away and apart. So it has been for us, and we hope you will find it so too.

ॐ

If you have children near at hand, let them take part in your baking days. It's a great way to spend time together, and no moppet is so small that he or she doesn't like to get fingers into dough, make a small shape to bake, and enjoy eating it, too. Bigger children can manage real jobs, beginning with greasing pans or measuring ingredients. Even before they were teenagers, some we know could handle a family baking all by themselves—a source of considerable pride.

Some Words About Ingredients

Before we get into the recipes, there are a few things to know about the ingredients. If you are going to go to the trouble to make bread, you want to be sure that your efforts are supported by the quality of your flour and yeast. Even the most skillful baker can't get good bread from bad ingredients.

Flour

FRESHNESS

Unlike white flour, whole wheat flour is perishable and must be fresh to make good bread. If you buy packaged flour and can't decipher the "pull date" on it, ask your storekeeper. Don't try to make bread with whole-grain flour that has been on the shelf for more than two months. If you are in doubt, taste a pinch: there should be no bitterness. At home, store whole-grain flour in a cool place; if you are likely to have it around longer than a couple of weeks, keep it sealed airtight in the refrigerator. The day before you bake, take what you will need out of the refrigerator so it can come to room temperature before you use it.

To make a light, airy loaf, you have to have flour that is high in protein—specifically, gluten protein, because gluten is what makes a stretchy structure that lets your bread rise high. Only wheat, of all the grains, has enough gluten to make light yeasted bread; and good-quality whole wheat flour has plenty of it: you don't have to add refined flour to get a light loaf. When you shop, look for "bread flour" milled from *hard red spring wheat, hard red winter wheat,* or *hard white wheat.* Hard red spring wheat usually makes the highest loaves. If the bag doesn't have this information but does give a nutritional profile, the protein content should be 14 percent or more by weight. Whole wheat flours labeled "all purpose" or "pastry flour" are milled from low-protein wheat. They can make tender quick breads, muffins, and pancakes, but they do not have enough gluten protein to make light yeasted breads.

Stone-ground flour is often considered superior for breadmaking, and indeed we prefer it. The coarser grinds especially lend a delightful texture to the bread, and the rough fiber is ideal for digestive health. But if you want a *really* light loaf, very finely ground flour will help you achieve it. In past years, stone grinding was preferable because faster methods of grinding produced enough heat to degrade the flour. Nowadays, careful millers air-cool both stone mills and hammer mills so that nutrients and baking quality are protected, and you can choose the grind that will suit your recipe best.

Home mills offer many advantages, especially to people who do not have a reliable source of high-quality flour near at hand. Since all whole grains properly stored will keep perfectly fresh until they are ground, having a home mill means that you can store wheat, corn, rye, and buckwheat until you need them, then grind them to order. There is a big difference in baking performance and flavor when the flour is very fresh, no matter what you are baking.

Salt

Salt strengthens the gluten and regulates the growth of the yeast, helping to make a light, even-textured loaf. If you want to cut back, we suggest first reducing the salt in whatever you put *on* the bread rather than *in* it.

If you do want to make bread without salt, though, here are some tips: Don't omit the sweetener. Expect a much faster rise. Keep the dough a little stiff, and be sure to knead very well to compensate for the strength the salt would give the gluten. Put the bread in the oven a little early to ensure an even texture. Saltless loaves may not rise so high, but that's all to the good because denser bread has more flavor.

Sweeteners

We usually call for honey, but nearly any non-artificial sweetener will please the yeast and sweeten your loaf. Yeast, by the way, *can* make its own food from natural sugars and starch in the flour, so unsweetened loaves rise perfectly well.

Oil or Butter

Oil or butter will make your loaves tender and help them stay soft longer. If you add what bakers call a "conditioning amount"— 2 tablespoons oil *or* 1 tablespoon butter *per loaf*—the bread will rise higher for it. On the other hand, if you leave it out, few people will notice any difference. (Everyone will notice if the oil or butter was rancid, however; the bread will be horrid.)

Add oil along with the other liquids. To reap the full benefit of butter, though, add it soft *but not melted*, about halfway through the kneading time.

Grains Other than Wheat

As we mentioned earlier, wheat is the only grain that contains substantial amounts of the proteins that make gluten, the stretchy substance that lets your yeasted breads rise high. For quick breads, especially muffins, gluten is not essential, and other flours work well. (If no wheat flour is used, eggs help to keep the bread from being crumbly.)

Corn makes delicious quick bread and muffins. (See page 81.) In yeasted bread, we have best success using as much as a cup of polenta (coarsely ground cornmeal), softened first in a cup of boiling water and allowed to stand until cool. Knead into two loaves' worth of dough after the gluten is developed. (More about corn and its ways on page 286.)

Buckwheat, millet, rice, oats, and barley, added as whole cooked grains, lend interesting texture to yeasted breads and help keep the loaf moist and fresh. (See page 73.) Flours ground from these grains make heavy yeasted breads, but they shine in other places: buckwheat flour and oats make super pancakes, for example (see page 95).

Rye flour has a little gluten, and a rye-wheat mix from the field was probably the rule rather than the exception in most leavened breads until the last century—hence the magnificent traditional rye breads of Eastern and Northern Europe. Rye is harder to work with than wheat, but a little bit added to wheat flour can make a satisfyingly hearty loaf even for the beginning baker. (If you want people to think "rye," add caraway seeds.) (See page 71.)

Bean flours can be included in small quantities to increase the nutritional value of yeasted and quick breads alike, but they do not improve the flavor or texture. (More on page 72.)

Yeast

We call for *active dry yeast* because it is readily available and reliable, but if you like to use moist (or cake) yeast, that's fine too—use a ½-ounce cake wherever we call for ¼ ounce of active dry.

If you buy yeast in bulk, ¼ ounce of active dry yeast is now just 2 teaspoons, though a few years ago it was a full tablespoon. The leavening power, however, is about the same. Not all active dry yeasts are alike; it's worth shopping around for one that works best for you. The "fast-acting" yeasts, for example, have a special talent: they tolerate higher temperatures, which gives a faster rise. But if you aren't in such a hurry, lower-temperature rising, which is slower, gives superior flavor, nutrition, and keeping quality to your loaves.

In fact, the time your dough takes to rise is up to you, and depends entirely on how much yeast you use and how warm you keep the dough. The chart on the next page shows how you can arrange your rising times to make bread that accommodates your schedule.

Whatever kind of yeast you use, be sure it is fresh. If it isn't, it can't raise your bread. To check its leavening power, stir the yeast into the proper temperature water. For active dry yeast, follow directions on the package; if there is no recommendation, use water at 110°F. For moist yeast, about 80°F is good. Be sure that the yeast is completely dissolved; then stir in ¼ teaspoon honey or a tablespoon of flour. If the yeast hasn't foamed to the top within about ten minutes, it has lost its leavening power and you should throw it out. If you bake regularly and have a reliable source for your yeast, you won't need to test it every time.

STORAGE Store yeast airtight in the refrigerator. Active dry yeast in packets should be good until the date on the package. (Since air, light, and moisture damage yeast, bulk yeast is sometimes not such a bargain, depending on how it has been handled by the storekeeper.) Moist yeast is very perishable and will keep only about a week, even refrigerated. If you freeze it in foil-wrapped, baking-sized packets, it will be good much longer.

RISING TIMES FOR TWO LOAVES

Yeast	Rising temperature	First rise	Second rise	Shaping and proof	Time (plus bake)	Bread characteristics
4 teaspoons	90°F	1 hour	½ hour	½ hour	2½ hours	very light bland flavor poor keeper
2 teaspoons	80°F	1½–2 hours	1 hour	1 hour	4 hours	light good flavor moderate keeper
2 teaspoons	70°F	3–4 hours	1½–2 hours	1 hour	6–7 hours	excellent flavor very good keeper

---

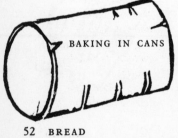

BAKING IN CANS   We used to like to bake our bread in the big juice cans—they have many advantages over loaf pans. But not long ago it was discovered that the seams of these cans can leach lead into food that is stored (and, presumably, baked) in them. Now, most of the lead-soldered cans have been replaced with leadless ones. If you bake in cans, look for smooth seams—avoid using cans with a soldered bump down the side.

Making Whole-Grain Bread

The method we present here is slightly different from what you might have encountered in other books (except our *Bread Book*). So far as we have been able to tell, written recipes for bread— even the ones for whole wheat bread—are based on the way *white* flour acts. But using whole wheat in a white-flour manner often doesn't work, and that has unfairly given whole wheat a bad name. White flour is not only milled to remove the bran and wheat germ, but blended and chemically treated to make it utterly uniform from bag to bag. Whole wheat flour can't be blended and standardized, so each batch has its own personality.

Our method is based on a traditional one developed long before white flour came along. It accommodates whole wheat flour's variability and makes the most of its great goodness. Beyond drawing on tradition, we have benefited a good deal from the knowledge and experience of professional bakers and bread scientists, who have helped make the whole process more understandable and controllable—especially in timing the risings and making the bread come out the way you want.

If you are a beginner, you will find the kneading easier if you make only one loaf. Divide the ingredients *and the kneading time* in half. Keep all the rest the same.

Some kind of a bowl, a pan, and a reasonable oven are all you really need by way of equipment. But because modern active dry yeast works best if it is dissolved in plain water at its favorite temperature, we suggest adding a thermometer to your supplies. A "chef's thermometer," with a steel spike and a dial that registers from 0° to 212°F, is the best.

Recipes for quick breads and muffins begin on page 79

*non-metal cup for
    dissolving yeast
thermometer
mixing bowl
    (about 4 quarts)
small mixing bowl
measuring cups, spoons
rubber spatula
dough cutter or spatula
comfortable kneading
    surface
rolling pin (optional)
2 greased loaf pans, 8" × 4"*

GREASE: If you want to avoid using solid shortening, make super-grease: 1 cup oil blended with ½ cup lecithin. Great anywhere you need to grease; use just a thin layer.

Basic Bread Recipe

2 teaspoons active dry yeast
(1 packet, ¼ oz, or 7 g)
½ cup warm water (about
110°F)
6 cups whole wheat
bread flour (2 pounds)
2½ teaspoons salt

2¼ cups lukewarm water
(2 tablespoons honey
or other sweetener)
(2 tablespoons oil or butter)

Warm your yeast-dissolving cup by rinsing it with warm tap water; then measure the ½ cup warm water into it. If there are directions on the yeast package, follow them; otherwise, the water should be 110°F, which feels just-warm to your fingers. Sprinkle yeast into water while stirring with spoon, being sure each granule is individually wetted. Be sure the yeast is completely dissolved.

To get the best from your yeast, be sure the dissolving water has no salt or sweetener in it and that the temperature is right. If you need to test the yeast for liveliness, refer to page 52 for instructions.

Stir the flour in its container and measure 6 cups into your large bowl. (Freshly ground flour will be fluffier, so tap it down in the cup.)

Measure salt and stir it into the flour, making a well in the center. Mix oil and honey, if used, into the 2¼ cups water and pour it and the yeast mixture into the well you have made in the flour. Stir the liquid mixture into the flour, beginning in the center and working outward so that you first make a smooth batter, then gradually mix in the rest of the flour to make a soft dough. Squeeze with your wet fingers to make sure the dough is evenly mixed; it will be sticky.

Adjusting the Consistency

Now is the time to adjust the consistency of the dough. Because whole wheat flour varies in the amount of liquid it will absorb, the dough may be too soft or too stiff to make perfect loaves, and learning to adjust the dough at this stage makes all the difference.

Pick up the dough and squeeze it. Feel deep into the dough, not just on the surface. Just-mixed dough is sure to be sticky and wet, but is it soft or is it stiff? Does it resist your touch? Do you feel a strain in the muscles of your fingers? Then it is too stiff. Soft dough makes lighter loaves; but it can be too soft: it has to have enough flour to hold its shape. Does it feel waterlogged, sort of runny, as if the flour wasn't contributing much substance to it? Then it is too soft.

If the dough is too soft or too stiff, put it back into the bowl and flatten it out. If it is too soft, dust with ¼ cup more flour; if too stiff, sprinkle with 2 tablespoons more water. Fold the dough over, mix it again, and re-evaluate, adjusting until it does seem right. Even perfect dough will seem sticky at this stage, so don't try for a firm, clay-like touch or you'll end up with a brick.

Kneading

Kneading makes the dough resilient and stretchy so that the loaves can rise high. There are many styles and methods, but the thing to aim for is a pleasant, easy rhythm that doesn't tire you. What you are doing is knitting together the proteins from wheat that make gluten, and forming the gluten into a structure that can hold the gas released by the yeast. Depending on how much gluten protein is in the flour you use, it will take an efficient kneader about 20 to 30 minutes to knead two loaves' worth of dough to perfection. A food processor can do it in minutes (usually in two parts, sometimes three); a mixer with a dough hook takes 8 to 15 minutes.

If you like, you can use a little flour or a little water on the kneading surface to keep the dough from sticking. If you use flour on the board, try to use the tiniest amount possible; the commonest cause of bricky loaves is simply too much flour. (The next commonest is too little kneading.) You can avoid extra flour and water and just use a dough cutter or spatula as shown to pick up the dough and turn it over as you work, until the dough loses most of its stickiness.

Kneading is a matter of pushing and turning. Handle the dough lightly at first, until it loses some of its stickiness; then you can be more vigorous. Keeping the dough as much in a ball as possible, press down on it with the heel and palm of your hands, using your whole body rather than only your arms to give power to the push. Lift, turn the dough, and repeat in a rhythm that is natural to you. If the dough becomes stiff, add a little water by wetting your hands while you work.

It is hard to overknead by hand, but not by machine. Overkneaded dough gets gooey and can't regain its elasticity. Dough made from flour that is low in gluten, or flour that's not fresh, will break down after only a few minutes of kneading.

Somewhere around halfway through kneading, the dough loses its stickiness and begins to get springy and elastic, though if you try to stretch it out it still rips easily. If you look closely at the surface, especially if the flour is stone-ground, you'll see tiny flecks of bran against a beige background. Try pulling the dough out as shown. You should see little craters all over, and it still tears easily.

If you stopped kneading now, the bread *would* rise, but not nearly so well as if you continue kneading until the dough is silky smooth. Then, when you pull and tug gently, it will stretch without tearing. The surface will still be sticky, but the dough will have lost its wet quality. If the flour you used was coarse, when you look closely you'll be able to see that the dough itself is bright white, with the bran embedded in the gluten sheet like freckles on fair skin. Even with finely ground flour, the dough is bright and has a whitish cast. If you pull gently as illustrated here, the dough will make a paper-thin, translucent sheet without tearing. How satisfying!

When you have finished kneading, it's time for you to rest while the yeast does its work. You can decide how long the rising times will be by how warm or cool you keep the dough: look at the chart on page 52 for your options.

Clean the bowl and shape the dough into a smooth ball, putting it in the bowl seam-side down. Cover with a platter or a plastic sheet to keep the dough from drying out, being sure that there's plenty of room for it to double or even triple. Don't oil or grease the bowl; unabsorbed fat can make holes in the finished loaf. Keep the bowl in a draft-free place at the temperature you need to give you the rising time you want.

Rising

When the dough has finished rising, it's time to deflate it. How to know when it is ready? Letting it double in volume is one way, but bakers know that doughs vary in the amount they can rise, so they use another test: wet your finger and gently poke it into the dough about one knuckle deep. Look at the hole you've made, and the dough around it. Does the dough begin to swell to fill in the hole? Then it needs more time. Does the hole remain, and the dough sigh slightly? Ready! (If the dough sighs profoundly and collapses, with alcohol on its breath, then you know that you have let it rise too long for the temperature it was resting in, and for the second rise, keep it in a cooler place, and/or allow *less than* half as long as the first rise.)

Deflating the dough and letting it rise again before shaping make a big difference in the the bread's texture, its keeping quality, and how high the final loaves will be. To deflate, wet your hand and press the dough flat; then form a ball again with the same top surface as before. Cover as before and let rise again. The second rise will take about half as long as the first at the same temperature.

At the end of the second rise, you should have what bakers call "ripe dough"—the kind that makes loaves which rise highest, taste best, and keep fresh longest. Feel the dough: it should have lost its stickiness and be pleasantly dry. When you pull on it, the strands of gluten should be thread-thin, where before they were thick and wet. Newly-kneaded dough is strong but not resilient; ripe dough is elastic. If you were to let it go even longer, the gluten would pass its prime and become brittle and "old," making grayish bread with poor flavor.

Turn the dough out on a very lightly floured board and flatten it with your hands. If you are making two loaves, divide it in half. Shape the dough pieces into smooth rounds again and cover them up while they rest. Use the time to rinse out the bowl and grease the pans: depending on the dough, it will take about 10 minutes for the dough to "relax" and be ready to shape.

Shaping

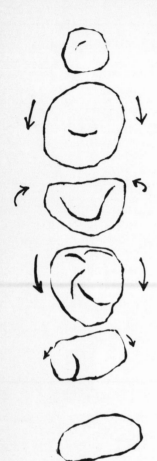

There are many ways to shape bread. Shape the relaxed dough gently, in easy stages. Dust the board lightly with flour if the dough seems sticky at all. (Honey, milk and some other ingredients, if they were included, will keep dough sticky even if it is ripe).

🥐 Turn the rounded loaf upside down and press or roll it into a circle about an inch thick.

🥐 Fold the top of the circle down not quite in half, making a smile. Press from one side to the other, letting the gas pop when it comes out the edge.

🥐 Fold in the sides, overlapping the ends slightly, so that the dough is about two-thirds the length of your loaf pan; press again, until the dough is about the length of the loaf pan.

🥐 Pull the top of the dough toward you as if you were curling it up jellyroll fashion. Since the piece is not very long, it may not roll up but just sort of fold in half. Either way is fine so long as it is tight and there's no air trapped in pockets.

🥐 Press the seam to seal it, and press the ends down to seal them.

🥐 Place the shaped loaf in the center of the greased pan, with the seam on the bottom, in the middle. Push the dough down with your hand to help it cover the bottom of the pan.

Perfect shaping takes practice, and if your early attempts aren't what they might be, take heart. Some of the most bizarre-looking loaves are most delicious, because they're so crusty.

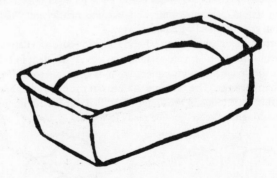

The Last Rise, or "Proof"

Let the loaves rise as before, protected from drafts, and contrive to keep the top surface of the dough from drying out. One way to do this is to set each loaf in a plastic bag that has been rinsed with water. Puff out the bag so the loaf can rise up; then seal it and set the balloon in its draft-free spot to rise. An ice chest (without ice) or even a roasting pan with plenty of room will also work well. This may seem like fussing, but a little more care at this last, most delicate part of the job can make all the difference in how high and even-textured your loaves come out.

This last rising will take a little less time than the one before if you maintain the same temperature. Keep the proof temperature about the same as before, or only a little warmer: otherwise the loaves will rise unevenly. About halfway along, preheat the oven.

Knowing when to put the bread in the oven is a learned skill. If the loaves have risen enough to arch above the top of the pan, well and good; but to be really sure, the best test is a gentler version of the finger-poke test you used before. Wet your finger and press lightly on the dough. When it's first shaped, it springs quickly back; as time passes, your fingerprint will fill in less quickly. The bread is ready for the oven when the dough returns slowly.

You have quite a bit of leeway here, but this is a moment for alertness because *underproofed* loaves won't be as high as they should, and may split drastically along one side in the oven; *overproofed* loaves will be holey at the top and dense on the bottom, and may even collapse.

Baking

A well-insulated oven that recovers its heat quickly after the door has been opened is a great boon for a baker. Ovens that recover slowly may allow bread to overproof before the heat can set the loaves. If yours is like that, put the bread in a little early. Another trick is to preheat to 400°F, turning the heat down just after the bread goes in. You can improve your oven for any kind of baking by lining the bottom with quarry tiles or firebrick. A less drastic step, but useful, is to set a pizza stone in the oven when you start to preheat. For sure, adjust the oven racks and tiles or whatever before you turn on the oven.

Handle the fully-risen loaves very gently. Center them on their racks in the oven, and *after half an hour* take a peek. Ideally it will take an hour to bake the loaves at 350°F, but ovens vary, and some of them bake unevenly. If the bread seems to need it, you can move the loaves around at this point, or lower the temperature to 325°F if the crust seems too brown. If you think the bread may be done a little early, check again after it's been in for 45 minutes.

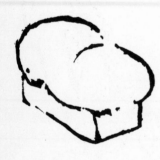

Is it done? A tricky question, especially if you haven't been baking long enough to learn the quirks of your oven. Here are some characteristics of a loaf that has baked long enough:

🍞 it slides out of the pan easily

🍞 it has an even, golden-brown color (darker if you included milk or much sweetener)

🍞 if you tap the bottom sharply with your fingertips, the sound is hollow rather than thick

🍞 when sliced, the crumb (all that's not crust is crumb) springs back to the touch rather than making a wettish dent that stays there*

*Some breadmakers are horrified at the very idea of slicing a loaf hot from the oven because any loaf, especially a fluffy one, can be mauled by all but the most skillful early slicing. But it *is* possible, with a *very* sharp, thin, long knife, to slice bread hot from the oven: use lots of gentle sawing and not too much downward pressure.

French Bread

French Bread is just the opposite of "fast-rise" breads that get flavor from sugar, fat, and other added things. With only the essentials—flour, water, salt, and yeast—it develops its splendid flavor naturally during a long, cool rising period. A hot, steamy bake gives French Bread its high rise and crisp, chewy crust.

2 teaspoons active dry yeast (1 packet, 1/4 oz, or 7 g)
1/2 cup warm water (about 110°F)

୨ବ

Follow the recipe for Basic Bread, omitting the sweetener and fat; make the dough soft by cutting back on the flour. Use icy cold water except for dissolving the yeast.

5 1/2 cups whole wheat bread flour (1 3/4 pounds)
2 1/2 teaspoons salt

Let the dough rise in a cool place, 65 to 70°F, until it is ready to deflate; this should take 2 1/2 to 3 hours. (You can give it more time in a cooler place, but if you let it get warmer, it won't have time to develop good flavor.) Deflate and let rise again, this time about 2 hours.

2 1/4 cups very cold water (iced if you knead with a food processor)

Press the risen dough flat and divide into pieces sized for the shapes you want to make. Round the pieces and set them to rest. Prepare the baking pans and then shape the dough, taking into account the suggestions below. Give the dough its final rise *in the same cool place as before*. It will take an hour.

୨ବ

Before you shape the dough, consider how to make the best use of the equipment you have so that you can give the bread the steamy-hot bake it needs. Because French Bread has no added milk or sugar, normal baking temperatures won't even brown the crust, let alone provide the characteristic beauty and flavor.

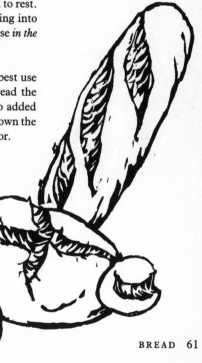

"Reduce the oven heat," does not mean "turn the thermostat down." If the heat stays high after the water is gone, the bread will burn very quickly. If your oven retains heat well, you may want to turn the thermostat down earlier and even open the door for a minute or so.

Whatever method you use for steaming, please be careful. The temperatures are high and the presence of steam makes the heat intense. Before heating the oven, put the racks in their places and figure out where you are going to put each pan or dish when baking time comes.

What you want to mimic in French Bread is the traditional wood-fired brick oven, which has very high heat and humidity when the bread is put in and loses both slowly as the bread bakes out. Sounds impossible, but actually, there are simple and effective ways of coming close to these conditions in a home oven. Some suggestions are given on the next page. Choose one of them, and allow plenty of time for the oven to preheat.

Shape your bread or rolls and place them on the baking sheet or oven stone, or in the covered dish you will use for baking them. If the bread will be free form, you need only give the surface beneath it a moderate dusting of cornmeal. Casseroles or loaf pans, because the bread will touch their sides, must be greased, with cornmeal coming after.

Just before baking, wet your loaves or rolls, and slash their tops to encourage their best rise in the oven. It's the slashing that leaves the characteristic open-leaf pattern on the crust. Use a very sharp knife and hold the blade at an angle to the surface of the bread, rather than cutting straight downward, so that the slashed part will open up rather than spread out.

Bake big loaves as long as an hour; long thin ones, or rolls, need just 20 to 30 minutes, depending on their size.

Steaming Methods

COVERED CASSEROLE

This is the easiest and most surefire way of steaming, and the least nerve-racking. Glass, pottery, or even heavy metal works fine, so long as it is big enough to allow the dough to do all the rising it wants to (including a final "spring" in the oven). A clay baking cloche is great. The key is the snug fitting lid; if it has air spaces the steam will escape without doing its job. You can remedy leaks in lids—or even fabricate a lid—using foil. (Ceramic, by the way, tends to burn and stick: use plenty of grease and lots of cornmeal.)

Preheat the oven to 450°F. When the bread is ready to bake, pour ¼ cup of warm water over the loaf, slash, cover, and put into the oven. After about 20 minutes the crust should be a nice, rosy brown. Reduce the oven heat to 350°F and bake until done.

WETTING THE LOAF

If you want to bake loaves that won't fit into a covered casserole, and if your oven is a well-insulated one that quickly recovers the heat lost when its door is opened, here is the simplest way to wet the loaf: Preheat the oven to 450°F; then spray or paint the fully risen bread with warm water, slash it, and put it into the oven as quickly as calm efficiency allows. Repeat the spraying or painting every 3 to 5 minutes until the crust begins to brown nicely—probably three or four times, depending on your oven and your dough. Reduce oven heat to 350°F and bake until the bread is done.

STEAMING THE OVEN

This method requires a pretty well-insulated oven too, and also a heavy skillet or other flat pan that you don't mind possibly ruining for any other use. Preheat the oven to 450°F with the skillet on the bottom. When you put the bread in the oven, pour one cup of boiling water into the skillet and shut the oven door quickly. After ten minutes, peek. As soon as the water is gone, reduce the heat. You can use this method to heighten the effect of the previous one. And both are enhanced by lining the oven with quarry tiles or using a baking stone instead of a cookie sheet under the bread.

Raisin Bread, and Such

The simplest way to make raisin bread—or any fruit or nut bread, for that matter—is to spread handfuls of the goodies on the dough when you shape it and then curl it up jelly roll fashion, being careful not to let any air get trapped in the curl. Ease the roll into a a well-greased loaf pan or bake free-form on a cookie sheet, or cut the roll into swirly rolls with a loop of strong thread. The rising time will be a little longer than usual.

If you prefer, you can incorporate sweet dried fruits into the dough when you mix it up. To prevent active enzymes in the fruit from harming the dough, and to make the fruit softer and more appealing, steam raisins and other firm dried fruits long enough to heat thoroughly, then drain and cool before you start. Use the broth as part of the liquid measure. (Incidentally, soggy fruit will make holes in the bread and present difficulties in baking too, so swirly rolls are a better option if your fruit is wetter than the dough.)

You'll find much, much more about ingredients and techniques in The Laurel's Kitchen Bread Book *(Random House, 1984).*

Cinnamon, when added to the dough too early, can develop a metallic taste. It gives its best flavor if incorporated at shaping time, or sprinkled on the top of the moistened loaf just before baking.

Seeded Bread

Sprinkle seeds on the board while you shape any plain dough, letting them get folded and rolled into the loaf and stuck to the outside. You can use any seeds you like—sesame or poppy, of course, or sunflower, chia, caraway, cumin, fennel, dill, anise. Sesame and cumin really sing out if they are toasted in advance, and sunflower seeds have two entirely different personalities toasted and raw.

EGG WASH

If you want stronger sesame flavor, include a tablespoon of unrefined sesame oil in the dough as part of the oil measure. To achieve a seedier crust, brush it just before baking with water, milk, or a mixture of a lightly beaten egg and a tablespoon of water; then sprinkle with seeds. The egg will make the loaf very shiny too.

Breads With Milk

You can use milk for part of the liquid in any loaf. Milk mellows the wheaty flavor, makes the crumb tender in texture, adds protein and minerals, enhances the keeping quality of the loaf, and gives a pretty, warm color to the crust. If scalded, it can also improve the rise.

Why scalded? Scalding denatures some of the proteins in milk which otherwise make bread dough sticky and keep it from rising high. To get the benefits without the drawbacks, scald the milk first, or else limit the amount you use to less than half the liquid measure. (With milk powder, this means using not more than ¼ cup powdered milk per 2 loaves. Stir dry milk powder into the flour along with the salt.)

Even more than fresh milk, we like buttermilk in bread—again, though, not contributing more than half the liquid. Buttermilk Bread is one of our top favorite recipes. It makes light, tender rolls too—fancy enough for royalty if you double the butter. Yogurt is good here too, but since it's much stronger-flavored than buttermilk, we recommend using even less: ⅔ cup for 2 loaves is a good amount. Follow the Basic Bread instructions, using these ingredients:

BUTTERMILK BREAD

2 teaspoons active dry yeast
(1 packet, ¼ oz, 7 g)
1¼ cups warm water

1¼ cups buttermilk
¼ cup honey

5½ cups whole wheat
bread flour
2 teaspoons salt

2 tablespoons soft butter

YOGURT BREAD

2 teaspoons active dry yeast
(1 packet, ¼ oz, 7 g)
1⅔ cups warm water

¼ cup oil
⅔ cup yogurt
3 tablespoons honey

6 cups whole wheat
bread flour
2 teaspoons salt

FRESH MILK BREAD

2 teaspoons active dry yeast
(1 packet, ¼ oz, 7 g)
½ cup warm water

2 cups fresh milk,
scalded and cooled
¼ cup honey

6 cups whole wheat
bread flour
2½ teaspoons salt

2 tablespoons soft butter

Rolls & Breadsticks

We like to make some rolls whenever we bake, to hand around fresh out of the oven or to serve for dinner. Plain round cushion rolls are probably the best eating, but fancy shapes delight the eye and can make a meal special.

For grand occasions—especially if you are serving Aunt Agatha, who finds whole wheat so, well, *unrefined*, you know— you'll want to call up all your skills to make the rolls really light. Choose a dependably light recipe like Buttermilk Bread and double the butter; you can also include an egg if you want to. The buttermilk, the fat, and the egg will all help lighten the dough. Choosing fine flour helps too. But good kneading makes the biggest difference of all, and careful timing comes next. Let rolls have plenty of time in the last rising; unlike loaves, they don't run the danger of collapsing, because they're small.

If you are making rolls at the same time as a loaf, you can bake them at the same temperature; the rolls will take about half as long. If they are by themselves, rolls (smaller ones especially) and breadsticks will be crustier and less likely to dry out inside if you bake them at a higher temperature: as high as 400°F for the smallest ones. They're done when golden brown, about 15 minutes at these higher temperatures. Brush with butter, if you like, when they come out of the oven. You can make truly mouthwatering, featherlight rolls this way.

BREADSTICKS Breadsticks are just long, thin rolls. To make them crunchy, let them dry out at 200°F for an hour or so after baking. (How long it takes will depend on how big you make them.) We generally go for chewy-soft, which is how they turn out if you bake them just until done: about ½ hour at 350°F.

Pine Nut Pinwheels

This truly original recipe can be planned ahead to star for company, or just as happily use up the end-of-the-week Soy Spread for the delight of your Inner Circle. In a pinch, sunflower seeds can substitute surprisingly well for the pine nuts.

bread dough for one loaf

1½ cups Soy Spread
½ cup toasted pine nuts

ॐ

You will need half a recipe's worth of any not-too-sweet bread dough. If you are in a hurry, make up half a recipe using the full 2 teaspoons of yeast. Keep the dough quite warm and expect a very fast rise. Proceed as usual until shaping time. (See page 52 for timing.)

Roll the risen dough out on a lightly floured surface, making an 11″ × 14″ rectangle. Spread the dough with the soy spread and sprinkle with pine nuts. Roll up tightly and seal the seam. Use a sharp knife or a loop of strong thread to cut the log into 1″ slices. Place the swirls in a greased baking dish with their sides just touching and let them rise. The final rise, in a warm place, should take about ½ hour.

Preheat oven to 375°F. Bake pinwheels ½ hour or a little longer.

Makes 16.

CINNAMON ROLLS

Follow the directions for Pine Nut Pinwheels, only use a sprinkling of cinnamon and brown sugar instead of pine nuts and soy spread. Nuts and raisins can also figure in. After baking, brush with butter.

Pocket Bread (Pita)

Here the trick is the baking, and that isn't as tricky as it has been made out to be. Ovens differ, though, so it may take a little experimentation to figure out your own best setup. You need fast bottom heat, so bake the breads on the floor of the oven, with or without a cookie sheet or pizza stone. Electric ovens and many gas ovens work fine with a cookie sheet on the bottom rack.

Use plain Basic Bread dough. A good method for the first try is to make a normal loaf of half the dough and Pocket Bread out of the rest. That way you will have about a dozen pitas, which is probably plenty for the nerves if not for the cupboard. After you master the process, you can easily make dozens and stay calm and cool.

When the dough has nearly finished its second rise, preheat the oven to 450°F. When the dough is ready, divide it and shape your loaf and set it in its pan to rise in a cool, draft-free place. Of the remaining dough, form about a dozen small *smooth* balls. Keep them in order as you shape them, so that you can take them on to the next step in order too. Let the rounds rest about 10 minutes, protected from drafts. *This is essential.*

If they are too thick, they won't puff (though they will be nice buns). If they are too thin, or if you are too rough with the rolling pin, they may puff in places but not make balloons.

Use flour on the board to keep the breads from sticking. Roll the first three or five or so rounds into flat circles about as thick as a heavy wool blanket and 6″ or so across. Put the rolled-out circles on the floor of the hot oven, or on the cookie sheet or hot pizza stone, and quickly close the door. Roll a few more, but don't get distracted.

Check the breads in the oven in 3 minutes. They should have puffed; if they are brown on the bottom, open one up and check to see if the inside is done. It will be moist, but it shouldn't be shiny-wet. If you think your breads need a little more time, you can bake them for a minute more on the top rack while the next batch bakes on the bottom. But don't let them get crisp and brown or they'll break when you try to fill them. They bake from the steam inside them, which cooks very fast without browning the top.

From here on out, work as efficiently as you can, rolling and baking in a comfortable rhythm, adjusting your oven setup to get the ideal pita. When you finish all the pitas, you should have time to cool the oven a bit and have it ready to bake that loaf.

Making Rye Bread

Rye is the only grain besides wheat that has substantial amounts of gluten, so it has been used along with wheat for centuries to make the superb breads of Eastern and Northern Europe. But rye not only has a lot less gluten than wheat, it also has carbohydrates called *pentosans* which weaken the gluten, making the dough sticky and the bread heavy. To get the lightest and best-textured rye bread, a different technique from the standard wheat-bread method is helpful.

If you simply want to let the wheat gluten carry the bread, you can mix the liquids into the wheat flour, making a thick batter, and beat the batter until it is elastic; then mix in the rye flour to make your dough. But there is a way to get the rye gluten to help too. Mix the rye, wheat flour, and salt; then add the bread's liquid measure to the flour mixture in stages, beginning with just enough to get the dough to stick together. Knead this very stiff dough, using the rest of the recipe's liquid measure to wet your hands as you work, so that within about 10 minutes of kneading you have used most of it. Depending on the dough, 5 to 10 minutes more will finish the kneading—but stop when the dough becomes dramatically sticky, no matter how long you've been working.

The reason for the stiff first stage is that the rye's pentosans compete with the gluten proteins for liquids, and the gluten has a better chance if the dough starts out less wet. It is the pentosans glomming onto the water that makes rye dough so sticky. Adding acid to the dough, by the way, helps counter this, and that is why you'll see vinegar in the recipes.

Once the dough is mixed and kneaded, it can follow the usual pattern for bread dough—with the caution that rye dough is less tolerant of either very slow (cool) or very fast (warm) rising times than wheat dough. Handle rye dough gently, and don't expect it to rise sky-high. Bake it thoroughly.

About rye flour: you will see "light," "medium," and "dark" rye flours. All of them are refined: light rye has had all of the bran and germ removed, dark rye has only lost a good deal of it. If you want whole-grain rye flour, you need to ask for 100 percent whole rye flour, which usually means stone-ground. Rye flour is even more perishable than wheat flour, so try to get and use it

RYE FLOUR

when it is really fresh. If you like rye bread very much, we would go so far as to suggest home grinding; it makes a marvelous difference in the bread.

The following recipes are meant to be prototypes for the basic kinds of rye breads. You can flavor them with grated orange peel, use chili-flavored cumin seeds instead of the traditional caraway, or leave the seeds out altogether. Add raisins, following the suggestions on page 64; or darken the bread by using 2 table-spoons carob powder, Postum, or cocoa (but maybe not all at once!) Give your creation a fancy name and keep careful notes so you can make it again. This we can testify: if it has caraway seeds, people will think it is rye, whether it is or not; if it doesn't, they won't, whether it is or not.

Light Rye Bread

Dissolve the yeast in the warm water.

Mix the flours, salt, and caraway seeds in a big bowl. Stir the honey, buttermilk, vinegar, and oil together and mix them into the flour mixture. Add the dissolved yeast next, mixing the whole into a stiff dough. Knead, adding the additional water gradually by dipping your hands into it as you work the dough. Kneading time should be 15 to 20 minutes. At the end you should have a soft, supple dough just beginning to become sticky.

Let rise twice and shape as described in Basic Bread. Let rise once more. Preheat oven to 425°F. Before baking, spray or paint loaves with warm water. Place in hot oven and immediately turn heat down to 325°F. Bake about 1 hour.

VARIATION

Substitute ¾ cup water for buttermilk and increase cider vinegar to ½ cup.

2 teaspoons active dry yeast
(1 packet, ¼ oz, 7 g)
½ cup warm water

4½ cups whole wheat
bread flour, preferably
finely ground
2 cups whole rye flour
2½ teaspoons salt
1 tablespoon caraway seeds

3 tablespoons honey
1 cup cool buttermilk
2 tablespoons cider vinegar
2 tablespoons oil

about ¾ cup water

Pumpernickel

This is a very old-fashioned rye bread, dark, tender, and hefty.

&

Dissolve the yeast in the warm water. Mix the flours, salt, and seeds together and stir in the molasses and vinegar. Add the dissolved yeast to make a stiff dough. Knead about 10 to 20 minutes, working the remaining water in gradually by wetting your hands, until the dough is supple.

Let rise twice as described in the Basic recipe, shaping the bread into rounds. Let rise again and bake for about 1 hour, using one of the steaming methods described on page 63.

2 teaspoons active dry yeast
(1 packet, ¼ oz, 7 g)
1½ cups warm water

4 cups whole rye flour
3 cups whole wheat
bread flour
2½ teaspoons salt
1 teaspoon caraway seeds

1 tablespoon molasses
2 tablespoons cider vinegar

1 to 1½ cups more water

Bean Breads

GARBANZO BREAD

*2 teaspoons active dry yeast
 (1 packet, ¼ oz or 7 g)
½ cup warm water*

*5 cups whole wheat
 bread flour
2½ teaspoons salt*

*2 tablespoons honey
garbanzo cooking broth,
 plus cold water to make
 2 cups liquid, about 70°F
(2 tablespoons oil)*

*2 cups freshly-cooked
 garbanzos, mashed*

SOYBEAN BREAD

*2 teaspoons active dry yeast
 (1 packet, ¼ oz or 7 g)
2½ cups warm water*

*5 cups whole wheat
 bread flour
2½ teaspoons salt*

*3 tablespoons honey
2 cups freshly-cooked
 mashed soybeans,
 or cooked soy grits*

¼ cup oil

If you want to work beans into your family's diet but find resistance in the ranks, adding beans or bean flour when you prepare your bread dough can make a small but significant contribution. With a little art, not a soul will guess what extra nutrients that delicious slice contains.

Our preference is for cooked, mashed soybeans or garbanzos—up to a cup per loaf, kneaded into the dough after the gluten is formed. That way the beans really do disappear into the dough, and the bread has very good flavor.

BEAN FLOURS

Garbanzo flour will disappear too: add as much as ½ cup per 2-loaf recipe, along with the wheat flour. But soy flour is different. Not only can it be very bitter, soy (bean or flour) also has dramatic effects on bread dough because of enzymes it contains. Professional bakers make use of this quality by adding soy flour in minute quantities as a dough conditioner. But when you use enough to make its nutrients count, the loaf can be so "conditioned" that it can't rise. Here are some ways to get around this if you really want to work soy in.

USING SOY

Use a maximum of ⅓ cup fresh soy flour in a 2-loaf recipe, or add as much as 2 cups of cooked, mashed soybeans or cooked grits. Either way, if you want to counteract the binding properties of soy, you have to include fat: 2 tablespoons oil or butter per loaf, minimum, for a good rise. In addition, because of the conditioning effect, let soy-enhanced breads rise only once before shaping, instead of twice.

Soymilk, by the way, makes lovely bread. Dissolve the yeast in warm water and use soy milk for part or all the remaining liquid measure. Unless it is first-day fresh, be sure to scald and cool the milk before using. Here too, for a good rise, include butter or oil and let rise only once before shaping.

Cracked Wheat Bread

When most people dream of cracked wheat bread, it's the light, sweet honey–wheatberry type sold in supermarkets. If you want to duplicate this, you need a very light version of Basic—perhaps Buttermilk Bread—and maybe even an egg or two as part of the liquid.

For the cracked grain to make its best showing, use either very coarsely cracked bulgur wheat or sprouted wheat berries two to three days along, chopped with a knife. You can use as much as 1 cup cooked or sprouted grain per loaf, adding it either when you mix the dough or later as you knead. Sprouts probably do best, but chew carefully: the ones on the crust can be hard enough to crack a tooth.

2 teaspoons active dry yeast
  (1 packet, ¼ oz or 7 g)
½ cup warm water

¾ cup hot water
¼ cup honey
1¼ cups cold buttermilk

5½ cups finely ground
  whole wheat bread flour
2½ teaspoons salt
1 cup chopped sprouted
  wheat berries or
  1 cup cooked bulgur wheat

2 tablespoons butter
  or ¼ cup oil

Oatmeal or Barley Bread

With whole wheat flour, the taste of the oats or barley takes a back seat. Still, this is one of our most frequently-made breads, because it is so mellow and light and such a good keeper. We usually just use leftover oatmeal (or cooked barley cereal) as the "liquid" in Basic Bread, increasing the honey a little and decreasing the salt by whatever is in the cereal. Dissolve the yeast in plain water only, of course.

The only quirk is that at first the bread seems absurdly stiff and sticky at the same time, making it hard to resist the temptation to add extra water. After a little kneading, though, the dough smooths out and becomes almost normal. From there on it's smooth sailing.

To let the fans know it's Oatmeal Bread, sprinkle rolled oats in the greased pan before you put in the loaf. Soak a handful of rolled oats in warm milk, and just before baking, pat the mixture all over the top crust.

This bread takes kindly to the flavor of walnuts and sunflower seeds too. Knead them in when you shape the loaves.

2 teaspoons active dry yeast
  (1 packet, ¼ oz or 7 g)
½ cup warm water

5 cups finely ground
  whole wheat bread flour
2½ teaspoons salt

2 cups cooked oatmeal
  or barley cereal
3 tablespoons honey

(¼ cup oil)
(½ cup toasted
  sunflower seeds or
  walnuts)

English Muffins

English muffins—in fact, excellent English muffins—are not hard to make. It doesn't take special equipment, either, just your bread dough and a griddle. The secrets are in the mixing, kneading, and the final rising time.

Use any kind of dough that suits the mood of the muffin you would like to make. If you like 'em tangy, Yogurt Bread is a good choice; for *really* tangy muffins, even cut back the honey. Basic Bread with chopped wheat sprouts kneaded in makes a muffin that's nubbly and slightly sweet. Doughs with a lot of sweetener or milk will be very dark on top and bottom by the time they are cooked, but delicious nevertheless.

You can make eight muffins from one loaf's worth of dough—one loaf of bread and a batch of muffins from one 2-loaf recipe. Knead the dough as usual for bread; then divide it in two and set the loaf half in its draft-free place to rise. Put a cup or so of warm water in a small bowl, take the muffin half of the dough in hand, and knead more, wetting your hands as you do. Keep kneading until the dough is really quite *over*kneaded. It should become quite flabby, with no elasticity at all. It might stretch out like regular dough, but if so, it will pull apart gooily rather than tear the way unkneaded dough will. When you finish, you should be worried that you have kneaded it too much and that you might have worked in too much water: it should be pretty darn wet.

(Overkneading and making the dough wet are the first two of three Great English Muffin Secrets. Number three comes later.)

Let the muffin dough have its first two rises as if it were normal bread. Because it is so wet, though, the muffin dough will ferment much faster than its sister bread dough. If you want them to follow the same schedule, keep the muffin dough in a cooler place: for example, if the loaf is rising in the oven with the door propped open to keep it at about 80°F, then set the muffin dough on a countertop at about 70°F.

After the muffin dough has had its second rise, turn it onto a well-floured board, flatten it out, and divide it into eight parts. Form each into a round and set on a well-*floured* tray or cookie sheet for the final rise. Protect the muffins from drafts and let them rise until the rounds are quite saggy, not higher than an inch. This last step—a very, *very* full proof—is the third secret.

Heat your griddle or skillet moderately hot, a little cooler than you'd want for pancakes. Unless it is completely unseasoned, you won't need to grease the surface. Use a wide spatula to pick up the first muffin and, deft as a magician, transfer it flour-side-down to the griddle. Fill the griddle with the first four or so and let them bake until they are getting brown on the bottom; then turn over. Keep turning as they bake, to prevent them from getting too dark. They are done when the sides, which will not brown, are springy. If you are in doubt, split one open with a fork: when done, it will be moist but not wet. How long this takes depends a lot on the dough—very light, holey muffins bake the fastest. It's fine to make the second four wait for their turn on the griddle, so long as they aren't in a place that is so warm they'll overproof.

TROUBLESHOOTING

When they cool, the muffins will be impressively smaller than they were after baking. Eight muffins from this recipe should be the right size, but if you want them larger, next time make only seven—or even six.

If there aren't enough holes, next time knead longer and add more water. It's hard to believe how much it takes.

If the inside is a little gray and the flavor beery, you have let them rise too long or too warm. The wet dough ferments much faster than stiffer bread dough.

Sebastopol Pizza

2 or more cups whole wheat
    flour
1 teaspoon salt
½ teaspoon cardamom

2 teaspoons active dry yeast
    (1 packet, ¼ oz, 7 g)
⅞ cup warm water

1 tablespoon butter, soft

6 cups firm, tart apples,
    sliced thin
1 cup apple juice
(2–4 tablespoons honey)
(2 tablespoons lemon juice)
1 tablespoon cornstarch or
    arrowroot

⅔ cup chopped walnuts
2 cups grated mozzarella,
    jack, or other favorite
    cheese

In northern California, Sebastopol means apples: Gravensteins in particular, which folks who live anywhere nearby think can't be beat. But this recipe works well with any fresh local apple—best with a crisp, flavorful, sweet-sour variety that will counterpoint the cheese.

This concoction is both showy and surefire, the kind of thing you serve to provide conversation and good eating at a festive lunch. It also makes a great project to do with kids on a lazy Saturday morning.

Combine flour, salt, and cardamom.

Dissolve yeast in water.

Add yeast mixture to flour mixture, adding flour or water if necessary to make a soft dough. Knead about 5 minutes, and then work in the soft butter, kneading another 5 minutes or so, to make a silky dough. Set to rise, covered, in a very warm place (90°–95°F) about 1 hour. Deflate and let rise again ½ hour.

Cook sliced apples in ¾ cup of the apple juice just until tender, not quite translucent. Drain, reserving the liquid. You should have a cup of juice; if not, add more. Stir in honey if desired, and lemon juice if needed, to produce a balanced sweet-sour flavor. Dissolve cornstarch in remaining quarter-cup of cold apple juice and stir into the hot juice mixture. Cook over medium heat, stirring, until clear.

Preheat oven to 425°F.

Roll dough out to fill a 14″ greased pizza pan. Turn up an edge to hold sauce. Spread apples over crust, then pour thickened sauce over that. Sprinkle nuts over top and bake for 15 to 20 minutes, until crust begins to turn color. Spread cheese over the pizza and return to oven for another 5 minutes. Serve hot.

Find Pizza on page 266, along with some interesting variations.

Puffs

Puffs are light, airy, yeast-raised muffins, nutritious and easy to make in spite of the time they need to rise. The first version is for caraway puffs, but try the poppy and herb puffs too—and make up your own.

2 teaspoons fresh minced
   onion
1 tablespoon oil or butter
1 cup cottage cheese
2 tablespoons honey
1 teaspoon salt

Sauté onion in oil or butter. Add the cottage cheese, honey, and salt, and heat mixture to lukewarm (100°F).

In a medium-sized bowl, dissolve the yeast in the warm water. Stir in the egg, seeds, 1¼ cups of the flour, and the warm cottage cheese mixture. Mix this batter well, then add the remaining flour as needed to make a very soft dough. Knead lightly until elastic.

2 teaspoons active dry yeast
   (1 packet, ¼ oz, 7 g)
¼ cup warm water

Let the dough rise in a warm place (85°–95°F) for about 1½ hours. Grease a 12-cup muffin pan.

Flatten the dough and divide it into 12 balls. Place these in the muffin cups and let the dough rise again, about 40 minutes this time. Preheat the oven to 400°F. Bake for 15 minutes—a little longer if they are not terribly puffy.

Makes 12 puffs.

1 egg, beaten
2 teaspoons caraway seeds
2¼ cups whole wheat flour

POPPY PUFFS

Substitute poppy seeds for the caraway seeds, grated lemon peel for sautéed onion, butter for oil. Melt the butter and heat the cottage cheese gently in the same pan.

HERB PUFFS

Increase the onion to two tablespoons. For the seeds, substitute a selection of your favorite herbs. Dill weed, basil, parsley, and celery seed or leaves all make good puff flavorings.

Everyone's Muffins

OATMEAL VARIETY

2 teaspoons active dry yeast
  (1 packet, ¼ oz, 7 g)
1½ cups warm water

1¾ cups whole wheat flour
1½ cups rolled oats

1¼ teaspoons salt
2 tablespoons oil
2 tablespoons honey
2 pinches nutmeg

BUCKWHEAT VARIETY

2 teaspoons active dry yeast
  (1 packet, ¼ oz, 7 g)
1½ cups warm water

2 cups whole wheat flour

1¼ teaspoons salt
2 tablespoons oil
¾ cup buckwheat flour
½ cup raisins
¼ cup toasted sunflower
  seeds

Most muffin recipes call for eggs and milk, but not these! Like other muffins, they are at their best served hot from the oven.

For either variety, dissolve the yeast in the water in a large bowl. Mix in whole wheat flour (and oats, if desired) and beat well.

Add the remaining ingredients and beat vigorously. Cover the batter with a towel and let the dough rise for an hour in a warm place (about 90°–95°F). Stir down the batter and spoon it into greased muffin tins, filling each cup full. Let the muffins rise again.

Preheat the oven to 400°F. When the muffins have risen nicely rounded above the muffin cups, bake them about 25 minutes.

Each recipe makes 12 large, crusty muffins.

About Quick Breads & Muffins

Because they do not have the long fermentation of yeasted breads, quick breads and muffins require more fat and sweetener to give them flavor and texture. In addition, the use of soda destroys the B vitamin thiamin, which you have a right to expect to be richly supplied in a whole-grain food. Despite these nutritional drawbacks, though, quick breads aren't likely to disappear from the scene. Quick to fix, scrumptious, and often happily nonwheat in a wheaty world, muffins, corn bread, and their ilk provide variety and—well—people really *like* them.

For whole-grain muffins, smaller muffin cups succeed better than large ones, though either will do.

Ordinary double-acting baking powder is probably the most effective and the least bitter tasting. If you want to avoid aluminum, though, look for old-fashioned cream of tartar baking powders, or make your own: use ⅝ teaspoon cream of tartar plus ¼ teaspoon soda per cup of flour.

Soymilk may be used in place of milk.

Use ¼ cup soymilk to replace one egg.

To replace buttermilk, sour sweet milk or soymilk with 1 tablespoon vinegar or lemon juice; fill to one cup and let stand five minutes.

Poppyseed Muffins

Preheat oven to 375°F. Grease a 12-cup muffin pan.

Soak raisins 5 minutes in ¼ cup boiling water. Chop coarsely in blender or by hand.

Make the oats into a coarse flour in blender or food processor (in blender, do ½ cup at a time). You will need 2 cups of coarse flour.

Put oat flour in bowl and sift in the other dry ingredients. Beat eggs, oil, and honey together, then stir in the milk, raisins and water, poppy seeds, and lemon peel.

Add dry ingredients to liquid ones, stirring just enough to mix well. Spoon into muffin cups and bake about 15 minutes. The muffins will be a sunny yellow on top and delicate brown on bottom when done.

Makes 12.

½ cup raisins
¼ cup boiling water

2¾ cups rolled oats (about)
½ cup whole wheat flour
2½ teaspoons baking powder
½ teaspoon salt
¼ teaspoon mace or nutmeg

2 eggs
2 tablespoons oil or butter
¼ cup honey

1 cup milk
2 tablespoons poppy seeds
2 teaspoons grated lemon peel

Apple Bran Muffins

1 cup whole wheat flour
¾ cup wheat bran
¼ teaspoon salt
½ teaspoon baking soda
¼ teaspoon nutmeg
1½ teaspoons grated
   orange rind
½ cup chopped apple
¼ cup raisins
¼ cup chopped nuts
   or sunflower seeds

juice of ½ orange
⅞ cup buttermilk
   or sour milk
1 beaten egg
¼ cup blackstrap molasses
1 tablespoon oil

Moist, dark, and fruity, these are a long-standing favorite.

Preheat oven to 350°F. Grease a 12-cup muffin pan.

Toss flour, bran, salt, soda, and nutmeg together with a fork. Stir in orange rind, apples, raisins, and nuts or seeds.

Combine the orange juice, buttermilk, egg, molasses, and oil. Stir the liquid ingredients into dry in a few swift strokes. Pour into greased muffin cups, filling them at least two-thirds full, and bake for 25 minutes.

Makes 12.

Cinnamuffins

¼ cup oil
½ cup dark molasses
1 cup applesauce

1½ cups whole wheat
   (pastry) flour
½ teaspoon soda
1½ teaspoons baking powder
¾ teaspoon cinnamon
pinch cloves
½ teaspoon salt
½ cup raisins

Preheat oven to 375°F. Grease a 12-cup muffin tin—use the smallish-sized cups with this recipe.

Mix oil, molasses, and applesauce. Sift together the flour, soda, baking powder, cinnamon, cloves, and salt. Stir together wet and dry ingredients and raisins. Drop into muffin cups and bake 18 to 20 minutes.

Lynne's Muffins

Nutty in flavor and texture, these favorite unsweet muffins are wonderfully simple to make. Start them ahead of time, however, or they will taste of soda and not be so light.

ಎ

Soak the oats in the sour milk overnight, or at least several hours. Preheat oven to 400°F.

Sift together the flour, baking soda, and salt. Combine dry ingredients, honey, and beaten eggs with the oats and stir lightly just until the batter is mixed. Drop batter into well-greased muffin tins, filling each cup two-thirds full.

Bake for 20 minutes.

Makes 12 muffins.

2 cups rolled oats
1½ cups sour milk
* or buttermilk*
1 cup whole wheat flour
1 teaspoon baking soda
1 teaspoon salt
¼ cup honey
1 or 2 beaten eggs

Corn Bread

Preheat oven to 425°F.

In a large bowl stir the dry ingredients together, making sure there are no lumps of baking soda or powder.

Mix liquids together and add to the dry ingredients, stirring smooth. Turn into a greased 8″ × 8″ pan. Bake 20 to 25 minutes. (Or make corn muffins: spoon into muffin tin and bake about 20 minutes.)

VARIATIONS

For a grainy, Southern-style corn bread, use 2½ cups freshly ground corn and omit the wheat flour and honey. Use butter. If you want to use very coarse cornmeal, it is a good idea to let the batter stand for an hour before baking. Keep the eggs and leavenings to add, blended smooth, at the last minute.

For a light, delicate New England–style corn bread, use 1½ cups cornmeal and 1 cup whole wheat pastry flour, plus the maximum of eggs, honey, and butter. You can even separate the eggs, folding the whites in after mixing the rest.

A cup of grated raw carrot makes a sweet, pretty addition; a cup of grated raw yellow zucchini or winter squash will disappear completely. Parsley, peppers, grated cheese, onions sauteed in the oil measure with a teaspoon of chili powder . . . these are all tasty ways to add interest.

2 cups cornmeal
½ cup whole wheat pastry
* flour*
1 teaspoon salt
½ teaspoon baking soda
1 teaspoon baking powder

1–3 tablespoons honey
1–2 large eggs, beaten
1–2 tablespoons oil
* or melted butter*
2 cups buttermilk

(When you use 2 eggs or add grated carrot, reduce the buttermilk to 1¾ cup. When you add raw squash, reduce it to 1½ cup.)

Boston Brown Bread

1½ cups whole wheat flour
½ cup rye flour
1 cup cornmeal
1½ teaspoons baking powder
½ teaspoon baking soda
1 teaspoon salt

2 cups buttermilk
¼ cup milk
½ cup blackstrap molasses
½ cup raisins
½ cup toasted sunflower
    seeds, lightly chopped

So moist and tender you'd imagine it to be terribly rich, but not so! The secret is in the steaming. This bread is easy to prepare and certainly easy to eat. It takes as long as three hours to cook, though, so start early.

❧

Grease and dust with flour or cornmeal one 2-pound coffee can, or three 20-ounce cans, or five 12-ounce cans. *Use seamless cans;* the ones with a seam down the side may leak lead onto the side of the loaf.

Sift dry ingredients to make sure there are no lumps of soda or baking powder. If some bran or cornmeal stay behind in the sifter, tip them back into the mixture.

Stir liquid ingredients together with the seeds and raisins. Add to the dry ingredients, stirring just enough to moisten thoroughly. Fill cans to two-thirds full.

Cover the cans with greased foil or greased heavy paper and tie with string. Set the cans in a large pot or slow cooker on top of a trivet or a cooling rack. (Even crumpled foil will do, or old jar lids.) Fill the pot with boiling water to halfway up the cans. Cover the pot and let the bread simmer on very low heat for 3 hours—check after 1½ hours if you're using small cans.

Let the bread cool uncovered for 1 hour before removing it from the cans.

Boston Brown Bread keeps well wrapped in foil and refrigerated. To reheat it, steam lightly.

Oat Crackers

Place all dry ingredients in blender and blend until they are the consistency of cornmeal. Stop frequently to stir ingredients if they stick. (If you use a food processor, you may need to double the recipe.)

Stir in the milk. Use a frosting knife or rubber spatula to spread batter thinly and evenly on a well-greased baking sheet. Be sure the batter is not thicker at the center of the sheet.

Place in cold or preheated 325°F oven and bake slowly until delicately golden. After about 10 minutes, use a pastry wheel or sharp knife to score the dough in squares or rectangles. If the outside crackers bake faster, take them off and return the others to the oven.

Crackers become much crisper when they cool, so loosen them from the baking sheet as soon as they come out of the oven to keep them from crumbling.

½ cup walnuts, chopped
1¾ cups rolled oats
½ teaspoon salt
1 teaspoon baking powder

1 cup milk

To make sure that these come off the pan easily, use a few drops of lecithin along with the oil or shortening you use for greasing the pan.

Crispy Seed Wafers

These large, tasty, paper-thin crackers keep for several days if stored airtight.

೩

Preheat the oven to 400°F.

Mix dry ingredients together. Add 2 tablespoons of the melted butter, the warm water, and the vinegar, and mix thoroughly. Knead for a minute or two in the bowl until the mixture forms a stiff dough.

Grease your hands lightly and shape the dough into a 12″ cylinder. With a sharp knife, slice the roll into 16 pieces.

For each piece spread ¼ teaspoon of seeds on a table top or counter and then press the dough into the seeds. Roll with a rolling pin into a paper-thin wafer. Spread another ¼ teaspoon of seeds and turn the wafer onto them.

When you've finished 4 or 5 wafers, slide them onto an ungreased cookie sheet, using a long, wide knife with a sharp edge. Brush the wafers lightly with the remaining butter or oil and bake them for 5 to 7 minutes, until golden brown. Repeat with the rest of the wafers.

Makes 16 wafers.

1 cup whole wheat flour
¼ cup cornmeal
¼ teaspoon baking soda
¼ teaspoon salt
1 teaspoon brown sugar

¼ cup melted butter or
*   oil, divided*
¼ cup warm water
1 tablespoon apple cider
*   vinegar*

poppy or sesame seeds

Chapatis

3 cups whole wheat flour
1 teaspoon salt
1½ cups warm water

USEFUL EQUIPMENT:

a rolling pin
a griddle
long thick oven mitts
a dish towel or other cloth,
* white linen or muslin*

PLEASE BE CAREFUL!

*In India, even the youngest
cook can make chapatis,
but we who did not learn
these skills at mother's
knee have a challenge
before us. Protect your
hands with mitts and your
arms with long sleeves,
and go slowly at first.*

Chapatis are the North Indian version of tortillas, made from stone-ground wheat flour. They're a most delicious bread for eating with curries, or with peanut butter and honey, or cheese and tomato, or any which way. ❧

Mix the flour and salt in a bowl. Slowly add the water, working it into the flour until the dough comes together, soft but not wet. Knead until silky, about 20 minutes. If possible, let the dough rest at room temperature for an hour or so.

Pinch the dough into 12 balls, golf-ball size. Keep covered with a damp cloth while you round each one smooth and then, one at a time, flatten them with a rolling pin on a floured board, making each one about 7 inches across. Don't roll the pin off the edge of the round or the rim of the bread will get too thin. Stack with flour and waxed paper between. Heat the griddle medium-high—if it is too hot, the chapatis will burn; if too cool, they won't puff up. Best of all is to work together with a friend, one rolling and the other baking.

If your griddle is not well seasoned, put a thin film of oil on it. You will be using the dish towel for pressing on the chapatis to encourage them to puff up, so make the towel into a smooth wad that is easy to hold.

Place the first chapati on the hot griddle and let it sit for one second, then turn it over. Use the cloth to press on the top of the bread as it cooks. The object is to help the chapati form steam pockets. Ideally each chapati will puff up round like a balloon, filled with its own steam, though at first it may blister in just a few places. Press gently on the small bubbles to enlarge them. Turn the chapati over as soon as the bottom browns lightly. It won't brown evenly, but will be a pretty pattern of brown and beige. It is done when delicately beige and brown on both sides, with no wet-pinkish places. (Flour will accumulate on the griddle as you cook; wipe it off so it doesn't burn.)

These wonderful breads are best served immediately, but you can wrap them in towels and keep them warm in the oven until time to eat. Don't let them dry out, though.

Breakfast

To eat or not to eat a hearty breakfast is something that goes in and out of fashion. Most important is to work out a way to get your nutrients in a pattern that's comfortable for you, whatever the fashion is. There is some scientific evidence in favor of a good breakfast, though, and our own experience supports it.

For one thing, metabolism is most efficient when we are moving around. Calories, and even demon fat, taken when you'll be exercising, are more likely to be used instead of being stored as fat. The fact that the digestive system rests when we sleep, working slowly or not at all, argues against eating a heavy supper: anyone can attest that going to bed stuffed makes for a sour, sluggish awakening.

Maybe the key to enjoying a substantial breakfast is to be up and around for at least an hour beforehand. There are hidden dividends in getting up early. The first hours of the day are the loveliest. The air is fresh then, and once you've broken free of the pillow your mind is likely to be at its clearest too. The silence of early morning is a perfect background for studying, writing letters, or taking a walk or run. In many traditions, it is the time of day thought to be most auspicious for meditation.

The earlier you get up, the more leisurely your morning can be. That's all-important, because the pace you set in the morning is the pace you'll maintain all day. If there are children about, try especially to keep breakfast time as slow and tranquil as can be. If eyelids are heavy, offer them some incentive: a fresh camellia, or a bowl of bright purple plums.

If you've been up long enough to get breakfast well underway before the family appears, you can actually sit down and eat with them instead of flying around the kitchen bagging lunches, burning toast, and feeding the cat. Children are much more likely to eat a well-balanced breakfast if their parents eat with them. Beyond a few gentle queries, it doesn't seem to matter if you say much. Just being together in a peaceful, warm atmosphere makes all the difference in how everyone gets through the day. Food eaten calmly, without hurry, will be digested much better than when one eye is on the plate and the other on the kitchen clock.

Our own breakfast mainstay during the week is hot whole-grain cereal and toast. Eggs we have only seldom. Buttermilk or

Oatmeal Pancakes turn up maybe one morning a week, or sometimes bagels. We like dry cereal, and granola is a favorite, but we think of such foods more often for snacks than for breakfast because of the nutritional advantages of cooked cereal. Dry toasting, whether of bread or of grains for cereal, destroys substantial amounts of the B vitamins thiamin and folacin and the amino acid lysine, all of which are protected in the kind of cooking that porridge gets. Since low, light toasting minimizes such losses, making your own granola (see page 88) and toasting your bread lightly can make a real difference.

If you can't find time to make your own granola, try to find a local bakery that prepares it with low heat, and without added fat. Nutrition-conscious people often turn away from big-name breakfast cereals to buy granola, only to realize that most commercial granolas are simply loaded with fat—often highly saturated fat—and sugar. Homemade granola can be custom-tailored to your family's needs. It'll taste better, too, because all the ingredients are fresher—and the money saved is impressive.

HOT BREAD

Leftover muffins or rolls, or even not-so-fresh bread, can be revived for breakfast by steaming. Wrap the bread in a damp towel and put it in a covered glass pan in the oven for 20 minutes at 325°, or in the microwave for about 30 seconds. If you get your setup worked out, the results can be nearly as appealing as fresh-baked.

BREAKFAST BEANS

Beans for breakfast might seem odd. Our first adventure with them was many years ago, during a visit to the Tassajara Monastery near Santa Cruz. We were startled to encounter a steaming hot bowl of adzuki beans at the breakfast table, served with a pungent pickled radish and a chunk of Tassajara's hefty, whole-grain bread. Maybe it was the mountain air, but nothing could have tasted better, and since then, beans have become a staple breakfast item. Electric slow-cookers cook them perfectly overnight. Strange as it sounds, morning is the ideal time to eat beans, because problems digesting them are minimized by the physical activity of the day.

❧

Besides breakfast recipes, this chapter includes some miscellaneous recipes that might be used throughout the day—instructions for preparing yogurt, buttermilk, and soy milk, and for toasting nuts, wheat germ, and seeds.

Porridge

Hard to believe that anything so satisfying could also be nourishing, inexpensive, and simple to prepare. But then, half the appeal does seem to come from what you put on top. We make our choices from a smorgasbord of healthful garnishes, so every bowl looks a little different.

The cereal we eat most often is an earthy commercial nine-grain, milled nearby, and very fresh. Probably we'd be satisfied if it were the only cereal we ever had. But since receiving a little electric stone mill, we have discovered how amazingly different, and delightfully better, *really* freshly milled grain tastes. Some mixtures that seem especially good to us are listed here for you to try. Some can be mixed from already-cracked grains in your pantry. Rice Cream, though, whose delicate flavor is truly remarkable, can be had only by those who grind their own.

Usually breakfasters expect their porridge to be softer than a dinner grain, and so it is cooked with extra water. As a general rule, unless the cereal is rolled, use 3 to 4 cups water to 1 cup cereal, making about 4 cups of porridge. For rolled cereals follow the directions on the package, or start with 2 cups water to 1 cup grain.

Finely cracked cereals tend to settle in the pot and burn more easily than bigger grains do. For long-cooked porridge with no burning, use a double boiler. Cook and stir over direct heat for just a few minutes first, until the cereal thickens; then put the pot over water. Allow 20 minutes or more, depending on how fine the grain is: the smaller the pieces, the faster they'll cook. If you are pressed for time in the morning, try the thermos method: bring cereal to a boil and stir till it thickens; then put it into a preheated wide-mouthed thermos, cap it, and let it stand overnight. By breakfast time the cereal will be cooked and piping hot. If it's thick, thin it to your liking with more hot water.

SOME GARNISHES FOR
BREAKFAST PORRIDGE

toasted sunflower seeds,
sesame meal, nuts,
wheat germ
stewed prunes or other
dried fruit
dates or raisins
fresh fruit in season
yogurt, cottage cheese,
milk or buttermilk
beans

CEREAL MIXES TO TRY

LIGHT AND BRIGHT

Equal parts lightly
toasted millet, cracked
barley, rice, and oats

ALL—GRAIN

Equal parts (or not!)
cracked wheat, rye, corn,
barley, rice, oats,
millet, triticale

RICE CREAM CEREAL

7 parts cracked brown rice
1 part cracked brown
basmati rice

STUART'S CHOICE

2 parts cracked wheat
1 part coarse cornmeal

Granola

4 cups rolled oats
1 cup toasted wheat germ
½ cup chopped toasted nuts
½ cup raisins or
  chopped dried fruits
(½ cup warmed honey)

We have listed the ingredients so simply because granola can be good in so many different variations, and your own will be the very best of all.

ঽ৯

Toast the oats in a 300°F oven in a big baking pan. Stir them often until they are fragrant and barely beginning to turn golden. How long this takes will depend on how thick your oats are.

When the oats are done, stir in the other ingredients. *Let cool completely* and store airtight in the refrigerator.

Makes 5½ cups.

TIPS

OATS You can buy rolled oats (and other rolled grains) in several thicknesses, from very thin (Instant) through Quick, Regular, and the thickest, Old-fashioned. If you are making granola for small children, choose one of the thin kinds; children often don't chew well enough to render the thicker ones digestible. Some of our crustier friends really do prefer the chewy natural-foods-store kind, but for most of us a big bowl of that sort of granola can mean a pretty tired jaw. Maybe start with Regular?

TOASTING Once you get your timing down, you may be able to toast oats, nuts, and even wheat germ together, adding each one at the right time so that they are all done at the same moment.

FRUIT Adding the fruit while the other ingredients are still hot lets the fruit get extra-dry and chewy. We like it this way, and it has the added advantage of preventing moisture in the fruit from softening the cereal in storage. If you want fruit that is soft, best add it when you eat.

Raisins or currants are obvious choices, but apricots add something really special, too. For very fancy cereal, add bits of dried pineapple, monukka raisins, chopped pitted prunes, or whatever you think is special.

Nuts add flavor and crunch. Almonds or filberts are our first choice. Or try peanuts, soy nuts, and pumpkin and sunflower seeds. All of these are most flavorful if toasted. NUTS

Bran is often added to granola, and if you feel the need to add extra fiber to your diet, this is a good a place to do it—though a diet that includes plenty of whole grains, vegetables, and fruits, probably has adequate fiber already. BRAN

For sweeter granola, stir warmed honey into the oats before toasting, or brown sugar or date sugar after toasting. How much to use is up to you, but ½ cup is a good place to start. Honey toasted with the oats has the advantage of making the cereal crunchier, too, which can make the difference between thumbs-up and thumbs-down on homemade granola. You'll want to adjust the amount to your family's tastes. Less is better *unless* it means that they reach for the sugar bowl to take matters into their own spoons! Then less usually means more. SWEETNESS

A high percentage of fat calories is one of the most telling arguments against most commercial granolas. When you make your own, it will be delicious without added oil. If you do add oil, however—or shredded coconut—keep the granola in the refrigerator and use it soon; oil that has been treated this way doesn't keep its freshness long. OIL

Toasting Wheat Germ

Raw wheat germ, with its abundance of unsaturated oil, goes rancid very quickly. The low heat of careful toasting helps preserve freshness in two ways, by inactivating enzymes that speed rancidity, and by reducing moisture content.

Unless you can get wheat germ that is freshly milled (very rare indeed), we recommend buying the kind that is toasted where it is milled. If you want to toast your own, the secret to preserving nutrients is to keep the oven temperature low, about 300°F. Use a wide, flat baking dish and stir the toasting wheat germ away from the sides and bottom frequently—it will brown there the fastest. When it is all golden brown, remove from the oven and allow to cool completely before storing airtight in the refrigerator.

Nuts & Seeds, Butters & Meals

TOASTING

Toasting brings out the flavor of nuts and seeds, and makes them crunchier. If it is done carefully, damage to the protein and unsaturated oils is minimal. Always toast *before* chopping. Use a big shallow pan, and keep the oven heat low, not above 325°F; stir often. Roasting in a pan, and oven toasting at higher temperatures, are quicker, but more nutrients will be destroyed and neither flavor nor texture will be quite as good.

NUT AND SEED MEALS

For garnishes, and for some recipes, nut and seed meals are called for. A grain mill with cleanable grinding plates—not most stone mills—or an electric blender or food processor will make meals quite easily. The trick with the blender is to chop the nuts first if they are smooth ones like almonds or filberts, and then do just ½ cup at a time, blending briefly, stopping the motor, stirring from the bottom, and repeating until the grind is right and you have the amount you want.

Nut and seed butters offer a delicious whole-food alternative to butter and margarine, though keeping them on hand may result in eating *more* fat calories rather than less, because people like them so much and spread them so thick. Still, unlike butter or margarine, they are real foods and do provide nutrients. Fresh, locally-made nut or seed butters often cost less to buy than the nuts or seeds would, to buy and do it yourself. Just read the label to be sure the one you buy has no added oil, salt, sugar, or additives.

BUTTERS

Peanut butter presents a special concern. Commercial peanut butter is often made from poor-quality peanuts that are dirty or broken in harvest or storage. Such nuts may be contaminated with the potent liver carcinogen aflatoxin. Whole, sound, clean nuts are likely to be safe, because the mold that produces the toxin requires damaged tissues to grow. Peanuts, which grow under the ground, are especially susceptible to infection when harvested by machine, because so many of them get broken or crushed. Whole, sound nuts are usually reserved for selling as peanuts, while the "splits" are used for making peanut butter. There are ways of checking for the presence of mold, but how carefully this is done is largely up to the processor. (Irradiation of food, incidentally, does not inhibit this mold but greatly stimulates its growth.)

Many natural foods suppliers are extremely conscientious about their peanuts. If you like a particular brand, write or call the company and ask them what precautions they take to protect the consumer. Do they use broken peanuts? Are the nuts tested for presence of the mold that produces aflatoxin? How are they stored? How is the equipment kept clean? If their answers satisfy you, you can probably eat their peanut butter with confidence. Otherwise, we suggest grinding your own from peanuts you know are clean and whole, or switching to almond butter. Happily, bumper crops of almonds in California in recent years have made almond butter an affordable, and delicious, alternative. (Since almonds do not grow under the ground, they are much less subject to damage and to contamination by molds that produce aflatoxin.)

To grind your own peanut or almond butter, use a grinder as described above for making nut meals, but grind finer; or use a food processor, following the manufacturer's directions. Most ordinary blenders are not powerful enough to make smooth nut butter.

SEED BUTTERS

Sesame is wonderfully flavorful, and uniquely resistant to rancidity, so sesame butter—tahini—has been enjoyed in other cultures for many centuries. Tahini is available in various degrees of toastedness in natural foods stores. Usually it is made from hulled seeds, because they make a smoother, less bitter spread. As you would expect, much is lost with the hulls, including B vitamins and minerals. (More about sesame seeds on page 116.) Sunflower seeds make tasty butter, too, but they don't contain a natural antioxidant, as sesame seeds do. Unless preservatives are added, sunflower seeds become rancid quickly after they are ground, so grind just what you'll use in a few days.

Stewed Prunes

An old-fashioned favorite, stewed prunes are a regular item on our breakfast menu. Some of the few remaining prune orchards in California are just a morning's drive away, so we can buy fresh dried prunes in bulk at a good price. Any food cooperative can probably do the same.

For a nutritional bonus, stew the prunes in an iron pot. They take up perfectly usable iron, making them an even richer source of this important mineral.

ᕕ

Cover a pound of dried prunes with cold water and bring to a boil. Simmer for about 20 minutes, until puffy; then, if you like, add a piece of cinnamon stick or half a lemon, scrubbed and sliced, and cook for another 10 minutes or longer, depending on your prunes and your taste. Some of us like to let them stand long enough to make the juice really thick and syrupy—good enough for pancakes, even.

Makes 3½ cups.

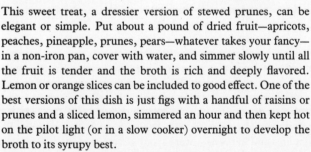

Fruit Compote

This sweet treat, a dressier version of stewed prunes, can be elegant or simple. Put about a pound of dried fruit—apricots, peaches, pineapple, prunes, pears—whatever takes your fancy—in a non-iron pan, cover with water, and simmer slowly until all the fruit is tender and the broth is rich and deeply flavored. Lemon or orange slices can be included to good effect. One of the best versions of this dish is just figs with a handful of raisins or prunes and a sliced lemon, simmered an hour and then kept hot on the pilot light (or in a slow cooker) overnight to develop the broth to its syrupy best.

Spoon over hot cereal or pancakes; for dessert, serve compote with yogurt or vanilla pudding—or all by itself in tiny cut-glass dishes. For quick, flavorful homemade jam, puree stewed fruit with some of its juice. Store in the refrigerator.

Better-Butter 🥨

This is surely one of the most popular of all our recipes. It offers an easy-spreading alternative to margarine, which can otherwise be the most highly processed—and salted—food in a natural foods kitchen.

Better-Butter combines butter (for flavor) with the unsaturated fats of good-quality oil. The result is a spread that's as low in saturated fat as margarine, but without hydrogenation, processing, and additives. You probably won't need to add the salt unless you have been using a salty margarine up until now.

1 cup canola or corn oil
1 cup (1/2 pound) butter
2 tablespoons water
2 tablespoons powdered nonfat milk
1/4 teaspoon lecithin
(1/2 teaspoon salt)

ૐ

Use butter that is soft but not melted. One version of Better-Butter can be made by simply blending equal parts of oil and butter together, pouring into covered containers, and storing in the refrigerator. By including the other ingredients, though, you will have a spread that stays firm a little longer at room temperature.

Blend all ingredients until smooth. Refrigerate. Makes just over 2 cups.

Apple Butter

Here is another kind of "butter"—strangely, it really does work as a spread all by itself. Adjust the honey and the cider vinegar to the tartness of the apples you have.

ૐ

Core and quarter apples and place in a saucepan with apple juice (or water), and vinegar. Bring to a boil, then lower heat, cover, and simmer until apples are soft—perhaps as long as 1/2 hour.

2 pounds flavorful apples
1/2 cup apple juice or water
1/4 to 1/2 cup cider vinegar
2 to 3 tablespoons honey or brown sugar
1 teaspoon cinnamon
1/4 teaspoon allspice
dash cloves

Press apples through a food mill or strainer and return to saucepan along with honey, cinnamon, allspice, and cloves. Bring to a boil, then lower heat to a brisk simmer, stirring frequently, as mixture reduces. When it "sheets" as you drop it from a spoon, it is ready. Refrigerate to store.

Makes 2 to 3 cups.

Old-Fashioned Pancakes

2 cups whole wheat flour
½ cup wheat germ
  (or just use more flour)
2 teaspoons baking powder
1 tablespoon brown sugar
1 teaspoon salt

2 large eggs
2½ to 3 cups fresh milk

2 tablespoons oil

Add interest to these or other kinds of pancakes by sprinkling the the griddle first with sesame, sunflower, or poppy seeds. Using wheat germ is optional, but it does improve the pancakes' texture, especially if your flour is finely ground. (Bran works too.) Coarser flours—like most stone-ground flours—make tender, light pancakes.

With coarse flour, it is entirely possible to make light, tasty pancakes without dairy products: simply use the dry ingredients as listed, plus water in place of the egg and milk measure. Leaving out the oil is also an option, though there, the character of the cakes is quite different. Let oil-free pancakes cook longer, over slightly lower heat.

Friends who make pancakes often like to stir up 3 or 4 batches of dry ingredients and store them airtight in the refrigerator, ready to mix with liquid as the occasion arises.

❧

Stir together all the dry ingredients.

Beat the eggs lightly and combine with the milk, then add to the dry ingredients and stir briefly. Stir in oil.

Heat the griddle. It should be hot enough so that when you sprinkle water drops on the surface, they dance. Unless the griddle is hopelessly unseasoned, it shouldn't need any grease. Pour the batter onto griddle by large spoonfuls. Cook over medium heat, turning once when bubbles come to the surface and pop, and the edges are slightly dry.

Makes 18 pancakes.

BUTTERMILK PANCAKES

Replace baking powder with 1 teaspoon baking soda and substitute buttermilk for sweet milk. These tender delicacies are a great favorite.

FRESH CORN PANCAKES

Add a cup of cooked corn kernels to either of the above.

Oatmeal Pancakes

Combine the milk and rolled oats in a bowl and let stand at least 5 minutes.

Add the oil and beaten eggs, mixing well; stir in the flour, sugar, baking powder, and salt. Mix just until the dry ingredients are moistened.

Bake on a hot, lightly oiled griddle, using ¼ cup of batter for each pancake. Turn them when the top is bubbly and the edges are slightly dry.

Makes 10 to 12 four-inch pancakes.

WHEATLESS OAT CAKES

Make 1¾ cups of flaky meal by spinning 2 cups or so of rolled oats in blender. Use instead of the combined oat and wheat measure.

Mix ingredients and let stand about 5 minutes. If griddle is not well seasoned, oil it lightly, as these pancakes tend to stick.

Makes 12.

1¼ cups milk
1 cup rolled oats

1 tablespoon oil
2 eggs, beaten

½ cup whole wheat flour
1 tablespoon brown sugar
1 teaspoon baking powder
¼ teaspoon salt

Buckwheat Pancakes

Sift the buckwheat flour (it tends to be lumpy) and stir the other dry ingredients in lightly with a fork.

Add the oil, beaten egg, and milk, and mix briefly. Include orange peel for a gourmet touch.

Cook the pancakes on a medium-hot, lightly oiled griddle. Buckwheat pancakes take a little extra cooking, so wait until bubbles appear all over the surface before turning them.

Makes 18 four-inch pancakes.

1 cup buckwheat flour
2 teaspoons baking powder
1 cup whole wheat flour
  (use whole wheat pastry
  flour for very tender
  cakes)
½ teaspoon salt
1 tablespoon brown sugar

1 tablespoon oil
2 eggs, beaten
2 cups fresh milk
(grated peel of 1 orange)

Potato Latkes

1 tablespoon onion, or more
1 tablespoon oil

2 teaspoons active dry yeast
1 cup warm milk, stock,
   or water

1 medium potato
1 egg, beaten
1 teaspoon salt (scant)
½ cup whole wheat flour
¼ cup wheat germ

These richly flavored yeast-raised potato pancakes are light, delicious, and not at all greasy—wonderful not only for breakfast, but at any time of day. Easy to make, too—a favorite for Sunday supper with a big spinach salad.

🍃

Sauté onion in oil. Dissolve yeast in liquid. Grate potato and mix together with egg, salt, flour, and wheat germ. Add the onion with its oil.

Let rise 30 minutes. Stir down. Cook over medium heat on lightly oiled griddle until browned on each side, about 6 to 7 minutes.

Serve with applesauce and yogurt or Mock Sour Cream.
Makes 8 pancakes.

Stewed Apples or Applesauce

6 flavorful apples
handful raisins
½ cup water or apple juice

(lemon juice or peel)

Core apples and cut into chunks. Add raisins and water or apple juice, bring to a boil, and simmer until tender. To make applesauce, mash with a fork.

Lemon lends a piquant touch to complement the raisins' sweetness.

Makes 3 or 4 cups.

Fresh Fruit Sauce

4 ripe bananas
1 orange, peeled
juice of 1 lemon
¼ cup raisins
¼ cup boiling water

A pancake topping that really can compete with syrup, this is quick to prepare, too. Since bananas tend to darken, eat this soon after preparing it.

🍃

Pour boiling water over raisins and let stand a moment until raisins are plump. Combine all ingredients in blender and puree until smooth.

Makes 1½ to 2 cups.

Dosas

Dosas are a classic South Indian pancake and an adventure in a whole other way of thinking about meal preparation. They must be set up two days in advance, and brought along in stages, and the cook—usually a mother, grandmother, or aunt—proudly insists on serving them hot from the griddle, so she doesn't get to sit down until the happy eaters can eat no more.

ঽৡ

Soak the dal (or garbanzos), fenugreek, and rice overnight in ample water to cover.

The next morning, drain most of the water off and, using only as much water as necessary, grind the mixture in blender or processor to make a paste that is light and frothy. When smooth, add the salt and water to make a thick pouring consistency—a little thinner than normal pancake batter. Let stand about 24 hours, loosely covered, at warm room temperature.

To cook the dosas you will need a griddle, a serving spoon with a round, shallow scoop, a saucer with a small amount of oil in it, and a pancake turner.

The griddle should be a little cooler than for pancakes, or the batter will "pick up" and you won't be able to make the dosas thin enough. Unless the griddle's surface is very well seasoned, wipe it with a cloth dipped in oil. Stir the batter as you make the dosas.

Pour about 3 tablespoons of batter in the middle of the pan. Using the back of your big spoon, and starting in the center, spread the batter in a spiral from the center outwards to make a very thin pancake about 9" to 10" across. It will show a slight pinwheel from the track of your spoon. Next, dip the tip of your spatula in the oil and flick tiny droplets over the dosa—that helps it cook. When the top surface has dried, loosen the cake from the griddle with your spatula, and turn it over. You can turn it more than once. Dosas can be made paper-thin and very crisp or slightly thicker and soft. They are done if you can press the dosa with the back of your spatula, without a sizzling sound. Thin dosas cook much faster than thick ones.

Serve hot from the griddle with Tomato or Coconut Chutney; or make MASALA DOSAS: spoon a couple of tablespoons of Masala Potatoes or Dal (next page) on the dosa, and fold it in half.

Makes about 12.

⅓ cup hulled split
  black gram (urid dal)
  or garbanzo beans
pinch whole fenugreek seeds
1 cup brown rice
scant ½ teaspoon salt
⅓–½ cup water
oil

Masala Potatoes

3 large potatoes

1–2 large onions,
1 tablespoon minced ginger
1 green chili
   (or ¼ green bell pepper)

1–2 tablespoons oil
1 teaspoon black mustard
   seeds

1 teaspoon turmeric
½ teaspoon salt

juice of ½ lemon
chopped fresh coriander
   leaves

The proportions of onion and potato in this dish can vary. If you want to serve it as a vegetable dish, tasty but not overpowering, use the measures as they are given; if it is to be a relish for dosas or a filling for stuffed eggplant, use more onion and less potato.

Steam the potatoes until tender. While they are cooking, cut up the other vegetables: the onions should be cut in ½" cubes; the ginger and chili minced. (If you use a whole chili the dish will be fiery beyond belief. To make it merely hot, take out the seeds; use only part, and it will be nippy. Green pepper without any chili at all is fine for most Western palates.) Peel and mash the potato, or cut into cubes.

Heat the oil in a heavy skillet and drop in the mustard seed. Cover and let the seeds pop; the moment the sound of popping quiets down, add the onions. Stir and sauté until the onions are soft; then add the ginger and chili or green pepper, continuing to sauté gently for about a minute. Stir in the turmeric and salt, then the potatoes, and half a cup of water or so. Cook and stir until the water evaporates and the mixture is dry. Add lemon juice and coriander leaves, stir well, and remove from heat. Serve with Dosas or Chapatis; or use as a side dish, or as a stuffing for peppers or small eggplants.

Makes about 3 cups.

Dal

1½ cups yellow split peas
1 teaspoon salt
1 onion
½ green pepper
1 teaspoon turmeric
½ teaspoon curry powder
2 tablespoons oil
1½ teaspoons black
   mustard seeds
juice of 1 lemon

In one form or another, this simple, delicious dish is popular all over India—and anywhere else it has been served.

Boil the yellow split peas for about 30 minutes—until they are tender, but not so long that they lose their shape. They should be rather dry, like mashed potatoes. Stir in salt. While the peas are cooking, chop onion and green pepper. Combine with turmeric and curry powder.

Heat oil in a large, heavy pan with a lid. When oil is hot, add mustard seed and cover. The seeds will pop noisily; when the sound quiets down, immediately add onion mixture. Sauté until onion is transparent and golden, and stir into peas along with the lemon juice. Serve with Dosas or Chapatis or over rice or other grains. Makes about 4 cups.

About Cultured Milk

Culturing milk—letting carefully chosen bacteria grow in it, producing various magical changes—is one of the oldest methods of food preservation, practiced by dairying people all over the world. Products like yogurt, buttermilk, and most kinds of cheese, make use of the talents of one or more microorganisms.

Since 1908, when the Nobel Prize-winning Russian scientist Elie Metchnikoff suggested that Bulgarian peasants owed their unusual longevity to the large amounts of yogurt in their diet, scientists have studied the benefits that yogurt offers for health. One discovery is that the microorganisms which culture dairy products make them more digestible: proteins are partially broken down and thus more easily assimilated.

Yogurt is similar to milk in its vitamin and mineral content except that the fermenting bacteria do consume some vitamins—especially B-12, which is reduced by about half. On the other hand, folic acid is synthesized in yogurt by the lactic cultures so that the amount is greatly increased. Calcium, phosphorus, and iron are easier to absorb.

Cultured milk bacteria can supply a digestive enzyme, *lactase*, that most people—except those of northern European stock—cannot make for themselves after childhood. Lactase is responsible for breaking down the natural sugar in milk, *lactose*. People who are deficient in the enzyme find that milk gives them stomachache, gas, and diarrhea. The lactase enzymes in yogurt (and to some extent in other cultured milks) slightly reduce the amount of lactose. Yogurt usually contains *Lactobacillus bulgaricus* and *Streptococcus thermophilus*. These two remain active for some time after they have been eaten, continuing to help with the digestion of milk sugar in the small intestine. *S. thermophilus* has about three times as much lactase as *L. bulgaricus*. If you have trouble digesting milk products, look for the names of these cultures on the label when you buy yogurt.

Buttermilk and sour cream are cultured, but with different organisms that don't reduce lactose. In cheese and cottage cheese, lactose may be diminished both by the culturing bacteria, if any, and by the removal of whey in cheesemaking.

Cultured dairy products can inhibit the growth of harmful bacteria that cause intestinal infection, diarrhea, flatulence, and

LACTOSE INTOLERANCE

If you are lactose-intolerant and want to continue using dairy products, ask your pharmacist about tablets or drops containing lactase enzyme.

other problems. *Lactobacillus acidophilus* culture (contained in some but not all yogurts) may also help to reestablish a beneficial balance in the intestines after the natural flora have been destroyed by antibiotic medication.

Research has shown that milk lowers blood cholesterol levels, and that cultured milk is more effective in this than uncultured. Other studies indicate that some cultured dairy foods are anti-carcinogenic: in animals, eating yogurt has dramatically reduced tumor cell proliferation; and in both animal and human studies, bacterial enzymes associated with bowel cancer were reduced by eating *L. acidophilus*.

The ways microorganisms work for us—in yogurt, wine, miso, tempeh, bread, cheese, and many other foods—is a vast topic for study. A great deal remains to be learned.

Foolproof Yogurt

Homemade yogurt is cheaper than the commercial kind, and can be as good as the best. Because your own yogurt is fresher, the culture will be more vigorous and enzyme activity greater. And when you make your own, you can control the flavor and tartness to suit your taste.

If you use commercial yogurt as your starter, be sure that it has an active culture. If the label says it's pasteurized or stabilized, the contents won't make new yogurt. Best is if the label says "active culture"—unless the container has been on the shelf for weeks. Once you get your own yogurt-making system going, you will always have a lively starter, and the time each batch of yogurt takes to set will be less.

Using powdered milk makes the process much simpler because there's no milk to heat, no pan to wash; you just use tap water at the right temperature. To us, yogurt made this way is so good that there's no need for the added fat and cholesterol of whole milk. But yogurt made from fresh milk *is* delicious. To make low-fat or whole milk yogurt, use the same recipe, but scald the milk and cool it to 120°F beforehand. Heat the milk gently because scorching spoils the flavor; a double boiler is best, if you have one. Fresh milk makes tender yogurt; if you want it firmer, blend in 2 tablespoons of milk powder along with the starter.

If your oven has a pilot or electric light, the temperature inside may be just right for incubating yogurt during times when you have nothing to bake. Or keep the yogurt on a heating pad in a warm nook, covering it with towels or newspapers to keep in the warmth. Some people like to use a Styrofoam box filled with warm water, and set the jars in that. Many things work, so long as the temperature stays steady long enough: 90° to 120°F. Above 120°F the culturing bacteria will die.

MISCELLANEOUS TIDBITS

Powdered low-fat and whole milks are available, but there is concern that the drying process damages the cholesterol in these products, making it especially harmful.

POWDERED WHOLE MILK

We recommend using non-instant milk powder because sometimes the instant kind is tricky for making yogurt. If you can get only instant, you will need more powder than we call for here. For making yogurt, use one-eighth more milk powder than the package directs for mixing regular-strength milk. (1½ cups milk powder instead of the normal 1⅓ to make a quart, for example.) If you find that you have trouble making yogurt, try reconstituting the milk and letting it stand overnight in the refrigerator. Warm it to temperature the next day to make yogurt.

INSTANT POWDERED MILK

To keep your starter free from stray organisms, sterilize the jar before you start. A run through the dishwasher will do it, or you can soak the container in this bleach solution for 30 seconds or more. Rinse thoroughly, because residual bleach can kill the yogurt culture. (By the way, this solution will sanitize eating utensils, too.)

STERILIZING CONTAINERS

1 tablespoon 5% chlorine bleach
2 gallons warm (not hot) water

YOGURT RECIPE

¼ cup plain yogurt
1 cup non-instant powdered
*   skim milk*
3½ cups water, 100–110°F

EQUIPMENT

1 one-quart glass
*   or plastic jar with lid*
electric blender
a warm place

Fill the jar with warm water to about 2 inches from the top. Pour 1 cup of the warm water into the blender. Turn the blender on low and add the milk powder and the yogurt. The instant the mixture is smooth, stop blending and return it to its jar. This prevents the milk from foaming.

Set the filled jar in a warm place and leave undisturbed for 3½ to 8 hours. The livelier the culture and the warmer the place, the more quickly the yogurt will set. Check from time to time. As soon as the surface of the yogurt resists a light touch of your finger even slightly, it is ready; but if you want a tart flavor, leave it another hour.

Refrigerate and let cool completely before you dip into it.

The first spoonful of yogurt from each jar can be set aside to be the starter for the next batch. To keep your starter fresh, plan your amounts to make yogurt at least once a week.

TROUBLESHOOTING YOGURT

The yogurt didn't set up

—Is your milk powder fresh? Fresh dried milk is odorless—take a sniff to see.

—Was the water too hot? Below 95°F the yogurt bacteria are not active; above 120°F, they die. The water should feel just warm to your hand. A dairy or chef's thermometer can be helpful here.

—Was your culture too old, or was your starter from a stabilized commercial brand? Try again with a different kind. Cheap local brands are often fresher and livelier than their more expensive and long-traveling colleagues.

—Did you sterilize the container with bleach and not rinse it well enough?

The yogurt tastes chalky

—The milk mixture might have been too concentrated. If you allow foam to build up when you're mixing powdered milk, it will fill your container and can trick you into including less water than is needed.

The yogurt is very soft or tender

—Either the milk solution is too dilute or the yogurt needed more time to set up. You can make yogurt extremely firm, if you want to, by increasing the amount of milk; but skim milk yogurt that is made very concentrated may taste chalky.

The yogurt separates and tastes sour

—Probably it was warm too long. Sometimes this happens if your refrigerator can't cool it fast enough; try cooling as suggested for soymilk on page 107, or just remove it from the heat promptly as soon as it has set.

—Another possibility is that your heat source is too intense. Prop the oven door open with a roll of towel or turn the heating pad down a notch.

The yogurt tastes off

—Some stray bacteria might have set up housekeeping. Start over with a new culture, and be careful to keep your starter and containers absolutely clean. Merely gamy yogurt isn't harmful, but if your batch smells really hideous, don't taste it, toss it.

Yogurt Cheese 🍶

Yogurt cheese made with low-fat yogurt is a slim version of sour cream or cream cheese (depending how stiff you make it), useful in many ways. The nonfat version can taste overwhelmingly yogurty by itself, but still be useful for such dishes as Jaji (page 118), Yogurt Cheese Pie (page 326), or Topping (page 318)—anywhere there are other flavors going.

ᕯ

Line a colander or strainer with a large cloth napkin. Turn a quart of yogurt into it and allow to drain until the cheese is as stiff as you want, anywhere from 6 to 24 hours. You can hang it over a sink by tying the napkin closed and fastening it to the faucet, but outside the refrigerator the cheese will become very tart. Another option is to suspend the yogurt over a bowl in the refrigerator.

No matter how stiff it is, when yogurt cheese is beaten hard it becomes liquid, so handle it gently when mixing.

Makes about 2 cups.

Buttermilk 🍶

We find that powdered milk doesn't make tasty buttermilk. If you can get good buttermilk for about the same price as fresh skim milk, there may be no reason to culture your own. But if splendid unsalted or skim-milk buttermilk is hard to find in your area, here's a dependable, simple method for making it:

ᕯ

To 2 quarts fresh skim milk, add ⅓ cup delicious buttermilk. Let stand at 65°–70°F for 24 to 36 hours. How long it takes will depend on how vigorous your starter is and whether the milk was straight from the refrigerator. When it tastes good to you, refrigerate it.

Soymilk

Soymilk is not a whole food, and it is far from being a nutritional substitute for milk, but for people to whom milk is not acceptable, what a boon!

Bottled soymilk has improved a lot in the last few years, and if you can get fresh liquid soymilk from a soy dairy nearby, you may find it quite good. The unflavored kind can be used in cooking wherever milk is called for; the flavored versions provide a reasonable alternative to milk for drinking. We really can't recommend any powdered variety we know of: the flavors are either too strong and beany or overly sweet. The list of additives can be amazing, and the price sky-high. Highly commercialized liquid soymilks have some of these problems too: more incentive for buying from a small local soy dairy, or making your own. The homemade version is wonderfully cheap and far more delicious than any you can buy, though it's decidedly not a "quick and easy" recipe.

COMPARING SOYMILK

1 cup	Calories kcal	Protein g	Riboflavin mg	B-12 mg	Calcium mg	Fat g	% cals as fat	Sat. Fat g	Unsat. Fat g
Soymilk: plain	73	7.5	0.1	0	46	3.3	40	0.5	2.4
sweetened	115	7.5	0.1	0	46	3.3	30	0.5	2.4
Skim milk	86	8.4	0.3	0.9	300	0.4	10	0.3	0.1
Whole milk	150	8.0	0.4	0.9	290	8.2	50	5.0	2.7
Goat's milk	168	8.7	0.3	0.2	320	10.0	50	6.5	3.1
Broccoli	46	4.6	0.3	0	140	0.4	10	0.1	0.2

Soymilk is a food in its own right, and maybe it's unfair to compare it with cow's milk. Still, since people use it as if it were cow's milk, knowing the nutritional differences is important, especially when considering the needs of children.

Soymilk has the same amount of protein as cow's milk and less fat than whole milk; almost all its fat is unsaturated. So much carbohydrate is removed from the soybeans when soymilk is made that almost none remains. One reason we suggest adding honey or barley malt syrup is that many people who drink soymilk are vegans—that is, vegetarians who avoid all foods of animal origin, including milk—and one of their nutritional needs is plain old calories.Soymilk is low or lacking in certain other nutrients richly supplied in milk: calcium, vitamin B-12, and riboflavin. (See suggestions for fortification on page 108.)

The basic procedure for making soymilk is to soak the beans in water for 4 to 16 hours until they are saturated, then grind them up fine in a blender, with more water. The "milk" is then strained off, flavored, cooked, and refrigerated.

Soymilk can have a bitter beany taste, the result of an enzyme (lipoxygenase or lipoxidase) that goes into action when the bean is broken in the presence of air and water. Scientists at Cornell University developed a way to inactivate the lipoxidase, and it is on their method—along with our own years of weekly soymilk production—that the following recipe is based.

ॐ

METHOD

The secret of the Cornell process is to grind the beans in *hot* water, at least 180°F, which inactivates the lipoxidase. (Cooking the beans first and *then* grinding them inactivates lipoxidase too, but the protein is thereby rendered insoluble, so it won't make milk.) This boiling–water grind process yields a soymilk that is bland and pleasant-tasting. But you have to be careful that the water you use is at a good rolling boil; it won't work if you let the water boil and then set the kettle aside for even a few minutes. This takes extra effort and time, but the result is well worth it.

1 cup dry soybeans
6 cups boiling water
  (plus 2 cups boiling
  water to heat blender)

FOR FLAVORING

¼ cup honey
  OR
2 tablespoons honey and
2 tablespoons barley malt
  extract

The quality of the soybeans you use will affect the amount and flavor of the milk they yield, so choose beans that are clean and sound. Wash them thoroughly and soak in 3 cups cold water for 4 to 16 hours; in warm weather, you can leave them in the refrigerator. The beans will double in size, so allow room in the container. If the water bubbles a little, it means that the beans fermented slightly: no problem.

Drain the beans well and rinse them in warm (not hot) water. If they were kept in the refrigerator, rinse them long enough to warm them through; this will help you maintain the required heat while the beans are in the blender.

Put a large kettle full of water on to boil. Divide the beans into three equal parts. Preheat the blender by blending 2 cups of boiling water for approximately 1 minute. Stainless steel blender containers are the best. Plastic ones cannot withstand boiling water. Glass tops should be warmed before pouring in boiling water to prevent their cracking.

Grind each portion of beans with 2 full cups of boiling water for 2 to 3 minutes. During the grinding, insulate the blender with a towel to keep the temperature high.

Strain the mixture in a muslin bag to remove the insoluble residue. Squeeze the bag to get as much of the milk as you can.

Mix in the sweetener and take note of the quantity. Heat the milk uncovered for 30 minutes in a double boiler, stirring occasionally to keep it from forming a film on top. Add water to the original quantity, replacing the amount lost to evaporation. This extra heating is important because it deactivates enzymes that interfere with the digestion of protein, soybean trypsin inhibitors (SBTI). Their presence in soybeans makes thorough cooking of any soy product essential.

This recipe makes 6 to 7 cups of soymilk.

A couple of tips to help your soymilk keep fresh longer:

[1] What makes the milk turn sour near the end of the week is the presence of bacteria. Be very careful to keep all your soymilk equipment extremely clean, and sterilize anything that will touch it after it is cooked, even the funnel, if you use one. This should extend the "sweet life" of your soymilk by several days.

[2] If you make a large quantity of soymilk at once, or if your refrigerator isn't up to cooling it in an hour or so, pre-chill the milk by setting it in its jar or pitcher in a dishpan of cold water for about half an hour. Keep the water cold by icing it, or by letting the faucet run in it. If the soymilk is in a plastic or glass container, this process will take longer; metal is best.

A NOTE ON CLEANING
UP AFTER

For easy cleanup, soak the muslin bag and all your equipment in a solution of washing soda immediately after you are through using them. Soda is very strong, so wear rubber gloves, and rinse everything thoroughly.

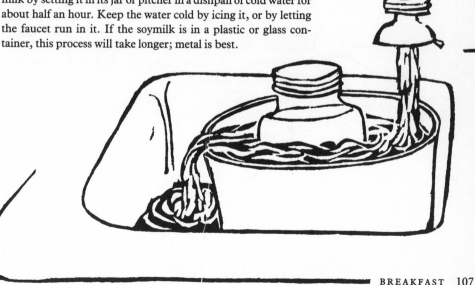

FORTIFICATION

Because of the nutritional differences mentioned above, soymilk can't entirely take the place of milk. If you don't use dairy products, be sure to eat plenty of green vegetables each day for calcium and riboflavin, and include a source of vitamin B-12 also. Special care is necessary in planning food for the vegan child, since children often resist eating vegetables.

Soymilk can provide an alternate source of some nutrients. It is not practical to add riboflavin to soymilk, but you can add B-12 by crushing and stirring in one tablet (the smallest size is 25 milligrams, which is far more than two quarts of milk would supply). Calcium can be added by mixing calcium carbonate, which is available in drug stores, into the soymilk, ½ teaspoonful per cup. The amount of calcium will then be comparable to that of milk, though it will not be absorbed so well and may cause constipation. Calcium lactate can also be used—it dissolves, which is an advantage over carbonate—but if the soymilk is heated, calcium lactate will make it curdle.

FLAVORING

The flavoring we suggest makes a drink that is sweet and delicious to our taste, but there's no reason not to experiment with other sweeteners and flavorings too: molasses, brown sugar, maple syrup; vanilla, or a pinch of cardamom or nutmeg. Keep some unflavored if you want to use it in place of milk in soups, cream sauces, quick breads.

Lunch

Not so long ago most people either ate at home or carried a brown-bag lunch. It's not uncommon now to stop at a deli or fast-food place for something quick that goes down easy. Americans spend 40 cents of their food dollar eating out—an average of 3.7 meals a week. But eating out, while it can be an enjoyable change of pace, isn't the best way to get your nourishment on a regular basis.

The chief nutritional complaints against restaurant food, from fast food to gourmet cuisine, are excessive fat and salt. Fast food in particular is loaded with both. One burger can exceed an adult's recommended daily maximum of salt, and a fast-food meal is not unlikely to have considerably more than half the day's allotment of fat—usually of the worst kind. (That rare vegetarian option, the "cheese"-stuffed potato, may have even more fat and calories than a burger.) Fast-food means frying, often in beef tallow or lard (even for fries, doughnuts, and turnovers), and the fat is used over and over again. Fast-food companies also employ the full array of additives: colorings, thickeners, flavorings, preservatives, emulsifiers. There is consumer pressure to require ingredient labels on fast foods, but at this writing, even if you ask, it's hard to discover what's in a particular item.

The best restaurant meals, of course, are to be had in individually owned places that use fresh, natural ingredients and cook without inordinate amounts of salt or fat. Next best may be a salad bar, where with care you can select a genuinely nutritious meal. But much depends on who's running the show. If the management is not committed to freshness, salad fixings—even lettuce—may be laced with preservatives of many kinds, and the dressings and cheeses can be of the most processed, chemicalized sort.

For such reasons, we and most of our friends prefer to bag our own: it's tastier, cheaper, and more nutritious, and you can take just what you want.

Incidentally, if lunchtime for you means a perfunctory affair with nobody else around—grabbing some bread and whatever, eating between jobs, paying no attention—why should the brown-baggers get all the delights? Even if you don't need much food in

the middle of the day, take the time to treat yourself to some of these suggestions; a home luncher needs pick-me-ups too. If you are tired of sandwiches, a fresh, tasty soup or a really worthy vegetable, grain, or fruit salad doesn't take long to prepare. Everyone deserves a lunch that satisfies aesthetic as well as nutritional needs, however simple it may be—and even aside from the food, it's worth taking time to make a break.

Carry-Out Lunches

Even for brown-baggers who like a streamlined lunch, with nothing to carry home when you're done, there are lots of possibilities beyond the standard sandwich and apple. Carrot and celery sticks, of course, but why not green peas in the pod, cherry tomatoes, whole little lemon cucumbers (easy to grow, very digestible)? Besides fruit bars and "real" cookies, try a simple bag of dried fruit and toasted nuts—whether its raisins and peanuts or medjool dates and pecans. Toasting the nuts yourself saves money, avoids oil and salt, and guarantees freshness.

If a small plastic container will come home afterward, a substantial salad—potato, grain, or pasta—makes an interesting break from the usual fare. Or pack some chilled, lightly steamed vegetables from the night before, with a little salad dressing. One of our friends takes a really righteous green salad every day, with the dressing packed separately in a tiny jar. It travels fine.

Special mention goes to grain salads—Tabouli, Yogurt Rice, and the like—which pack well and go down easily. Any grain left over from the night before can make a scrumptious salad with the help of a tad of yogurt, maybe a little olive oil and lemon, some chopped celery or pepper, chives. Or skip the grain and pack crisp-tender broccoli with a few leftover noodles, a lace of red bell pepper, Vinaigrette, and a sprinkle of Parmesan cheese or toasted sesame seeds.

When the weather turns cool, we want a hot meal. If you can microwave at work, bringing a container of vegetables or pasta to keep in the refrigerator until lunchtime makes a really good lunch easy. If there's no microwave, soups, saucy pasta, and many vegetable dishes will keep hot or cold for hours in a widemouth thermos. (Keep thermos jugs sweet by washing them well, and never storing them with their lids on.)

When packing lunches, keep in mind that food-borne bacteria grow quickly at warm room temperatures, especially when the food is nonacidic; potato salad is the classic example. Even if they'll be going into the microwave, take care that your leftovers don't sit in a warm place for hours before you eat.

Sandwiches

Sandwiches are a practical favorite, the challenge being to make them delicious and easy-to-eat without lots of mayonnaise or butter. Made with bean spreads, and even with moderate amounts of cheese, they're quite respectably low in fat. Soy spread on whole wheat, for example, is 19 percent fat without mayonnaise; add a tablespoon of mayo and it becomes 41 percent fat. A sandwich with 1 ounce of jack cheese on rye is only 32 percent fat without, 48 percent with. Our conclusion: try to cut back on the mayo. Tomato slices, alfalfa sprouts, sunflower greens, lettuce, pickle, mustard, sliced olives, and such all add juiciness without so many fat calories.

If you do want to use mayonnaise, try cutting it half and half with yogurt, or try our tofu mayonnaises on page 241 for a version much lower in fat. Careful packing, with a double wrap of waxed paper if needed, helps keep bagged sandwiches from drying out.

OTHER PLOYS:

🍂 For cheese sandwiches, include lots of goodies—tomato, lettuce, sliced mushroom, cucumber, onion, whatever—and then slice the cheese with the potato peeler, using enough to taste great but not enough to add much fat.

🍂 Make cheese spreads by mixing cottage cheese with grated hard cheese for a slightly lower-fat and less expensive cheese filling. (See page 118.)

🍂 For egg salad, lower the fat by adding low-fat cottage cheese or chopped firm tofu. You can even substitute tofu for the egg altogether, but since tofu is only slightly lower in fat, its main advantage is that the fat is less saturated and there is no cholesterol.

CHEESE: GRAMS OF
FAT PER 1¼ OUNCE

= piece 4" × 4" × ⅛"
= two 1" cubes
= scant ⅓ cup grated

12.4	Cream cheese
11.8	Cheddar
11.5	Gruyère
11.1	American (processed)
10.9	Roquefort
10.7	Jack, Muenster
10.6	Parmesan, *dry, grated*
10.2	Blue
10.0	Port du Salut
9.9	Edam, Brie
9.7	Swiss, Gouda
9.4	Provolone
9.2	Parmesan, *hard*
8.7	Mozzarella, *full fat, low moisture*
8.3	Neufchâtel
7.7	Mozzarella, *full fat*
7.5	Feta
6.1	Mozzarella, *part skim, low moisture*
5.6	Mozzarella, *part skim*

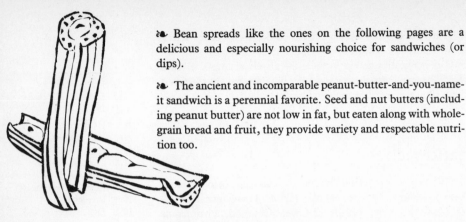

 Bean spreads like the ones on the following pages are a delicious and especially nourishing choice for sandwiches (or dips).

 The ancient and incomparable peanut-butter-and-you-name-it sandwich is a perennial favorite. Seed and nut butters (including peanut butter) are not low in fat, but eaten along with whole-grain bread and fruit, they provide variety and respectable nutrition too.

Sandwich Suggestions

Peanut butter and: chopped dates, sliced apple or banana, raisins, or stewed prunes; lettuce and tomato, or pickle

Almond butter and any of these; or try it with Dijon mustard, raisins, spinach leaf, dill pickle

Tofu Bars with pickle and lettuce on Whole Wheat

Pizza sandwich: on a slice of bread, Pocket Bread, or English Muffin, spread fresh tomato slices, pepper ring, oregano; sprinkle with olive oil, add grated cheese and grill until melted

Soy Spread, sprouts, tomato, on any whole-grain bread

Jaji and cucumber slices on Pumpernickel

Lentil Loaf slices, thinly shredded cabbage, and Dijon mustard on Light Rye

Walnut Oatmeal Burgers, mustard, ketchup, pickles, lettuce on a bun

Soy Pâté, cucumber slices, grated carrot on Pumpernickel

Split Pea–Parmesan Spread, red pepper rings, spinach leaves on Cracked Wheat

Garbanzo Spread, cucumbers, and lettuce on Whole Wheat

Reuben's Revenge: Swissy Spread and Vegetable Relish on Rye

Ricotta cheese, toasted walnuts, and Apple Butter on Oatmeal Bread

Yogurt Cheese, chopped dried apricots, and toasted almonds with a dash of cinnamon on Raisin Bread

Refrito Spread, tomato slices, and lettuce rolled in a Chapati

Jaji, grated carrot, cherry tomato, cucumber slices, and Tempeh Bars in Pocket Bread

Sesame spread and banana slices on Buttermilk Bread

Sliced mushrooms, tomato, spinach leaves, and Tofu Mayonnaise on Garbanzo Bread

Chili-Cheddar Spread, sliced olives, tomato, lettuce on Sesame Bread

Bean Spreads

Sandwiches with spreads made from cooked, mashed beans are a delicious addition to the lunch scene. Soy spread has been a staple at our house for years now. We like it best with lettuce or alfalfa sprouts and sliced tomato or pickle.

Beans—even soybeans if they are well-cooked—are easy to mash with a potato masher if you drain them hot from the cooking pot and set to work at once. (If you can't mash them right away, use a meat grinder or food processor; but drain them hot or the spread will be too runny.)

Bean spreads keep for about a week in the refrigerator. If you've made more than you can use up in sandwiches, stir the rest into soups or make Neat Balls or Pine Nut Pinwheels.

Soy Spread

Sauté onion and garlic in oil until onion is soft; then add celery (and green pepper if desired) and continue to cook until onion is transparent. Crush the garlic clove with a fork. Add tomato paste and herbs. Simmer briefly. Stir the sauce into the mashed beans and add vinegar, salt and pepper to taste.

Makes about 1½ cups.

½ onion, minced
1 tablespoon oil (or less)
1 clove garlic
1 small stalk celery,
*   chopped fine*
(¼ cup chopped green
*   pepper)*

2 tablespoons tomato paste
1 teaspoon basil
½ teaspoon oregano

ZIPPY SOY SPREAD

Omit basil. When onion is nearly cooked, stir in ½ teaspoon cumin and a dash of cayenne. If you have coriander powder, add 1 teaspoon of that, too.

QUICK SOY SPREAD

Stir ¼–½ cup flavorful tomato sauce into mashed beans; correct for salt.

1 cup cooked, mashed
*   soybeans*
1–2 teaspoons vinegar
½ teaspoon salt
dash pepper

SOY SPREAD WITH PARSLEY

Omit the tomato paste and herbs. Add ¼ cup chopped fresh parsley to the onion and celery before taking off heat. Add 1 teaspoon soy sauce and the juice of ½ lemon as you mix the ingredients together.

Garbanzo Spread

½ onion, chopped
1 clove garlic
1 tablespoon oil
dash cumin
salt to taste
1 teaspoon basil
½ teaspoon oregano
(½ bunch parsley,
    chopped fine)
juice of 1 lemon
3 cups cooked garbanzo
    beans, mashed

(⅔ cup toasted sesame
    seeds, ground)

Garbanzo Spread is an enduring favorite. Try it as an open-face sandwich with cucumber and tomato slices, or thin it with a little vegetable or bean stock and serve as a dip with whole wheat crackers.

&

Sauté onion and garlic in oil until onion is transparent. Add cumin and cook until fragrant. Crush garlic with a fork. Add herbs (and parsley) at the last minute, cooking just enough to soften parsley. Mix with the lemon and mashed beans (and sesame), stirring together thoroughly.

Makes about 3 cups.

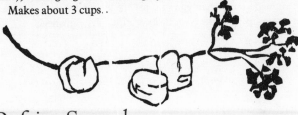

Refrito Spread

1½ cups cooked,
    well-drained pinto,
    kidney, or black beans

1 bunch scallions
    or a big onion
1 tablespoon oil

1 or 2 cloves garlic
½ teaspoon cumin powder
1 teaspoon chili powder
¼ chopped green pepper
    or chopped green chili
    peppers

½ cup grated cheddar cheese
½ teaspoon salt

Mash the beans. You should end up with about a cup.

Chop the onion and sauté with whole garlic cloves in oil. When the onion is done, crush the garlic with a fork. Add the spices and the green pepper. (If you are a chili fan, you can use green chilies instead of pepper.) Cook until the pepper is softened and the spices are fragrant.

Remove from heat and cool slightly. Add beans and mix. Add cheese and salt, and check the flavor: if the beans were unsalted, you may need more salt.

Makes about 1¾ cups.

Split Pea Spreads

When you make these spreads, you can use either plain cooked split peas (cooked with less water than you would use for soup) or very thick leftover pea soup (much tastier!). In either case, the peas should be cool when you mix the spread so that you can judge the consistency accurately. If you don't use soup, you can make the spread tastier by sautéeing onion and garlic in the oil measure before adding the peas, or by adding shoyu or miso to taste.

❧

Mash split peas and mix with other ingredients. Refrigerate.

SPLIT PEA—PARMESAN

1 cup cooked green split peas
2 tablespoons oil (or less)
2 tablespoons Parmesan cheese
2 tablespoons cottage cheese
¼ teaspoon basil
salt to taste
dash pepper

SPLIT PEA—SUNSEED

1 cup cooked green split peas
2 tablespoons oil (or less)
¾ to 1 cup toasted
   sunflower seeds, ground
salt to taste
dash pepper
(2 tablespoons lemon juice)
(2 tablespoons whole
   toasted sunflower seeds)

SPLIT PEA—TOFU DIP

1 cup cooked green split peas
2 tablespoons oil
1 pound firm tofu
1 cup toasted sunflower
   or sesame seeds, ground
1 tablespoon light miso,
   or salt to taste

Soy Pâté

This delicious and very savory pâté makes a sophisticated sandwich spread, very easy to make once the soybeans are at hand.

❧

Sauté the onion in oil, adding the garlic once the onion is transparent and beginning to turn golden. Continue to sauté briefly, taking care not to burn the garlic. Remove from heat. Put the seeds in the blender, whirling them until they are ground. (You can grind them any way you want, but this is very fast.)

Mix all the ingredients together. The pâté will be stiff, which is fine if you are going to serve it on pumpernickel bread; otherwise, stir in water or stock until the consistency is more to your liking. Adjust salt.

Without the optional added liquid, the recipe makes a little over a cup.

1 onion, chopped fine
1 tablespoon oil
2 cloves garlic, minced

½ cup toasted
   sunflower seeds
1 cup cooked, mashed
   soybeans
¾ teaspoon salt
pepper

Sesame Seeds

Natural sesame seeds are sometimes called "brown" because they are a darker color than the hulled and bleached supermarket variety. They lose some important nutrients along with the hulls. Looking at food charts, you'd think the most important loss is calcium, which is present in very large amounts in sesame hulls. But the calcium in the hulls is in a form that is unavailable, so calcium is really not the issue: probably you get the same small amount whether the seeds are hulled or not. More significant are the losses of folacin and vitamin B-6; and thiamin if the seeds are alkali processed. Minerals go, too, especially iron and potassium.

Since most sesame seeds grow in Latin America, what about pesticide residues? Arizona sesame producer Ray Langham told us that sesame seeds grow well without pesticides in Arizona and northern Mexico, but farther south, where a large part of the supply comes from, this is not usually possible. Importers seldom distinguish which batch comes from where. The tiny seeds are difficult to clean, too, and so may have traces of natural as well as chemical activity. To ameliorate both problems, toast before using. Conserve nutrients by using low heat, 300° to 325°F, stirring often. They are done when a shade darker, and too hot to hold in your hand.

Some natural foods companies are beginning to market domestic, organically grown seeds. Why not see whether your co-op or store carries them?

Sesame Spread

¾ cup natural sesame seeds
1 tablespoon honey
    or other sweetener
¼ cup water
    or apple juice
⅛ teaspoon salt

Toast sesame seeds and grind into a meal in blender; remove to bowl and add honey, water, and salt. The mixture will thicken as it cools, so you may want to thin it by adding more water or juice.

Slightly less quick, but very good, is to use raisins for sweetener. Pour boiling water over ½ cup raisins, and let them stand until cool. Blend or process the soaked raisins along with the seeds, adding the soaking water as needed to achieve a reasonably smooth grind.

Makes ¾ cup with honey, 1 cup with raisins.

Tofu or Tempeh Bars

The saucy bars are delicious hot from the pot over rice or toast, and the remains may be even tastier the next day or two in sandwiches. Leftover tempeh bars are good to crumble and stir into spaghetti sauce or chili.

Use either tofu or tempeh in this recipe. The difference is that tempeh takes longer to absorb the flavors of the sauce. It tastes best and is tenderer after a really long simmer, so its sauce needs extra liquid at the beginning.

1 pound firm tofu
  or tempeh

1 onion
2 tablespoons oil

2 tablespoons shoyu
2 tablespoons vinegar
¼ cup tomato paste
1½–2 cups water or broth
¼ teaspoon mustard
pepper

ò.

If you are using tofu, rinse it first. For sandwiches, slice tempeh or tofu into bars about ¼″ thick and somewhere around the size of half the slice of bread. If you are serving the dish hot, cut the pieces any size that appeals to you.

Chop onion and sauté in oil in a large skillet until golden. Stir in the shoyu, vinegar, tomato paste, water or broth, and mustard. Bring to a boil. Arrange tofu or tempeh slices in the pan, spooning the sauce over them as you do. Be sure they are covered with sauce.

If you will be serving the dish hot, cover and simmer about 20 minutes for tofu, ½ hour or longer for tempeh. Serve over toast or rice.

If you want to use the bars for cold sandwiches, cook uncovered until the sauce is evaporated and absorbed, making a glaze on the bars. Keep an eagle eye on them while you do this to prevent their sticking and burning.

FOR A PEPPIER SAUCE add a clove of garlic and pinch of cayenne to the onion when sautéeing. Toward the end of the sautéeing time, crush the garlic with a fork and add a tablespoon of chopped fresh ginger.

SERVE OVER RICE or noodles, or with spaghetti: When the onions are nearly done, add 2 cups or so of sliced mushrooms and ½ cup diced celery if desired. Increase the broth or water and add more salt or shoyu to taste.

Cheese Spreads 🍶

1 cup grated natural cheese
1 or more cups
   low-fat cottage cheese

OPTIONAL ADDITIONS

finely chopped celery or
   green or red pepper
minced parsley, chives
chopped tomatoes
paprika
mustard powder
dill weed

Cheese is high in fat and natural cheeses are expensive, but cost and fat both go down when you grate the cheese and mix it with low-fat cottage cheese to make a flavorful spread. Start with a half-and-half mixture and experiment. You can raise the portion of cottage cheese much higher and still have good results.

Below are some spreads fancy enough to serve on a buffet platter. For everyday sandwich making, a plain mixture is fine: Swiss, jack, or good sharp cheddar with low-fat cottage cheese. The spread will keep as long as the cottage cheese stays fresh, and it can be used to make sandwiches of many moods.

🍂

Mix the ingredients together and refrigerate. If you add fresh vegetables—tomatoes, for example, or peppers—make only what you will use in a day or two.

SWISSY SPREAD

½ cup grated Swiss
½ cup low-fat cottage cheese
¼ cup chopped green pepper
½ teaspoon dill weed
salt and pepper to taste

JACK AND DILL SPREAD

½ cup grated jack cheese
½ cup low-fat cottage cheese
½ teaspoon dill weed
1 tablespoon chopped
   toasted almonds
1 tablespoon minced chives
   or scallion tops
(½ teaspoon Dijon mustard)

CHILI–CHEDDAR SPREAD

½ cup grated cheddar
½ cup low-fat cottage cheese
1 small onion, chopped
   and well sautéed with
   a clove of garlic and
1 teaspoon chili powder

Jaji 🍶

1 cup cottage cheese
1 cup yogurt cheese
⅓ cup finely chopped
   green pepper
3' scallions, chopped
⅓ cup finely chopped celery
½ teaspoon dill weed

Jaji is Armenian and unabashedly oniony, so if your tastes are for milder fare, start with only the inner leaves of one scallion rather than three whole ones, or use chives. Nippy as it is, Jaji is very refreshing. It can be either a dip or sandwich spread, depending on how stiff you make the yogurt cheese.

🍂

Blend cottage and yogurt cheese with potato masher or put through food mill. Add green pepper, scallions, celery, and dill weed.

Makes 2½ cups.

Smoothie

This versatile summertime beverage easily accommodates many needs. It can be a quick, light lunch when you're at home; when you're packing a meal, smoothie travels better in a thermos than plain milk does. Dieters can enjoy the low-calorie version made with skim milk or buttermilk, while those who need to gain weight find that a smoothie (made calorie-rich with nut butter) goes down easily when other food might seem overwhelming.

৯৮

Blend in blender until smooth. Makes one serving, about 1½ cups.

*1 cup milk or buttermilk
or soymilk*
*½ cup or so fresh fruit:
one banana, a peach,
strawberries, apricots;
or combinations:
orange and banana,
date and banana, etc.*

EXTRAS

*(1 or 2 of the following,
—or none—but not all!)
1 tablespoon almond
butter
1 teaspoon nutritional
yeast
2 tablespoons wheat germ
1 tablespoon soy powder
1 tablespoon milk powder*

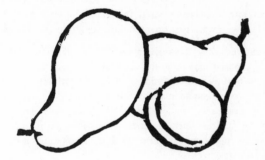

Mock Rarebit

Serve this rather zippy sauce over toast or as a dip for chunks of French Bread, fondue-style. Not bad on veggies either.

৯৮

Mix the cornstarch into ½ cup of the milk and set aside.

Blend the cottage cheese smooth in blender with 1 cup of the milk, or heat cottage cheese in the top of a double boiler until melted, stirring until it is smooth. Stir in the remaining ingredients except the cheddar and heat gently, letting them simmer very slowly for 10 minutes. Stir in the grated cheese and serve.

Makes 2¼ cups, enough for about 6 slices of toast.

*1 tablespoon cornstarch
1½ cups milk, divided*

*¾ cup cottage cheese
¼ teaspoon salt
1 teaspoon mustard powder*

*½ cup grated sharp
cheddar cheese*

Sprouts

The classics for sprouting are mung beans, garbanzos, lentils, wheat berries, and alfalfa seeds; but if you get into sprouting, try fenugreek, watercress, sunflower, radish, or mustard seeds, or other whole grains or beans. Be sure that the seeds you sprout were meant for food and haven't been treated for planting. For best nutrition, use your sprouts within a couple of days.

[1] Check your seeds or beans and remove rocks or other interlopers. Soak about ⅓ cup of your selection in a quart jar of cool to tepid water overnight. Choose a wide-mouthed jar if you have one. A quart jar is big enough to hold the ⅓ cup of most seeds or beans after they are sprouted, though not big enough for mung sprouts (if you want to grow them long) or alfalfa (see below).

[2] Next day, rinse the seeds in cool water and drain them thoroughly. An easy way to do this is to fasten a piece of cheesecloth or nylon netting over the mouth of the jar with a thick rubber band: the water can go in and out, but the seeds will stay behind. (You'll need pretty fine netting for alfalfa seeds, of course!) Keep the jar in a darkish place—if possible, on its side—and protect the mouth with a damp towel; the seeds want air but they don't want to dry out.

[3] Rinse the sprouts two times a day—three if the weather is hot. Be sure to drain them well each time.

[4] Depending on what you are sprouting, your crop may be ready by the second or third day. Sunflower seeds are sweetest when the sprout is only one-third the length of the seed. Sprouts from mung beans, lentils, and most other beans can be eaten the third day. Alfalfa sprouts take about five.

SOME SPECIAL CASES:

ALFALFA SPROUTS During the winter when the lettuce supply isn't the best, we are grateful for the freshness of alfalfa sprouts in salads and sandwiches. Their virtues may have been overpraised, but their nutritional assets are respectable—they compare quite favorably with lettuce!

The sprouter trays sold in natural foods stores are terrific because you can rinse and green your sprouts in the same tray. It's easy to do a good job with everyday home equipment, though, and here's a simple method.

For the first three days, follow the method suggested for other sprouts, above.

The third day, pour the sprouts into a 3–quart (or bigger) bowl and flood with water. If the sprouts have clumped, separate them gently. Pour the sprouts and water into another bowl, leaving the unsprouted seeds behind at the bottom of the first bowl. Strain and drain well, letting them grow as before. Keep the bowl covered with a small towel or with plastic.

Continue to rinse the sprouts a couple of times a day and keep them in a darkish, cool place until each one has two tiny leaves. Now, when you flood them with water, you can swish them gently to wash off the brown seed casings—not required, but elegant.

Drain the sprouts for the last time and spread them out on a glass or plastic dish (a 9″ × 13″ baking dish is fine). Cover with clear plastic or waxed paper and set them in a *cool* place where they have a source of light. (Don't let them get too warm or they will quickly rot.) In a few hours they will be bright green and ready to enjoy. Store in the refrigerator, closely covered.

Alfalfa sprouts are delicate and pretty, delightful on a sandwich or salad. But don't eat pounds a day. Alfalfa contains small amounts of a natural toxin, saponins. Such natural toxins do occur in foods; usually, as with alfalfa sprouts, they do no harm if the food is not eaten in abnormally large quantities.

BEAN SPROUTS

Sprout soaking water is vitamin candy for houseplants.

Soybeans require special attention because the sprouts mold easily. Remove the nonsprouters as soon as they make themselves known. Rinse the sprouting beans *at least* three times daily, and disentangle them when you do. Don't expect a long tail to develop. Sprouted soybeans are ready to eat after three days.

To get longer tails on mung bean sprouts, keep them in utter darkness while they sprout. Seed casings will float off if you swish sprouts gently in a basin of water during the last rinsings.

Soy sprouts must be cooked at least 5 minutes to destroy harmful enzymes. Other bean sprouts do not require cooking, but they will have better flavor if you dip them for 5 seconds or so in very hot water just before adding them to your salad or sandwich. Rinse quickly in cold water, pat dry, and serve.

Dinner

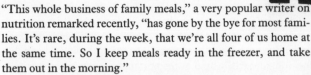

"This whole business of family meals," a very popular writer on nutrition remarked recently, "has gone by the bye for most families. It's rare, during the week, that we're all four of us home at the same time. So I keep meals ready in the freezer, and take them out in the morning."

It is true, of course, that the competing claims on our evening time are many and powerful. Meetings, workshops, dates, dance lessons, exercise classes, late work at the office or just Wanting to Get Away pull family members in different directions. There is more going on now, for people of every age, than a generation ago, and none of us wants to miss out. Little by little, the family dinner hour has indeed fallen on hard times.

The drift is clear, but that we're happier this way —that we'd really have *chosen* it—is not clear at all. Life has skidded dramatically toward the mechanized and impersonal in recent years. We bank with automated tellers, we assess political leaders by their performance on television, we accept finally that most of our telephone conversations will be with recorded message devices. Surely the personal relationships we do have today are more precious than ever. Surely they are worth sustaining—and to date, no one's come up with a more universally effective way to achieve this than by sharing a meal.

Granted, there will be nights when you look back at the time you just shared—maybe it wasn't all grace notes —wince a little, and wonder whether it's worth the effort. Maybe that one evening you *would* have been better off at haunts of your respective choices. But the rewards don't come on any one evening, and really can't be measured over the short run. It's the cumulative effect you're after: the continuity itself, and what comes with it. By setting off that one hour and drawing a circle around it, you are creating a situation where, over time, some very important processes can take place: where subtle connections can be forged, and the kind of wordless understandings established that allow human beings to be of real use to one another.

Just as there is an art to breadmaking and gardening and other old-timey skills, there is also an art to the convivial dinner hour. Don't be discouraged if everyone comes off a little callow at first. Gradually, you learn to draw one another out about the day's adventures, and to keep an eye open during your own day for table-worthy anecdotes. An eight-year-old's version of such stories can be pretty roundabout, but an attentive listener asking the right questions can gradually make him a real spellbinder—and give him convincing proof that you do care.

It's an institution too valuable to be reserved for "families" strictly defined. In the days before singles apartments and frozen entrees, most families had a single aunt or uncle to supper regularly—or just a friend of long standing—and it worked to everyone's advantage, especially the children's. We know individuals who get together once or more a week for potluck suppers—especially helpful for people who love "from-scratch" meals but find it's a lot to do for just one person.

We don't just differ politely, then, from those who would dismiss the family dinner hour without a backward glance. We flat-out *adamantly* protest. Eat late if you must, if that's what it takes to get everyone together. Keep the menus simple, and involve every able body in the preparation. Buy a gorgeous new tablecloth, go the candlelight route if you have to, but get them ranged 'round that table and eating what*ever* it takes.

The single most insidious opposition to a civilizing meal hour, incidentally, is probably television. Besides absorbing attention so we don't really see or hear one another, it fills the mind with trivia, and its backdrop of continual violence exerts a disintegrating influence on personal relationships and family unity. Whatever you think of TV, it surely doesn't have a place at the dinner table, and wonderful things happen when you start easing it out of your life. For a delightful rundown on other families' experiences, read *What to Do After You Turn Off the TV*, by Frances Moore Lappé and her children, Anthony and Anna (New York: Ballantine, 1985).

Salads

Whether you like yours at the beginning of the meal as most Americans do, or served just before dessert in the Italian fashion; whether it makes a graceful complement to the meal or *is* the meal, salad makes a vital nutritional contribution to anyone's diet. Raw leafy greens provide the essential B vitamin folacin in abundance. When salad greens are homegrown, or at least really *green*, they supply other members of the B vitamin complex, too, and vitamins A, C, E, and K, as well as a respectable amount of minerals: calcium, iron, and magnesium.

Fresh-picked greens require only light and simple dressing, but there is always some odd or end that will make the salad special: a bit of cheese, a spark of bell pepper, a handful of new green peas. If you aren't already a salad nut, do experiment with some of the fancies on the next page and see whether a little extra pizzazz doesn't make twice as much salad disappear.

Use our ideas as a springboard for your imagination, and you will come up with dozens of variations on our variations. I like remembering the lady who rushed up and told us, "I just *love* your book! Your recipes are wonderful." Then looking a little abashed, she added, "Of course, I never *follow* them." Hurray for her! I bet she makes great salads.

Making Irresistible Salads

≈ Use salad greens that are fresh, crisp, clean, cold, and dry. Wash lettuce in cold water and dry gently by spreading it out on a clean terry towel and rolling it up, or by putting it in a lettuce spinner. You can wash and dry lots of lettuce and put it in its towel in a plastic bag or crisper in the refrigerator, ready to be cut (or torn) and dressed as needed just before serving.

≈ For zest and variety, use a medley of salad greens in your bowl. Romaine, red, green leaf and butter lettuce, escarole, napa cabbage, watercress and spinach are seasonally available in most supermarkets. Gardeners and farmer's market shoppers will have even more of a selection.

❧ Don't toss salads until you're ready to serve the meal. Use dressing at room temperature; it spreads further and coats the greens more evenly. Start with a little and toss well—a lot of extra salad dressing gets eaten just because it's dumped on top.

❧ To make a salad into a light meal that's perfect for lunch or dinner on a hot summer evening, select some of these additions:

Cooked chilled garbanzo or kidney beans

Sprouted garbanzos, lentils, or red beans

Small chunks of cheese or marinated tofu

Lightly cooked vegetables like fresh corn, string beans, sliced carrots, broccoli florets and slices, or beets (Chill with or without a marinade and add to the salad before tossing)

Raw vegetables like thinly sliced zucchini, celery, cucumber, cabbage, green or red pepper, parsley, finely grated carrot, avocado chunks, or (best of all) tiny fresh green peas

Croutons (page 158)

❧ Fresh herbs add a lot to salads, and to other dishes as well. Grow them in a window box or in a plot near your kitchen. Mince fresh herbs and crush dried ones to bring out all their flavor.

❧ Nasturtiums grow easily nearly anywhere, and their bright petals add color to salad long before the tomatoes ripen. Nasturtium leaves too can be chopped for peppery zest in salads. (Other flowers add color too—johnny jump-ups, calendula, borage— but nasturtiums *taste* especially good.) For best effect, sprinkle on top after dressing.

To get salad greens in really dazzling variety, try growing your own. Lettuce is particularly easy, and seed catalogs provide countless gorgeous and tasty varieties you'll never find in the store. Many of the smaller seed companies offer interesting varieties that aren't available anywhere else; perhaps the most fun of all is to get lettuce from other gardeners who save and exchange heirloom seeds with each other. To learn more, write to Seed Saver's Exchange, Rural Route 3, Box 239, Decorah, IA 52101.

Oil for Salads & Cooking

From a nutritional standpoint, by far the most important thing about salad oils is not what kind you use but how little. Make sure that what you do use is fresh; beyond that, what oil to buy is mostly a matter of taste. We use canola oil for salads and sautéing and for making Better-Butter; for flavoring salads and sauces, good olive oil. Here are the main options with some of their distinguishing characteristics. All are high in polyunsaturated fatty acids and low in saturated ones. If refined, all are pale and nearly tasteless.

Safflower oil: Highest in polyunsaturates, therefore somewhat more prone to rancidity unless it has preservatives added. The smoke point is very low, so safflower oil is not good for frying.

Canola and Corn oils: versatile, all-around oils. Canola is one of the few vegetarian sources of beneficial omega-3 fatty acids.

Soy oil: Unrefined soy oil has a very strong flavor and is especially prone to rancidity.

Peanut oil: Higher than other oils in saturated fats, lower in polyunsaturated ones. If you do fry (we don't), peanut oil is best because it has a high smoke point. Research on rabbits and primates has shown peanut oil to be uniquely atherogenic—more so than butter. These results have not been supported by studies with humans, but the finding has cast a shadow on peanut oil's reputation.

Sesame, walnut, avocado, sunflower, and other special oils: Refined, these are as stable and mild in flavor as other refined oils. Unrefined, each has its own distinct flavor from the nut or seed of its source. All unrefined oils have to be protected from light, air, and heat. Don't expect them to keep for a long time.

Olive oil: For flavor, nothing can match good olive oil. There is evidence that nothing can match it nutritionally either. The top grades are labeled "virgin," which means that the oil is pressed from the fruit (rather than extracted by solvents) and unrefined. "Pure" means only that all the oil in the bottle is from olives, usually solvent-extracted. Very much less expensive are blends of some cheap refined oil with a very small amount of good olive oil for flavor, which can be called "blended olive oil." We think it's worth getting a small bottle of the real thing for flavor; if you like, you can blend it yourself with an all-purpose oil like corn oil for salad making. As the demand for good-quality domestic olive oil increases, it should become more widely available and cheaper. Our co-op now carries really good California virgin olive oil (under the Co-op label) at a rather moderate price; maybe your co-op can get it too.

"Salad oil" blends containing cottonseed oil, palm oil, or the preservatives BHA, BHT, or EDTA, are best avoided.

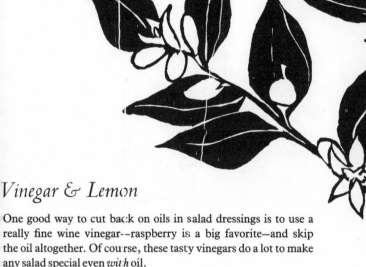

Vinegar & Lemon

One good way to cut back on oils in salad dressings is to use a really fine wine vinegar—raspberry is a big favorite—and skip the oil altogether. Of course, these tasty vinegars do a lot to make any salad special even *with* oil.

Juice from homegrown lemons can vie with the most exquisite vinegar in nearly any dressing, especially if you include the finely grated peel. If you have sunshine and a place you can protect from frost, a dwarf lemon may be the most rewarding thing you plant. One small tree, even in a tub, can provide plenty of its delicious lemons nearly all year round. Fragrant and pretty to look at, too. Ask your nursery to help you choose the right variety for your climate.

Salad Dressings

We suggest making these quickly-mixed dressings fresh each day or two. One good no-muss way to blend up just the right amount is to lay in a supply of half-pint-sized blender jars so that instead of using the usual big blender container, you can just put all your ingredients in the little jar, screw on the blade unit, invert, and blend. Any dressing left over can be stored right in the jar, ready for the next day. (The small glass jars make it easy to grind spices in the blender too.) There have been some awful accidents when people used ordinary jars in this way, however, so get ones made for your own blender.

Marinade

Sometimes cooked beans and vegetables are marinated for extra flavor before being used in salads. Most often, the marinade is a combination of oil and vinegar or lemon juice with salt and herbs, or perhaps the same dressing that will be used on the salad. We find that you can get excellent flavor by skipping the oil and simply tossing the cooked beans or vegetables in fresh lemon juice, with salt and pepper, herbs, and perhaps a little garlic. The taste is great, and there's a considerable saving on the fat quota.

Lowering the Fat

In experimenting with dressings that make a mouth-watering salad with less oil, we have found two basic extenders. One is cultured dairy products—especially buttermilk, but also cottage cheese and yogurt. The other is vegetables, especially tomatoes, blended smooth. Mixing one of these into a well-seasoned normal dressing will usually make a tasty dressing that covers much more salad with fewer calories from fat. The catch is that when there is a lot of liquid that is not oil, the dressing doesn't keep well, so these dressings need to be made fresh in small quantities.

On the next page are some of our favorite dressings with variations. If you are very serious about lowering fat in your diet, most of these taste fine without any oil at all.

Our own approach might be of interest here. We discuss on page 45 our usual way of keeping control of the amount of fat that goes into dinner. By the time soup or sauce is done, the meal's fat allotment leaves maybe ½ teaspoon of oil per person to use in salad dressing. That's the amount that goes in, no more. You can experiment in the same direction by adjusting the recipe to your own limit (or by using only a part of the dressing). One nice thing about this approach is that it leaves room even for the classic vinaigrette.

Vinaigrette

Mix the vinegar or wine, mustard, and salt. Add other herbs if desired.

When salad-making time comes, measure the amount of oil you want to use for the whole salad. Either mix in the flavored vinegar to taste or, for the freshest possible salad, toss the oil with the greens first and follow that with the vinegar mixture, to taste. Even a tiny amount of oil will cover a lot of lettuce that way, and protect it from the wilting effects of the vinegar too.

2 tablespoons wine vinegar
or ¼ cup dry red wine
½ teaspoon Dijon mustard
¼ teaspoon salt

olive oil
pepper

Favorite Salad Dressings

We draw on these dressings every day in all possible variations. Mix the ingredients by hand, chopping as necessary, or put everything in the blender.

We often call for lemon zest. "Zest" is the colored part of the citrus peel only; the white inner peel is bitter. To get the zest, either use a potato peeler and then chop the peeling fine, or take advantage of technology and use a *zester*.

*1 medium lemon
= 3 tablespoons juice
and 1 tablespoon zest*

LEMON-PARSLEY DRESSING

*2 tablespoons oil
zest of one lemon
2 tablespoons lemon juice
1/2 cup parsley, chopped
1/4 teaspoon salt
1 tablespoon chopped
    green pepper
dash black pepper*

Makes about 1/2 cup.

ya

BLUE CHEESE DRESSING

*1 ounce blue cheese
1 tablespoon oil
    or mayonnaise
2 tablespoons cottage cheese
1/4 cup buttermilk
pinch salt and pepper
a drop of pressed garlic
(chopped scallion leaves,
    chives, and/or coriander
    leaves)*

Makes 1/2 cup.

ORANGE-PARSLEY DRESSING

IN BLENDER:
*1 orange, cut up, and
    1 tablespoon zest
2 tablespoon oil
1 tablespoon cider vinegar
1/4 teaspoon salt*

ADD:
*2 tablespoons chopped
    parsley*

Makes 2/3 cup.

ya

SESAME DRESSING

*1/4 cup freshly toasted
    sesame seeds, ground
    in blender into meal
1 tablespoon oil
1 tablespoon lemon juice
    (or more, to taste)
1/8 teaspoon salt
1/4 cup buttermilk
    or orange juice*

Makes 1/3 to 1/2 cup.

BASIC BUTTERMILK DRESSING

2 tablespoons oil
1/2 small lemon,
    juice and zest
1/3 cup buttermilk
(2 or 3 chives
    or a scallion leaf)
(1/4 cup tender parsley
    and/or other fresh herbs)
(drop of pressed garlic)
pinch salt, dash pepper

Makes 1/2 cup.
❧

CURRY DRESSING

Make Buttermilk Dressing
but omit herbs and use
cider or white wine vinegar
instead of lemon. Add 1/4
teaspoon curry powder.
❧

ARTICHOKE DRESSING

Make Buttermilk Dressing,
using olive oil if possible, and
include garlic. Add cooked,
cut-up artichoke hearts and
leaf-scrapings, letting the
mixture marinate for an hour
or more before tossing salad.
Allow 1/4 cup dressing and
1/4 cup artichoke per person.

FRESH TOMATO DRESSING

1 tomato, fresh and ripe
2 tablespoons olive oil
1 tablespoon vinegar
1/8 teaspoon salt
1 teaspoon fresh
    or 1/2 teaspoon dry
    chopped basil

Makes about 3/4 cup.
❧

EVERYDAY DRESSING

Make Fresh Tomato
Dressing, using
red wine vinegar and
great handfuls of
fresh basil and parsley.
Add pepper and dry
mustard, a dash each.
❧

FEROZ'S DRESSING

Blend smooth:
1 medium lemon, juice
    and zest
1/2 teaspoon salt
1 large peeled tomato
dash cayenne
2 small cloves garlic
2 tablespoons olive oil
1/4 teaspoon each
    ground coriander,
    cumin, dry mustard,
    paprika
1/2 teaspoon brown sugar

Makes 3/4 cup.

COTTAGE DRESSING

1/4 cup cottage cheese
1/4 cup buttermilk
2 teaspoons lemon juice
1 tablespoon oil
pinch salt
pinch pepper
1 teaspoon fresh herbs

Makes 1/2 cup.
❧

GARDEN COTTAGE DRESSING

Make Cottage Dressing and
mix in a tomato (cut up),
1 tablespoon fresh chopped
basil, and a pinch more salt.

RUSSIAN DRESSING

1 tablespoon mayonnaise
1 tablespoon tomato paste
1 tablespoon cottage cheese
1/3 cup buttermilk
1 tablespoon wine vinegar
1/4 teaspoon salt
1/8 teaspoon each
   mustard and paprika

Makes 1/2 cup.

THOUSAND ISLAND DRESSING

Make Russian Dressing;
chop and add pickles,
celery, and hard-boiled egg.

AVOCADO DRESSING

1/2 large ripe avocado
1 tablespoon lemon juice
1/8 teaspoon salt
1/8 teaspoon chili powder
squeeze garlic
1/4 cup buttermilk

Makes 1/2 cup.

AVOCADO DIP OR
SANDWICH SPREAD
*Omit the buttermilk and
double the recipe (except
the salt).*

YOGURT SALAD DRESSING

1/2 cup yogurt
2 tablespoons oil
   or mayonnaise
1 tablespoon lemon juice
1/8 teaspoon salt
grate pepper

Makes 2/3 cup.

BRIGHT MINTY DRESSING

Add to Yogurt Dressing
   and blend smooth:
1/2 cucumber, sliced
2 tablespoons fresh
   mint leaves
2 scallion leaves

GREEN GODDESS DRESSING

1/2 cup yogurt
2 tablespoons oil
   or mayonnaise
1/4 cup chopped parsley,
   basil, and/or
   coriander leaves
1 teaspoon chopped chives
1 tablespoon lemon juice
1/4 teaspoon salt
(scallion leaf)
(squeeze garlic)

Makes about 3/4 cup.

Astonishing Salad

A truly impressive, unusual, and delicious salad.

 је

In a small pot, heat wine and lemon juice to a bare simmer. Turn off the heat and add the apricots. Cover and let apricots soak for about ½ hour, turning occasionally if liquid doesn't cover.

Wash spinach and drain well. Quarter and core apples and slice paper-thin. If the salad won't be eaten right away, cover apples with orange or other fruit juice, draining thoroughly before you add them to the salad.

Over a bowl, drain the apricots through a sieve. Reserve liquid and cut apricots into bite-sized pieces. Add the oil, salt, and pepper to the apricot liquid and whip with a fork. In a salad bowl, mix spinach and apple slices, add dressing, and toss thoroughly. Sprinkle apricots and walnuts on top. Toss again just before serving.

Makes 4 servings or a light meal for two, with muffins and a creamy soup.

½ cup dry white wine
2 tablespoons lemon juice
½ cup dried apricots

1½ pounds fresh tender
   spinach leaves
2 apples
2 tablespoons olive oil
¼ teaspoon salt
pinch pepper
½ cup chopped walnuts

Greek Salad

Like our other Greek recipes, this one comes from our friend Sultana, and provides an utterly satisfying balance of flavors, colors, and textures.

 је

Wash and cut lettuce. Crumble cheese over the top and add the olives, tomatoes, cucumber, and green pepper.

Pour olive oil over salad and toss well to coat; then add the wine vinegar, salt, and pepper and toss.

Serves 4—or two salad connoisseurs.

leafy lettuce or mixed greens
2 or more ounces feta cheese
1 handful black olives
   (Greek, if available)
1 tomato, chopped
1 small cucumber, sliced
1 green pepper, diced
1 tablespoon olive oil
2 teaspoons wine vinegar
salt and pepper to taste

Dilled Cucumber & Yogurt Salad

1 cup water
1/4 cup vinegar
1 teaspoon dill weed
1 slice raw onion
2 cucumbers, thinly sliced

1 cup yogurt
1/2 teaspoon salt
dash pepper
1/8 teaspoon turmeric

leafy lettuce, or mixed greens

Combine water, vinegar, dill, and onion. Add cucumber slices and let stand half an hour or longer. Drain, and discard the onion.

Mix yogurt, salt, pepper, and turmeric. Stir cucumbers into the mixture and serve on beds of salad greens, cut into bite-sized pieces.

Serves 4.

Ceci Salad

2 cups raw garbanzo beans
1/3 cup wine vinegar
2 tablespoons olive oil
1/2 teaspoon salt
1/4 teaspoon paprika
1/4 teaspoon oregano
pinch cayenne
1 clove garlic
1/4 cup chopped chives
    or 1 minced scallion

4 quarts tender fresh
    spinach leaves
1 small avocado
black pepper

Cook garbanzos until tender. Drain and toss with vinegar, oil, and seasonings. Marinate for an hour or more. (If you want to use already-cooked beans, warm them first or just allow them longer to marinate.)

Wash and dry spinach leaves, and cut or tear to bite-size. Cube avocado and toss all together. Check salt.

Makes salad for 4 or more. Served with crackers and chilled tomato juice, Ceci Salad also makes a fine, light meal.

Some Good Salad Combinations

MEXICAN SALAD BOWL

MARINATE:

¾ cup cooked kidney beans
juice of 1 lemon
salt and pepper

TOSS:

leafy lettuce or mixed greens
¼ cup Everyday Dressing
¼ teaspoon crushed oregano
¼ teaspoon lightly toasted
   cumin seeds or ground cumin

TOP WITH:

½ avocado, cubed
½ green pepper, diced
1 tomato, cut up

(½ cup grated cheddar)
ɜ

SHADES OF GREEN SALAD

MARINATE:

½ cup green peas
½ cup cooked lima beans
lemon juice, salt, and pepper

TOSS TOGETHER:

leafy lettuce or mixed greens
   and tender spinach leaves
¼ cup toasted sunflower seeds
Green Goddess Dressing

CHEF'S SALAD

MARINATE:

½ cup cooked garbanzos
juice of 1 lemon
salt and pepper

TOSS:

Big bowlful romaine lettuce
dressing of your choice

ARRANGE ON TOP:

8 cherry tomatoes
½ cucumber, sliced
½ bell pepper, in rounds
cheeses in strips
1 hard-cooked egg, quartered
fresh black pepper
ɜ

SPINACH AND MUSHROOM SALAD

Big bowlful tender spinach
leaves
raw mushrooms, thinly sliced
Parmesan cheese
garlic-flavored whole-wheat
   Croutons
Fresh Tomato Dressing
   (or your choice)

CALIFORNIA TOSSED SALAD

leafy lettuce or mixed greens
¼ cup watercress leaves
½ avocado, cut up
½ cup sliced cucumber
8 cherry tomatoes, halved
1 cup herbed croutons
2 tablespoons Parmesan cheese
Vinaigrette
ɜ

TOMATO PEPPER SALAD

DICE AND TOSS TOGETHER:

fresh and ripe tomatoes
crisp green peppers

parsley and/or fresh
   basil, finely chopped
ɜ

NAVY BEAN AND CASHEW SALAD

MARINATE TOGETHER:

1 cup broccoli or cauliflower
   pieces, steamed
½ cup cooked navy beans
juice of 1 lemon
salt and pepper

TOSS WITH:

leafy lettuce or mixed greens
¼ cup chopped toasted cashews
Avocado or Blue Cheese
Dressing

Antipasto

whole small mushrooms
broccoli florets
*   and sliced stems*
cauliflower pieces
asparagus spears
whole green beans
artichoke hearts
zucchini
green pepper
celery sticks
scallions
tomato wedges
*   or cherry tomatoes*
olives
garbanzo or kidney beans
cubes of cheese

BABA GANOUJ

Peel and mash a baked eggplant, add a few tablespoons tahini, a minced garlic clove, and the juice of half a lemon; salt to taste; let stand half an hour, at least. Just before serving, sprinkle with a few drops of olive oil and dashes of ground cumin. Wow.

Traditionally served to whet the appetite, any of a number of beautifully arranged and tasty dishes can be an antipasto. In American translation, the appetizer may grow to become most of a light meal, perhaps preceding a good soup and fresh bread. The idea is to present a feast for the eye as well as the palate, so indulge your artistry to its utmost in arranging the vegetables and other dishes. The choices can be light or rich, and as varied as you choose, so Antipasto Americano offers a splendid answer to what to serve when dieters come or when your guests have widely different eating preferences. ("Adelaide, it's all low-cal except the pâté." "Vergil, there's no dairy in anything except the cheese sticks!")

Some antipasti are traditional: *Misto*, fried vegetables (we substitute lightly steamed ones, marinated or not); Greek Peppers (next page); Caponata (also next page), *crostini* (toasted slices of bread, with spicy or cheesy toppings, served hot); stuffed artichokes or tomatoes; deviled eggs; mushrooms; and, for their beauty, an assortment of young, fresh raw vegetables, olives, and scallions.

Some other ideas: any of the spreads from our Lunch section, stuffed into small tomatoes or celery boats or mounded and garnished for spreading on bread or dipping. Or make the classic dip, Baba Ganouj. Hot food is quite welcome, especially if it is bite-sized—for example, trays of hot Potato Poppers or Neat Balls.

Caponata

Caponata is a traditional antipasto dish, but it can hold its own as a dip for crackers or vegetables any day.

❧

If you are able to get the long, thin Japanese eggplants, steam them in their jackets until tender. The most effective way to deal with the fat, round, normal kind is to halve and bake it at about 350°F. When tender, set aside to cool.

Chop the onion rather fine and sauté it in the olive oil. Chop the celery similarly and stir it in when the onion is beginning to get translucent. Cook until the onion is soft and barely golden.

Add the bell peppers, if used, and tomatoes, capers, honey, vinegar, and olives. Simmer, stirring frequently, until most of the liquid has evaporated.

Meantime, peel and dice the eggplant. When the tomato mixture has lost most of its liquid, remove it from heat and add the eggplant, salt, and pepper. Correct the salt: how much you need will depend on how salty your olives were. Serve chilled.

4 long thin eggplants
or one big one
(about 1 pound)

1 big onion
2 tablespoons olive oil
8 center stalks of celery
(1 cup chopped)

(1 bell pepper, diced)
1¼ cups tomatoes,
peeled, seeded, chopped
¼ cup capers
1 tablespoon honey
¼ cup red wine vinegar
½ cup olives, chopped
¼ teaspoon salt
fresh black pepper

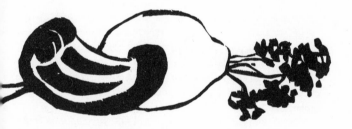

Grilled Peppers

The easiest way to grill peppers is to cut them in half and remove the seeds and supporting membranes. Place face down on a metal pie tin or some such, and broil until the skins are blistered and black. Remove from heat and cover tightly with a bowl or lid, letting them steam in their own heat until cool enough to handle; then slip the skins off. Roasting peppers smell heavenly and taste great; use anywhere canned chilis or cooked peppers are wanted. To make GREEK PEPPERS: cut in strips and marinate lightly with olive oil, lemon juice, salt and pepper.

Coleslaw

½ head cabbage,
green or red (about
4 cups shredded)

½ cup Basic Buttermilk or
Yogurt Dressing,
or any dressing that
harmonizes with the
ingredients you have
chosen.

Cabbage is a rich source of vitamin C and is available year-round at low cost. For slaw, use any kind of cabbage and shred coarse or fine as suits you. The dressings suggested are considerably lower in fat than the standard mayonnaise dressing, and you can extend them even more with extra yogurt or buttermilk.

Unlike green salad, coleslaw can be dressed ahead of serving time—in fact, it is still very good the next day. When the cabbage is fresh, slaw is good made very plain; but you can alter its mood in many ways. We list some tasty additions below.

Serves 4 to 6.

dill weed
tarragon
caraway seeds
poppy seeds
toasted sunflower seeds
chopped walnuts
slivered almonds

chopped fresh pineapple
orange chunks
grated apples
raisins
dates or dried apricots

minced green pepper
chopped celery
minced parsley
grated carrots
cooked green beans
shoestring beets
corn off the cob
pickle

Slaw Chez Nous

2 tablespoons almonds
2 tablespoons sesame seeds
2½ cups shredded cabbage,
white or Chinese
(2 scallions or chives)
½ small red bell pepper

1 tablespoon oil
1 tablespoon rice vinegar
or ½ teaspoon cider
vinegar
1 teaspoon honey
⅛ teaspoon pepper
¼ teaspoon salt

Toast nuts and chop them; toast seeds. Allow to cool. Shred the cabbage, chop the scallion, and dice the pepper. Toss the vegetables together.

Mix oil, vinegar, honey, pepper, and salt. Just before serving, combine vegetables, dressing, seeds, and nuts.

Makes 3 cups.

Red Rogue's Delight

This pretty slaw can be exceedingly zippy unless the red onion is just-picked. If you aren't a raw onion enthusiast, the salad's good without it, or with just a thin slice. (Sweet white onions will do the trick too.)

🍃

Shred cabbage thin or grate coarse and combine with onion. Mix oil, lemon juice, orange juice, mustard, salt, and pepper and stir them into the cabbage and onion. Sprinkle sunflower seeds on top.

Makes 4 servings.

½ medium red cabbage
(3 cups shredded)
¼ cup chopped
red bermuda onion
2 tablespoons oil
1 tablespoon lemon juice
¼ cup orange juice
1 teaspoon Dijon mustard
½ teaspoon salt
freshly ground black pepper
¼ cup toasted
sunflower seeds

Carrot Salad

We used to drown carrot salad in mayonnaise, but we like this version much better. If the carrots aren't very sweet, grate apples in too. Or, for a carrot slaw, substitute grated cabbage for half the carrots. For a savory version, omit the raisins and orange zest and add finely chopped parsley and chives instead.

🍃

Mix well. To be fancy, top with nuts before serving.

Makes 3 cups, to serve 4.

3 cups carrots, grated fine
½ cup raisins or currants
½ cup orange juice
1 tablespoon lemon juice
1 teaspoon each: zest of
orange and lemon
(¼ cup nuts,
toasted and chopped)

Disappearing Carrot Salad

Almost a light chutney, it's so gingery and sweet. Very good packed up in tomorrow's lunchbox too.

🍃

Toast walnut pieces and coconut in a low (300°F) oven. The walnuts will take about 10 minutes and the coconut 5. Chill.

Combine grated carrots, apple, lemon zest, orange and lemon juices, currants, salt, and ginger. Add walnuts and coconut and serve.

Makes 3 cups, to serve 4.

¼ cup walnut pieces
1 tablespoon shredded
coconut
2 cups grated carrot
1 apple, cored and grated
zest and juice of ½ lemon
½ cup orange juice
½ cup currants
dash salt
1½ teaspoons grated
fresh ginger

Russian Salad

2 cups diced cooked potatoes
2 cups diced cooked beets
½ cup peas
2 tablespoons chopped
    fresh parsley
2 scallions, thinly sliced

2 tablespoons mayonnaise
6 tablespoons yogurt
2 tablespoons vinegar
dash black pepper
½ teaspoon salt

A classic that eclipses plain old potato salad.

All vegetables should be cold; if you use frozen peas, let them thaw. Put potatoes, beets, peas, parsley, and scallions in salad bowl. Mix together mayonnaise, yogurt, vinegar, salt, and pepper. Toss together.

Makes 6 servings (4½ cups).

Fruity Beety

4 beets
3 oranges
2 tablespoons coconut
1 teaspoon honey
juice of ½ lemon
grated peel of ½ lemon
2 tablespoons currants
(1 teaspoon vinegar)
pinch salt

This sweet and deeply colorful salad adds a bright touch to any plate; it's especially fine alongside green vegetables and rice. Many people who ordinarily avoid beets will eat an astonishing amount of Fruity Beety.

Wash beets and steam whole until tender; then peel. Grate on ripple-shaped grater or slice in long, thin sticks.

Peel, seed, and cut up oranges. Place half the oranges in blender with coconut, honey, lemon juice, and peel, and blend 2 minutes.

Mix all ingredients, balancing the sweetness with the additional vinegar if needed. Chill, letting the flavors blend for 2 hours or so.

Makes 3 cups.

Sweet Potato Salad 🥗

Place sweet potato, green pepper, celery, scallions, and walnuts in a small salad bowl.

Stir together mayonnaise, yogurt, lemon zest and juice (about 3 tablespoons), and salt. If you're fond of fresh ginger, try it in this dish: peel it, cut in three pieces, and press the pieces in a garlic press to extract the juice. (It will well up in the upper part of the press—pour from there, loosen with a fork, and squeeze again.) Mix the juice into the dressing, adding to taste. Combine with sweet potato mixture and adjust salt and lemon juice to taste.

Makes 3 cups, to serve 4.

2 cups cubed cooked
sweet potato
1/2 cup chopped green pepper
1/2 cup chopped celery
3 scallions, sliced thin
1/2 cup chopped walnuts

2 tablespoons mayonnaise
1/4 cup yogurt
zest and juice of 1 lemon
1/4 teaspoon salt
(nubbin of ginger, thumb-tip
size)

Winter Salad

Quarter potatoes lengthwise and steam only until tender. Remove peel if you want to and cut in 1/2-inch chunks.

Steam broccoli pieces ever so briefly, until they cook just tender. The scallions can be added either raw or cooked. If you want to sauté them, use some of the oil to do it. Place broccoli, scallions, and potatoes in a salad bowl.

Combine olive oil, sesame seeds, ginger, honey, salt, and vinegar. Pour over the potatoes and broccoli and toss lightly. Taste to see whether it needs a little more vinegar. Serve at room temperature.

Makes about 4 cups, to serve from 4 to 6.

2 medium potatoes
(red if possible)
3 cups broccoli florets
(and peeled, sliced stems)
1 bunch scallions, sliced thin

1–2 tablespoons olive oil
2 tablespoons toasted
sesame seeds
1 1/4" fresh ginger, minced
1/2 teaspoon honey
3/4–1 teaspoon salt
3 or more tablespoons
vinegar

WINTER SALAD WITH ARAME

Before starting the potatoes, soak 1/2 cup dried arame sea vegetable in water to cover. Let stand 15 minutes while you prepare the potatoes and broccoli. After you mix the dressing, drain the arame and stir it in. Combine with the vegetables as described above.

Tomato Aspic

1/4 cup agar flakes*
1 quart tomato juice
  or 1 cup tomato paste
  dissolved in 3 cups water
1 teaspoon honey
1/2 teaspoon curry powder
1 teaspoon dried basil
1 teaspoon salt

1 cup chopped celery
1/4 cup chopped green pepper
1 cup grated carrot
3 green onions, chopped

3 tablespoons lemon juice

1 cup chopped walnuts

A flavorful vegetarian version of the classic aspic usually made with animal gelatin. The quantities given here produce a slightly soft, spoonable result; if you like yours stiffer, increase the agar to 6 tablespoons.

Because Tomato Aspic is usually considered holiday fare, this recipe is sized for a crowd. But it's simple enough to prepare for everyday use in half-size amounts.

❧

Dissolve agar in 1 cup tomato juice and let stand 1 minute. Put remaining juice in saucepan with honey, curry powder, basil, and salt. Heat to boiling. Mix in vegetables. Add dissolved agar and chopped onions and boil for 2 minutes. Cool slightly, add lemon juice, and pour into a 2-quart bowl or flat baking dish. Top with walnuts when partly set (about 15 minutes) and press down lightly with your palm.

Allow to set at cool room temperature for 1 hour.

Cut into squares, or spoon out. Serves 6 to 8.

*If you have agar in a different form than flakes, follow the manufacturer's recommendation for the amount to use for jelling 4 cups of juice.

VARIATIONS

A teaspoon of grated fresh ginger adds zest.
1 teaspoon soy sauce lends a deeper, heartier flavor.
2 tablespoons of fresh parsley gives a springy lift.
Try Florence fennel instead of celery; or use 1/4 teaspoon fennel seeds with or without celery.

Finocchio Salad

An especially mouth-watering pasta salad.

ð

Cook macaroni until tender in salted boiling water. Cool and combine with fennel, parsley, bell pepper, mushrooms, chives, and olives.

Mix 2 tablespoons lemon juice, olive oil, salt, and pepper. Toss salad in dressing, taste, and add remaining tablespoon of lemon juice if desired.

Makes 5½ cups.

*No fennel in sight?
Substitute raw celery or
blanched green beans, or
crisp-tender broccoli.*

*1½ cups raw whole
    wheat macaroni*
*½ cup sliced Florence
    fennel**
*¼ cup chopped Italian
    parsley*
¼ cup diced bell pepper
1 cup sliced raw mushrooms
2 tablespoons chopped chives
(⅓ cup sliced black olives)

*2 to 3 tablespoons lemon
    juice*
2 tablespoons olive oil
½ teaspoon salt
freshly ground black pepper

Yogurt Rice

Traditional in South India for tiffin, and as delicious at home as on the road.

ð

Heat the oil in a heavy skillet that has a lid. Add the mustard seeds to the hot oil and cover the pan. As soon as the wild sound of popping dies down—it only takes a few seconds—add the ginger, the chili if used, and then the rice, yogurt, and salt. (If you use rice that was already salted in cooking, use less salt than the recipe calls for.) Stir and cook gently for 5 minutes; then remove from heat and chill. Serve cool.

Makes 4 cups.

1 tablespoon oil
*2 teaspoons black
    mustard seeds*

*2 teaspoons finely minced
    fresh ginger*
*(1 small green chili,
    seeded and minced)*
*4 cups well-cooked, cooled
    brown rice*
*1½ cups yogurt,
    beaten smooth*
1 teaspoon salt

Tabouli

3 cups water
¾ teaspoon salt
1½ cups raw bulgur wheat
½ cup cooked white beans
2 tomatoes, chopped
3 tablespoons olive oil
pepper to taste
1 garlic clove, minced
2 tablespoons chopped chives
2 teaspoons chopped
  fresh mint leaves
juice of at least 2 lemons
¼–½ cup chopped parsley

This classic Lebanese salad makes a truly delicious luncheon dish. The combination of garlic, lemon, and fresh mint reverberates delightfully on the palate. Beans are not traditional but definitely tasty; omit them if you prefer.

રત

Bring water to a boil with salt. Add bulgur and return to boil. Remove from heat, cover pot tightly, and set aside for 15 minutes.

Drain off any excess water and chill the grain. Toss thoroughly with all ingredients, adjusting salt and lemon if needed.

Makes 6 generous servings (6 ½ cups).

Pineapple-Bulgur Wheat Salad

1 cup water
¼ teaspoon salt
1 cup raw bulgur wheat

1 medium avocado
1 cup fresh pineapple chunks
½ cup chopped red bell
  pepper
2 inside stalks celery,
  chopped, or
  ½ cup cucumber,
  chopped
3 or 4 scallions, thinly
  sliced
chopped chives
1 tablespoon oil
3 tablespoons lemon
  juice, or
  2 tablespoons cider
  vinegar

This fresh and sweetly satisfying salad makes a friendly lunch all by itself. If you need to prepare it ahead, try to leave at least the avocado and pineapple till the last moment; this one doesn't keep.

રત

Bring water to boil with salt. Add bulgur and return to a boil. Remove from heat, cover pot tightly, and set aside for 15 minutes or until water is absorbed. Cool to room temperature.

Peel and cube avocado and stir into pineapple chunks so that the juice from the pineapple will keep the avocado from discoloring. Combine with bell pepper, celery, scallions, oil and lemon juice or vinegar. Stir in bulgur wheat and serve.

Makes 6 generous servings.

Sideways Sushi

Not to be confused with the more familiar Nori Maki Sushi (page 274), this is "O-sushi" or "Big Sushi." It comes to you "sideways" because we have taken some liberties with this classic dish, which we first tasted at the hands of an honored and beloved friend, Fukuda-Sensei, many years ago.

ಶ

Bring water to boil with salt. Add rice and boil uncovered 5 minutes. Cover and reduce heat to low. Cook for 45 minutes. Turn off heat, cover, and allow to rest for another 10 minutes.

While rice is cooking, steam carrot until crisp-tender and prepare cucumber and almonds.

Spread hot rice out quickly on the biggest tray or platter you have (but not one made of metal!). Toss rice with a fork for several minutes while you or a helper fan the steam away with a fan or a folded newspaper. This helps make the rice as dry and fluffy as possible.

Sprinkle vinegar over rice as you toss it. Lightly stir in the cucumber, carrot, and almonds. Taste and add more vinegar if you like. Do not refrigerate. Cover with a damp cloth and serve warm or at room temperature.

Makes 8 servings.

3¾ cups water
1 teaspoon salt
2 cups raw long-grain brown rice

1 medium carrot, diced
1 cucumber, peeled and diced
½ cup chopped toasted almonds
⅓ cup rice vinegar

Other options for additions (use three or four only, about 2 cups total):

> *tiny strips of omelette*
> *diced sautéed mushroom*
> *thin-sliced steamed green beans*
> *minced scallion*
> *diced green bell pepper*
> *nori sea vegetable, toasted and crumbled*

Persian Rice Salad

This sophisticated salad is sweet and tangy. Perfect for carry-outs too.

ಶ

Dress rice with combined olive oil, lemon juice, and dill weed. Add salt to taste. Combine with scallions, cashew pieces, and dates and serve immediately. (If you can't serve right away, set the cashews aside and add them just beforehand.)

Makes 4 servings (2½ cups).

2 cups cold cooked long-grain brown rice
1 tablespoon olive oil
3 tablespoons lemon juice
¼ to ½ teaspoon dill weed, by taste
½ teaspoon salt, optional
3 thin scallions, sliced thin
⅓ cup toasted cashew pieces
4 to 6 medium dates, cut up

Soups

Because we like to serve light suppers, soup appears frequently on our table, often with nothing more than fresh bread or muffins and a big green salad alongside.

Our soups usually take form around what is fresh and wonderful from the garden (or sometimes it's What Really Needs Using from the refrigerator). The recipes here reflect that, and we feel sure their usefulness for us will make them helpful to you, either as they are or as inspiration for your own creations.

Truly splendid broth can transform an ordinary soup into a great event, and it's not hard to make; some suggestions follow. But truth to tell, *most* of the time, plain old water is all you need. Daily-fare soups that have a dose of onion and celery, garlic, or herbs will make their own broth in the pot and be delicious. Like the stone soup of the fairy tale, they develop their character along the way.

With soup, even more than most dishes, there is a lot of leeway where fat is concerned. Most of the soups here start with sautéed onion because that is the surest, quickest way to a delicious base that we know. But if you have more time and are trying to bring your fat intake to a real minimum, boil the onion instead of sautéeing, adding seasonings or other vegetables if you like for extra flavor. When the onion is very well cooked, you can use it and its broth, or puree them, or strain out the onion and use just the broth by itself. The onion's flavor will be different than if it had been sautéed, but still sweet and satisfying. A variation on this theme is spelled out in the Corn Chowder recipe.

Because soup is so good the next day for lunch, either at home or in a thermos, we have scaled many of the soup recipes generously. Check the serving size before you start; if your household is very small, you may want either to cut the recipe in half, or plan to freeze part for using another time.

INSTANT SOUP A little leftover sauce, thinned with broth or milk or tomato juice (whichever seems appropriate) and heated with leftover vegetables and/or noodles, makes fine soup in a trice.

Basic Vegetable Soup

In a big soup pot, sauté a chopped onion until golden, adding garlic and some chopped celery or green pepper if you like. Add stock or water and bring to a boil. Stir in whatever vegetables are in season, chopped attractively—start with slower-cooking ones like potatoes, carrots, and green beans, and end with delicate greens like spinach or parsley and fresh herbs. Leftover grains, beans, or noodles are welcome and contribute substance to the pot; so does tomato sauce or other leftover sauce. A simple and low-calorie way to make the soup thicker is to put part of its cooked vegetables (and grain) into the blender and blend smooth, returning the puree to the pot.

Especially when you're preparing soup for more than four people, you may prefer to cook all or part of the vegetables separately, adding them with their cooking water to the pot toward the end. This insures that each one will be perfectly cooked, and preserves individual colors—especially helpful when the soup is tomato-based. Cooking separately like this can save time too, because the vegetables can be simmering while you prepare the rest.

This simple soup is a perfect way to use up odds and ends from the garden, but made with a delicately flavored broth and just the right herbs, it can be superb.

Stock

When you simmer vegetable trimmings to make stock, you preserve both useful nutrients and rich flavors that would otherwise be lost. It's a thrifty procedure that can become such a habit that the little work involved slips unnoticed into your routine.

Collect clean vegetable trimmings for a week, storing them in a covered jar in the refrigerator. To make stock, take stock: what kinds of trimmings have you collected? Balance the flavors: if it's all spinach and parsley stems, for example, slice in some carrot or potato or winter squash to sweeten the pot. Don't include anything that is over the hill, and take time to add whatever extras you think will insure that your brew tastes great. Cover with cold water and add a small spoonful of salt, if you like, to draw out the flavors. Bring to a boil and simmer gently about half an hour, or until the vegetables are very soft. Let the pot sit as long as is convenient, or until cool. Drain, discarding the vegetables. Use at once, preferably, or keep in the refrigerator for a day or two at most.

TIPS   ❧ Some things can tolerate more cooking than others. Onions, potatoes, and the like can simmer for hours. But don't overcook the green things; their flavors become drab and harsh. Grate the carrot and potato when you are in a hurry; smaller pieces cook faster.

❧ Very good for stock are pea pods, trimmings of green beans, squashes of all sorts (including their seeds) parsley, carrot and potato bits (but not eyes and bad spots!), any edible part of any member of the onion family, celery leaves, and mushroom bits.

❧ Take advantage of the the sea vegetable kombu, which has a wealth of minerals and also a natural glutamic acid which MSG was invented to imitate. Wash and soak a piece of kombu in cold water for several hours or overnight, or put a four-inch square in a quart of cold water and heat slowly, removing the kombu as soon as the water comes to a boil. You can include a small piece of kombu with other vegetables when you make stock in the normal way, but don't let it stay in after the stock boils.

ᕮ Some things do more harm than good: artichoke trimmings and bell pepper innards, for example, are bitter, and the whole brassica family from cabbage to cauliflower overcooks quickly, giving a heavy, sulfury taste.

ᕮ Adjust the stock to its purpose, seasoning or flavoring it according to its proposed use. Try adding one or more of the following: a few fennel or cumin seeds, peppercorns, turmeric, bay leaves, onion, garlic, ginger.

Special Broths

BROTH FOR PEOPLE WITH COLDS OR FLU

"Get lots of rest and drink plenty of *fluids*." Fruit juice and herb teas are fine, but after a while what tastes best is good, hot broth. Golden Broth (page 151), strained and thinned, is good for colds. Or try Rasam (next page) if your snuffly patient has good digestion and an adventurous palate. The broth described below, with onion, garlic, cumin, and perhaps tomato added for extra flavor, also hits the spot when you have a cold.

But when the patient is recovering from flu and has a sore, touchy stomach, a light, soothing broth seems to help most. These ingredients can be varied to suit, but when nothing else seems good, this mild broth can be heavenly just as it is.

ᕮ

Wash and cut up the vegetables. Place in a saucepan and cover with cold water, adding salt if desired—even a little bit makes a big difference in flavor. Bring to a boil and simmer gently until the vegetables are very soft—about 20 minutes or so, depending on how small they were chopped. Add the leaves and simmer 10 more minutes, then drain, discarding the vegetables. Serve soon, refrigerating and reheating the rest as needed—but this broth is best when used within a day or two.

2 small zucchini
   or use winter squash,
   potatoes, or carrot
handful green beans
handful parsley stems
   and/or spinach stems
⅛ teaspoon salt
2 quarts water

1 cup parsley and/or
   spinach leaves

Rasam

4 small cloves garlic
1/4 teaspoon cumin powder
1/2 teaspoon black
  peppercorns

1 tablespoon oil
2 teaspoons black mustard
  seed
1/2 teaspoon cumin seed

2 tomatoes, quartered
1 cup water
1 teaspoon turmeric
1/2 teaspoon salt
2 teaspoons tamarind
  concentrate dissolved
  in 1 cup hot water
    OR
  juice of one lemon
  in 1 cup hot water

1 cup well-cooked yellow
  split peas

(chopped coriander leaves)

This exceedingly spicy broth is credited with curing colds in South India, and if it seems to do the same in North America, who can complain? The cures are undocumented, but the brew is breathtaking, no doubt about it. For a less fiery version (and more soup) use 6 tomatoes and add extra water. For LEMON RASAM, omit the tomatoes—and stand back!

❧

Crush the garlic, cumin, and peppercorns with a mortar and pestle or in a blender, using just enough water to cover the blades.

Heat the oil in a very heavy small pan. Add the mustard seeds, coating the bottom of the pan evenly. Cover the pan quickly and listen for the moment when the furious sound of popping slows dramatically. Then add the cumin seeds so that they brown, but almost immediately *turn off the flame* and add the tomato, water, and turmeric, then the garlic mixture.

Bring to a boil and add the tamarind or lemon and salt. Mash the peas and add them too. Simmer gently until the tomatoes are soft, about ten minutes. In Kerala they take advantage of the way this soup separates, serving the liquid top part over rice at the beginning of the meal and the thick bottom part over rice at the end of it. If you want a uniformly creamy soup, give the finished version a spin in the blender. Serve with a garnish of chopped coriander leaves on top, if you have them.

Makes 2 cups as written, 6 cups with extra tomato and water.

Golden Broth

This is a hearty broth that is useful wherever you think you need chicken stock. If you want to make it without the fat, the flavor is quite satisfactory with everything just boiled together. You can't strain it, however.

1 onion, chopped
1 clove garlic
½ cup yellow split peas
2 tablespoons oil

½ teaspoon turmeric
2 quarts hot water

ૐ

Sauté onion, whole garlic clove, and split peas in oil until delicately brown. Stir in turmeric and add water. Simmer at least half an hour. Strain for a thin stock, puree for a thick one.

GREEN BROTH: substitute green peas for yellow. Add a bay leaf and omit the turmeric. For a very full flavored broth, add a carrot and potato, cut up. Celery leaves are good too.

Golden Noodle Soup

Golden Noodle Soup is our answer to Mother Campbell, and to all the colds, malaises, and depressions usually remedied at the expense of our feathered friends. This is wonderful, elemental, satisfying soup. Easy, too.

2 quarts Golden Broth
big handful whole wheat
  ribbon noodles
1 cup each diced celery,
  potatoes, carrots
1 teaspoon salt
½ cup finely chopped
  parsley

ૐ

Bring broth to a boil in a heavy pan. Add noodles, celery, potatoes, carrots, and salt. Reduce heat and simmer gently until the vegetables are tender, about half an hour. Stir in the parsley, adjust seasoning, and serve.

Makes about 10 cups of soup (and you won't be sorry.)

TIMESAVING VARIATION: If you don't already have the broth, cook the noodles and vegetables in another pot while the broth simmers, combining them after you puree or strain the broth. Total cooking time is about half an hour.

Gumbo

1 onion, chopped
3 cloves
2 tablespoons oil
1 green pepper, diced
2 cups diced tomatoes
4 cups vegetable stock
1 cup cooked lima beans
1 cup fresh corn
1 1/2 cups sliced okra
1 teaspoon salt
1/4 teaspoon allspice

(1/2 cup cooked brown rice)

You won't feel diffident about serving a vegetarian gumbo when you taste this soup. (Who says it isn't gumbo, anyway?) Fresh tomatoes are wonderful, but canned work fine.

❧

Sauté the onion and cloves in oil until the onions are soft. Remove the cloves.

Add green pepper and stir over medium heat for several minutes; then stir in the tomatoes. Bring the mixture to a boil, turn down the heat, and let simmer for 5 minutes.

Add the rest of the ingredients. Bring soup to a boil again, cover, and simmer for 15 minutes. Add rice if desired.

Makes about 8 cups.

Whole Beet Borscht

1 small onion
1 clove garlic
2 teaspoons oil
2 tablespoons flour
5 cups stock or water

1 bunch beets and greens
   (3 large or 6 small)
1 potato
1 carrot
1 stalk celery
1/2 small cabbage
1 bay leaf
1 1/2 teaspoons salt
1/4 teaspoon pepper
1 teaspoon honey
2 tablespoons tomato paste
   or 2 fresh tomatoes,
   chopped

This is *good*, especially served with Mock Sour Cream.

❧

Chop onion and sauté with garlic clove in oil. Mash garlic clove when onion is translucent and browning. Stir in flour and cook gently for a minute. Add stock or water and bring to a boil.

Meantime, trim roots of beets, saving the good leaves and stems. Grate beets, potato, and carrot, or slice them thin. Slice celery thin. Add these and simmer 10 minutes while you shred the cabbage and chop the beet leaves and stems small. Add these and bay leaf, salt, pepper, honey, and tomato to the vegetable mixture. Simmer until all vegetables are tender. Remove bay leaf.

Makes 10 cups.

Minestrone

Minestrone is a general name for a richly flavored tomato-based soup that welcomes infinite variation, according to the season's taste and needs. It can appear as a light, fragrant vegetable soup on summer evenings or, most memorably, as a hearty stew for a cold winter day. Either way, minestrone is a wonderful meal in itself with green salad and crusty fresh bread. Begin with the tomato soup base and include any of the suggested grains, beans, and vegetables.

❧

Sauté onion, garlic and celery in oil until soft. Crush garlic. Add tomatoes, or tomato paste and stock, and herbs. Simmer the soup gently while you prepare whatever vegetables, beans, or grains you wish to add.

At least 30 minutes before serving soup, add beans, noodles, and/or the grain.

Minestrone welcomes leftover steamed vegetables, but if you are cooking them fresh, we suggest steaming or simmering them before adding to the soup because vegetables cooked with tomato will lose their color. Incorporate the vegetable cooking water into the soup. Parsley and tender greens will keep their color and not be overcooked if you add them just a few minutes before serving. Don't count them as part of the 2 cups of vegetables because they cook down so much; just add them as extras.

After combining all the ingredients, bring the soup to a boil, simmer briefly, and correct the seasonings. If you like, garnish each bowl with a spoonful of Parmesan cheese.

Makes about 10 cups—all to the good because it's even better the next day. Serves 6 generously.

1 onion, finely chopped
1–2 cloves garlic
1½ cups chopped celery
1½ tablespoons olive oil
4 cups chopped tomatoes
* with juice, or*
* 1 six-ounce can tomato*
* paste and 3 cups*
* vegetable stock*
2 bay leaves
1 teaspoon oregano
2 teaspoons basil
pinch fennel seed

2 cups or more, chopped:
* carrot, zucchini, potato,*
* broccoli, green*
* beans, green pepper,*
* cabbage, peas, corn,*
* sautéed mushrooms*

1 cup cooked beans:
* lima, kidney, pinto,*
* black, or garbanzo*

handful of raw or cooked
* whole wheat pasta*

(½ cup cooked grain)
salt to taste
plenty of pepper

(tender greens, cut up)
½ cup chopped parsley

Puree

"Puree" means to reduce whatever it is to a smooth, thick liquid. You can do this with a food mill (or a strainer and spoon), or a blender or food processor—whichever you find most convenient. A few recipes specify one of them if the others aren't practical for that particular step. If a food mill is called for, you can always use the strainer-and-spoon method, but food mills are inexpensive, and so handy that we can hardly imagine cooking without one.

Blender companies are very stern in their instruction booklets about the danger of blending hot liquids. *They're right!* If you are making soup or sauce and can't wait for the temperature to go down to lukewarm before popping the brew in the blender, *please* fill the container not more than half full, cover tightly, and hold the cover in place with a large, half-folded towel. Stainless steel blender jars won't break, but besides cracking glass and plastic blender jars, hot liquids can cause bad burns if they come spewing out the top.

Xergis

3 cucumbers
3 scallions or
   ½ small onion
(1 clove garlic)
5 cups yogurt
(1 teaspoon oil)
4 teaspoons dill weed
1 teaspoon salt
dash pepper

On hot summer evenings, this flavorful Levantine beverage is a refreshing first course.

Peel cucumbers and remove seeds. Chop cucumbers, onion, and garlic. Mix all ingredients and divide in 3 parts. Place in blender one part at a time and blend very smooth. Chill.
   Makes 6 to 8 cups.

Creamy Green Soup

At its simplest—and some say its best—Creamy Green Soup is just cooked, garden-fresh zucchini blended with its own broth with salt, pepper, and a dab of butter. You can enliven it if you like with bright red bell peppers or corn off the cob, sautéed scallions or chives, parsley or chopped greens. For added heft, you can blend in a spoonful of milk powder, cottage cheese, cooked green split peas, or a little nutritional yeast.

Vary the texture by blending some ingredients and leaving others chopped or shredded. Thin with good vegetable stock or milk, or thicken by adding half a cup or more of well-cooked brown rice that has been blended smooth with a small amount of the soup.

To complete its versatility, Green Soup can be served chilled. Top it with a spoonful of yogurt and add crackers with Garbanzo Spread for a refreshing supper on a hot summer evening.

The following versions are some current favorites.

Old Favorite Green Soup

Sauté the onion and celery in oil until soft. Add 4 cups of stock, split peas, and bay leaf. Bring to a boil; then cover loosely and simmer over low heat for about 40 minutes.

Add zucchini, remaining stock, and seasonings. Cook for another 10 minutes, until zucchini is tender.

Remove bay leaf and discard. Puree soup, return to the soup pot and stir in the spinach and parsley. Cook over medium heat for several minutes. Adjust seasonings and serve.

Makes 7 to 8 cups.

½ onion, chopped
2 stalks celery, diced
1 tablespoons oil

6 cups vegetable stock
¾ cup green split peas, rinsed
1 bay leaf

6 cups diced zucchini
¼ teaspoon basil
⅛ teaspoon pepper
1 teaspoon salt

1 pound spinach, washed and chopped
¼ cup chopped fresh parsley

New Favorite Green Soup

1 onion or 1 bunch scallions
1 tablespoon oil or butter
2 or 3 potatoes, cut up
6–8 cups chopped fresh
    greens—chard, spinach,
    etc.

broth or milk
salt and pepper

Sauté onion in oil or butter until very soft. Add the potatoes and water to cover. Cook until tender and remove peels if you desire. Add greens and simmer until they wilt. Puree all. Add broth or milk to thin and extend as desired, then add salt and pepper to taste.

Asparagus Soup

½ onion or 6 scallions
1 tablespoon oil or butter
1 medium potato
2 cups vegetable stock
    or water

1–1½ pounds fresh
    asparagus
4 stalks celery
1–1½ teaspoons salt
⅛ teaspoon pepper
(milk or broth)

For an elegant touch, set aside the asparagus tips and stir them in just a little before serving. This delicate, spring-fresh soup makes good use of slender, stringy asparagus as well as fat, succulent spears.

❧

Sauté onion in oil or butter. Dice potato and add along with 1 cup of stock. Simmer until potatoes are soft.

Wash the asparagus and snap off the tough ends. Slice. (If you have a lot of tough ends but the spears seem fresh and good, peel and include the tender inside parts, or cook the spears along with the rest and put the finished soup through a food mill to remove the tough fibers.)

Chop celery small, including leaves. Add asparagus, celery, and remaining vegetable stock to potatoes and onions. Cook for 10 minutes, until the vegetables are quite tender. Add salt and pepper and puree. Add milk or broth to thin or extend soup as desired.

Makes about 6 cups.

Creamy Cauliflower Soup

The cauliflower disappears completely, making a warm-flavored soup as thick and white as heavy cream—but much tastier and better for you!

🍃

Cook the potato in the broth. Chop the celery and add. When the potato is nearly done, add the cauliflower and cook until tender. As always in blended soups, the potato must be very well cooked; otherwise the soup will be gluey.

While the vegetables are cooking, chop the onion and sauté it and the garlic clove in the olive oil. Cook them gently until very well done but don't let them brown.

Puree all the cooked vegetables and the onion and garlic in blender or food processor until smooth. To get a very smooth soup, blend or process in small batches.

Stir in the wine, if you choose, and the salt and pepper. Reheat gently, adjust seasoning as needed, and serve.

Makes 10 cups.

🍃

This soup is lovely as is, pure white. If you want to add color or other interest, though, stir in one or more of the following a few minutes before serving:

*1/2 pound fresh mushrooms, sliced and sautéed,
    with 1 teaspoon each marjoram and savory*
1/2 cup chopped fresh parsley
1/2 cup diced red bell pepper
1 cup fresh corn off the cob

*1 1/2 cups potato
    chunks (no peels)*
4 cups light broth or water
*1 1/4 cups chopped pale
    celery*
*5 cups cauliflower
    pieces (1 head)*

1 small onion
1 whole clove garlic
*1 tablespoon olive oil
    or butter*

(1/2 cup dry white wine)

1 teaspoon salt
pinch pepper

Lynne's Spiced Pumpkin Soup

1 small pumpkin
  (about 10 cups diced)
3 carrots

1½ tablespoons oil
¾ teaspoon black mustard
  seed
½ onion, chopped
½ teaspoon turmeric
½ teaspoon cumin
½ teaspoon cinnamon
¼ teaspoon ginger

¾ cup powdered milk
2 teaspoons honey
1 teaspoon salt

Truly remarkable with pumpkin, but if you haven't any, substitute winter squash. A light, flavorful soup that finds favor even with squash haters. It's worth growing pumpkins for.

≥●

Peel and chop pumpkin and carrots, and simmer in water to cover until tender.

Toward the end of the cooking time, heat oil in a small, heavy skillet. When hot, add mustard seeds. Cover pan and keep over high heat until the sound of popping dies down a bit, then *immediately* add the onion and reduce heat. Cook and stir until onion is clear. Measure the spices while the onion is cooking; then stir them into the mixture and allow to cook on low heat for a minute or so until they are fragrant. Turn into the pumpkin pot, using a cup or so of cooking water to rinse the spice pan into the soup pot.

Puree the seasoned pumpkin and carrots in their cooking water, adding the milk, honey, and salt to the mixture in the blender or processor. Add salt to taste.

Makes 10 cups.

ALTERNATE METHOD: If you have leftover cooked pumpkin, or prefer to use fresh milk, warm the squash and milk and then puree them, using the milk instead of the cooking broth to provide the liquid.

Croutons

The best croutons come from bread that is airy and not too sweet. Light sourdoughs are great.

For croutons in a hurry, toast bread slices, butter them, and cut into cubes. Croutons made in this way will be soft in the middle and are not meant for storing, but for eating up right away.

To make plain croutons that will keep a long time, cut bread into ½" to 1" cubes, spread on a shallow pan, and bake very slowly until they become 100 percent crunchy. (Chomp on one; there's no other way to be sure that we know of.) Cool thoroughly and store airtight.

Squash Soup

A wintertime standby of many interpretations, this hearty soup provides a useful role for leftover baked squash.

❧

If you use raw squash or pumpkin, simmer in water until tender. Puree the cooked squash.

Sauté the onion in the oil. When the onion is golden, add the parsley. Cook just long enough to soften parsley; then combine with squash and add salt.

Bring the soup to a simmer—don't boil or it will stick.

Near the end of the cooking time, if you like, add fresh spinach or other tender greens, chopped bite-size. Colorful and tasty too.

Makes about 7 cups.

5 cups cubed raw winter
*   squash or pumpkin, or*
3 cups cooked winter
*   squash*
2½ cups water

1 cup chopped onion
1 tablespoon oil or butter
½ cup chopped parsley
2 teaspoons salt
(2–4 cups tender greens)

Carrot Soup

Cut carrots in 1″ chunks, quarter the potatoes, and place both in a 2-quart sauce pan. Add just enough water to cover. Bring to a boil and simmer, covered, until vegetables are tender. Remove and discard potato peels.

Meanwhile, wash leeks thoroughly and chop them coarsely. If they are very muddy, chop them first and rinse well in a sieve after chopping. Sauté in butter along with the tarragon. Use blender or food processor to puree the vegetables in batches, adding the milk, stock, and salt. Return soup to pot; add pepper and wine, and reheat.

Makes 8 cups.

5 medium-large carrots
2 small potatoes or one large
1 bunch leeks
*   (or 1 large onion)*
2 tablespoons butter or oil
1 teaspoon dry tarragon
*   leaves, or*
*   1 tablespoon fresh*
*   tarragon*
2 cups milk
2 cups vegetable stock
*   or water*
1 teaspoon salt
pinch black pepper
½ cup dry white wine

Kale-Potato Soup

1 large onion
1 tablespoon butter
1 clove garlic

2 big potatoes
1 large bunch kale
5 cups hot water or stock

½ teaspoon salt, to taste
black pepper

An utterly satisfying soup. How many winter nights does this seem to be the only possible choice? A classic, a favorite, a stand-by. With fresh young kale, it is, perhaps, even a world-class soup.

&

Sauté onion in butter, cooking and stirring until clear and slightly golden. About halfway, add the garlic; when the onion is done, crush the garlic with a fork.

Add the potatoes and 2 cups of water. Simmer, covered, until potatoes start to soften around the edges. Meantime, wash the kale, remove stems, chop, and steam. (Don't try to cook it with the potatoes; the flavor will be too strong. Really.)

When the potatoes are very well done, puree half of them with remaining water and the salt and pepper. Combine all and heat gently, correcting the consistency if necessary by adding hot water or milk.

Makes about 6 cups and serves 4 if no extra water is added.

Potato-Cheese Soup

4 medium potatoes
2 carrots

1 onion, chopped
(1 whole clove garlic)
1–2 tablespoons oil or butter

3 cups milk
½–1 cup grated sharp
    cheddar
2 teaspoons salt
¼ teaspoon pepper
1 tablespoon chopped parsley

"Your Potato-Cheese Soup gets us through the Minnesota winter," writes a friend. What a tribute! What a soup!

&

Cook the potatoes and carrots in water to cover in a large, heavy pan. Remove potato skins. Meantime, sauté the onion—and garlic, if desired—in the oil or butter and combine with potatoes, carrots, and cooking water. Puree in batches.

Return puree to pan and add milk, cheese, and seasonings. Heat until cheese is melted and soup is piping hot—but don't let it boil.

Makes 8 to 10 cups.

Corn Chowder

When a recipe has been with you as long as you can remember, and enjoyed so much, it can be hard to think what to say about it. This is an elemental, wonderful chowder.

❧

Simmer the water, onion, celery, potato, and parsley until half cooked, about 10 minutes.

Add the corn. Simmer gently with the other vegetables until nearly done, not more than a few minutes.

Add the milk or Cream Sauce, and bring the soup just to the boiling point without actually boiling. Add seasonings and correct to taste.

Serve piping hot, with a dot of Better-Butter. Serves 4 to 6.

VARIATION: Instead of milk or cream sauce, you can use 1 cup tomato sauce and 1 cup broth. Presto, MANHATTAN CORN CHOWDER!

2 cups water
½ chopped onion
½ cup chopped celery
½ cup diced potato
½ cup chopped parsley
1 cup fresh raw corn
  off the cob
2 cups milk
  or light Cream Sauce
1 teaspoon salt
¼ teaspoon pepper
Better-Butter

Cream of Celery Soup

A warming, soothing brew for chasing chills on cold winter evenings. Homey and good.

❧

In a large soup pot, sauté onion and garlic in oil until soft. Add 4 cups stock and bring to boil.

Stir in potatoes, celery, and celery seed. Cover and simmer for 10 to 15 minutes, until potatoes are very soft. Add cabbage if you want and simmer 5 more minutes. Puree half of the soup mixture. (If you use a blender, do it in 2 portions of 2 cups each.) Add pureed soup, salt, parsley, pepper, and paprika to soup pot and reheat. Thin with milk or broth if desired.

Makes about 8 cups, to serve 4 to 6.

½ onion, chopped
1 garlic clove
1 tablespoon oil
4 cups water or broth

2 medium potatoes, diced
½ bunch celery, diced
¼ teaspoon celery seed
(¼ head cabbage, chopped)

1½ teaspoons salt
¼ cup finely chopped
  parsley
dash pepper
¼ teaspoon paprika
(2 cups milk, or more broth)

Tomato Soup

1 medium onion
2 stalks celery
1 carrot
1 tablespoon oil

¾ teaspoon oregano
1½ teaspoons basil
4 cups cut-up tomatoes★

2–3 cups hot vegetable stock
¾ teaspoon salt
pepper to taste

★Here and anywhere we call
for tomatoes, use fresh
if you have them, canned
if you don't.

A fine basic tomato soup, spectacularly good when the tomatoes are garden-fresh and ripe. Delicious as is, or a fine base for any kind of red-brothed soup.

In a big soup pot, sauté the onion in oil, adding the celery and carrot when the onion is partly cooked. Cook together until the onion is soft.

Add oregano, basil, and tomatoes to the pot and simmer gently until the tomatoes are very soft. If you want a smooth, creamy texture, puree the soup. (Using a food mill for pureeing will remove the tomato seeds and skins, making a velvety soup.)

Add the hot stock, adjusting the amount to get the quantity and thickness you want. Bring to a boil and simmer on low heat for 5 minutes. Season with salt and pepper to taste.

Makes about 8 cups.

Cream of Tomato Soup

Follow the Tomato Soup recipe but tone down the herbs, using just ¼ teaspoon oregano and ½ teaspoon basil—and perhaps a little extra salt.

Blend 1 cup of dried skim milk with part of the stock or with the tomato mixture. Pour it back into the pot, add salt and pepper, and heat thoroughly (but *don't boil*). For a heartier soup, add a cup of cooked brown rice.

Makes about 8 cups.

Gingery Tomato Soup

A tangy, fruity soup, very light and refreshing.

ᨓ

Sauté shallots or onion and whole garlic in oil; add ginger. Add tomatoes and stock and simmer until tomatoes are soft. Put through sieve or food mill.

Add black pepper and shoyu to taste, starting with 1 teaspoon shoyu.

Makes about 5 cups.

2 teaspoons oil
3 shallots
   or 1 onion
2 cloves garlic
1 tablespoon minced ginger
3 cups tomatoes
2 cups stock
1 tablespoon shoyu
fresh black pepper

TOMATO–PEPPER SOUP

Make Gingery Tomato Soup, omitting ginger and shoyu. While soup simmers, roast, peel, seed, and chop 2 red bell peppers (see page 137). Sieve the tomato soup as described in the recipe, then puree the peppers with part of the soup. Mix together, adding ½ cup sherry. Simmer 10 minutes gently, then adjust seasoning.

TOMATO–PEPPER SAUCE: Don't add extra stock; simmer soup gently to reduce volume to 2 cups.

Fresh Corn & Tomato Soup

A thick, creamy, coral-colored soup with truly superb flavor.

ᨓ

Sauté onion, celery, cayenne if desired, and garlic in oil in a heavy 2-quart pan until tender. (This amount of oil will be enough if you keep the heat low and stir frequently.)

Strip corn from cobs with a small, sharp knife. Remove stem end of tomatoes and cut up coarsely.

Add corn and tomatoes, water, and salt to sautéed vegetables. Bring to a boil; then reduce heat to low and simmer, covered, until corn is tender, about ½ hour.

The soup is pretty now, but even better if you take your courage in hand and proceed with the next step: puree it all. Return to pot, thinning with a little more water if you want, and correct the salt. Heat, stirring in coriander leaves just at serving time.

Serves 4.

½ onion, chopped
1 stalk celery, chopped
(dash cayenne pepper)
1 whole clove garlic
1 tablespoon oil

5 ears corn
   (4 cups off the cob)
4 good-sized tomatoes
½ cup water
½–1 teaspoon salt

(handful fresh coriander
   leaves, lightly chopped)

Miso Soup

How much salt does miso have?

½ teaspoon salt
= 2 teaspoons shoyu
= 1 tablespoon salty miso:
  (red, barley, light-yellow,
  soybean, or Hatcho)
= 1½ to 2 tablespoons
  "mellow miso"
= 2½ to 3 tablespoons
  sweet miso

SOURCE: *The Book of Miso, by William Shurtleff and Akiko Aoyagi (Berkeley: Ten Speed Press, 1983)*

Flavorful and salty, miso is a brown, golden, or reddish paste made by fermenting soybeans with or without rice or other grains. A staple in Japanese cuisine, it is a versatile seasoning with considerable nutritive value—one that Americans are finding increasingly useful.

In traditional Japanese families, hot miso soup is served every morning alongside a steaming bowl of rice cereal. In their splendid *Book of Miso,* Bill and Akiko Shurtleff describe the place miso has in the Japanese consciousness: its warming aroma is as nostalgic and comforting as the fragrance of baking bread is to us of European extraction. They also describe miso's versatility: to give just an idea, one Japanese firm publishes a calendar with a different seasonal miso soup for each and every day! Here and elsewhere in this book we present some simple ways to let miso work its magic.

Like yogurt, miso contains beneficial organisms—and like yogurt, it is often pasteurized, so that these organisms are not available to the eater. If you can buy unpasteurized miso, cook it as little as possible so that you don't pasteurize it yourself: if you want to use it to flavor a soup, for example, stir the miso smooth in a small amount of broth and add at the last possible moment before serving.

In this context, researchers who have spent decades studying miso at the USDA Northern Regional Research Center in Peoria, Illinois, say that although miso bacteria may well be helpful to the eater while they are present in the digestive system, they are not the kind of organisms that would be able to colonize the intestines with beneficial flora after a course of antibiotic drugs, as is sometimes claimed.

Store miso airtight in the refrigerator; it can spoil.

Some Ways to Use Miso

Traditional soups are composed of miso broth with one main vegetable and two garnishing vegetables, the latter being freely interpreted to include such things as tofu pieces or lemon zest besides zucchini, spinach, mushrooms, and the like. The ingredients are cut with mindful artistry and simmered in stock; then the miso is stirred in as described above and the soup is served. With unsalted broth, 1 or 2 teaspoons per person of miso is about the right amount, depending on the variety.

Untraditional soup can be literally any liquid that tastes better with miso in it. Its flavor in soup is deep and hearty, with the darker varieties almost like a vegetarian bouillion.

TO MAKE SOUP

Since miso is flavorful and salty, it can be used to enhance many dishes where you would use salt or shoyu. Sandwich spreads made from beans or tofu would be a good example.

AS A SEASONING

A more concentrated version of miso soup, thickened with flour or cornstarch or with cooked rice or vegetables pureed smooth, makes a very convincing brown gravy.

TO MAKE GRAVY

Some of our friends swear by miso as a coffee substitute. A spoonful stirred into hot water makes a satisfying hot drink, with or without a garnish of crumbled, toasted nori. Commercial instant miso soups that come in packets may lack the living cultures of unpasteurized miso, but they travel easily and need no refrigeration, so they are convenient pick-me-ups when you're away from home.

AS A HOT DRINK

Catalina Soup

1 onion
1 clove garlic
1 tablespoon oil

¼ cup tomato paste
4 cups water or stock
2 large potatoes
½ teaspoon oregano
1 teaspoon salt
black pepper

(handful of fresh
    chopped coriander leaves)
½–1 cup grated jack cheese

Like all often-made favorite dishes, this soup adapts to the needs of the day. For tomato paste, you can use tomatoes—or less, or much more—and the amount of potatoes can go up or down to make the soup heartier or lighter.

᳜

Chop the onion and sauté it and the garlic in oil until the onion is soft; then crush the garlic with a fork. Add the tomato paste and water or stock, stirring to mix. Bring to a boil.

Meanwhile, cut potatoes into ½″ cubes and add to the soup pot. Simmer until potatoes are tender but not mushy. Add oregano, salt, and pepper (if you used seasoned broth, you may want less salt).

Just before serving, stir in the coriander leaves, if desired, and the cheese.

Makes about 7 cups, a meal for 4 or more.

VARIATION: Before adding cheese and coriander, stir in a quart of chopped fresh spinach or tender chard leaves. Simmer just until tender.

Black Bean Soup

1½ cups black beans
6 cups water
1 onion
2 tablespoons oil
2 large cloves garlic
2 stalks celery
1 potato
1 carrot
1 bay leaf
1 teaspoon oregano
¼ teaspoon savory
2 teaspoons salt
⅛ teaspoon pepper
2 lemons

Wash the beans and put them in a saucepan along with the water. Cover loosely, bring to a boil, and simmer for 2½ hours or so, until beans are quite tender.

Meantime, chop the onion and sauté in the oil with garlic until soft. Crush the garlic. Chop the celery, including the leaves. Dice potato and carrot or grate on large grater. Add celery, potato, and carrot to onion and heat for several minutes, stirring all the while.

Add the vegetables to the beans, along with the seasonings, in the last hour of their cooking. Bring the soup to a boil and lower the heat to simmer until the beans and vegetables are done. Puree half or all the soup if you want a thick, hearty broth.

Juice one lemon and slice the other. Stir in juice and add slices just before serving.

Makes about 9 cups, to serve 6.

Hearty Pea Soup

It's easy enough to make plain pea soup with just onion, potato, and carrot—and it's good, too. But this fine soup is the perfected model, worth the extra hour of simmering.

❧

Sauté onion in oil until soft, along with bay leaf and celery seed. Stir in peas, barley, and limas. Add 2 quarts water and bring to a boil. Cook on low heat, partially covered, for about an hour and a half.

Add salt, pepper, vegetables, and herbs. Turn heat down as low as possible and simmer another 30 to 45 minutes. Thin with additional water or stock as you like. Correct seasonings.

Makes about 8 to 9 cups.

1 onion, diced
2 tablespoons oil
1 bay leaf
1 teaspoon celery seed

1 cup green split peas
1/4 cup barley
1/2 cup lima beans
2 quarts water

2 teaspoons salt
dash pepper
1 carrot, chopped
3 stalks celery, diced
1/2 cup chopped parsley
1 potato, diced
1/2 teaspoon basil
1/2 teaspoon thyme

Greek Lentil Soup

A thinner, more flavorful version of lentil soup than the usual stewy kind.

❧

Pick over lentils and wash.

Mix all ingredients except the vinegar in a soup pot and cook until the lentils are very soft, about one hour. Stir in vinegar at the end and serve.

Makes about 8 cups, to serve 6.

2 cups uncooked lentils
8 cups water or
*   vegetable stock*
1/2 onion, chopped
1 small carrot, chopped
1 celery stalk, chopped
1 small potato, chopped
2 tablespoons olive oil
2 bay leaves
1 1/2 to 2 teaspoons salt

2 teaspoons red wine vinegar

Fruit Soups

Fruit soups are sweet, but not very. They are a whimsical, enjoyable way to start just about any meal—like brunch, for instance. There's a distinctly Old European mood about fruit soups. In Scandinavia they are likely to be made with buttermilk and fresh raspberries, then topped with meringue and slivered almonds. That's in the summertime. Come winter, a mixture of dried fruits is stewed—a happy commingling of apples, prunes, pears, raisins, lemon peel—then sweetened lightly and pureed. Cinnamon, allspice, nutmeg, or cardamom are often added.

Fruit soups are a great way to use fruit that isn't quite showy enough to serve as is. They can be delicate and modestly caloried or downright devastating. Whatever recipe you use, you'll want an accompanying crunch: a crisp wafer or cookie, or a sprinkling of toasted nuts on top. Use full-flavored cooking apples and pears for the following recipe.

Early Autumn Fruit Soup

*1 pound ripe cooking apples
    and/or pears
1 quart water
strips of peel from ¼ lemon
    and ¼ orange
1 tablespoon cornstarch
¼ cup cold water
3 tablespoons light honey
¼ teaspoon ground
    cardamom
½ teaspoon orange zest
2 tablespoons lemon juice
juice from one orange*

Cut apples and pears in chunks. Place in a pan (cores, peel, and all) with quart of water.

Use a potato peeler to take a strip from the orange and lemon peel; use a zester or fine grater to take zest from the rest of the orange, making ½ teaspoon. Juice the orange and lemon and combine the orange zest and juices, setting them aside. Add the strips of orange and lemon peel to the cooking soup and bring to a boil. Lower heat and simmer for 10 minutes, or until the fruit is soft.

Remove strips of rind and put the soup through a food mill or strainer.

Mix the cornstarch with ¼ cup cold water and stir it into the puree. Add honey and cardamom.

Return soup to clean pan, bring to a boil again, then lower heat and simmer for five minutes, stirring frequently. Allow it to cool slightly, then add grated orange rind, lemon and orange juice. Chill and serve with a dollop of yogurt or a thin slice of orange on top.

Makes 5 cups.

Vegetables

Soon after people become vegetarians, they are likely to make a marvelous discovery: vegetables. No longer relegated to the role of second-class citizens, these best of foods can shine out as the fascinating individuals they are: stalwarts like broccoli and butternut squash, arty types like asparagus and artichokes, gnarly characters like rutabaga, and the town zany, kohlrabi.

Quick on the heels of that discovery comes a second: the spiffiest recipes in the world won't compensate for lack of freshness. Then the chase is on for the freshest, most flavorful vegetables you can lay hands on. That chase can take you in some unexpected directions: to the early-morning uproar of a big city produce terminal, armed with the buying power of a cooperative food buying club; to the merry hubbub of a farmer's market; or, best of all, to your own backyard, newly dug and ready to plant exactly the vegetables you want.

The produce section in a typical supermarket has doubled in size over the past ten years. If looks were everything, no one would need to go further; these aisles heaped and banked with bright eggplants and peppers, gleaming onions and ruffled lettuce, are a feast for the eye. Actually, the quality *can* be quite good too. But often it isn't. For one thing, the produce sold to supermarkets is generally bred to travel well cross-country. It is sturdy, often to a fault. If, in addition, it has been grown in one of those countries where winter never comes, it has not only spent a long time on the road but might have residues of pesticides not permitted in this country. Third, a really knowledgeable produce manager is a rare treasure, and without someone who knows a lot about how to do it, produce isn't always stored or handled well, particularly the more fragile things like leafy greens and uncommon varieties of fruits and vegetables. Finally—and this drawback you won't see or taste—much out-of-season produce comes from places in the Third World where giant multinationals grow export crops on land that's needed for staple foods for the local people. The price may seem right, but the hidden costs are high.

The answer to all these problems is to strengthen our food supply system at the local level: to learn to use and enjoy what your region will produce. Support your local farmers by being faithful customers. Even among supermarkets there are some that try to buy from local farmers. Patronize them, and tell them why you're doing it.

Implicit in the mandate to buy local is a corollary: buy seasonal. Far from being a constraint, the choice to eat foods in season can enhance your life. The first warmth of spring brings fresh asparagus to mind, and then peas and new potatoes. With the chill of autumn you start to hanker after heartier fare—baked winter squash and cabbagey stews. Even if you can't grow your own vegetables, it's satisfying to feel in tune with the growing cycle of the year.

Having said this, though, we'd like to put in a special word for home gardening. The vegetables are incomparably better, you'll save oodles of money, but above all, the work is a joy. If you are a latent gardener who needs encouragement, or if you're deterred because you think you have to have a back yard, or if you're already gardening and just want a host of practical ideas, try some of the inspiring reading listed in the margin.

The New Organic Grower and The New Organic Grower's Four-Season Harvest, by Eliot Coleman (Chelsea Green Publishing Company, Post Mills, Vermont, 1989 and 1992)

How to Grow More Vegetables Than You Ever Thought Possible on Less Land Than You Can Imagine, by John Jeavons (Berkeley: Ten Speed Press, 1993)

Designing and Maintaining Your Edible Landscape Naturally, by Robert Kourik (Metamorphosis Press, 1986)

Organic Gardening magazine (write to: Rodale Press, 33 East Minor Street, Emmaus, PA 18049)

STORAGE

Even the most vitamin-rich, mineral-rich, organically grown, vine-ripened tomato or string bean can be denuded of its nutritional value if not treated properly. Good handling starts with harvesting: when you're picking vegetables, don't let them stand in the sun to wilt; whisk them into the refrigerator right away, or at least into the shade. If you're harvesting them from a supermarket, the principle is the same: even if the price is right, don't buy wilted-looking produce. It's no bargain. If possible, buy only a few days' supply of perishable things like greens and eggplant. If you buy for a week, plan to eat the most perishable things first.

Store potatoes, onions, and uncut winter squashes outside the refrigerator in cool, well-ventilated cupboards or cellars. To keep other vegetables crisp and vitamin-rich, store them in the refrigerator in plastic bags or in a humidifier. Tomatoes that are not overripe may be stored at cool room temperature (not on a hot windowsill) for up to a week. Keep bunches of especially fragile green things like spinach, parsley, and coriander upright in a cottage cheese carton in the refrigerator—line the cartons with a moist cloth beforehand and cover the top with a plastic bag. You'll find other storage suggestions where we talk about each vegetable in turn.

The nutrients that are most likely to be lost in cooking are the water-soluble vitamins: vitamin C and the B vitamins folacin, riboflavin, and pyridoxine. Air (oxygen, to be exact), light, heat, and water are the vitamin thieves, so try to protect vegetables from these four as you work. Wash vegetables as quickly as you can, and avoid soaking them. If you aren't going to cook them immediately, cover them and put them back in the refrigerator.

Peeling vegetables is usually unnecessary and a waste of time and food, as well as nutrients, which usually concentrate just beneath the skin. Try to peel only when the skin is unpalatably tough (most broccoli stems), bitter (oldish turnips), or so rough-skinned that it can't be thoroughly scrubbed (an infrequent twisty carrot). To preserve nutrients, you can cook potatoes and beets first and peel and chop afterwards.

Cutting vegetables in large chunks exposes minimum surface area to the vitamin thieves and preserves flavor and juices as well. On the other hand, smaller pieces cook more quickly; so if they're called for, chop away, especially if you're careful to preserve cooking liquids. Broth from cooking many vegetables —corn, winter squash, zucchini, carrots, string beans, spinach —is delicious and contains significant amounts of the water-soluble vitamins. Save it to use in place of water for cooking grain or making soup or sauce. (Broth from some other vegetables may be vitamin-rich but too strong-tasting to use.)

Some vegetables are so attractive in their native shape that it's nice to steam them and serve them whole: not only artichokes but tiny crookneck and patty pan squashes, carrots, beets, asparagus, and broccoli spears. Tender green beans can be cooked whole or with just the ends snipped off. Serve an assortment of these vegetables with Mock Sour Cream and crackers for an ultra-simple dinner.

We've found that carefully cut vegetables are appealing to the eye and therefore more appetizing. You can cut a carrot in at least eight ways, each one appropriate for a particular dish. Vegetable chopping has never been quite the same for us since we watched a Japanese friend prepare a lavish supper for twenty-five people. As her knife flashed swiftly and rhythmically across the board, her expression was completely concentrated. She didn't say a word. In just half an hour she had filled several big bowls with vegetables, all cut in pretty, perfectly uniform little shapes. In other parts of the world, like India or China, this humble art is

The microwave oven is energy efficient and cooks vegetables quickly, retaining most nutrients very well. Until much more research has been completed, we strongly recommend microwaving only in heat-proof glass or lead-free pottery or china containers, rather than any plastic.

taken for granted. You don't need to worry about the swiftness, but the artistry is certainly worth emulating: proof again that even the simplest daily act is worth our full attention.

It might seem that the best way to preserve nutrients in vegetables would be to eat them raw. It's true that vitamin C and folacin are both vulnerable to heat (hence the importance of fresh fruit and green salads). Fortunately, though, it's easy to defend cooked vegetables too. Cooking breaks down a food's cellulose structure and makes other vitamins, as well as minerals, *more* accessible than they would be otherwise. Proper cooking methods can preserve 90 percent of the nutrients your food offers.

COOKING METHODS

The cooking methods we prefer are steaming and the so-called waterless method, where vegetables actually steam in their own juices. In both these methods, steam fills the space in the pan around the vegetables so that oxygen can't rob them of their vitamins. Since the vegetables aren't standing in water, the water-soluble vitamins and minerals stay put.

PRESSURE COOKING

Pressure cooking is an alternative that offers real advantages to anyone constrained by time. Grains and beans can be ready in half their usual time, and vegetables often in just seconds. An added advantage of pressure cooking is that it conserves some vitamins better than ordinary methods can. The color of cooked vegetables is preserved too. If you are thinking of buying a pressure cooker, try to get one of the newer stainless steel models with a safety gauge that absolutely prevents the kind of messy and even tragic explosions that some of us remember all too well in connection with the old-fashioned models.

STEAMING VEGETABLES

One of our favorite kitchen gizmos is the collapsible steamer basket, the kind that opens flowerlike to fit small or large pots. Nothing could be simpler to use. Bring ¾" of water to boil in a saucepan. Plunk your magic basket into the pan, put the vegetables into the basket, add a close-fitting lid, and reduce the heat so that it is just high enough to keep the water simmering. Vegetables cook quickly this way and require a minimum of fussing.

For the waterless method, the vital equipment is a pan which conducts heat well and has a close-fitting lid. Most vegetables contain enough water to steam by themselves once they are heated, as long as the heat is coming from all sides. Best of all for most kinds of vegetables is a good iron pot. This does entail the loss of a certain amount of vitamin C, which reacts with iron; but the gain in usable iron is so great—and dietary iron so much more critical for most of us—that it outweighs the partial loss of C. Watch out for acidic foods like tomatoes and walnuts, though; they interact more with iron and may get discolored or begin to taste rusty if you leave them in the pot very long.

WATERLESS METHOD

To cook by the waterless method, preheat the pot and place two tablespoons of water in it, to provide steam until the vegetables release their own. When the water boils, add the vegetables, stir, and cover. Turn the heat down after a couple of minutes. Cooking time is a little longer than with steaming, and the amount of water that different vegetables need will vary too; so give a stir from time to time, and keep a watchful eye and ear to prevent burning.

One thing to remember when using heavy cooking pots is that they retain heat for a long time. If you have to hold the vegetables for tardy biscuits or a late diner, take the pots off the flame well before the vegetables are cooked through. Left in the pots with the lid on, they will continue to cook gently.

Another waterless method is stir-frying, where the vegetables are placed in a hot pan with a little oil and sautéed before they are covered to steam, with a little added water if needed. Tenderer vegetables, especially spinach and the like, may not even need the steaming period, but can cook directly as you stir.

STIR-FRYING

The one disadvantage of this quick and tasty method is that it is easy to find yourself using a lot of oil. A happy answer is a *wok*, which is especially suited for stir-frying. Its round bottom keeps the oil where the heat is, so your vegetables cook neatly in the smallest possible amount of fat, and the depth and round shape make vigorous stirring easy too. In our experience, the wok is most effective when used on a gas stove with fairly large burners.

It isn't possible to give precise cooking times for vegetables. There are so many variables, not the least of which is that what is "done" is really a matter of taste. Suppose you're cooking green

COOKING TIMES

beans. How old are they? Were they picked young and tender, or tough and stringy, or in between? What size pieces were they cut into? How heavy and how big is the pan? What kind of burner are you using? With all this to consider, the cooking time can vary by half in either direction.

Generally, though, we encourage you to push back the timer little by little when cooking vegetables. You may discover that you have been missing a great deal of taste, to say nothing of vitamins, by overcooking. This is particularly true of the brassica family (cabbage, cauliflower, brussels sprouts, broccoli), whose sulfur compounds break down with very long or harsh cooking to release obnoxious flavors and aromas. Aim for tender, or crispy-tender, rather than mushy.

Cooking time for different vegetables will vary. Try 8 minutes or less for sliced asparagus, garden peas, or corn; roughly 10 minutes for ¼" pieces of zucchini, 12 minutes for ¼" pieces of carrot or broccoli stems, and up to 20 minutes for reasonably tender green beans or broccoli spears. Artichokes will take any-where from 30 to 45 minutes, depending on their size.

When you are steaming *mixed* vegetables, simply cut the ones that require longer cooking times into thinner pieces. If you want similar-sized chunks, add them at intervals, longest-cooking first.

With vegetables, in terms of nutrition and aesthetics too, simple is beautiful, especially if a vegetable is garden-grown. Freshly harvested spinach is so sweet and delectable that it begs to be enjoyed steamed as it is, with only the tiniest hint of flavoring. When we steam vegetables we like to serve them with just a little lemon and parsley, or salt and pepper, or a sprinkle of Parmesan cheese. Broccoli spears, new young chard, or the first harvest of garden zucchini are good eating with no embellishment at all. Growing your own vegetables, of course, is a good way to help your family enjoy them for themselves. Serving them with an eye to their visual appeal helps too.

Serve a wide variety of vegetables. If your local paper runs a greengrocer's column, check it regularly to learn about vege-tables new to you, and new ways to prepare the familiar ones. These columns can help you keep abreast of what's available in the stores too, and make suggestions for using seasonal produce. If you are a gardener, you know there are many delicious varieties of vegetables that simply aren't available in the supermarket, though many do find their way to farmer's markets.

Now we'd like to sing out the glories of our favorite friends from the vegetable patch one by one, and tell some of the ways they can be enjoyed. We've tried to stick to ingredients that are easily available and not expensive. Radicchio and enoki mushrooms may well add a lot to a salad, but you won't find them in our recipes. "To make something out of something is nothing," a friend who lived at Findhorn used to say. "To make something out of nothing—*that's* something!" Succulent "somethings" are possible every day from ordinary, inexpensive seasonal produce, when you stir them up with imagination.

Mingled here and there among the recipes and serving ideas that follow, you will find some intentionally rough suggestions. Don't be frustrated by their vagueness. When amounts are unspecified, it's because you have a lot of latitude and know better than we do how much squash you can eat at a sitting. We include these suggestions to convey our own approach to vegetables, which has almost nothing to do with recipes. Once you acquire a feel for characteristics and cooking times—and that doesn't take long—your imagination can take over. Then you won't be bound to recipes at all; they'll just be useful for inspiration, or as points of departure.

Artichokes

Artichokes are California's own. The highway south from Berkeley to Big Sur takes you through Castroville, with its funky banner telling you that you've finally made it to the Artichoke Capital of the World. Well might they brag. They're on to a good thing.

Trimming isn't necessary, but it reduces the mess at the table and prevents you and the eaters from getting stuck by those nasty little thorns. Use a sharp knife to cut off the top, with most of the thorns; use the knife or scissors to remove thorns from the remaining leaves. While you're at it, you might as well take off the tiny outside leaves—the great eating begins where the leaves are large—and trim the stem near the base too.

Steam artichokes (trimmed or not) upside-down in a steamer basket, or in a saucepan with an inch or so of boiling water. Depending on the size of the artichoke, it may take half an hour to a whole hour to steam. That's a long time, so check the pot now and again to be sure the water level is up. If you aren't going to be serving them whole, chokes will cook in half the time if they're cut in half. They are done when the outer leaves come off effortlessly or when a fork slides easily into the heart. Serve them hot or chilled. (To keep chilled artichokes or their cut parts from darkening, douse exposed places with lemon juice.)

Artichoke leaves dipped in mayonnaise or drawn butter are marvelous, but so are artichoke leaves dipped in absolutely nothing, or in one of the many delicious low-fat sauces in the next section. If artichokes become a regular item in your diet, this could be a critical discovery!

Although extracting the edible parts from an artichoke may seem a tedious task for a cook, it's really not bad, and the flavor is so rich that one or two artichokes can make good eating for up to four people. The following dishes are well worth the effort.

Artichokes Tellicherry

2 large artichokes, steamed
2 medium potatoes, steamed

3 shallots or 1 small onion
(1 clove garlic)
1 tablespoon butter

(½ teaspoon ground cumin
or fennel seed)

(½ cup tiny peas)
(1 big, fresh, ripe tomato,
chopped)
salt and plenty of pepper

Tellicherry in South India is famous for black pepper. Artichokes have probably never been seen there, but toasted cumin and fennel seeds often scent a vegetable dish. We use this combination in many ways to take full advantage of the long artichoke season. Some of the possibilities are outlined below. The ingredients in parentheses are optional, but they add a lot.

è

Prepare cooked artichokes by removing the outer leaves and scraping them with a spoon to get the tender meat. The middle leaves will come off together and the tender portion can be cut off and chopped. Discard the leaves. Pull or spoon out the thistly top from the center of each choke and discard. Trim away the stringy stem and dice the heart, putting it with the other good gleanings from the artichoke parts. All together, this should measure about a cup.

Peel and dice the steamed potatoes. They should measure about a cup or a little more.

Sauté the shallot or onion (and garlic) in butter in a sizable skillet, cooking until soft. Add the cumin or fennel if desired and heat and stir until fragrant. Lightly stir in the remaining ingredients, and heat through.

This is a very flexible recipe, as you can see, and the quantities are changeable. Plain—without the optional additions—it makes 2 cups or stuffs 4 medium tomatoes, which will serve two people generously or four as a tidbit. With the peas and whatnot, you'll have more.

VARIATIONS

TOMATOES TELLICHERRY If you have pretty tomatoes, instead of chopping one, hollow out one for each person and use the artichoke mixture to stuff them. Cut the top off the tomatoes and scoop out the insides with a spoon, leaving at least ¼″ of tomato on the skin. Fill with hot artichoke mixture and top with buttered bread crumbs; heat in moderate oven about 15 minutes.

ARTICHOKE PATTIES With the optional ingredients (but without the tomato), the mixture can be formed into patties. Adding a beaten egg helps hold them together but isn't really necessary. Press both sides of each patty into a dish of whole grain bread crumbs and cook them on a lightly buttered griddle or in the oven, turning once.

STUFFED ARTICHOKE HEARTS Instead of chopping the heart, trim it and scoop it out carefully; then dip in lemon juice to keep it from darkening. Mix the rest of the ingredients (no tomatoes) to make the filling. Pile it into the heart and decorate the top with sliced olives, tiny pearl onions, pine nuts, or sliced cherry tomatoes. Small artichokes work well for this version, but if yours are large you can quarter the choke after you stuff it. Good hot or cold.

Asparagus

Asparagus ranks right alongside the hyacinth as a sure, spriggy herald of spring. Its season is so brief (at least, its affordable season!) that we never have time to tire of its delicate appeal.

Have you considered growing asparagus? Even a narrow strip against a wall at the back of a flower bed is a good place, because by midsummer, asparagus makes tall, feathery ferns that provide a beautiful backdrop for decorative plantings. Needless to say, homegrown asparagus is wonderfully special. You can pick it when the shoots are less than six inches long and closed up tight, so sweet that cooking seems superfluous.

Whether you grow your own or find it in the supermarket, the fattest spears will be the most succulent. Look for heads that are tightly closed, firm, and fresh-looking; the bottoms shouldn't be dried up or moldy. Break the stalks just above the white part at the place where they choose to snap. Save the bottom for making stock, or if there is a sizeable green portion, peel it and cook it along with the tops. Use your steamer basket or a skillet with a tight lid (and a minimum of water!) to steam the asparagus; or try the old-fashioned trick of standing the spears straight up in a coffeepot with an inch of water in the bottom. Never overcook asparagus.

Serve fresh spears with Lemon Butter (or just lemon) or a sprinkle of Parmesan cheese. If you want the piquancy of hollandaise with less fat, try Sunshine Sauce or Dijon Sauce, or Mock Sour Cream. Sliced toasted almonds make a pretty and harmonious garnish.

For ASPARAGUS PATTIES, slice an onion very thin, and sauté with a couple of cloves of garlic. Crush the garlic gloves with a fork. Add a cup each of lightly steamed, thin-sliced asparagus and steamed, grated potato. Grated cheese is optional; salt and pepper to taste. A beaten egg helps hold the mixture together but isn't necessary. Cook on bread crumbs on a buttered griddle, turning once onto more crumbs. An easy way to form the patties is to put a tablespoon of crumbs into a ⅓–cup measure and press the mixture into that, turning it out onto crumbs on the griddle.

Chinese Asparagus

A classic dish that fits in anywhere. Use tiny snow peas or sliced sugar snap peas instead of asparagus later in the season.

Have you ever tasted *fresh* water chestnuts? They are as much better than the canned ones as fresh asparagus is better than canned. Chinese groceries often have them even if others don't, and they are worth looking for. Choose firm nuts that haven't shriveled at all. Peel and rinse, then use as you would the canned ones, allowing a couple of extras for the cook to nibble raw.

*Combine the shoyu, honey, cornstarch, and water and set aside.

Trim the asparagus and cut diagonally into 1″ slices. Have the remaining ingredients ready. Heat a wok or big heavy skillet; when hot, add the oil and then the leek. Cook just a minute, then add ginger and garlic, stirring for only a few seconds. Add water chestnuts and asparagus, stir once more, and add the broth. Reduce heat, cover, and simmer gently only until the asparagus is tender.

Stir the sauce to dissolve the cornstarch completely. (If you have Chinese sesame oil, add that to the sauce.) Turn the heat to high, uncover vegetables, and pour the sauce over them. Bring to a boil, stirring constantly about a minute or until the sauce is thick. Serve at once, sprinkled with sesame seeds if you like.

Serves 4.

1 tablespoon shoyu
½ teaspoon honey
2 teaspoons cornstarch
1 tablespoon water

1 pound asparagus
2 teaspoons oil
1 medium leek, sliced thin
1 tablespoon ginger, minced
2 cloves garlic, minced
8 water chestnuts
½ cup flavorful broth

2 teaspoons toasted
  sesame seeds or
  Chinese sesame oil

Green Beans

Green beans are one of the most versatile and delicious of vegetables. They are incomparably good when freshly picked, and their growing habits are varied enough that you can have them early and late, tall and short, green or yellow, in whatever clime and soil and space is available.

But store-bought beans are plenty good too. Look for the young and crisp. The tender, tasty Blue Lake variety that used to be available only to home gardeners now appears in produce sections from time to time. And don't think of them as "string beans"—the stringiness was bred out years ago, thank goodness.

Green Beans Hellenika

*1 pound green beans,
cut bite-size
(about 4 cups)
1 small onion, chopped
3 tomatoes, chopped
1/2 bunch parsley, chopped
1 tablespoon olive oil
1/2 teaspoon salt
dash pepper
about 1 cup water or stock*

Cook all ingredients together at least 20 minutes, until the beans are tender, using just enough water to prevent sticking. Stir from time to time.

Makes 3 cups, to serve 4 to 6 people.

Green Bean Stroganoff

Take yogurt (and buttermilk, if used) out of refrigerator to warm to room temperature. Wash green beans and cut into bite-sized pieces. Steam until tender.

While the beans cook, chop the onion and sauté in oil or butter. Slice mushrooms in thick pieces and add them to the onion. Cook and stir until tender.

Cube eggplant and add to mushrooms. Cover and steam until tender, stirring as necessary to prevent sticking. Add green beans and season with salt and pepper.

Beat yogurt (or yogurt and buttermilk) smooth. Stir cornstarch into the beaten yogurt and bring it to a boil, stirring vigorously; it will separate and then smooth out again. Add to the bean mixture.

Serves 4 to 6 over rice, noodles, or kasha.

CABBAGE STROGANOFF Use a whole large onion and substitute 2 cups packed shredded cabbage for the beans and eggplant.

2 cups yogurt, or yogurt and buttermilk

1 pound green beans

½ large onion
2 tablespoons oil or butter
½ pound mushrooms

2 small or ½ large eggplant (½–¾ pound)
1 teaspoon salt
pinch pepper

2 teaspoons cornstarch

Spicy Green Beans

Bring water, garlic, onion, bay leaf, tomato, and green beans to boil. Cover pan and simmer over low heat for about 20 minutes, or until the beans are tender. Remove garlic and cloves and stir in vinegar, salt, and cinnamon. Cook, uncovered, for 2 to 3 minutes.

Serves 4 to 6.

½ cup water
1 clove garlic, studded with 3 whole cloves
½ onion, chopped
bay leaf
1 small tomato, peeled and diced
1 pound green beans, cut in 1" pieces

2 teaspoons cider vinegar
½ teaspoon salt
¼ teaspoon cinnamon

Beets

Charmed by the rich red of its root, most people give short shrift to the beet's greatest asset: its leaves, where an abundant store of vitamins and minerals is tucked away. Cook the greens like chard: they are tart and lovely.

Beet leaves, incidentally, share their red color liberally with whatever is cooked along with them—a quirk that can take you off guard in mixed vegetables, but one you can turn to your advantage in a tomato-based soup. (For that matter, beet greens or a little grated beet root will correct the color of any tomato sauce that's turned out too orangish. Don't add so much that it goes purple, though!)

If you are a gardener, do you know about golden beets? They are sweet and as pretty as the red ones without that uncontrollable red juice. Especially good for salads.

If you steam mature beets until they're tender, the skins slip off in the most cooperative way you could imagine. Slice them and serve hot with a dollop of Mock Sour Cream or a sauce of a little warmed honey and orange juice. Chilled and marinated, they are good cut up in green salad or simply served as is.

The following recipe is meant to use beet thinnings from the garden. We like it so much that we now pluck many more of our baby beets than we would normally, and just keep planting new ones. Mature beets too can be cut up and cooked in the same way.

Whole Beets

12 to 15 tiny beets,
  tops and all
2 tablespoons oil
juice of 1 lemon
1 green onion, chopped
½ teaspoon dill weed
½ teaspoon tarragon
½ teaspoon salt
(a squeeze of garlic)

Wash beets well and remove inedible parts, leaving them whole and keeping the skin and leaves.

Heat oil, lemon juice, onion, and seasonings in a heavy pan with a tight-fitting lid. Add beets and steam over medium heat. Check after 5 minutes, and add a small amount of water to prevent burning if necessary. Cook until tender.

Serves 4 to 6.

Broccoli

We don't usually think of green vegetables as a source of protein, but 1 cup of steamed broccoli provides 5 grams, not to mention that it also has 140 milligrams each of calcium and vitamin C! We serve plain spears, or bite-sized chunks with a little lemon, very often. Here's a vegetable that is universally loved in its simplest manifestation—a special boon for balancing dinners with some other dish that's a little rich.

Fresh broccoli is one vegetable that almost always needs some peeling. The outer skin of the stalk can be quite fibrous and tough, and if you cook broccoli long enough to cook the skin tender, you risk overcooking the other parts, losing more vitamin C in the process than you've saved by keeping the skin. On the other hand, do save the leaves; they are a mine of vitamins and minerals. Cook them along with stems and tops; or, if they look untidy to you, snip them off and save them to add to a soup or casserole the next day.

If you peel the stem and cut it into ¼″ slices, it will cook right along with the flowers in the same amount of time. Serve broccoli cut up or in spears with salt and fresh-ground black pepper; with lemon, Lemon Butter, Sunshine Sauce, or Potato Dill Sauce; with a sprinkling of Sesame Salt, or with any cheese or cheese sauce. But don't be surprised if you find yourself coming back to the simplest and very best: fresh, bright green, crispy-tender spears with no ornament but their own reputation.

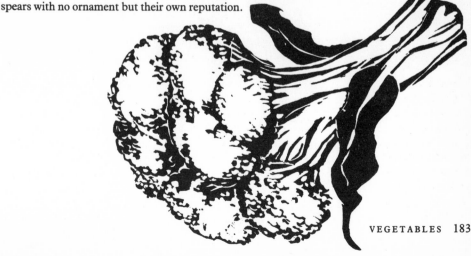

King Cole Curry

1 bunch broccoli, cut into
  flowers and sliced stems
1/2 head cauliflower, cut
  into florets
1 medium potato, sliced
  small

SAUCE

1/2 onion, chopped
1 tablespoon oil
2 tablespoons whole
  wheat flour
3/4 teaspoon curry powder
1 1/2 cups water
3/4 pound tofu, rinsed
  and mashed
2–4 tablespoons lemon juice
1 tablespoon shoyu
3/4 teaspoon salt

TOPPING

1/2 cup bread crumbs
pinch salt, pepper, paprika

This colorful vegetable curry looks and tastes as creamy and rich as it could be, but it has no dairy products at all; its creaminess comes from tofu. Serve it with bulgur wheat or whole wheat noodles, marinated beets on a bed of romaine, and a fresh fruit salad.

≈

Steam broccoli, cauliflower, and potatoes.

Sauté onion in oil. Add flour and curry powder and stir two minutes over medium heat. Stir in 1 cup of the water and cook until thickened.

Preheat oven to 350°F.

Blend or mash tofu with lemon juice, shoyu, and remaining 1/2 cup water until smooth. Stir into onion mixture. Add more salt or lemon juice to taste.

In a 2 1/2-quart casserole dish, spread half the vegetables. Top with half the sauce and repeat. Mix topping ingredients and sprinkle over casserole. Bake covered for 10 to 15 minutes, uncovered for 10 minutes more or until the sauce is bubbly.

Serves 4 to 6.

Brussels Sprouts

These days the visual glories of fresh vegetables are well established; whole calendars are given over to translucent cross-sections of cucumbers and interior shots of bell peppers. But when vegetable art was in its first blush, one photographer with a sense of whimsy circulated a striking picture of a cabbage perched atop a grater box while tiny brussels sprouts tumbled out from underneath. Mini-cabbages they may be, but aristocrats for all that, and delectable.

Arresting, too, is the brussels sprout *plant*: a mighty three or four-foot stalk stuck all over with round knobs peeking out from where the long leaf connects. You pick from the bottom up as they ripen, and one plant can supply a whole family. You end up with an elegant miniature palm tree, complete with little green "coconuts." (There are reasons why gardeners are a little daffy about the whole affair.)

Sweet, tender young brussels sprouts can be cooked intact, but if the core seems hefty, you will want to trim it off. Score any but the tiniest brussels sprouts by cutting an × in the bottom ¼" deep, to ensure a quicker, evener cooking time. The outermost leaves should go if they are yellowish or spotty.

Steamed whole, or simmered gently in milk, brussels sprouts are delectable, and when they're first in season it never occurs to us to eat them any other way. After the initial thrill subsides, we start dressing them up: a light sprinkling of grated hard cheese, or Cream Sauce or Potato Dill Sauce (with nutmeg or thyme replacing the dill) to complement their very special flavor.

One of our favorite fancy winter dishes is BRUSSELS SPROUTS WITH CHESTNUTS. Roast and peel chestnuts and cut them into chunks; then stir them into steamed sprouts with the tiniest bit of Better-Butter. The mild, nutty flavor and somewhat mealy texture of the chestnuts complements the sprouts beautifully. Try the following recipes too; the first one has a real holiday air.

Brussels Sprout–Squash Casserole

1 pound brussels sprouts
1½ cups winter squash,
  peeled and cubed
1 medium onion, minced
1 cup chopped celery
1 tablespoon butter
2 tablespoons oil
¼ cup whole wheat flour
2 cups milk
½ teaspoon salt
½ teaspoon marjoram
dash pepper
dash nutmeg

Clean, trim, and score brussels sprouts; cut large ones in half. Steam sprouts and squash separately until barely tender. Set aside.

Preheat oven to 350°F.

While squash and sprouts cook, chop onion and celery. Sauté onion in butter and oil. Add flour and cook slowly for about 3 minutes, stirring continually. Add milk and spices slowly, stirring to keep mixture smooth. Bring to a boil and remove from heat. Correct seasonings.

In a greased 8″ × 8″ baking dish, arrange cubed squash on bottom and spread over it an even layer of brussels sprouts. Sprinkle chopped celery over the top. Pour the sauce over the vegetables and sprinkle with nutmeg.

Bake for 30 minutes. Serves 4 to 6.

Brussels Sprouts & Bell Peppers

1 pound brussels sprouts
2 small red bell peppers
½ small onion, chopped
2 teaspoons oil
1 bay leaf
¼ cup vegetable stock
  or water or milk
1 small potato, cubed
salt to taste

The bright sweetness of red bell peppers complements the nippy taste of brussels sprouts perfectly.

❧

Clean, trim, and score brussels sprouts. Cut large ones in half. Cut peppers into ½″ pieces.

Sauté onion in oil with bay leaf until onion is soft; add pepper pieces and stir for a few seconds. Add the brussels sprouts and stir again.

Add ¼ cup of stock and simmer, covered, until just tender. (Probably about 7 minutes, but keep checking.)

Steam or boil potato cubes separately and puree, using some of the juice from the vegetables if needed. Stir together with sprouts and peppers. Season with salt.

Serves 4 to 6.

Cabbage

Because cabbage can endure a certain amount of winter storage, most people think of it as strong-flavored, and often it is served in a sweet or sweet-and-sour sauce or dressing that makes it even more assertive. But try another tack. Steamed and cooked in milk, especially when freshly picked, cabbage can be as sweet and pleasing as you'd ever want a vegetable to be, and as digestible as well. Always cook it gently, not too hot and not too long. Simmered in milk, then tossed with a dab of butter, salt and pepper, and maybe a handful of chopped parsley, cabbage gets surprised requests for seconds even from devout cabbage-loathers.

Chinese Cabbage

Chinese cabbage has pale, curly leaves and is taller and far more elegant than its plump occidental cousins. With its lighter, subtler flavor it is delicious raw, and it makes a truly fluffy slaw. Or try it Chinese style, sliced thin and stir-fried in a little oil, a dribble of shoyu, and sesame salt or Chinese parsley for garnish. Very good added to mixed Chinese vegetables, too.

Bubble & Squeak

Traditionally, Bubble and Squeak is a thick "pancake" of mashed potato and cooked cabbage, fried in lots of fat. The fat bubbles, the cabbage squeaks. Listen closely, and you might hear the cabbage squeak as you stir-fry this much lighter contemporary variation. The flavors combine splendidly.

1 medium head curly-leafed cabbage (about 7–8 cups)
3 medium leeks
1 tablespoon oil
1 or 2 cloves garlic
1 large potato, quartered, steamed, and peeled
2 tablespoons shoyu
1 tablespoon cider vinegar

❧

Cut the cabbage in strips. Quarter leeks and slice in ½″ pieces. Cut potato in ½″ pieces.

If you have a wok, use it to cook this dish; otherwise a heavy skillet or dutch oven is good (not iron, though, if possible). Stir-fry the cabbage and leeks over medium-high heat for 3 or 4 minutes. Add garlic. Cover and reduce heat to low until cabbage is crispy-tender, about 5 minutes. Add the potato and stir another minute or so until warmed through.

Sprinkle with shoyu and vinegar and serve immediately.
Makes about 4 servings (5 cups).

Carrots

Carrots are one of those staples we always have on hand for soups and mixed vegetables, but which we don't have real recipes for. That's probably because we more often use winter squash, which grow more easily in our gardens, to provide that spot of sweetness or color in winter menus. Carrots often substitute very nicely for winter squash—they have a smoother, less sweet presence. The lacy green tops, by the way, are great for soup stock.

Orange or lemon juice gives a boost to carrots that aren't garden fresh: add a tablespoonful or so for 2 cups of carrots while you're cutting or grating. It enlivens their flavor considerably and keeps them from turning brown if they have to wait a while before cooking or serving.

Most people are fond of carrots. Try them in some of these ways, which we like very much:

❧ Cut in thin sticks and cook by the waterless method. Just before serving, stir together with a small dab of butter and a handful of chopped parsley.

❧ Glaze just-cooked carrots lightly by stirring in a tablespoon or two of honey; remove from pan and add a handful of chopped, lightly toasted walnuts.

❧ Glaze with orange juice, honey, and a small spoonful of minced fresh ginger, or with applesauce and lemon.

❧ Grate carrots and cook, seasoning with tarragon, nutmeg, dill weed, or chervil.

❧ Sauté chopped onion in oil, stir in cut carrots, cover, and cook on low until tender.

Crumby Carrots

A surprisingly delicious dish, much more so than you would think from the simplicity of the ingredients. If you want to make more than one recipe, plan to do it in batches, because the breaded carrots can't cook properly if they are deeper than one layer in the skillet.

ða

Cut carrots in ½″ sticks and steam until crispy-tender. Meantime, mince garlic and add with cumin to butter in a large skillet. Heat briefly and gently to cook the spices, being careful not to brown the garlic. Stir in the bread crumbs and set aside.

Use two shallow bowls, one to mix the flour and salt, the other for the egg and milk. Line the bowls up, with the skillet making number three, and dip the carrot sticks a few at a time, first in the flour and salt mixture, then in the egg and milk; then roll them in the bread crumbs. Try to get each one completely covered. When you are finished, put all the carrots in the pan and cook over low heat, turning occasionally with a spatula. When all sides are crisp, they are ready to serve.

Serve the carrots at once in a warmed dish, with the yogurt as sauce.

3 medium carrots
 (about 2 cups cut)
1 clove garlic, minced
¼ teaspoon cumin powder
2 teaspoons butter

⅔ cup whole wheat
 bread crumbs

¼ cup whole wheat flour
pinch salt

1 beaten egg
2 tablespoons milk

⅓ cup plain yogurt, beaten
 smooth

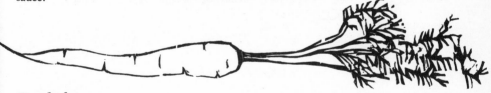

Cauliflower

Snowy white it is, but don't be fooled: cauliflower is a good choice nutritionally. It's a versatile addition to mixed vegetables because of its color, mild flavor, and pretty shape, but it's also good on its own with parsley or basil, a little sesame salt, chopped toasted cashews or almonds, seasoned bread crumbs, or a grating of hard cheese.

For an impressive entrée, steam a head of cauliflower whole and serve it surrounded by green vegetables on a platter, topped with a generous grating of sharp cheddar cheese.

Cauliflower is tasty raw too, or lightly cooked to serve on relish trays or in salad.

Greek Cauliflower

1 head cauliflower
juice of ½ lemon
   (about 1 tablespoon)
1–2 teaspoons olive oil
¼ teaspoon salt (scant)
2 tablespoons chopped
   parsley

Our favorite way of serving cauliflower.

❧

Wash, trim, and cut cauliflower into bite-sized florets. (From a smallish head you will get about 4 cups.) Steam gently until tender. Sprinkle with lemon juice, olive oil, salt, and parsley. Toss gently and then adjust the flavorings to taste. Heat gently, just to soften the parsley, and serve at once.

Serves 4.

Celery

We keep celery on hand for soups, Chinese-style vegetables, casseroles, sandwich spreads, and stuffings for this or that. With its assertive flavor and negligible nutritional contribution, it is really more of a seasoning than a vegetable. For crunchiness, though, nothing is so handy. And when the larder is nearly bare, or the winter seems very long, sometimes a light, creamy celery soup can provide just the break you need from strong greens and sweet squashes.

Swiss Chard

Gardeners all know chard because it grows undaunted from spring through the first hard frosts, letting its outer leaves be taken while the plant continues on. For sheer beauty, there may be nothing quite like a big tender ruby chard leaf against the morning sun, with the light shining through its red stem and showing up the deep curly forest-green of the leaf. Not all chard is red-veined, of course, and most of what you buy in the market has white stems. It may be less gorgeous, but it can be a lot more useful in vegetable combinations or soups where the red color isn't wanted. Chard doesn't have quite the delicacy of spinach, but it is so much easier to grow that we find ourselves using its leaves virtually everywhere we would use spinach.

When the leaves are very young, the stems can be chopped and cooked along with them. But as they get more mature, the stems become thicker and need extra cooking time; trim them off the leaf, chop them, and give them a head start in the pan or steamer basket. Chard stems are similar enough to celery that they can substitute for it in many cooked dishes. Like spinach, chard contains oxalic acid and will discolor if cooked in an iron pot.

For a simple and very tasty chard dish, sauté chopped onion and stir in chard, cut bite-size, and a handful of raisins. Cook until chard is tender; then toss in a handful of toasted sunflower seeds.

Or sauté onion and garlic and add a tablespoonful of minced fresh ginger; add chopped chard, and when it is tender, add a tablespoon of shoyu and a cup of chopped tomato. This dish is good with steamed diced potato, or over rice.

Nearly any sauce is good on chard, particularly those with a milk or cheese base. For a real treat, try Stuffed Chard Leaves—they don't take as much time as you'd think—or Chard Pita.

Chard can sub in any kale or spinach recipe too—and don't overlook the chard variation of Hijiki Stir-Fry.

Chard Cheese Pie

6 cups lightly cooked chard,
   well drained
2 cups low-fat cottage cheese
2 eggs, beaten
juice of 1 lemon
½ teaspoon salt
½ cup whole-grain
   bread crumbs
paprika

We developed this fine recipe when the garden produced its first enormous chard crop, and we've cooked it regularly ever since, throughout the long chard season. If you are enjoying a bumper crop, you can make Chard Cheese Pie with leaves only, but it is good with some stems included too. Either way you will need a scant 6 cups of cooked, well-drained chard.

Preheat oven to 350°F.

Beat together the cottage cheese, eggs, lemon, and salt. Stir a cup of this mixture into the chard and press it down in a well-greased 8″ × 8″ pan. Spread the remaining cottage cheese mixture evenly over the top and sprinkle on the bread crumbs and paprika.

Bake for about half an hour, or until set. Allow to stand for several minutes before cutting into squares.

Serves 4 to 6.

VARIATIONS

Chill and serve with red-ripe garden tomatoes and a sprinkling of crumbled blue cheese.

Add ¾ cup grated Swiss cheese to the chard mixture. Omit lemon.

To make more from less, add a cup of buttermilk and another egg.

Substitute spinach or kale for the chard.

Add a chopped, sautéed onion.

Corn

Remember all that stuff about how the only way to eat corn is to pick it at five minutes to six, *run* from the garden, shucking all the way, drop it into a pot of boiling water, snatch it out again, and skid into the dining room by six sharp? Remember? Well, it was all true until a couple of years ago when science broke through corn's tendency to convert sugar to starch as soon as it was picked, and managed to produce a whole new breed of corn—now available to gardeners, and probably very soon in stores. Its sugar stays unstarched for hours and days after picking. Meantime, even with the old-fashioned kind, the arrival of the first corn is one of the great events each summer.

For the first week or two, no one thinks of eating corn any way but straight off the cob. But when the enthusiasm begins to flag, try gilding the lily in any of the following ways. Remove the kernels from the cob with a sharp knife, being careful not to cut down deeply into the cob. Then, using the back of the knife, scrape the cob to force the nutritious germ of the grain out into your bowl.

  Chop an onion, a bell pepper, and a tomato. Sauté the pepper and onion in oil until soft, then stir in fresh corn and tomato. Cover and cook briefly. Add salt and pepper to taste.

  For a summer garden treat, sauté sliced green onions; add snow peas and then fresh corn. Cover and cook till tender— just the twinkling of an eye.

  Cook cabbage in milk, add fresh corn and parsley.

  For a corny liquid to flavor pancakes or sauces—or to make the base of a delicious soup with red and green peppers—sauté a big white onion, adding a spoonful of chili powder once the onion is soft. Stir in 2 cups corn kernels and add water to cover. Simmer until tender; then puree. (To get a smooth liquid, strain through a sieve or put it through your food mill.)

Eggplant

These jewel-toned fruits are a traditional and delicious substitute for meat. They are so spongelike that they absorb whatever oil or juices are nearby while they're cooking, so eggplant dishes can be heavily greasy. We have designed our recipes to take a minimum of oil, usually by steaming or baking the eggplant rather than frying it.

It isn't hard to adapt old favorite recipes that call for frying. Use the guidelines in the recipes that follow, or try the simple technique of cutting the eggplant in half and baking it face down on a greased baking pan at 350°F until it's tender—about half an hour for a medium eggplant. At that time it can be cooled and chopped or sliced or scooped out for stuffing. Eggplants cooked this way have marvelous flavor without any fat at all. An added advantage is that if the eggplant is a little over-mature, the bitter seeds separate out easily after baking and you can discard them. A medium eggplant will give about a cup of well-cooked pulp. (The peel will be tough and you'll probably want to discard it).

You will see the most amazing tips about choosing eggplants, but it isn't all that hard. The skin should be firm and glossy, and if you press the eggplant, it should give and then bounce back. If it doesn't give, it's immature (only gardeners are likely to encounter that); if it doesn't bounce back, it's over the hill. Unfortunately, this is not unusual in market eggplants, since they don't keep very well.

Some cooks like to slice and salt eggplant, letting it drain for an hour, before cooking. This removes some of the liquid, which makes frying easier, but that's not necessary when you are using other cooking techniques. Salting also removes some bitterness when you have to use an eggplant that is older than you would like.

Eggplant Parmesan

This is a truly delicious Eggplant Parmesan, and easily the lowest in calories. To make an even lighter dish, you can use 3 egg whites instead of the 2 whole eggs, or omit the mozzarella—or both.

If you use cracker crumbs, adjust the salt to compensate for the saltiness of the crackers. This recipe is written for the moderate saltiness of bread, and normally crackers are much saltier.

❧

Prepare three bowls for dipping the eggplant:

[1] ½ cup whole wheat flour
    ½ teaspoon salt

[2] 2 eggs, slightly beaten
    ¼ cup milk

[3] 2½ cups crumbs
    ½ teaspoon salt
    pepper and oregano

Preheat oven to 350°F.

Cut eggplant into ¼″ rounds and dip slices in each mixture in turn, coating them completely.

Layer slices in a greased 9″ × 13″ glass baking pan. Slices may overlap but should not cover each other completely. Sprinkle each layer with tomato sauce and Parmesan cheese. Cover tightly and bake for 30 to 45 minutes, or until a fork pierces middle slices easily. Remove from oven, top with mozzarella, and return dish to oven until the cheese melts and bubbles.

Serves 6.

½ cup whole wheat flour
1 teaspoon salt, divided

2 eggs
¼ cup milk

2½ cups whole wheat bread crumbs
or cracker crumbs
¼ teaspoon oregano
dash pepper

1 medium-sized eggplant
2 cups Tomato Sauce
½ cup Parmesan cheese

1 cup grated mozzarella cheese

Florence Fennel

"Common" fennel is an herb: you use just the seeds and young leaves. Cousin Florence (also called finocchio) is actually a vegetable, one that looks like a cross between a teardrop and a head of celery, with fancifully feathery headdress. This is one of the peasant-hearty vegetables which gourmets claim but won't be able to keep from ordinary folks like us because it's so easy to grow. In Italy, where fennel is a great favorite, it is enjoyed raw like celery or cooked in tomato dishes where its mildly aniselike flavor can add a lot. It's often served raw for dessert with creamy cheeses, too; its sweet crunchiness clears the palate.

Fennel is available throughout the fall and into the winter, but quality deteriorates after December. Serve it as you would celery in salads, on platters of "finger food," or in tomato soup or sauce. Very lightly cooked, its unusual flavor can add a graceful dimension to simple stir-fried vegetables or rice or lentil pilaf. Cooked longer, the flavor becomes pretty strong.

Kale

Trying to talk about kale is a little like describing a very dear friend: there are so many nice things to tell, and yet all of them together don't really add up to what is so endearing. Kale is delicious and spectacularly nutritious, especially because it has little oxalic acid to prevent absorption of its rich supply of minerals. Besides that, it is *pretty*: its lacy, ruffled leaves, the subtlest grayed-down green, are beautiful enough to make a border for a flower bed, if you are into edible landscaping. Northerners, Scottish or not, have a special fondness for kale because it grows bravely all winter, surviving even snow and frost to provide its goodness when nothing else is fresh. (In fact, the Scottish word for kitchen garden is "kailyard.") Its nippy flavor makes a perfect foil for the sweetness of starchy winter vegetables like potatoes and winter squash.

Like most vegetables, kale is exceedingly good straight from the garden. (As with other greens and leaf lettuce, you can pick the outer leaves and let the plant keep growing.) But if you're at the grocery store and the kale looks a little tough and gray, don't be deterred. Unless the leaves are actually yellowish, it will cook tender and reward you with a bright green, ruffly vegetable dish that is simply unbeatable.

Before some of our favorite serving suggestions, a few general words on preparation. Wash the leaves by submerging them in a sink full of water, swishing them around to remove dirt and any incidental aphids. Bugs are a problem only in late summer; one drop of detergent in the water usually sends them to the bottom of the sink. Rinse very well. (This method works well with any kind of buggy vegetables.) Strip and discard the stems; they are tough and stringy. You can cook very young, tender kale by the waterless method or stir-fry it, but steaming is better for kale slightly older than baby-size because of its strong flavor. Kale cooks down as all greens do—though less than most—and keeps its ruffly texture. A one-pound bunch will serve two kale fanatics, or a family of four in a dish that includes potatoes or other mitigations.

Since kale is so rich in flavor and nutrients, we frequently combine it with other vegetables, especially the sweet ones: for example, with potatoes and Tangy Cheese Sauce; with potatoes, tomatoes, ginger and soy sauce; with winter squash or yams, and a handful of raisins; chopped fine and floated in Squash Soup or Potato Cheese Soup; sauced with Potato Dill Sauce, Stroganoff Sauce, Sunshine Sauce. . . .

If you have both kale and spinach, for example, cooking both and serving them mixed together makes a third dish with quite a different flavor—and the virtues of both.

MIXING GREENS

Colcannon

Quarter potatoes and put them on to steam; put kale also on to steam separately. Meantime, chop leeks or onion and sauté in butter, stirring frequently to prevent sticking. If they start to stick, add a little water and cook them until soft.

When potatoes are tender, peel and mash them. When kale is tender, drain it very well. Combine potatoes, kale, leeks, milk, parsley, salt, and pepper. If you need to reheat, you can do it by stirring in the skillet you used for the onions, or by the traditional method of making a mound of colcannon on a platter and baking it in the oven with a dollop of butter on top. Since the dish is plenty good without the extra fat, we use the nontraditional method.

4 medium potatoes
3–12 cups chopped kale
3 leeks or 1 large onion
1 tablespoon butter

1/3 cup milk
1/4 cup chopped parsley
3/4 teaspoon salt, to taste
black pepper to taste

Tomato Kale

1½ bunches kale
(1–2 pounds)

1 small onion
(1 clove garlic)
1 tablespoon olive oil
1 teaspoon cumin seeds
or ground cumin
½ cup tomato paste
1 cup tomatoes, chopped

½ cup peas

salt if needed

Wash kale, strip off stems, and chop. You should have 12 cups, more or less. Steam until tender and drain.

Meantime, sauté onion (and garlic, if desired) in oil, adding cumin when onion is soft. Continue to cook a moment more until the cumin is fragrant. Add the tomato paste and tomatoes, and stir to heat through. Add peas, cooking until tender, then add kale. If you have used canned tomatoes or frozen peas, you may not need to add more salt; check, and adjust salt to taste.

Makes about 4 cups.

VARIATION: Instead of peas, add a cup of cubed steamed potato or winter squash.

Crumby Greens

1 leek or a medium onion,
chopped
1 tablespoon oil
½" slice of fresh ginger,
minced fine
1½ cups cooked chard
or kale
or other greens, very
well drained
1 cup lightly toasted
crumbs
salt and pepper to taste

A delicious way to use garden greens, whether you serve as is, use it to stuff tomatoes or steamed ripe bell peppers, or make into patties.

❧

Sauté the leek or onion in the oil until soft. Remove from heat and stir in the remaining ingredients.

If you want to make patties, add a beaten egg, form 6 small patties, coat with more crumbs, and grill on a lightly greased skillet until the crumbs are nicely browned; turn once.

This recipe is a happening; add whatever sweet vegetables are in season. These are good: fresh corn off the cob, diced red bell pepper, chopped coriander leaves.

Serves 4 to 6.

Okra

Okra has a tendency to yield a mucilaginous goo as it cooks—a plus or minus, depending on the dish! But with a little art in cooking, this nutritious and wonderfully tasty vegetable can become a favorite.

Choose fresh okra carefully. It should be a really clear green, with no dark spots, and if you press the pointy end slightly, the tip shouldn't bend over. As with mushrooms, wiping is better than washing, because water is what makes okra gluey. (If you do wash them, dry at once with a towel.)

In soup, where a little glueyness does no harm, okra is enormously good, and its little wheels make a sparky point of interest in rice or millet pilaf. One of our favorite ways of serving okra eludes formal recipe-writing: slice it thin and toss with a beaten egg white, then gently coat with fine cornmeal. Cook very slowly in a very lightly oiled skillet, until nicely browned. Season with salt and pepper. Utterly delicious.

Whole Okra

Clean okra and trim it as needed. Cutting a tiny bit off the tip tells you whether that pod is tender or tough.

Sauté the onion and garlic in oil, cooking gently until soft. Crush garlic with a fork. Add okra and stir and cook until it changes color slightly, about 5 minutes. Add just enough water to cover the bottom of the pan, cover, and cook gently until the okra is almost tender. Add tomatoes, salt and pepper, and cook uncovered until the okra is tender and tomatoes are done.

Serves 6.

1½ pounds small young okra
1 large onion, minced
3 whole cloves garlic
1 tablespoon oil
1½ cups tomatoes, peeled, seeded, chopped
1 teaspoon salt
pepper

Onions

The most common crime against onions is to undercook them so that they have a harsh aftertaste. People who don't like onions have often been victims of this kind of cookery.

For the record, the word *sauté* means to cook something in a little fat while stirring. *Fry* requires more fat; no stirring required. Sometimes you will hear that you can sauté with water instead of oil. Cooking without oil isn't sautéeing: the effect on flavor is different. But you *can* sauté in less fat than you are used to. The trick is to keep the fire lower, use a heavy skillet, and stir vigorously, with attention. If the onions begin to brown before they cook as much as you want them to, lower the heat; *then* add a little water and keep stirring until the water evaporates. Do this more than once, if necessary; it's called "candying" and makes a sweet, deeply rounded flavor. Scallions (green onions) and shallots cook quickly, so they are easy to sauté in very little oil.

From winter to spring, the onions you see are varieties that store well, which are usually stronger tasting. In the fall, big purple bermudas are sweet and mild; green or spring onions (scallions are the smaller version) give nip and freshness year-round. Both are great for salads. Scallions are welcome in any vegetable or grain dish where color and zip, rather than sweetness, is wanted. Delicate and less oniony than scallions are chives, which grow easily even in pots and lend zing to salads or soups with no cooking needed.

On the other end of the scale is the gourmet's onion, the shallot, which combines sweetness and pungency in one tiny, flavorful bundle. Shallots grow easily wherever there is full sun, so there is no reason for them to be so rare, except that unlike their larger cousins, they do not store well. You can use the leaves of shallots as you would chives or scallions—an added bonus for the gardener.

The onion that is an eating vegetable—and another easy-to-grow member of the family—is the leek. Leeks are sweet and mild and green in their flavor, so they often don't play a supporting role but star in dishes like leek soup, patties, or pita.

Garlic

Is there anyone who doesn't have a strong opinion about garlic? Some people believe it will cure anything, and that life without it is a hollow shell. Others can't abide even a hint of its strident flavor and would rather starve than meet a whiff in dinner. If you are a fan, you know how you like to use it; if you are a foe, you will know how to leave it alone. The following paragraphs are addressed to everyone else.

Garlic gives heft and heartiness as no other ordinary seasoning can. Its warmth enhances certain vegetable dishes where a deeper, rounder flavor is wanted; it provides a bass note in bean dishes and an added dimension to both bean and grain concoctions.

The most common crime against garlic is to use garlic powder or salt, both of which invariably taste rancid and have a characteristic sour afterbite that is quite horrid. The second most common mistake is to add minced garlic along with onions while you sauté them. Garlic is fragile and burns easily; once burned, it makes the whole dish bitter. Try these techniques and see whether you don't find that they work better for you:

[1] Add the whole uncut clove of garlic while you sauté the onion. When the onion is done, use a fork to mash the clove, which should be perfectly cooked.

[2] Mince the garlic and add it once the onion is done; then continue to sauté only briefly to cook the garlic.

[3] Use a garlic press, squeezing the garlic into the onion as in method [2].

[4] A drop or two from the press can add a lot to salad dressings—but this is controversial.

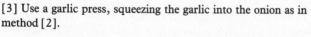

Parsnips

Parsnips are one of those old-fashioned vegetables being redis-covered now that complex carbohydrates are high chic. Their sweetness combines well with other root vegetables, as well as with sharp-flavored greens or with green beans in mixed vege-table dishes. They add an unmatchable note to winter stews. Young, tender parsnips can be steamed but older ones will get rubbery, so stir-frying is better. If the top center is pithy, cut it out.

Sesame-Glazed Parsnips

1–1½ cups parsnips, peeled
    and cut in ¾" chunks
1–1½ cups carrots,
    cut in ¾" chunks
1 tablespoon sesame seeds
2 teaspoons butter or oil
2 tablespoons maple syrup
½ teaspoon salt
juice of 1 orange (½ cup)

Sweet and scrumptious.

Steam parsnips and carrots together until barely done.

Toast sesame seeds in a medium-sized skillet over medium flame. When they begin to turn color slightly, add oil or butter, maple syrup, salt, and orange juice. Stir in carrots and parsnips. Turn heat up to medium high and cook, stirring with increasing frequency, until liquid is reduced to a glaze.

Makes 4 servings (about 2 cups).

Parsnip Patties 🐷

4 cups raw parsnips, peeled
    and cut in chunks
1 onion, minced
1 tablespoon oil
1 teaspoon dried tarragon
2 eggs, beaten briefly
1 teaspoon salt
½ cup finely chopped
    walnuts
2 cups whole-grain bread
    crumbs

These are truly outstanding. *Don't* leave out the walnuts. Along-side broccoli, green beans or kale, and a dollop of applesauce, very fine eating indeed.

Steam parsnips until tender—10 or 15 minutes. While parsnips are cooking, sauté onion in oil. Add tarragon.

Mash parsnips with potato masher (a few lumps are okay). Stir onion into mashed parsnips with egg, salt, and walnuts.

Preheat oven to 350°F.

Form parsnip mixture into patties, using about ⅓ cup for each. Spread half the bread crumbs on a greased baking sheet and place patties on crumbs. Press remaining crumbs on top. Bake for 20 minutes.

Makes 12 patties. Serves 6.

Bell Peppers

Green peppers are a familiar favorite, quite indispensable for dishes of Spanish or Creole persuasion. Red bell peppers, though, are really special. They're the same vegetable, only riper, and hence much more quickly perishable. Their season is brief—just a few months in autumn—but how we treasure their bright, sweet tartness and color! They combine perfectly with the quieter autumn vegetables like squash and brussels sprouts. Wonderfully good too are golden yellow peppers, pretty for salads, stuffing, or light cooking, like their red counterparts.

If you want to enjoy peppers of any color year-round, you can find them at amazing prices in specialty groceries, imported from places as far away as Holland—or you could consider giving them growing space indoors. One of our greenhouse pepper plants is three years old, and our very most prolific bearer. Even without a greenhouse, some of the smaller peppers will grow happily in pots. Commercial peppers, especially imported ones, are usually coated with a pesticide-impregnated wax, and the peels are very tough and sometimes bitter. We usually peel them with a sharp potato peeler—or roast them; see page 137.

Stuffed Peppers

Pepper cases give a sense of purpose to untidy grains and miscellaneous mixtures, and they make leftover Spanish Rice a feast. Or try filling them with Stuffing, Rice-Lentil Polou, Bulgar Wheat Pilaf, or any similar dish. Filled with lightly creamed greens, pretty red or yellow cups are dazzling—one of those little touches that make a meal special.

If the filling wants the extra baking, the peppers can be stuffed raw, but usually you'll want to steam them first. For small ones, just cut the top off; otherwise, cut in half lengthwise. Remove the seeds and membranes and cook upside down in a steamer basket until barely tender—about 5 to 10 minutes, depending on the pepper.

To keep the surface of the filling from drying out, and for artistic effect, top the filled peppers before baking. If you steam them along with the peppers, you can use the tops you cut off; or try almost any combination of bread or cracker crumbs, nut or seed meal, grated cheese, and tomato slices.

Chinese Peppers & Sprouts

1 pound fresh mung bean
  sprouts
½ each, large red and
  green bell peppers
(1 head baby bok choy)
1 leek

2 tablespoons sherry
½ teaspoon honey
1 teaspoon salt

1 tablespoon oil

Crunchy, pretty, and fresh-tasting, this dish graces a Chinese
dinner or an American one equally well. Bean sprouts are very
perishable, so buy them only if they show no signs of brown and
use them right away. (Or sprout your own: see page 120.)

☙

Rinse the sprouts in cold water and drain. Cut the peppers into
thin strips somewhat the size of sprouts; do the same with the bok
choy, if you use it. Slice the leek into thin strips also, and rinse in
cold water until clean. Drain well.

Mix sherry, honey, and salt in small dish.

Heat oil in a wok or large skillet; when hot, add the leek and
stir-fry for about a minute, letting it soften but not brown. Add
peppers (and bok choy, if desired); stir about half a minute, until
hot. Add sprouts, tossing as they cook, until hot—another half
minute. Pour sauce over all, again stirring and tossing. Vegetables are ready when they are coated with sauce.

Serves 4 to 6.

Potatoes

Potatoes have gained prestige recently because of the discovery
that complex carbohydrates are Good For You. Partly because of
this renewed interest, friends who didn't grow up back in the last
century have asked that we tell a few basic things about this
wonderful vegetable—such as, for example, what's the secret of
really fluffy mashed potatoes (Cook them well, mash with milk
and some of the cooking water, and never, never let them cool
off. We like to use buttermilk instead of the standard milk and

omit the butter: it makes a rich-tasting mashed potato with much less fat.)

Besides their other nutritional virtues—vitamin C and minerals, modest calorie count, etc.—potatoes are *versatile*. For example, cooked very well and blended smooth, they thicken sauces and soups in place of cream sauce. The flavor is good, the fat much less.

Another useful role: grated potato will hold patties together nearly as well as an egg. Add it raw if the patties will cook long enough, or lightly steamed: ½ to 1 cup for half a dozen patties to cook on a griddle or in the oven. (See pages 177, 178, 215.)

With their sweet, mellow taste, potatoes (either chunky or saucy) are a perfect balance for the assertiveness of dark greens. Colcannon is a delicious case in point.

In late spring, wherever you shop, there'll be "new" potatoes: small, freshly-dug potatoes with a flavor that's unbeatable, especially after the tired winter-storage potatoes that you've had for months before. With fresh peas, or maybe a little parsley, what could be better?

GREEN POTATOES: If a potato's skin is green, the toxin solanine may be present. It's bitter and can cause slight to serious illness. Peeling deeply will remove most of the poison, but if more than half of the skin is green, it's much better to throw the potato away.

French Bakes

These are a favorite around our house. They are enough like fries for most of us, with or without Homemade Ketchup.

3 large potatoes
1 tablespoon oil
½ teaspoon salt,
  or to taste

૨ᴥ

Preheat oven to 400°F.

Scrub potatoes and cut into french fry–sized pieces. Put them in a bowl with the oil and toss very well, so that each piece is coated with the oil. Spread them on greased cookie sheets one layer deep, and sprinkle with salt. Bake about 35 minutes, or until done to your taste.

Serves 4.

Parsley Stuffed Potatoes 🥔

4 baking potatoes

1 bunch scallions
  or 1 onion
1 tablespoon oil or butter

½ to 1 cup yogurt
  (not *tart*)
1 teaspoon salt
dash nutmeg
⅛ teaspoon black pepper
½ cup chopped parsley

Prepare potatoes as described in Green Potatoes for Six.

Meanwhile, sauté the scallion or onion in the oil. When the potatoes are done, scoop out their insides and mash while still hot with enough of the yogurt to make them fluffy—moist, but not soggy. Mix in the sautéed scallion and the remaining ingredients. Return the potato mixture to its jackets and bake for another 20 minutes.

Makes 8 stuffed potato halves—4 or more servings.

Green Potatoes for Six 🥔

6 medium or 3 large baking
  potatoes
3 stalks broccoli
  (about a pound)
¾ cup grated cheese
1 teaspoon salt
⅛ teaspoon pepper
¼ cup milk

This is a simple recipe, most enthusiastically received by the children.

Preheat oven to 400°F.

Scrub potatoes. Butter skins and make shallow slits around the middle as if you were cutting the potatoes in half lengthwise. Bake until done, 45 to 60 minutes depending on size.

Peel broccoli stems. Steam whole stalks until just tender and chop fine.

Carefully slice the potatoes in half (the slit helps) and scoop the insides into a bowl with the broccoli. Add ½ cup of the cheese and the salt, pepper, and milk. Mash all together until mixture is pale green with dark green flecks. Heap into the potato jackets and sprinkle with remaining cheese. Return to the oven for about 10 minutes.

Serves 6.

VARIATION

When you want to serve the broccoli alongside, use green peas and chopped parsley to "green" the potatoes.

Ishtu

This South Indian dish is almost a sauce. You serve it over rice with a green vegetable, curried or not, alongside. Add mint chutney, which makes a perfect foil for Ishtu's soothing sweetness, and you have a truly special meal.

1½ cups dried, unsweetened coconut
5 potatoes
3 medium onions
1 teaspoon salt
3 tablespoons chopped fresh ginger

❧

Soak coconut in 1 cup very hot water.

Peel potatoes (alas, yes) and cut them into 1″ cubes. Put them in a 3–quart saucepan with about 2 cups water. Bring to a boil and lower heat to a simmer. Meanwhile, cut onions in big chunks—about 1–1½″, cutting away the very top and bottom so the layers separate. Add to the potatoes after the first few minutes. Cover pot and cook potatoes and onions until they are just tender, about 15 minutes altogether.

Put chopped gingerroot in blender (use a small blender jar if you have one) with just enough water to cover, and blend smooth. Add to potato-onion mixture along with salt when potatoes are just about done (ginger is best when it's barely cooked). Check occasionally to be sure there's still enough water to prevent sticking.

Place coconut and its water in blender and blend for 2 to 3 minutes, stopping frequently and pushing coconut down into blades with rubber spatula. Use a cloth napkin, or your hands and a strainer, to squeeze out the milk and set it aside.

Return squeezed coconut to blender with another cup of very hot water. Blend for another few minutes and repeat the squeezing process. Add the second coconut milk to cooked potatoes and onions. Stir. Bring stew to a boil, then add the first milk (it is delicately flavored and best if not boiled). Add more salt if you think it needs it.

Makes 6 servings.

Potatoes Tarragon

1 large onion
1 tablespoon olive oil
3 large potatoes
1 bay leaf
3 tablespoons vinegar
1 teaspoon dried
   tarragon leaves
1 teaspoon salt
¼ teaspoon black pepper

A variation on hot potato salad, but much lower in fat.

%

Remove top and bottom of onion and slice down through center into long strips ¼″ wide. Sauté in olive oil in a good-sized skillet until transparent.

Slice potatoes in half lengthwise, then in semicircles ¼″ thick. Add to onions along with bay leaf, vinegar, tarragon, salt, and pepper. Add just enough water to barely cover potatoes. Bring to a boil, then cover and reduce heat. Simmer for 30 to 45 minutes—long enough to cook potatoes very well, so well they're beginning to crumble. Stir gently from time to time to make sure they aren't sticking. The pan sauce and potatoes should be commingling deliciously when you serve the dish.

Makes 4 generous servings.

Buttermilk Scalloped Potatoes 🍶

2 very large baking
   potatoes (1 quart packed
   when thinly sliced)
¼ cup whole wheat flour
1 teaspoon salt

1 medium onion, chopped
2 tablespoons butter
2 cups buttermilk
freshly ground black pepper
   to taste

Here's a delicious, rich-tasting scalloped potato dish with much less fat than you'd guess.

%

Peel potatoes and slice very thin. Combine salt and flour and dredge potato slices in that. Place them in a 9″ × 13″ casserole dish. Sauté onion in butter until tender, then add buttermilk to pan just long enough to warm but not boil. Pour mixture over the potatoes, grind pepper or paprika over them, and bake in a 350° oven for 1 hour or until potatoes poke tender with a fork.

Makes 6 servings.

Papas Chorreadas

If you include the green beans, this Latin American potato dish is a meal unto itself, needing only a pile of steamed tortillas to sop up the juices. Add a salad of green lettuce leaves, jicama, and avocado with a pinch of cumin in the dressing, and you have a feast for any day.

🍂

Quarter potatoes lengthwise and steam them. Remove skins and slice into ½" pieces. Cut green beans in 1" pieces and steam separately until barely done.

Meanwhile, heat butter in a skillet. Sauté onion over low heat until tender, then add green onions and garlic. Add chili if desired, along with cumin and oregano, and sauté a minute more. Add tomatoes and salt and simmer 10 minutes; then stir in cottage cheese, cheese, and coriander. Heat until cheese melts. Combine with potatoes and green beans and serve immediately.

Makes 4 to 6 servings.

4 medium potatoes
(½ pound fresh green beans)

1 tablespoon butter
1 medium onion, chopped
4 green onions, chopped
1 clove garlic, minced
(1 green chili, seeds out, minced)
½ teaspoon cumin
½ teaspoon oregano
2½ cups chopped tomatoes
1 teaspoon salt
½ cup cottage cheese
¾ cup grated jack cheese
(2 tablespoons chopped coriander leaves)

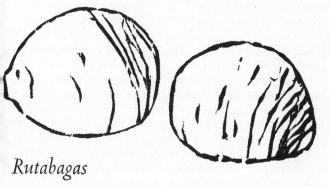

Rutabagas

A down-home Complex Carbohydrate if there ever was one. Peel and boil rutabagas until they turn orange, then mash them and beat in some salt and pepper (and milk, if you like), or mix them with equal parts of mashed potatoes to make Roota-Roota, the way Grandma Bauman used to do. Very good indeed on cold winter nights, whether you are in Sweden or the U.S.A.

Like parsnips, rutabagas make a flavorful addition to winter stews. Northern gardeners leave them in the ground all winter— no storage problem at all!—to use as needed. Dill and fennel are complementary seasonings.

Sea Vegetables

Most people think of edible seaweed as a characteristically Japanese food, but maritime cultures all over the world have made use of the tasty and nutritious vegetables collected from their shores. In Scotland, for example, dulse is used to make a cream soup not unlike New England clam chowder. In fact, Americans eat a lot of seaweed—mostly derivatives like agar, algin, and carrageenan that are used as thickeners in convenience foods.

Here we give only a brief introduction to some of the sea vegetables you can find in your natural food store. For the adventurous palate, these foods offer a new realm of flavors and textures; but even conservative cooks will find useful material here. Agar, for example, offers a vegetarian alternative to gelatin. Nori, the thin black wrapper around sushi, can be lightly roasted over a flame to make a blameless snack food that children love.

Sea vegetables have a lot to offer nutritionally, particularly for their trace mineral contribution. Kombu, for instance, has been used for centuries in China for treating goiter because of its dependably high iodine content, and laver is particularly rich in iron. Constant bathing with the mineral-rich waters of the sea probably guarantees to all marine vegetables a full spectrum of the elusive trace minerals.

Unfortunately, however, most sea vegetables available in stores today are grown in the polluted waters of the Japan Sea, and available research shows that heavy metal pollutants, pesticide residues, and other contaminants do find their way into edible seaweeds and algaes. From the extremely limited data available, it appears that the levels of heavy metals in products on the shelves are not greater than those found in land vegetables. Still, at this point we are wary of any vegetables grown in areas with significant pollution problems. We suggest that you buy from domestic growers, such as those whose sea vegetable farms are in Maine, and that you join in the efforts to cut down on the tragic pollution of our oceans. Ask your local oriental or natural foods stores for the names of companies that grow sea vegetables in domestic waters.

AGAR (also known as agar-agar or kanten) is a seaweed derivative that works like gelatin to make molded salads and aspics (pages 142 and 323) or can replace eggs in thickening anything that doesn't have to be served hot. Agar comes in bars, granules, or flakes, the flakes being the easiest to use. Unlike gelatin, which has to be chilled, agar thickens at 98°F and has nearly no calories.

KOMBU (*Laminaria*) is a member of the kelp family whose special talent is making soup stock (see page 148). It contains glutamic acid, the natural version of MSG. Added to beans, it reduces cooking time and may help to prevent flatulence.

HIJIKI (*Hizikia fusiforme*) is black, piney-looking, and exotic. Its hearty, salty marine flavor tastes best with sweet vegetables like carrot, squash, and onion, or with tofu. Try it in our Hijiki Stir-Fry (next page).

ARAME (*Eisenia bicyclis*) is fibrous and needs to be soaked before using. Try it in Winter Salad (page 141).

WAKAME (*Undaria pinnatifida*) is green and leafy and has a mild flavor close to that of leafy land vegetables. Like kombu, it tenderizes foods cooked with it.

DULSE (*Palmaria palmata*) is salty and makes a good snack food right out of the bag. It comes in thin sheets and has a beautiful purple color.

NORI has been cultivated by the Japanese for three hundred years, and was collected wild before that. The characteristic thin black sheets have a high concentration of nutrients, though the amounts are very small. Nori can be eaten as is, but it is usually toasted over a flame. We like it cut up and floated in miso broth as an instant snack. To preserve flavor, store airtight.

Many sea vegetables (particularly nori) can be toasted and then crushed or rolled into a flaky powder to use in the salt shaker. Nori has much less sodium than table salt, but equals it in flavoring strength: much of its salty flavor comes from potassium rather than sodium.

Hijiki Stir-Fry

½ cup dried hijiki
   or 2 cups chopped chard
1 small onion, sliced thin
3 cups thin-sliced hard
   vegetables (broccoli,
   carrots, green beans,
   celery, cauliflower, etc.)

2 tablespoons white or
   yellow miso
1 tablespoon honey
1 teaspoon fresh ginger,
   grated
¾ cup water
dash cayenne

2 tablespoons oil
   (corn or sesame)
(½ cup tofu cubes)
1 tablespoon toasted
   sesame seeds

If you aren't up to hijiki yet, use chard instead. Either way, we guarantee one of the tastiest stir-fry meals you can make. A very adventurous palate—or one that has developed a taste for sea vegetables—will enjoy the hijiki version. It makes a completely different dish, and a very good one also.

৵

If you use the hijiki, cover it with water to soak for ten minutes. Meanwhile, chop the vegetables.

Mix together in a cup: miso, honey, ginger, water, and cayenne. Drain and rinse the hijiki.

Stir-fry the sliced vegetables in oil for about 4 minutes, then add the hijiki or chard and stir-fry another minute. Add the miso mixture, and the tofu if you like. Stir briefly and cover. Steam over reduced heat another 5 minutes, or until the vegetables are cooked to your taste.

Sprinkle with sesame seeds and serve with brown rice. Makes 4 cups, enough for 4 people.

Spinach

It's hard to figure out how spinach ever got such a bad press, because fresh spinach is an enormous hit among the people we know, *especially* the children. Maybe the hangup is some primal recollection of canned spinach: gray, slimy, gritty stuff with its own unique bitterness.

Fresh spinach deserves to be handled with delicacy. Wash it carefully, especially if it is sandy or muddy, swishing it gently in a sinkful of cold water, draining, and repeating until the water is clean. Don't soak it or handle it roughly, or you'll get dark, soggy places where the vitamins have up and gone.

Cook and serve it whole, with just the roots taken off, or chop it before or after cooking to make the forkwork easier. Even a big pot of spinach leaves will cook in the water that clings after washing, if you stir from time to time. If you aren't used to cooking it, you'll be amazed to watch a bunch of spinach that makes 4 quarts of leaves cook down to a cup or so when it's done.

Like chard and beet greens, spinach contains oxalic acid, which makes the taste slightly sharp. To minimize this, you can cook it in milk or serve it with a creamy sauce (real cream isn't necessary), or accompany it with blander vegetables like potato or zucchini or winter squash, or with other salty or tart foods like shoyu, tomato, or lemon. Beyond the flavor, however, there has been concern that oxalic acid may bind minerals like calcium, limiting their availability to the eater. Recent studies indicate that although this does happen in the lab, probably it doesn't in the actual human digestive system. Still, if you depend on greens for your calcium—that is, if you don't include much milk in your diet—be sure to include oxalic-free greens from the cole family: kale, collards, broccoli, bok choy, and the like.

Spinach and eggs seem to have an affinity, and for special occasions we like to make Spanakopita, Quiche, or Crepes. For simpler "nutrient-dense" fare, garnish a serving of spinach with chopped hard-boiled egg along with a dash of vinegar. Or do it the way our friend Josh invented many years ago: pile up a lot of cooked, diced potatoes, about as much as a nine-year-old can eat and still have room for apple crisp; dot them with Better-Butter; add a layer of lightly cooked chopped spinach, and top wit̃ a poached egg. Perfect for filling a growing kid's "hollow leg."

Creamed Spinach

¾ cup milk
2 tablespoons powdered
milk

½ small onion
1–3 tablespoons butter
3 tablespoons whole wheat
flour
3 quarts fresh spinach,
washed, dried, and
chopped
(3 small bunches)
¼ teaspoon salt
pinch nutmeg

(½ cup grated Swiss cheese
or 2 tablespoons
Parmesan
or ¼ cup cream cheese
crumbled with a fork)

It's normal to cook the spinach separately and add it to the sauce, but here's a method which preserves nutrients that would be lost in the cooking water, and leaves one less pan to wash too.

This recipe has considerable sauce for the amount of spinach. When a very *spinachy* version is needed, we find we have better results cooking sauce and greens separately, and draining the spinach well before combining it with the sauce.

❧

Blend the milk and powdered milk and set aside. Chop onion fine and sauté in the butter in a large, heavy skillet. When the onion is clear, stir in the flour and cook and stir for about 2 minutes very gently. Don't let the flour brown. Add the milk and bring to a boil, stirring.

A handful at a time, stir in the spinach, adding more as the greens cook down. Simmer gently until tender, seasoning with salt and nutmeg. Add the cheese if wanted.

This recipe will make about 3 cups, enough for 4 generous servings. It is not a soupy creamed spinach but goes nicely on the plate by itself, or with mashed potatoes, or in crepes.

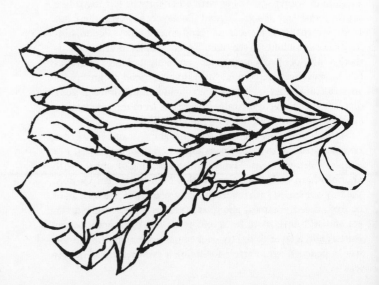

Summer Squash

Summer squashes are similar to each other in flavor and texture, but they vary in shape and color, so we like to cut up whatever's fresh and cook them together in chunks, perhaps with sautéed green onion and ripe tomatoes. Cooked crispy-tender, these bright yellow or dark or pale green squashes are light and refreshing after a hot summer day.

In the last few years, the yellow zucchini called "Goldrush" has replaced crooknecks in our patch. They fruit earlier, taste better, keep better, and produce longer. Because they are straight, they're easier to cut evenly, and they don't have big seeds like the crookneck. Whichever kind you have, the golden yellow squashes are pretty in tomato dishes and hide cleverly in corn bread and similar adventures if you happen to grow too much.

Patty pan squashes are fanciful, with their scalloped parasol look, and they are the sweetest-flavored too. We like them best picked when they're only 2″ to 2½″ across, steamed plain and served with a piquant sauce; or, at the 3″ stage, scooped out and stuffed with herbed bread crumbs.

And then—zucchini. What hasn't been said about this versatile vegetable? Welcome and delicious, and so outrageously productive in the garden that around the middle of August people start thinking of ways just to use it up. That's why you see zucchini recipes so farfetched as to boggle the imagination in every newspaper's late-summer food pages. Still, it may be at its best served simply—stir-fried, or sliced lengthwise and baked, then topped with cheese, herbs, crumbs, or just freshly ground pepper; or blended smooth in the dozen versions of Green Soup.

❧

ZUCCHINI PATTIES Slice and sauté a bunch of scallions (or slivered onion); add a grated potato, and let it cook about halfway, then add the same amount of grated zucchini, and a big handful of chopped parsley or coriander leaves. Mix well; salt and pepper to taste. (You can add beaten egg or grated cheese, if you want.) Form or spoon onto buttered crumbs on a griddle, and cook until the crumbs brown. Turn onto more crumbs, and brown the other side. You can make SPINACH PATTIES the same way.)

Zucchini Provencal

1 bunch green onions
1 whole garlic clove
1 tablespoon olive oil

1 potato, cubed
3 smallish zucchini, cubed
½ cup chopped celery
2 medium ripe tomatoes,
    in 1" chunks or
    ½ cup tomato sauce
1 teaspoon basil
½ teaspoon salt
pepper

Use a large skillet or stewpan. Chop the onion and sauté with the whole garlic clove in oil. When onions are transparent, crush garlic with fork. Add potato and a little water. Cover and simmer gently, stirring occasionally, for about 10 minutes. Add the zucchini (and the celery, if you want it soft rather than crunchy) and cook another 10 minutes, until tender. Stir in the celery (if you haven't already), tomatoes, and basil. Heat uncovered, stirring as necessary, until tomatoes are soft. Check seasoning.

Makes about 4 cups. Serves 4 to 6.

Baked Zucchini 🏺

5 to 8 small zucchini
1 egg
1 cup cottage cheese
(3 tablespoons buttermilk)
paprika or cayenne

EXTRAS

Add to the topping:
    ¼ cup grated cheese
    or this sautéed mixture:
    ½ onion, 1 clove garlic,
    and 2 tablespoons finely
    chopped parsley

Sprinkle on top before
    the second bake:
    Toasted bread crumbs
    Parmesan cheese

Another standby, dependable and infinitely variable.

Preheat oven to 350°F.

Slice zucchini in half lengthwise and place as many as will fit cut side up, sides touching, in a greased 9" × 13" glass baking dish (metal pans can give a metallic taste where they touch the zucchs). Cover with a cookie sheet and bake until half done—about 15 to 20 minutes, depending on the size of the zucchini.

Meantime, beat the egg and cottage cheese together (if you want it smooth, add the buttermilk and blend in blender). When the zucchini are ready, remove from oven and spoon the cottage cheese mixture over the top. Dust with paprika or cayenne and return uncovered to the oven for 15 minutes. When done, the zucchini will be tender (poke with fork) and the topping melted and bubbly-browned.

Greek Stuffed Zucchini

Yet another Macedonian specialty from the repertoire of our friend Sultana. This may just be the world's most delicious zucchini dish. If you don't have time for all the coring and stuffing, you can just chop the would-be stuffees into the rest and bake.

❧

Hollow out the zucchini. Make cylinders with an apple corer, or slice in half lengthwise and scoop out the insides to make little boats. In either case, you will need a pan large enough to arrange them side by side for baking.

Chop all of the vegetables very small. Chop insides of zucchini too, but keep separate.

Cook rice with water, onion, celery, salt, pepper, and oil for 25 minutes.

Add chopped zucchini and cook 5 minutes more.

Add parsley, bread crumbs, juice from 2 of the lemons, and slightly beaten whites of the eggs.

Preheat oven to 350°F.

Put the filling into the scooped-out zucchini shells. (If you chose the cylinder style, pack the filling in firmly with your fingers, keeping a bowl of cold water nearby to cool your hands.)

Arrange zucchini in a baking dish. If there is extra filling, spread it over and around the zucchini. Cover and bake for about 40 minutes.

Beat the egg yolks with remaining lemon juice. Spoon out some of the juices from the baking dish. Add slowly into egg yolk–lemon mixture, stirring briskly. Pour this sauce over the zucchini and bake for another 5 minutes.

Serves 6 to 8.

10 six-inch zucchini

1½ cups chopped onion
2 cups chopped celery
½ cup raw brown rice
1 cup boiling water
1 teaspoon salt
pepper
3 tablespoons olive oil

1 cup chopped parsley
1 cup bread crumbs
3 smallish lemons
2 eggs, separated

Winter Squash

Easy to grow, easy to store all winter and use as needed, these golden squashes provide reliable good food from October through April. Their warm sweetness is a nice complement to the other standard winter vegetables from broccoli through kale and on to cabbage, whether combined or served side by side.

Although most winter squashes are generally interchangeable in recipes—even in pumpkin pie—each has particular strengths that can make a difference. For example, small squashes like delicata, Lady Godiva, and acorn make the best individual-serving stuffers, especially with savory fillings. Sweet-meat and butternut are richly flavored and mealy, wonderful for baking in chunks. Pumpkin has its characteristic flavor, with a smooth, non-mealy texture; by itself it has only a few more calories than zucchini, where butternut and acorn have double. Even so, any winter squash is a calorie bargain: a good complex carbohydrate with lots of vitamin A and potassium for under 100 calories per cup. Satisfying fare for all of us who want to lower our fat intake: the really tasty varieties are good enough to eat plain.

Here is a bonus for small children on rainy winter days: take the seeds from a big pumpkin, and in a bowl of warm water, clean off all the slimy strings. Put the seeds on a towel to drain, then on a baking sheet to toast until crisp. A delicious treat very high in protein and minerals.

Sandy's Gingered Squash

3 cups hot, cooked,
    mashed winter squash
1½ teaspoons butter
pinch salt
2 tablespoons finely minced
    fresh ginger
juice of 1 lemon
2 tablespoons honey

A light, bright dish to serve alongside any dark green vegetable.

↊

Mix all ingredients, adjusting the amount of lemon and honey as required for balance. (It will depend on how sweet your squash is.)

Makes about 3 cups, or 4 to 6 servings.

Cranberry Squash

The pungency of the cranberries is a perfect foil for the mellowness of the squash. A pretty and lively variation on baked squash.

๛

Arrange pieces of squash in one layer in a baking dish with a cover (or use aluminum foil). Scatter cranberries, chopped apple, and raisins over and around squash. If you use acorn, butternut, or other small squash, you can halve them, mix all the other ingredients together, and pile the mixture into the cavities. Otherwise, mix orange juice, grated peel, honey, butter (if desired), and salt together and pour over squash.

Cover baking dish and bake until squash is tender—25 to 45 minutes, depending on variety.

Makes about 4 servings.

1½ pounds raw winter
squash, unpeeled,
cut in serving-size chunks
½ cup raw fresh cranberries
1 small apple, chopped
in ¾″ pieces
¼ cup chopped raisins

juice and grated peel of
1 small orange
1½ tablespoons honey
(1 tablespoon melted butter)
dash salt

Stuffed Acorn Squash

Use acorn squash, delicata, Lady Godiva, or any other small variety of winter squash. A handsome, colorful presentation.

๛

Preheat oven to 350°F. Halve and clean squash. Place cavity face-down in a greased baking dish and bake for 25 to 45 minutes, until tender to a fork. The time will depend on which squash you choose.

Meantime, sauté onions in oil until soft. Add chopped celery. Cover and simmer on medium heat until just tender. Add spinach; stir to wilt.

Stuff squashes with vegetable mixture. Sprinkle with salted bread crumbs. Return to oven for 10 to 15 minutes.

Serves 4 to 6, depending on size of squash.

3 small winter squashes

3 green onions, chopped
2 tablespoons oil
1 cup diced celery
1 bunch spinach, coarsely
chopped

½ to 1 cup whole wheat
bread crumbs
½ teaspoon salt

Hungarian Squash

1 small onion, chopped fine
(1 clove garlic)
2 tablespoons butter
1 quart cubed winter squash

1 teaspoon paprika
1 teaspoon dill weed
2 tablespoons chopped
   parsley
1 cup yogurt, beaten smooth
1 teaspoon salt

Best with a truly sweet and mealy squash so that you get a piquant, sweet-and-sour taste when combined with the yogurt.

❧

Sauté onion (and garlic, if desired) in butter. Add squash and cover; simmer for 15 to 20 minutes on low heat. If the squash is very starchy, it might need ½ cup water added midway. If any liquid is left after squash is cooked, uncover and cook and stir until it evaporates.

When squash is tender, stir in remaining ingredients. Heat very gently until warmed through. If you heat it too much, the yogurt will separate—still tasty, but less attractive.

Serves 4 to 6.

Squash Malagushim

⅓ cup coconut
½ cup very hot water
1 teaspoon ground cumin

½ cup yellow split peas
1 cup water

2¼ pounds winter squash
   (6 cups cut)

½ teaspoon turmeric
½ teaspoon salt

1 teaspoon black mustard
   seeds
2 teaspoons oil

This South Indian dish goes as beautifully with Western food as it does as part of an Indian dinner. We like to serve it in winter alongside broccoli or other green vegetables and rice.

❧

Cover coconut with very hot water. Add cumin and set aside.

Cook split peas in water until soft, about half an hour. Be sure they are covered with water as they cook, but try to end up with as little extra water as possible.

Peel squash, remove seeds, and cut in ¾" cubes. Cook in as little water as possible. When half cooked, add turmeric and salt.

Mash split peas with cooking water.

Puree coconut and soaking water in blender 3 minutes or until very smooth. (This step can be omitted, but it makes a much nicer dish.)

Mix peas, coconut, and squash. Simmer a few minutes.

In a small, heavy pan, heat oil and add mustard seeds. They will begin popping like popcorn. Cover and listen: the instant the frantic sound of popping dies down, turn the seeds into the squash dish and mix well.

Serves 4.

Butternut Tostada

Artist Alan Gussow works in several media, including vegetables. This hands-across-the-border dish reflects his eclectic approach nicely. The combination may sound strange, but this is one fine dish, a revelation for people who love Mexican food but can't eat beans.

❧

Cut and quarter the butternut and steam for 20 minutes. Meanwhile, toast the tortillas over gas burner or on a griddle until just softly crisp.

Remove the squash pulp from the skins. Heat oil in a heavy pan and sprinkle with chili powder, cumin, and garlic. Stir and fry until the spices are fragrant. Add squash and oregano, stirring while mixture heats through.

Place squash on tortillas, sprinkle with shredded cheese, and place under broiler until cheese melts. Remove, cover with lettuce or sprouts, and dot with salsa. A handful of toasted pumpkin seeds makes a delicious final touch.

Makes 4 rather unusual but very tasty tostadas.

*1 butternut squash
 (to make 2 cups cooked
 pulp)*
4 tortillas
1 tablespoon oil
1 teaspoon chili powder
½ teaspoon ground cumin
1 clove garlic, minced
*1 teaspoon well-rubbed
 oregano*
*1 cup shredded cheddar
 or jack cheese*
*4 cups shredded lettuce
 or alfalfa sprouts*
salsa (see below)
(toasted pumpkin seeds)

Salsa

Dice tomatoes, chop onions, mince garlic and chili; combine all these with herbs and mix well. If you are not an old chili hand, see page 236 for some tips about using them.

3 ripe, red tomatoes
4 green onions
2 cloves garlic
*1 jalapeño or yellow
 hot chili pepper*
*¼ cup chopped fresh
 coriander leaves*
1 teaspoon oregano

Sweet Potatoes & Yams

The controversy continues, so we looked them up. Yams proper are tuberous roots of tropical plants of the genus *discorea*, hardly ever available north of the tropics. All our so-called yams are probably really sweet potatoes, but when people say yams, usually they mean the moist, dark orange varieties that taste so terrific. Bake them in their jackets and serve piping hot, with or without Better-Butter. Some brown-baggers we know like to take the leftovers for lunch, to eat like fruit. But the competition for leftovers is keen because yams are so delicious chunked into dinnertime greens or used for Sweet Potato Salad.

For baking, allow about twice the time you'd give for similar-sized normal potatoes: 2 hours at 375°F for big ones. Scrub and trim as necessary, removing black spots. Since they are full of natural sugar, which tends to burst out in the oven, covering the baking sheet with clean brown paper or cooking parchment makes clean-up a lot easier.

South Indian Sweet Potatoes

3 cooked sweet potatoes
  or yams (2 cups mashed)
2 teaspoons oil
½ teaspoon black mustard
  seeds
½ cup green pepper, finely
  chopped (½ large pepper)
(1 fresh green chili, minced,
  or dash cayenne)
½ teaspoon ground cumin
lemon juice to taste
½ teaspoon salt, to taste

What could be better than plain baked yams? Maybe nothing, but this dish would definitely get votes. Why not bake extras and use them this way? Very different, and utterly delicious. Warm them up before proceeding with the recipe.

🍂

Peel and mash the yams and set aside.

Heat oil in a small skillet until faint lines form on the surface.

Sprinkle in mustard seeds and keep covered over high heat while they pop. When the wild noise dies down, immediately add the chopped green pepper. Return to a medium-low flame and sauté, adding chili (if desired) and cumin.

When green pepper is tender, add mashed sweet potato and heat through. Add lemon juice to taste. (A tablespoon or more is delicious, but if you're serving the dish with anything else that's piquant, you might want to use less.)

Makes 4 servings.

Tomatoes

Tomatoes are so basic to year-around cooking that it's hard to imagine doing without them. We give them much of our tiny greenhouse space, so that we have some fresh all year. Still, we use them so much that tomatoes are the one vegetable we buy canned. If you, like us, have to rely on canned tomatoes sometimes, be sure that you remove all the contents once you open the can. Most cans are still lead-soldered, and lead leaches into the food once the can is open. (That goes for tomato paste too, and any other food or juice in soldered cans.)

Much has been written lately about the poor eating quality of commercial fresh tomatoes, and all of it is true. The happy result of the flack is that local growers are actually bringing real home-grown tomatoes to market—red, ripe, luscious, and in season, mind you; the real thing. Ask for them if you can't grow them yourself. The salmon-colored, cubical lumps of papier-mâché that agribusiness calls tomatoes add nothing to any salad, sandwich, or casserole.

Our own tomato season is so short that we can seldom bring ourselves to cook with fresh tomatoes. Instead we enjoy them in salads, or stuffed with Tabouli, or in sandwiches. But sometimes, at peak of season, we get a chance to make Tomato Soup—simple, but what more satisfying?—or grilled tomato halves, with maybe a drizzle of olive oil, a sprinkling of parsley or fresh basil, and a grating of black pepper or hard cheese. Fresh-picked tomatoes usually inspire our version of a Mexican feast at least a few times each summer: fresh steamy-hot tortillas, Refritos, shredded lettuce, Mock Sour Cream, sliced tomatoes, Salsa, Avocado Dip, grated jack and cheddar cheeses, so everyone can construct tostadas to taste. (See pages 276–277 for more.)

If you had to pick one vegetable to spend the extra money to buy organic, tomatoes would be it. Commercial tomatoes have a bad record of pesticide contamination. The lab method routinely used by the federal government can detect only 55% of more than 100 pesticides used on tomatoes; yet nearly half of all domestic, and 70% of imported tomatoes tested contained residues of one or more pesticides.

Pesticide Alert, *by Mott, Lawrie, and Karen Snyder (National Resources Defense Council) (Sierra Club Books, 1987) p. 127*

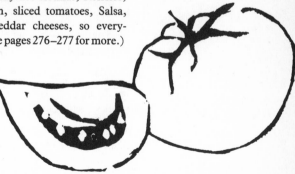

Mixed Vegetables

The next few recipes are for mixed vegetable dishes, most of which draw their inspiration from other cultures. Besides these, and too simple to be treated as real recipes, are the many delicious combinations of garden-fresh vegetables that one stumbles upon from day to day as the seasons change. Serve them in a colorful heap just as they are, or accompanied by lemon wedges or shoyu, or topped with Sesame Salt, chopped nuts, grated cheese, Lemon Butter, or your favorite sauce. Serve them with brown rice or millet, or fresh whole wheat rolls. Add a salad and your meal's complete.

You may choose to start with a sautéed onion, but from there on almost anything goes, though most cooks prefer to keep the number of vegetables down to three. Choose them with color, texture, and flavor in mind. Vary the way you cut the vegetables, and you'll be amazed what a difference it can make. Chop them, dice them, slice thin or thick, in rounds or diagonals or matchsticks; shred or grate them; fix some one way, some another; but make them as pretty as you can. If some will cook quicker than others, you can adjust the thickness of the slices or give the slower ones a head start.

The following combinations are a few that we enjoy often. Treat these suggestions as a jumping-off place: invent your own medleys, a different one each time.

ૐ Zucchini and broccoli stems cut in thick rounds; broccoli florets bite size; carrots in thinner rounds.

ૐ Cauliflower and green beans with red bell peppers for accent

ૐ Winter squash or leftover yams cubed, with celery crescents and chopped spinach or chard

ૐ Green beans, diced potato, and sautéed onion

ૐ Zucchini coarsely grated or sliced very thin, with corn and parsley (that's a quickie)

ૐ Carrots and zucchini grated large, with shredded cabbage and finely chopped parsley (add salt and lemon juice at serving time)

Ratatouille

Ratatouille (the word means "stew" or "soup" in French) makes use of a savory vegetable combination which is a favorite the world round. The exotic dishes from the Middle East which follow are variations on this basic theme.

If you can use fresh, perfect ingredients—not only the vegetables but the herbs too—this dish can be truly wonderful.

꙳

Dice eggplant into 1″ cubes and slice zucchini in ½″ rounds. Chop onion coarsely and cut green pepper into squares.

Use a heavy-bottomed saucepan with a lid. Sauté the onion, garlic, and green pepper until they are soft; stir in eggplant and zucchini and sauté a few minutes more. Crush garlic clove with a fork. Add tomato and seasonings. Cover and simmer gently for about 30 minutes or until all the vegetables are well cooked.

Uncover and turn the heat up to evaporate some of the liquid, stirring as necessary.

Serves 6 to 8.

1 large eggplant
2 medium zucchini
1 large onion
1 green pepper
1 whole clove fresh garlic
2 tablespoons olive oil
3 fresh, ripe tomatoes,
  chopped or
  5 tablespoons tomato paste
  and 3 tablespoons water
1 teaspoon salt
⅛ teaspoon pepper
½ teaspoon basil
½ teaspoon oregano

VARIATIONS

IMAM BAYILDI: Preheat oven to 350°F. Add a large potato cut in chunks, some sliced mushrooms if you wish, and a cup of hot water or stock. Instead of simmering on top of the stove, bake in a covered dish for 45 minutes.

GVETCH: Include not only potato chunks and sliced mushrooms, but also 4 carrots sliced in rounds and the juice of 1 lemon. Use only 2 tablespoons water instead of a whole cup and bake as for Imam Bayildi.

Aviyal 🐚

1/4 pound green beans
2 large carrots
2 large potatoes
2 medium zucchini
1 teaspoon turmeric powder
1 teaspoon salt

1 cup unsweetened
    coconut flakes
1 cup hot water
1 cup yogurt, beaten smooth
(1 small green chili)
juice of 1 lemon,
    if yogurt is not tart

Aviyal means "miscellaneous," so if this list isn't in season when you prepare your feast, choose from winter squash, broccoli stems, asparagus, or plantains. Serve with rice, other vegetable curries, and chutney.

ᴥ

Cut vegetables into strips the size of your little finger and cook in as little water as possible. Start with the green beans, then add carrots and potatoes after a few minutes. Zucchini should go in last, when the other vegetables are half cooked. Add turmeric. Stir the vegetables so they will cook evenly, but be careful not to break them. Add salt. Add water if necessary.

Grind coconut in blender or food processor with the hot water, adding the chili if you like things fiery. When all the vegetables are tender—not mushy—stir in the blended coconut. Remove from heat. There should be just a little water left. Stir in yogurt, adding lemon juice if needed: the sauce should be a little tart.

This makes 6 cups or more, to serve 4 to 6.

Cauliflower Eggplant Curry

1 cauliflower
1 eggplant
2 tablespoons oil
1 teaspoon black mustard
    seed
1/2 teaspoon turmeric powder
1 teaspoon curry powder
1 teaspoon salt
1/4 cup water
2 potatoes
1 cup peas
1 tomato, chopped
juice of 1 lemon

One of our favorite mixed vegetable dishes, whether the meal is Indian in mood or not.

ᴥ

Remove thick stems of cauliflower and cut them into small pieces. Separate the head into florets and slice.

Cut eggplant into 1/2" cubes.

Heat oil in heavy pot with a lid. When very hot, add mustard seed and cover quickly. The seeds will pop wildly; when the sound dies down, turn off the flame, open the lid, and immediately add the spices and the cauliflower. Stir to coat with spices and oil. Add 1/4 cup water and eggplant. Cube potatoes and boil them separately until partially cooked before adding them.

Continue cooking over medium heat, adding 1 or 2 tablespoons of water from time to time, stirring gently. Add peas about 5 minutes before serving. At the last minute, add finely chopped tomato. Turn off heat and add lemon juice.

Serves 6 to 8.

Middle Eastern Vegetables

eheat oven to 375°F.

Dice potato, carrot, and apple small. Separate cauliflower
to small florets. Cut zucchini into chunks.

Sauté onion in oil with bay leaf, mustard seed, celery seed,
d dill.

Stir in vegetables in this order, leaving 2 minutes or so
tween each addition: potato, carrots, cauliflower. Then add
ple.

Add tomato and zucchini. Heat quickly, sprinkle with salt and
prika, cover loosely, and transfer to oven for 20 minutes.

The trick of getting vegetables to bake evenly is to cut the
tato, carrot, and cauliflower quite small.

Serves 4 to 6 over rice, bulgur wheat, or millet.

1 potato
1 carrot
1 medium green apple
1/2 head cauliflower
2 zucchini
1/4 onion, chopped
1 tablespoon oil
1/2 bay leaf
3/4 teaspoon yellow
  mustard seed
1/4 teaspoon celery seed
1/2 teaspoon dill weed
1 tomato
1 teaspoon salt
1/2 teaspoon paprika

Chinese Vegetables

his recipe is not very authentic, but we make it often and enjoy
very much. Where amounts are given, they are for 4 to 6
ople.

હ્

llow at least 1 cup of vegetables per person. Cut attractively in
agonal shapes; cut the onion vertically in thin wedges. If a
getable doesn't lend itself to the diagonal cut—cabbage, for
ample—dice or cut in square pieces.

Heat the oil in a wok or a large skillet. Stir-fry the onion, then
ld minced garlic and ginger, stirring in the other vegetables in
rn, beginning with the longer-cooking ones and ending with
ch quick-cookers as peas and bean sprouts. If you want to use
fu, rinse and cut into 1" cubes and place on top of the vegetables
fore they are completely cooked. Cover and steam until tofu is
ot and vegetables crisp and tender.

Add shoyu to taste. Sprinkle with toasted sesame seeds and
rve right away, with a steaming bowl of brown rice.

THE MUSTS

1 onion
minced garlic
1 teaspoon minced ginger
2 tablespoons oil
green pepper, celery
1/2 cup water
shoyu to taste

THE VARIABLES

mushrooms
snow peas or green beans
carrots, peas
broccoli, cauliflower
zucchini
bok choy or chard
Chinese or Western cabbage
tofu chunks
mung bean sprouts

Mushrooms Petaluma

3 potatoes
3 carrots
¾ pound fresh mushrooms
  (ideally buttons)
2 bell peppers
1 large onion, chopped
2 tablespoons butter or
  butter and oil combined
2 tablespoons mustard
  (Dijon best)
3 tablespoons shoyu
3 tablespoons brown sugar
1 cup mellow red table wine
½ cup chopped fresh parsley
salt and pepper to taste

This rather purple stew may look odd, but it's quite delectable.

𝄞

Trim potatoes, quarter lengthwise, and slice in ½″ pieces. Slice carrots the same thickness. Steam potatoes and carrots together.

Clean mushrooms with a damp cloth and cut larger ones into good-sized chunks. Remove seeds and stem from peppers and cut in 1″ squares.

Sauté onion in butter in a heavy 2-quart pot until translucent. Add mushrooms and bell pepper and sauté, stirring, until mushrooms begin to sweat.

Mix mustard, shoyu, brown sugar, and wine. Add sauce to sautéed vegetables along with carrots, potatoes, and a cup of the water they steamed over (or other vegetable stock).

Bring mixture to a boil and add parsley. Reduce heat and simmer, covered, until vegetables are all quite tender. Cook uncovered then, if you want to, to reduce and thicken sauce. Serve with whole-grain noodles.

Makes 6 servings.

Winter Stew

8 cups kale, chopped
1 large or 2 small parsnips
1 rutabaga (¾ cup)
1 smallish turnip (½ cup)

SAUCE

1 onion, chopped
2 whole cloves garlic
2 stalks celery
2 tablespoons olive oil
3 tablespoons shoyu
1–2 tablespoons molasses
2 tablespoons lemon juice
2 teaspoons dried basil
2–4 cups stock

Just the thing to perk up a jaded winter appetite.

𝄞

Steam kale until nearly tender. It may take more or less time than the rest of the recipe ingredients, depending on whether it is tender or tough; if it cooks quickly, take it off earlier. You should have about 2 cups. Drain well. While kale is cooking, peel roots and dice in ½″ cubes.

Sauté onion, garlic, and celery in olive oil. Mash the garlic cloves with a fork and add the remaining sauce ingredients, as well as the parsnips, rutabaga, and turnip. Simmer 10 minutes. (Adjust the amount of stock to suit the way you will be serving the stew.) Simmer until parsnips etc. are nearly tender, about 20 minutes. Add kale and cook briefly, until everything is tender. Serve with grain, potatoes, hot rolls, or (maybe best of all) Spoon-bread, page 286.

Makes about 5 cups, to serve 4 to 6.

Sauces & Such

What better way than a fine sauce to brighten the flavors of your vegetables, or to join otherwise disparate ingredients in a happy marriage? But is there sauce after fat?

To enhance what is already good, and to make appealing what is nutritious but maybe not so immediately welcome, a little fat can be a big help for the magic it works in a skillet. But when you begin to lean on cream, butter, or even good olive oil, you soon notice that the stuff is addictive. Fortunately, there are alternatives.

There is, for example, the time-tested combination cherished by Greek cooks: parsley and lemon juice. Nothing simpler, nothing more appetizing, and nothing in the world more innocent. Always add lemon juice and parsley (and any other fresh herbs) at the last minute; they don't take kindly to long cooking.

The sauces that follow are meant to make good food even better without sending you to an early grave. Even so, use a light hand. We sauce only one dish per meal, as a rule, and do the saucing in the kitchen; it's tempting to ladle on too much at the table. Everyone can discover the exquisite flavors of vegetables and grains—but not when the food is drowned in sauce.

If you have a tiny bit left, it's well worth keeping. Those few spoonfuls might be just what tomorrow's soup needs for extra sparkle, or combine with leftover beans to make a delicious spread.

Flavoring

When your appetite is keen and the green peas were picked moments ago, it's a travesty to reach for the spices. But when you're trying to simplify your family's diet, or introducing them to Complex Carbohydrates, or when the midwinter gleanings from the garden seem monotonous beyond relief—at times like these, imaginative saucing and seasoning can change everybody's feeling about dinner, and make the difference between good nutrition and a secret raid on the local fast foods outlet. With this in mind, we have collected some of our favorite ways of adding appeal to praiseworthy dishes that might otherwise not get the top billing they deserve.

SALT   Try to use just enough in the kitchen that no one reaches for it at the table. Our recipes use the amount of salt that seems right to people who are used to lightly salted food. If you can use less, by all means do it!

PEPPER   Nicer when freshly ground. Pepper is aromatic when added just before serving; it becomes hot-tasting when it sits in cooked food.

BAY   A bay leaf adds dimension to soups, sauces, and stews. Be sure to remove it before serving time.

GINGER   Ginger adds nip and brightness. Use it to enhance dishes that already have a fruity mood, such as winter squash or tomato soups or sauces. Ginger gives ping to vegetables that might otherwise taste flat or heavy, and is often included along with garlic in Chinese and Indian cooking. Wonderful stuff. Don't overcook.

Growing Your Own

Few of us have time or space to grow all our own spices and herbs. But anybody who wants to can grow at least pots of basil, parsley, and chives. Garlic and onions are practical for gardeners, and oregano, marjoram, savory, rosemary, and thyme grow easily. Lemon thyme makes a beautiful green-and-yellow ground cover. Coriander, even more than basil, is best fresh, and its pretty, lacy flowers have a bonus: they support very tiny wasps that help keep the aphid population down. Growing herbs is a very satisfying thing.

PARSLEY

Parsley must be the friendliest herb of all. We keep it planted just outside the kitchen door, but it will flourish even in a pot (use a deep one) and provide plenty for salad dressings and more. Where many other herbs seem too strong-flavored for vegetarian fare, parsley adds freshness and sparkle to just about anything that isn't green already. To our taste, the tender Italian kind with flat leaves has the best flavor. No parsley wants much cooking, and the color is preserved too if the chopped leaves are added at the very end of cooking time.

To say that parsley is very nourishing may seem silly considering how little you use at a time, but there you are: it is. Good for freshening the breath after a garlicky dinner, too—just chew up a sprig.

CHINESE PARSLEY

Also called coriander or cilantro, these leaves make a brightly green topping for many Mexican, Indian, and Chinese dishes. It is one of our favorites for adding freshness to salads and grain dishes. Buy it in the produce section of supermarkets or in Mexican or Chinese groceries.

BASIL

Fresh or dried, basil adds perky sweetness to any tomato dish, as well as to peas and salad dressings. Its mild, sweet flavor is a perfect complement to the lighter flavor of meatless sauces and vegetables. The large-leafed kind grows and harvests easily and has a lovely, mellow flavor.

Seasoning Blends

Commercial blends can be a godsend for cooks who feel diffident about using herbs and spices. Try to choose for freshness, and read the label: some have a lot of salt (which you can add more cheaply in the kitchen!) and some contain MSG—an additive worth avoiding. It may be just as easy to create your own blends, either on the spot or at convenient times; they are likely to be fresher than commercial mixes and certainly will taste better.

MEXICAN FLAVORING

Cumin powder is the essence of Mexican flavoring. Add cayenne for hotness (to the extent that you want it), oregano, and garlic. Cayenne is what gives Mexican food that fine red color, but if you want to go light on cayenne you can add quite a lot of paprika instead; it's made of dried ripe bell peppers instead of chili peppers, and gives color without hotness. Cumin and chili powder give their best flavor when you add them as you sauté the onion.

Add fresh, chopped leaves of cilantro to salsa, and top your chili beans or guacamole with it.

ITALIAN FLAVORING

If spaghetti is a spur-of-the-moment standby, you may want to keep Italian Blend on hand. Mix 6 parts basil, 2 of oregano, 1 of thyme; use about a teaspoon per cup of sauce (for example), to taste. Include fresh garlic in your sauce too, and a bay leaf.

Indian cooks blend spices differently for each dish, but in the U.S. we have the convenience of prepared curry powder (coriander, cumin, ginger, cardamom, turmeric, etc.), a dash of which can save a vegetable stew from disaster or give interest to sauces that lack pizzazz. Shop around to find a curry blend that you particularly like. Most of the spices in curry powder require cooking to give their best flavor, so include it at the sauté-the-onion stage.

A spice blend often made in advance even by Indian cooks is *garam masala*. This mixture is sweeter than curry powder and wonderful for dishes with spinach or peas. Indian specialty stores stock different masalas in various degrees of hotness, but if you often use Indian recipes that require it, you may want to grind your own, using a recipe from a good Indian cookbook like Yamuna Devi's *Lord Krishna's Cuisine: The Art of Indian Vegetarian Cooking* (Bala Books, 1987). If you're caught short when a recipe calls for garam masala, use allspice.

Many South Indian dishes call for black mustard seeds. These are smaller than the familiar yellow seeds, and must be popped like popcorn for best flavor. Don't let them burn. Black mustard seeds give an unmatchable warmth to many vegetable curries and to Raita, page 239.

Three spices from the Indian palette that work together to make bean dishes and soups special are coriander powder, cumin, and turmeric. Use them as a team, a quarter to a half teaspoon turmeric, a teaspoon of cumin, and two or even three of coriander. Added when you sauté the onions, the mixture makes an event of a pot of pintos. All three are believed to help prevent flatulence, and all should be cooked well to give their best flavor.

Turmeric is an acrid yellow powder encountered mostly in prepared mustard, which would be only pale tan without it. Used in most curries in small amounts, it adds interest, an assertive curl, and a sunny color.

Cumin is familiar to anyone who enjoys Mexican cooking, but it appears as frequently in Indian dishes. It gives bright, warm piquance to bean and tomato dishes and greens.

Ground coriander seed may be a stranger, but once you try it with beans, you'll want to have it around regularly. Its sweet warmth rounds out the flavor of cumin, and when sautéed and added to bean dishes and such, it thickens the liquid into sauce.

Soy Sauce, Shoyu & Tamari

For counting sodium:
2 teaspoons shoyu
= ½ teaspoon salt

"Soy sauce" is a general term for the dark-brown flavoring liquids with a soybean base. *Shoyu,* the term we use throughout this book, is the naturally-fermented kind whose ingredients include soybeans and wheat (in nearly equal portions) and salt. Made in the traditional way by long fermentation, it has especially good flavor. Some of the finest of commercial Japanese shoyu is now available in the United States. When you are shopping, check the label for the ingredients mentioned, and be sure there are no preservatives.

The "other kind" of soy sauce is an unfermented preparation made from hydrolyzed vegetable protein (HVP), corn syrup, caramel color, salt, and monosodium glutamate. We don't use or recommend it.

To add to the confusion in terminology, for a decade or so some natural foods firms have been calling their shoyu *tamari.* Tamari is also a flavorful brown liquid, and not so different from shoyu that you couldn't use it as a substitute; but real tamari, a by-product of miso making, is not usually available commercially. What you may find called tamari is usually a Chinese version of shoyu that *may* be made without wheat. Again, the thing to watch for on the label is preservatives.

Aside from providing their own characteristic and delightful flavor, shoyu and tamari can be helpful to people who are trying to cut back on salt. The salty flavor of these products *does* come from actual salt, but they seem somehow saltier-tasting for an equivalent amount of sodium, enabling you to use less. You still have to be careful, though: it only works if you use less!

Homemade Ketchup

We like this version better than store-bought. It's free of additives and sugar, and much lower in salt—and cheap.

☙

Mix all the ingredients together. Store in a jar in the refrigerator.
Makes 1¾ cups.

1 twelve-ounce can
tomato paste
½ cup cider vinegar
½ cup water
½ teaspoon salt
1 teaspoon oregano
⅛ teaspoon cumin
⅛ teaspoon nutmeg
⅛ teaspoon pepper
½ teaspoon mustard powder
squeeze of garlic from press

Sesame Salt

A flavorful seasoning to add at table.

☙

Toast sesame seeds and grind in blender with salt, one part salt to eight *or more* parts seeds.

Quick Vegetable Relish

A crisp, tangy relish that goes well in sandwiches. Try it with Swiss cheese and mustard for a Vegetarian Reuben that's a real knockout; or use a spoonful alongside simple fare to add interest.

☙

Combine all ingredients and pack into a pint-size jar. Add enough water to cover, if needed—about ¼ cup. Cover tightly and refrigerate overnight.

Makes 2 cups (the vinegar shrinks the vegetables). Store in refrigerator.

2 cups shredded green
cabbage, packed
½ cup grated carrot, packed
½ cup very thinly
sliced red onion
½ cup very thinly
sliced green pepper
2 teaspoons salt
dash pepper
6 tablespoons distilled
vinegar

Margarita's Salsa

4 fresh medium tomatoes
½ smallish onion
1 mild jalapeño pepper*
½ teaspoon (rounded)
  oregano
½ teaspoon (level) cumin
½ teaspoon (scant) basil
½ teaspoon salt
dash black pepper

This is freshness itself, and best served shortly after its creation. A perfect garnish for any dish with Mexican antecedents, or with vegetable or bean concoctions where a little fire is called for. Even with mild jalapeno, however, this is a hot salsa by many people's standards. For a milder version, use just a few chives or one small scallion top instead of the onion; you might also omit the chili, or substitute ¼ green pepper.

Puree in blender or food processor, or just chop everything very fine and mix.

Makes about 2 cups.

*An aside to anyone who isn't used to chilis: the seeds and membranes are the hottest parts, and you can get flavor with less ferocity if you discard them. Cut the chili in half, being careful to handle it by its skin and trying not to touch the inside. Remove the seeds with knife or spoon—and don't flip one up into your eyes! After you have chopped the chili, wash your hands, knife, and chopping board, and don't touch your face for at least half an hour.

Chutneys

The recipes on this page are for fresh chutneys of the sort made daily in Indian homes; the bottled ones in stores are more in the category of pickles. Both can serve to pick up the palate and complement the other dishes at a meal.

If you have fresh coconut, remove the white flesh and grate it before you start. If not, use dried: soaking it beforehand in hot water to cover makes the chutney smoother; use part of the water from the recipe to do that.

Coriander Chutney

Place all the ingredients in the blender and blend smooth, using a minimum of water. This chutney should not be runny, so you will have to stop the blender frequently to stir, especially at first. Makes ¾ cup, enough for 4 at a feast or for 2 for Dosas.

MINT CHUTNEY: Substitute ¾ cup coarsely chopped mint leaves for the coriander. (For another delicious mint chutney, see the recipe on the next page.)

1 cup coriander leaves
½ cup shredded coconut
1 small shallot, chopped
*   or 2 tablespoons onion*
1 tablespoon chopped ginger
(½ green chili)
¼ teaspoon salt
1 tablespoon lemon juice
1 teaspoon brown sugar
about ¼ cup hot water

Coconut Chutney

This chutney comes from Tamilnadu, and is good for Dosas or —if you have our Bread Book—Iddlis. Blend all the ingredients except oil and seeds, using enough hot water to grind easily but well; it should be a thick smooth paste. Rinse the blender, using about ¾ cup hot water, and add that to the chutney to make about 2 cups.

Heat the oil in a small, heavy pan and add seeds. They will pop frantically; the moment the sound of popping dies down, add the chutney. Reduce heat and bring the chutney just to a simmer. Makes 2 cups.

1 cup coconut
1 tablespoon minced ginger
1 medium shallot, chopped,
*   or 3 tablespoons onion*
(½ small green chili)
½ teaspoon salt
¾ teaspoon brown sugar
1½ tablespoons lemon juice
hot water

1½ teaspoons oil
1 teaspoon black mustard
*   seed*

Tomato-Ginger Chutney

3 cups red ripe tomatoes,
   peeled, seeded, and diced
½ teaspoon turmeric
1 tablespoon minced ginger
3 garlic cloves, minced
½ teaspoon salt

1 tablespoon oil
1 teaspoon black mustard
   seeds
½ teaspoon cumin seeds

A very tasty general-purpose chutney, not too hot. If you want fire, add a dash of cayenne when the cumin seeds begin to brown.

❧

Combine tomatoes, turmeric, ginger, garlic, and salt, and set aside. Or, for a quicker, rather liquid version, put tomatoes in blender or processor along with the turmeric, ginger, and garlic; whirl briefly, then force the mixture through a food mill to remove seeds and skin. Add salt.

Heat a heavy skillet; when hot, put in oil. When the oil is hot, add mustard seeds. They will pop wildly. When the noise of the popping dies down slightly, remove the pan from the heat and add the cumin seed. Heat slowly, stirring, until the cumin is slightly darkened, then immediately add the tomato mixture. Simmer gently about 10 minutes to reduce and thicken.

Makes about 1¼ cups.

Apple Chutney

2½ cups (or more)
   diced tart apples
1 cup cider vinegar
½ lemon, chopped
¾ cup raisins
¾ cup brown sugar
⅓ cup minced ginger
1 or 2 cloves garlic,
   chopped
½ teaspoon salt
(dash cayenne)

Here is an easy "Anglo" chutney that can go alongside nearly anything that wants perk. We like it especially with kale.

❧

Combine all ingredients and simmer until fruit is soft, about ½ hour if the apples are crisp. Makes 2⅓ cups.

Mint Chutney / Raita 🫖

A cooling chutney, quite runny; delicious spooned next to any sort of rice or spicy vegetable dishes. If you are short on mint, you can use coriander leaves or spinach. Mint and coriander are used raw, but cook the spinach first and squeeze it dry, then chop small. Being milder, this dish is much more like raita than chutney.

⌘

Combine all the ingredients. Makes ⅔ cup, plenty for 4 at a feast; if you use it on iddlis (you really *should* have the *The Laurel's Kitchen Bread Book*), this will make enough for about 6 iddlis.

½ cup chopped mint leaves
½ cup mild yogurt,
* beaten smooth*
(thin slice green chili,
* or 1 teaspoon ginger)*
½ shallot, chopped, or
* 1 tablespoon onion*
¼ teaspoon salt

Raita 🫖

Raita is an Indian side dish that complements the flavors of the rest of the meal, adding tartness where needed for balance. It can do the same for Western-style meals.

Rai means mustard, and authenticity demands that raita include mustard seeds "popped" in the traditional way. You will see many raita recipes without the seeds, though, and as elsewhere, omitting them doesn't mean the dish won't turn out. However, there are few flavors so delicious.

If you omit the popped mustard seeds and use skim-milk yogurt, the raita can sometimes taste a little chalky. If you have this problem, stir in only a little cream, or a *little* oil.

⌘

Beat yogurt smooth and mix with all the vegetables. Heat a tiny, heavy pan very hot; add the oil and, when hot, the mustard seeds. Cover and listen for the sound of frantic popping. As soon as the sound diminishes, uncover the pan and turn its contents into the raita. Mix, and serve cool.

Makes about 2½ cups: enough for 4 people, more or less, depending on how much else there is for dinner.

1½ cups yogurt, beaten
* smooth*
½ cup diced tomato
½ cup diced cucumber
2 teaspoons minced fresh
* ginger*
¼ teaspoon salt, or to taste

(½ green chili, seeded and
* minced, or dash cayenne)*
chopped coriander leaves

1 teaspoon oil
½ teaspoon black mustard
* seed*

BANANA RAITA: Use bananas instead of tomatoes and cucumber. Omit ginger. Wow.

RED ONION RAITA: Use red onions and tomatoes for the vegetables. Add ½ teaspoon of honey and ½ teaspoon lightly toasted ground cumin. This one stands nicely with or without the mustard seed.

Mock Sour Cream 🍥

1 cup low-fat cottage
  cheese
2 tablespoons lemon juice
2 tablespoons mayonnaise
¼ cup buttermilk
zest of ½ lemon
pinch of salt if needed

Mock Sour Cream is easy to fix; it's dramatically lower in fat, saturated fat, and cholesterol than sour cream itself, and it's not half bad as a source of calcium. We make it often to serve with vegetables, on baked potatoes, Blintzes, and Whole Beet Borscht, with Mexican-style dinners, and for dressing potato salad. The taste is distinctly lemony; if you plan to use it with other flavorings, you can omit the lemon zest and reduce the juice.

Mock Sour Cream works reliably in most recipes that call for sour cream. Other options are to use soft Yogurt Cheese (page 104), stirred smooth; or thick Buttermilk Sauce (page 244).

🥄

Place cottage cheese, lemon juice, mayonnaise, buttermilk, and lemon zest in blender and blend thoroughly until creamy smooth.

Makes 1½ cups.

Homemade Mayonnaise 🍥

1 egg
½ teaspoon salt
½ teaspoon mustard powder
2 tablespoons cider vinegar
1 cup oil

This recipe has just as much fat as normal mayo, but it tastes better and has no harmful additives. If you are looking for alternatives, check your natural foods store for one of the good lowered-fat or nondairy mayonnaises. Or see the facing page.

🥄

Put egg, salt, mustard, and vinegar in blender with ¼ cup of the oil. Blend on low, uncover, and slowly but steadily pour in the remaining oil.

Atmospheric conditions will occasionally cause mayonnaise to curdle as you make it. If this should happen, remove it from the blender, put another egg in the blender, turn it on, and slowly pour in the curdled mayonnaise.

Makes 1¼ cups.

Tofu Sour Cream

This makes a tasty substitute for sour cream in cooking and other places that call for plain sour cream. For more emphatically flavored tofu-based concoctions to use as dips or in place of mayonnaise, see below.

You won't need the water with soft tofu, but with firm tofu you probably will.

1/4 cup lemon juice
2 tablespoons oil
1 tablespoon light miso
1/4 teaspoon mustard
(2 tablespoons water)
1 tablespoon shoyu
   (or other flavoring)
1 cup tofu (1/2 pound)

🍃

BLENDER: place all ingredients except tofu in blender. Add tofu bit by bit, blending smooth with each addition. If the mixture stops moving, turn off blender and stir, then blend again. Add tofu and repeat until all is included.

PROCESSOR: put it all in and process until creamy smooth.

Makes 1½ cups.

Tofu Mayonnaises

Follow the directions for Tofu Sour Cream above, using the ingredients listed.

RUSSIAN

1 tablespoon white miso
1 tablespoon prepared
   mustard
2 tablespoons oil
3 tablespoons cider vinegar
dash pepper
pinch chili powder
1/2 teaspoon dill weed
1/8 teaspoon paprika
1/2 pound tofu

ORIENTAL

1 tablespoon shoyu
   or dark miso
3 tablespoons rice vinegar
white part of 2 scallions,
   minced
2 teaspoons ginger, minced
sliver fresh garlic, minced
2 tablespoons oil
1/2 pound tofu

FRENCH ONION

2 tablespoons oil sautéed with:
   1/2 small onion, minced
   1 clove garlic
   1/2 small carrot, grated
   pinch chili powder
   1/8 teaspoon paprika
2 tablespoons cider vinegar
1/8 teaspoon black pepper
1/2 pound tofu

Cream Sauce

*1, 2, or 3 tablespoons
each butter and flour
(for thin, medium,
and thick sauces)
1 cup hot milk
¼ teaspoon salt
pinch nutmeg*

Cream sauce is unarguably delicious and versatile. We seldom use the whole amount of butter, and find that although cooking the flour with less butter requires more determined stirring, the sauce comes out tasting great. The best flour is whole wheat pastry flour, but any whole wheat flour works fine.

❧

Melt butter in pan. Stir in flour and cook 3 minutes over low-medium heat, stirring constantly. Add milk slowly while stirring, and bring to boil to thicken. If you can, set the pan over a very low heat or even in the oven for a while; the sauce will get richer and thicker. If the sauce lumps up, a spin in the blender will set it right.

Makes 1 cup; less if you simmer it afterward.

*Dairy-free "cream" sauce
can be made replacing
butter and milk with oil
and broth or soymilk. We
suggest enhancing the flavor
with sautéed onions,
mushrooms, etc.—or
perhaps as in the top two
recipes on the right.*

SWEET AND SOUR MUSTARD SAUCE: To 1 cup basic Cream Sauce, add this mixture: 1½ teaspoons cider vinegar, 1 teaspoon honey or brown sugar, 1 teaspoon mustard powder (or 1 tablespoon Dijon mustard). Very good on sweetish vegetables like carrots or green beans or on greens, especially chard.

SAUCE DIJON: Make the sauce above, omitting the sweetener and vinegar. Add 2 tomatoes, quartered, a sautéed onion, 2 cloves garlic, and ½ cup of Madeira or port. Simmer until tomatoes are tender, stirring often, and put through a sieve or food mill. Try this on asparagus!

CHEESE SAUCE: Stir ½ cup sharp grated cheese into 1 cup Cream Sauce, either the basic version or that which follows. If you're using cheddar cheese, you can enhance the cheddary flavor by adding ¼ teaspoon (or more) of chili powder, cooked briefly in a teaspoon of butter. Half a teaspoon of prepared mustard works to the same end. With Swiss cheese, a tablespoon of Parmesan rounds the flavor nicely, and a little dill weed complements it well. Either version can be further garnished with chopped parsley or peppers.

Cream Sauce with Onion

Even if you are going to use 3 tablespoons of flour for a very thick sauce, when you start with the sautéed onion it is easy to get away with using just 1 tablespoon of butter, because the onion will let the flour cook nicely without lumps. The onion supplies flavor too—a help with lower-fat sauces.

≥

Melt the butter as in the Cream Sauce recipe and add ¼ to 1 cup chopped onion. (Add garlic with the onion if you want to.) Sauté the onion in the butter very gently, until onion is soft and slightly golden—this takes some time and some stirring. Stir the flour into the sautéed onion and cook them together for 3 minutes, again stirring. Add milk and proceed in the usual way, bringing the milk to a boil—more stirring—and then simmer gently to enhance and marry the flavors if you have time. Puree if you like.

Cream Sauce without Butter

A cream sauce made without butter isn't really a sauce, but it can make a working base for cheese sauces or sauces with other very flavorful additions. If it lumps up on you, blend it.

≥

Toast flour lightly in a dry pan, then add the milk and boil to thicken. The flour needs toasting or it will taste raw, but if you toast it very much, the sauce will get brown. The more the flour is toasted, the less it will thicken your sauce. You can brown the flour and use this method to make brown gravy—a flavorful way to go—but you will need twice as much flour for the thickness you want.

For creamy sauces, you can also use corn flour (untoasted); or thicken milk with cornstarch, as suggested in the Buttermilk Sauces on the next page. As with the above, this makes a working base; it isn't flavorful enough to be a sauce on its own.

Buttermilk Sauces

Here is a genuinely satisfying alternative sauce. Good buttermilk has a taste reminiscent of sour cream, and in sauces this works very nicely, whether you make a normal cream sauce (using buttermilk instead of milk) or the cornstarch version below. If you use flour, the sauce will stand up better to reheating. The cornstarch version is a little quicker because you don't have to cook cornstarch before adding the liquid, as you do flour. If you prefer, you can use arrowroot instead of cornstarch, but arrowroot sauces can become gluey.

BASIC SAUCE

1 cup cold buttermilk
1 tablespoon cornstarch
2 teaspoons shoyu, to taste

For a medium sauce, mix ingredients and bring to boil in a heavy skillet. Use a spiral whisk or a fork and keep stirring vigorously as you bring the sauce to a boil. Let it simmer gently to thicken. It will curdle, but don't panic: as you stir, it will smooth out and come back together.

This quietly tangy sauce can stand on its own with anything interesting or flavorful—potatoes, say, or a pasta dish that has tasty vegetables in it and sesame crumbs or cheese on top.

Stroganoff Sauce

1 cup buttermilk
1 tablespoon cornstarch

1 small onion, chopped
(1 clove garlic)
1 tablespoon butter
1/3–1 1/2 cups mushrooms, sliced

1/4 teaspoon salt
 or 1 tablespoon shoyu
black pepper

Combine buttermilk and cornstarch and set aside. Sauté onion and garlic in butter until soft. Crush the garlic with a fork. Stir in mushrooms and cook just until tender. Remove mushrooms and juices from the pan and pour in the buttermilk mixture. Stir and cook until thickened, then return mushrooms and their juices to the pan. Season with salt (or shoyu) and pepper. This really tastes like a sour cream sauce, even with only a few mushrooms.

Tomato-Buttermilk Sauce 🍵

This delicious sauce is well received by the younger set. Its fruity, cheesy taste is especially good on noodles. Great for vegetables too.

&

Mix buttermilk and cornstarch and set aside. Sauté onion and garlic in oil. Crush garlic with a fork. Add tomato paste and basil, then buttermilk mixture. Bring to a boil, stirring, and cook until thick and smooth.

Makes 1 cup.

1 cup buttermilk
1 tablespoon cornstarch

½–1 small onion, chopped
(1 clove garlic)
2 teaspoons oil or butter

2 tablespoons tomato paste
½ teaspoon basil

Sunshine Sauce 🍵

Sauté onions in oil just until soft. Add turmeric and cook gently for a minute.

Stir cold buttermilk into cornstarch, then add to the spiced onions and bring to a boil, stirring. Cook and stir until smooth. Stir in the cheese, and when it has warmed enough to melt into the sauce, check to see if salt is wanted. Just before serving, stir in the coriander leaves if you have them.

A lovely piquant sauce for vegetables, especially those that are a little sweet, like broccoli.

2 green onions with tops,
chopped
2 teaspoons oil
⅛ teaspoon turmeric

1 cup buttermilk
1 tablespoon cornstarch

1 tablespoon grated
Parmesan cheese
(1 tablespoon chopped
fresh coriander leaves)

Tangy Cheese Sauce 🍵

Mix the buttermilk and cornstarch and stir while you bring to a boil. Simmer to smooth and thicken. Stir in cheeses and check for salt. Good additions: dill weed with Swiss cheese; chopped parsley with anything. Very good on greens, any of the cole family (broccoli, cauliflower, kale, etc.), on green beans, or even on toast.

HUNGARIAN SAUCE: Halve an onion lengthwise and slice it crosswise paper-thin. Sauté in butter or oil until golden. Set the onion aside while you prepare the sauce above, with or without the cheese. When the sauce is smooth, stir in the onions. Garnish the final serving liberally with paprika.

1 cup buttermilk
1 tablespoon cornstarch

½ cup cottage cheese
¼ cup grated sharp cheese
(but not cheddar)

Potato Dill Sauce

½ onion, chopped
1 clove garlic
1 tablespoon oil or butter
1 cup vegetable stock
1 potato, cubed
1 teaspoon dill weed

½ teaspoon salt, to taste
black pepper
1 tablespoon chopped parsley

Excellent on any winter greens: broccoli, Swiss chard, brussels sprouts, kale. This sauce, and Cheddy (below), are so low in fat that you can use rather a lot without getting too much. Both are good thinned with broth or milk to make soup.

৯

Sauté onion and garlic in oil. Add stock, potato, and dill weed. Cook partially covered until potato is soft, then puree. Add seasonings and parsley. Thin with stock or milk if desired.

Makes 2½ cups.

CHEDDY SAUCE: A delicious sauce that seems very rich and cheesy, even when you don't include the cheese!

৯

Follow the directions for the sauce above, except that when the onion is nearly done, add ½ to 1 teaspoon chili powder and cook about 1 minute. Add a small carrot, cut up, to the cooking vegetables. Omit dill weed.

Puree. Stir in ¼ cup grated cheddar cheese and check salt.
Makes 2¾ cup.

Mushroom Sauce

½ onion, chopped
1 clove garlic
1 tablespoon oil or butter
1 cup sliced mushrooms
3 tablespoons flour, toasted
1–1½ cups water
1 tablespoon shoyu
½ teaspoon molasses
¼ teaspoon savory
¼ teaspoon thyme
dash pepper

Sauté onions and garlic in oil or butter until soft. Mash the garlic with a fork. Add the mushrooms and simmer 5 minutes over low heat. Stir in the flour and add water, shoyu, and molasses. Cook, stirring, until thickened. Season with herbs and spices. Adjust to taste.

Makes 1 cup thick or 1½ cups medium.

Wickedly Good Sauce

Sauté onion in oil with the whole garlic. When the onion is tender, crush the garlic with a fork. Add the ginger and pepper and cook gently a minute more.

Stir in the peanut butter and shoyu, then water and celery leaves. Stir until smooth; then simmer about 5 minutes.

Add the tofu and cashews and heat through. Serve over steamed vegetables.

Makes ¾ to 1 cup.

¼ onion, chopped
1 teaspoon oil
1 clove garlic
½ teaspoon minced ginger
¼ green pepper

1 tablespoon peanut butter
1 tablespoon shoyu
½ cup water (or more)
2 tablespoons celery
*   leaves, chopped*

¼ pound firm tofu, cubed
2 tablespoons toasted
*   cashew pieces*

Yogurt Sauce

Serve this simple, surprisingly delicious sauce cold, at room temperature, or *gently* heated. Don't boil! Very good on vegetables, with falafel in Pocket Bread, or as a dip for raw vegetables. Makes a tasty dressing for potato salad too.

Sauté onion in oil. Toast sesame seeds in another skillet, stirring often to keep them from burning. Put all ingredients in blender or food processor and puree until smooth. Thin with additional yogurt or buttermilk if desired.

Makes 1 to 1½ cups.

1 chopped onion
1 tablespoon oil

¼ cup sesame seeds

1 tablespoon lemon juice
⅛ teaspoon salt
dash pepper
½–1 cup yogurt

Tomato Sauce

1/2 onion, chopped
1 clove garlic
2 tablespoons oil

1 small carrot, grated
2 tablespoons chopped
    green pepper
1 bay leaf
1/2 teaspoon oregano
1/2 teaspoon thyme
1 teaspoon basil
2 tablespoons chopped
    fresh parsley
2 cups tomatoes,
    coarsely chopped
1 six-ounce can tomato paste
1 teaspoon salt
1/8 teaspoon pepper
(1/4 teaspoon honey)

One of our most praised recipes. Use vegetable broth to thin it to the right consistency for spaghetti, or use it "as is" for dishes like pizza.

Fresh tomatoes are wonderful, of course, but if they aren't in season, use canned. (Check the label to avoid added salt and sugar.)

ᶻᵃ

Sauté onion and garlic clove in oil until onion is soft. Crush garlic with a fork.

Add carrot, green pepper, bay leaf, and herbs. Stir well, then add the tomatoes, tomato paste, and seasonings. Simmer 15 minutes. Remove the bay leaf.

Makes about 3 cups.

VARIATIONS

MEXICAN SAUCE: When onion is nearly done, stir in 1 teaspoon cumin and 1 teaspoon chili powder, or to taste. Increase oregano to 1 teaspoon.

ITALIAN SAUCE: Add a pinch of fennel. Increase oregano to 1 teaspoon.

Quick Spicy Tomato Sauce

1/2 cup chopped shallot
    or red onion
2 cloves garlic
1 tablespoon oil
1 tablespoon coriander
    powder
1 teaspoon cumin
1/4 teaspoon turmeric
1/2 teaspoon salt

3 cups chopped tomatoes

Sauté shallot or onion with whole garlic cloves until soft. Add spices and continue cooking and stirring for a minute or so, until spices are fragrant and onion begins to brown. Stir in the tomatoes, cover, and cook gently at least until tomatoes have turned to liquid. Force through food mill or sieve.

Makes 2 cups.

Good Gravy

Delicious, rich-tasting gravy, brown and fragrant with or without the mushrooms. If you cook beans for Soy Spread, you'll have plenty of the makings: the thick broth strained off after the beans are tender. Perfect with potatoes or on grain, even on vegetables.

ஓ

Toast and stir the flour in a dry pan until it is quite brown. Remove the flour and sauté the onion in oil, adding garlic and mushrooms if desired. Mash the garlic with a fork. Stir in the toasted flour, then the stock. Bring to a boil and simmer for a few minutes, adding the salt, marjoram, and pepper. Check the seasonings. Thin with water, broth, or more soy stock if desired.
  Makes 1 to 2 cups.

¼ cup whole wheat flour
1 small onion, chopped
(1 or more whole cloves garlic)
(¼ to 1 cup mushrooms, sliced)
1–2 tablespoons oil

1 cup soy stock (cooking water from soybeans)
½ teaspoon salt
½ teaspoon marjoram
black pepper

YEAST BUTTER We were going to let this sinfully rich sauce slink into oblivion with this edition, and no doubt it deserves the fate. But its advocates insist that Yeast Butter alone has made life possible on many a day. So here it is, just on the QT: the "health food" of the sixties.
  Melt a cube of (yes) margarine (½ cup). Add 2 tablespoons torula yeast and stir. Drizzle over broccoli or summer or winter squash; or let it cool and use on your toast the next day. Phew.

Lemon Butter

This is one of the nicest things that could happen to a pile of fresh, steamed asparagus spears. Try it on carrots, too, and broccoli, but use a light hand. It's rich.

ஓ

Juice the lemon and zest half of the peel. Melt the butter and pour it into a small blender jar along with the lemon juice and peel. Blend smooth and fluffy.
  Makes about ⅓ cup.

1 lemon, well scrubbed
¼ cup butter

Heartier Dishes

In this section are one-dish meals, international delicacies, casseroles—generally, fanciful or traditional preparations that are definitely greater than the sum of their parts. These are the recipes you pull out when you are stumped, when the refrigerator is full of leftovers, or when wary nonvegetarian relatives are coming to dinner. This section in particular really highlights the marvelous good fortune of today's vegetarian cook, who has access to such an array of ethnic cuisines that the possibilities are endless.

In their traditional form, many of these dishes are loaded with calories and fat. We have reduced butter, eggs, and cheese wherever possible, and substituted low-fat milk products. These dishes are unquestionably special, but they will let you walk away from the kitchen with a clear conscience—and from the table with clear arteries.

Whole-Grain Pasta

Whole-grain pasta is available everywhere now, and you can use it anywhere you used to use white-flour pasta, giving all the advantages of whole grain over white. If it is made from normal hard red wheat, the color of the noodles is a light brown. This makes tasty spaghetti and lasagna, and the ribbon noodles are very good. It usually needs longer cooking than its paler counterparts.

But just as hard red wheat is good for bread, and soft white wheat (the grains themselves are white, not red) good for pastry flour, there is durum wheat for pasta. (Semolina, from which the best white-flour pasta is made, is durum's refined version.) Durum wheat's grains are yellow instead of red, so it makes noodles that are a pale creamy-golden color—something that seems to reassure those who are new to whole-grain pastas. The noodles keep their shape well, and they are tender and mellow in taste. There *are* some who object to red-wheat whole wheat pasta, but nobody has anything but praise for durum whole wheat pasta. Try it—and if you make your own pasta, ask for whole wheat durum flour; you won't believe the difference there.

Pasta-making is challenging fun when you are just learning, and easy fun once you have mastered the art. There are pasta-making machines plain and fancy now, and if you hanker for exotic varieties or like to serve noodles often, they are a bargain. We have the oldest, simplest kind of machine, and use it frequently for some of the dishes that follow. Store-bought noodles are perfectly adequate substitutes, however, so if you are thrifty with your time, don't pass up the noodle recipes just because they say to make your own.

Buckwheat noodles deserve special mention. Their assertive flavor is an old favorite in Japan, but new to many of us in this country. If you get the 100 percent buckwheat flour noodles, expect them to be very fragile and *very* flavorful. For a milder-flavored noodle that is more resilient, look for a mixture of buckwheat and wheat flours. Serve them with Chinese Vegetables or in miso soup, or just stir into the cooked, drained noodles a cup or so of stir-fried vegetables like onion, peas, celery, or cauliflower; add shoyu and a sprinkling of sesame seeds.

Cooking Noodles

Cook noodles uncovered in a *big* pan with 1 quart of briskly boiling water and 1 teaspoon salt for each ¼ pound of dry noodles. Adding oil to the water helps keep the pot from boiling over, but isn't necessary if there is enough water and you keep it boiling. How long it takes will depend on the thickness of the pasta: 5 minutes for very thin, 20 minutes for thick! There are classic tests, including throwing the noodles against the wall (if it sticks, it is done); but the best is to bite a piece. There should be a trace of resistance to the teeth—*al dente*, as the Italians say. Drain the noodles, keeping them wet. No need to rinse unless they're to be used in a salad. Serve—or at least sauce—at once.

As a rule of thumb for a main dish, allow ½ pound of dry noodles and about 1 cup of sauce (depending on the sauce) for 4 people.

½ pound raw noodles = 4 cups cooked, approximately.

Homemade Noodles

It is easy to make good noodles, and in fact, fresh homemade noodles are as much better than the store-bought kind as your own bread is better than store-bought. If you are content with simple ribbon noodles, you need no more equipment than a rolling pin, a knife, and a table, and that's a good place to start.

Including whole eggs in your pasta adds a rich flavor, and noodles are surely one of the more delicious ways to eat eggs. Egg helps noodles hold their shape; to lower the fat and cholesterol, egg white serves this purpose as well as whole eggs. For simple noodling with a flavorful sauce—spaghetti, for example—the egg is completely unnecessary; and once you are adept at making noodles, even Canneloni and other ambitious performances can be achieved perfectly well without eggs.

ও৯

**FOR FOUR CUPS
COOKED NOODLES**

*1½ cups fine whole
    wheat flour
1 teaspoon salt
2 eggs
2 tablespoons water*

O R

*1½ cups fine whole
    wheat flour
1 teaspoon salt
¾ cup medium-hot water*

Measure the flour and salt and mix them in a bowl or on the tabletop, making a mound with a well in the center. Put the liquids (water and/or egg) in the well, and beginning in the center, mix them with flour to make a stiff dough—stiffer than bread dough. If it is too soft, you'll have trouble rolling them out, trouble moving them around, and trouble drying. If it is too stiff, however, there is a lot more work for you in rolling—so don't aim for a rock.

Knead the dough until it is supple, about 10 minutes. Large batches take more time. For easier rolling, cover the ball of dough after kneading and let it rest for about an hour. Use your rolling pin (if you don't have a machine) to roll the dough thin. If you are making more than just a small amount, keep the part of the dough you are not actually working on covered up so that it doesn't dry out. Use as much flour on the board (or with the machine) as you need to keep the dough from sticking—no harm done by that. In fact, as you come to the finishing stages, keep the noodles floury; they won't be likely to stick together.

Cut into ribbons or whatever shape suits your recipe. By hand, the little zig-zag rolling cutters make life easier in this department (even a pizza cutter is better than a knife). Cook at once, or let them rest a couple of hours; or dry thoroughly on cookie sheets, after which they will keep for weeks if stored in an airtight container kept in a cool place. Fresh is best of all, though. (Quaintly appealing as wooden chairbacks draped with drying noodles may be, we haven't found the practice very useful. If the noodles are thin enough to be tender, they are also fragile enough to break.)

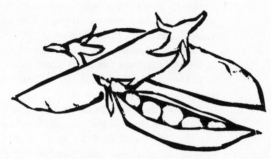

Hungarian Noodles

This delicious noodle dish is one of our longtime favorites. For everyday, we use vegetables on the sweet side—diced carrots, green beans, broccoli—but this dish really rises to magnificence with artichoke hearts (or asparagus), tiny fresh peas, and lots of coriander leaves.

Cut the onion into thin slivers and sauté in the butter until soft. Add the flour and cook, stirring, for 2 minutes. Stir in the buttermilk and cheeses and gently heat just until the mixture comes to a boil.

Preheat oven to 350°F.

Cook the noodles and drain them. Stir them and the vegetables (and coriander, if desired) into the sauce. Put into a greased baking dish and bake about 15 to 20 minutes, until bubbly.

Serves 4.

1 large onion
2 tablespoons butter
¼ cup whole wheat flour
2½ cups thick buttermilk
2 cups low-fat cottage cheese
¼ cup grated Parmesan cheese

noodles to make 2 cups cooked (¼ pound raw)
1½ cups cooked diced vegetables

(¼ cup chopped coriander leaves)

Vermicelli Florentine

1 large onion
1 tablespoon butter

3 medium red-ripe tomatoes
2/3 cup small peas
1–2 bunches spinach
   (12 oz; 3–4 quarts of
   leaves)

2¼ oz thin whole
   wheat vermicelli or
   linguine

½ cup buttermilk
2 teaspoons cornstarch
1–2 teaspoons shoyu
   or ¼ teaspoon salt

(grated Parmesan, if desired)

This is a delicate, satisfying dish that can be exceptional with excellent tomatoes and homemade noodles. As written, it makes a light meal for two; if you want to double the recipe, use a wide dutch oven instead of a skillet.

Cut the onion in half and slice paper-thin. Use a large, heavy skillet to sauté the onion in the butter, keeping heat low and stirring very frequently until the onion is golden. If the pan begins to brown, turn the onion out, wash the pan, add a little more butter, and resume. When the onion is soft and evenly cooked, remove from heat and set aside.

Prepare the tomatoes by removing seed and juice (and the peel, if you've a mind to). Cut into 1″ chunks.

Put water on to boil for the pasta. Wash and stem the spinach. Cut leaves into ¼″ strips.

Remove the onion from the pan, and with the golden film remaining in the cool pan, stir the buttermilk, cornstarch, and shoyu or salt together. Bring to a boil, stirring all the while. It will curdle and then come together into a smooth sauce. Add tomatoes and peas. Heat gently.

Add 1 teaspoon salt to the boiling noodle water and then add the noodles. Start stirring the spinach gently into the sauce and tomato mixture. When noodles are done, drain and stir them in also, working to get the spinach and noodles evenly dispersed. (A couple of oversized forks are useful here.) Taste for salt. Add cheese if desired and serve *at once*.

Serves 2 handily with salad, French Bread, and dessert.

Canneloni

These are large homemade noodles with a delicately flavored cheese filling. The saving grace of this admittedly time-consuming marvel (wait till you taste it!) is that it can be done in several steps ahead of time. The whole dish can be assembled early and baked later.

To make the filling, combine Parmesan, mozzarella, and cottage cheese or ricotta with 1 beaten egg, nutmeg, and ¼ cup of the cream sauce. Reserve remaining cream sauce for topping.

Wash spinach and steam briefly to wilt. Drain well and chop fine. Combine with cheese mixture and refrigerate.

To prepare noodles, mix flour and salt together and place in a mound on a flat surface. Make a well in the mound and drop in the 2 unbeaten eggs and the water. Use your fingers to work these ingredients together swiftly and knead well until smooth. This will take about 10 minutes. Cover the dough and let it rest 10 minutes before rolling it out.

Bring 3 quarts of water to a boil in a wide, shallow pan, and add a teaspoon of salt and a tablespoon of oil to keep the noodles from sticking together as they cook.

Divide dough into two balls. On a floured surface roll dough out paper-thin, turning it around and over frequently. Keep turning and rolling dough until it's about ¹⁄₁₆″ thick; or roll with a pasta-making machine at the second-thinnest setting.

Cut dough into ten 4″ × 6″ rectangles and drop a few at a time into simmering water. Keep pushing the noodles back under the water. When the noodles are tender, remove with slotted spoon. Put them carefully on a wet baking sheet.

Preheat oven to 350°F.

Fill noodles with a generous ¼ cup of filling each and roll them up. Place seam-side down in a greased casserole. Spoon the remaining cream sauce on top and dribble tomato sauce over all. Bake for 20 minutes, then sprinkle with parsley.

Serves 4 to 6.

FILLING

¾ cup grated Parmesan
    cheese
½ cup grated mozzarella
    cheese
2½ cups low-fat cottage
    cheese and/or ricotta
1 egg
¼ teaspoon nutmeg
1 cup medium Cream Sauce
    (page 242) seasoned with
    1 bay leaf and a pinch
    of nutmeg

1 bunch spinach

NOODLES

1¾ cups whole wheat flour
½ teaspoon salt
2 unbeaten eggs
4 tablespoons water

TOPPING

reserved cream sauce
1 cup Tomato Sauce
    (page 248)

½ cup chopped parsley

Lasagna al Forno 🍲

¾ pound whole wheat
  or whole wheat–soy
  lasagna noodles
6 cups Tomato Sauce,
  Italian Style (page 248)

2 cups cottage cheese
3 cups grated mozzarella
  or Swiss cheese (10 oz)
1–3 bunches spinach
½ cup grated Parmesan
  cheese
¾ cup chopped toasted
  walnuts or almonds

Perhaps the most favorite of all our casseroles, this lasagna is lighter than most but plenty fancy for company, and a sure hit even with nonvegetarian guests.

The spinach can be added either raw or cooked. If raw, one large bunch will be enough: wash, shake dry, and chop fine. Cooking ahead lets you use a larger amount—three big bunches or even more. Cook very briefly with only the water that clings to the leaves, drain well; chop fine.

For everyday dinners, the greens can be Swiss chard or even nippier ones like kale. Any kind of cheese is fine. In fact, crumbled tofu can be good, provided your sauce is very flavorful. A topping of bread crumbs tossed with a little olive oil is delicious and keeps the top from drying out. You can lower the fat further by cutting back on the cheese and using less oil in the sauce.

🍃

Cook noodles in a very large pan of boiling, salted water until *almost* tender: they will cook more in the oven, absorbing liquid from the sauce as they do, and if they are slightly undercooked at this point, they'll hold together better while you're assembling the dish. After draining the noodles, it can be helpful to spread them out on a towel or waxed paper, or submerge them in cold water.

Grease a 9″ × 13″ × 2½″ baking dish. Spread a thin layer of sauce in the bottom, and then a layer of noodles, lengthwise. Keep the best of the noodles for the top and use broken ones in the middle. Each layer of noodles should lie crosswise to the one below it.

On the layer of noodles, spread the first layer of filling: one half the cottage cheese, one third of the nuts, one fourth of the Parmesan; then a coating of sauce. Layer noodles again, then the spinach and most of the mozzarella, and sauce. More noodles, another cheese and nuts layer, and your prettiest noodles across the top. Add sauce and the rest of the nuts and cheese for the top.

Bake at 350°F for 30 to 45 minutes (if your ingredients were hot, the shorter time will be enough); then let stand 10 minutes before cutting—otherwise it will be too runny to hold together, and too hot to eat.

Serves 8.

Poppyseed Noodles

Quick and zippy. To make a dairy-free version, replace the Mock Sour Cream with Tofu Sour Cream (page 241).

❧

Cook noodles in boiling salted water until tender and drain.
Preheat oven to 350°F.
Combine Mock Sour Cream, poppy seeds, and noodles. Place in greased 9″ × 13″ baking dish. Sprinkle with Parmesan and paprika if desired.
Bake about 20 minutes.
Makes 4 servings.

½ pound whole wheat ribbon noodles
1½ cups Mock Sour Cream (page 240)
1 tablespoon poppy seeds
½ teaspoon salt
(grated Parmesan cheese)
(paprika)

Lazy Pirogi

A scrumptious cabbage dish to serve over whole wheat noodles. Many people who find cabbage hard to digest have no trouble with sauerkraut—the pickling fermentation has done some of the work already! Buy sauerkraut in jars rather than cans to prevent the possibility of getting lead from the can's seam. We suggest also that when you use a brand you haven't tried before, taste it before using. The salt level may be different from what you expect. If it's too salty, you can drain and rinse before using, if necessary—but often it will be going over potatoes (or noodles, as here), when it might supply the salt for the whole dish.

❧

Chop onion, celery, and mushrooms. Starting with onion, sauté in oil until onions are tender. Add ½ cup hot water and simmer for 10 minutes.
Meanwhile, cook noodles until tender in unsalted boiling water; drain.
Stir together sautéed vegetables with sauerkraut and noodles. Heat through and serve.
Makes 4 servings.

1 large onion
1 stalk celery
6 fresh mushrooms
2 tablespoons oil
1 cup (packed) drained sauerkraut
¼ pound whole wheat ribbon noodles

Sandy's Macaroni

1 small bunch scallions,
  sliced thin
1 or 2 garlic cloves, minced
1 bell pepper, diced (red,
  green, or some of each)
½ cup sliced mushrooms
1 stalk celery, diced
2 tablespoons butter
¾ teaspoon salt
dash black pepper
¼ cup chopped parsley

¼ cup whole wheat flour
2 cups low-fat milk
(2 tablespoons grated
  Parmesan cheese)
½ pound whole wheat
  macaroni or noodles

This is a very light, low-fat alternative to macaroni and cheese—one we serve often. Toasting the flour separately lets you use about half the fat you'd need otherwise. The long, slow simmering draws the flavors of the vegetables out into the sauce.

❧

Sauté scallions, garlic, bell pepper, mushrooms, and celery in butter in a heavy pan for 5 minutes; then add 1 cup of boiling water, salt, pepper, and parsley. Bring to a boil, reduce heat, and simmer covered for 20 to 30 minutes.

Meanwhile, toast flour in a small, dry skillet over low heat, stirring constantly, for 5 minutes or so—just until it starts to smell toasty. It shouldn't change color.

Add some of the vegetable–water mixture to the flour, stirring to avoid lumps; then add this back to the pot along with the milk (and cheese, if desired). Bring just to a boil; then reduce heat and simmer uncovered for 10 or 15 minutes, until sauce is creamy and reduced to about 2½ cups. Cook pasta; drain and mix with sauce. Serve immediately.

Makes 4 generous servings.

Blini 🥟

2 teaspoons active dry yeast
  (1 packet, ¼ oz or 7 g)
¼ cup warm water

½ cup buckwheat flour
½ cup whole wheat flour
1 cup milk, lukewarm
1 teaspoon honey
2 tablespoons oil
¼ teaspoon salt
2 egg whites and one yolk,
  beaten slightly

These are buckwheat crepes, served in Russia (long ago, at any rate) during the week before Lent. Serve with Mock Sour Cream, chopped hard-boiled egg, and chopped sweet onions. Very good alongside steamed beets or cabbage.

❧

Dissolve yeast in water. In a medium-size bowl, stir together buckwheat and whole wheat flour, milk, honey, oil, salt, eggs, and yeast mixture. Beat until smooth, cover, and let rise in warm place free from drafts until bubbly—about 1 hour.

Stir down. Heat a 6″ crepe pan or griddle, lightly oiled, until a drop of water dances on its surface. Drop batter by spoonfuls onto griddle, spreading it around by tilting the pan. If batter seems thick, more like pancake than crepe batter, add a bit more milk to thin it down. Cook crepes until top is beginning to look dry, then turn over and brown on second side. Keep blini warm in a damp towel placed in a warm oven until ready to serve.

Makes about 12.

Crepes

Crepes can turn nearly any vegetable dish into an event: not just creamed spinach but Ratatouille, or asparagus with grated Parmesan, or even more mundane choices like chopped broccoli and cauliflower, nicely cooked and seasoned. Top with a light cheese or mushroom sauce. Add tiny peas to nearly any filling if you need to make it go farther.

As soon as you roll them up in a crepe, vegetables become interesting to children (and others) who might otherwise not find them so, and since the batter is so easy to prepare, and nutritious, that's a bargain. Keep extra batter in the refrigerator to use in the next couple of days. If it turns dark on top, just shake the jar and forge ahead.

*1 cup milk (or half
water, half milk)*
*¾ cup whole wheat flour
(finely ground or with
bran sifted out)*
2 eggs or 3 egg whites
½ teaspoon salt

❧

Put all crepe ingredients in blender and mix on low speed, or use an electric or rotary beater. For best results let batter stand an hour, or refrigerate overnight.

Use a 7″ skillet with sloped sides, or a nonstick pan or seasoned griddle. Heat over medium-high flame as for pancakes. If there's any chance of sticking, use a little butter or oil spread thin with a paper napkin between pours.

Pour a scant ¼ cup of batter on the pan. Tilt pan as you pour so the batter spreads evenly on the bottom. Brown the bottom of the crepe lightly, and as the top becomes visibly dry—about 1 minute—turn it over and cook the second side until it too is lightly browned. Let each one cool, and overlap them on a platter. The pretty spotted side is the traditional outside for the crepe. (If you think the crepes could be thinner, add more milk or turn the pan faster.)

Makes about 12.

DAIRY-FREE CREPES

Both the egg and the milk make a significant contribution to the flavor and character of crepes, but you can produce a very satisfactory crepe without them, using the ingredients listed here. (If you really want *delicious* non-dairy crepes, though, learn to make Dosas, page 97.)

*1 cup finely ground
whole wheat flour*
1½ cups water
½ teaspoon baking powder
½ teaspoon salt
1 tablespoon oil

❧

Beat or blend very well. Follow the directions for pouring given above.

Blintzes

1 recipe Crepes

CHEESE FILLING
2 cups baker's cheese,
  ricotta cheese, or
  low-fat cottage cheese
1 tablespoon brown sugar
1 tablespoon melted butter
½ teaspoon salt
2 tablespoons chopped
  toasted almonds
1 tablespoon raisins
(Add ½ teaspoon cinnamon
  or ½ teaspoon vanilla
  or 1 tablespoon lemon
  juice.)
OR
(Substitute a dash of pepper
  and ½ teaspoon paprika
  for sugar and raisins.)

We like to serve cheese-filled blintzes with yogurt and apple-sauce. Tangy Cheese Sauce (page 245) goes well with either the savory or the simple vegetable fillings. Mock Sour Cream (page 240) is a fine topping for all three versions.

Prepare crepes as described in the recipe above, but *do not cook them on the second side, and don't stack them.*

Combine filling ingredients. Preheat oven to 400°F.

Put 2 big tablespoons of filling on the cooked side of each crepe. Turn in opposite sides and then roll up. Place seam-side down in a well-buttered baking pan and bake for 20 minutes. After the first 10 or 15 minutes, when the bottom is brown, turn to brown the other side. Some filling may escape from the crepes, but they will be just as good. Instead of baking the blintzes, you may brown them on a nonstick or iron skillet if you prefer.

Each filling recipe makes enough for about 12 crepes, which will serve 4 to 6.

SIMPLE VEGETABLE FILLING FOR BLINTZES

Prepare 1½ cups of your favorite combination of vegetables. Cut them quite small or grate them. Cook and season to taste. Try any of these:

Creamed spinach and celery
Asparagus and green onion
Green pepper and eggplant or okra
Shredded cabbage, carrots, and onions
Fresh corn, green onion, and parsley

Sauté onions in oil just lightly. Stir in green beans. Add stock and bring to a boil. Simmer for 10 minutes or more, until beans are tender. If there is too much liquid, drain and save for the sauce topping.

Combine beans and onions with remaining ingredients. Cool until ready to fill the blintzes.

3 small green onions, sliced fine
1 tablespoon oil
1 cup finely cut green beans
¼ cup vegetable stock or water
½ cup baker's cheese, ricotta cheese, or low-fat cottage cheese
½ teaspoon salt
1 tablespoon grated Parmesan cheese
½ cup well-cooked green split peas

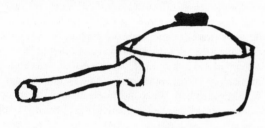

Spinach Crepes

This dressy, delicious dish is always well received, and because it can be prepared in stages ahead, it's great for special occasions. For every day, though, unless you cut some corners along the way, it is not a low-fat presentation. There *are* corners to cut: use whites instead of one or both yolks in the crepes; make a lower-fat cream sauce (we often use the Cream Sauce with Onion here, keeping the butter to a bare minimum.) Balance the meal by serving low-fat foods alongside: baked yams or winter squash, for example, and fruit salad for dessert.

1 recipe Crepes
1 double recipe Creamed Spinach (page 214)
1 cup thin Cream Sauce (or more) (page 242)
(grated Parmesan or Swiss cheese)
(nutmeg)

A little lemon zest blended into the crepe batter gives a nice lift to the flavor.

🍃

Preheat oven to 350°F. Grease a 9″ × 13″ baking dish. Place a generous ⅓ cup of creamed spinach across the lower middle of each crepe, roll it into a cylinder, and place in the baking dish, making two rows of 6 each. Pour the sauce over the top, down the middle of the rows of crepes—or, if you like plenty of sauce, thin the sauce with more milk and cover the crepes completely. Sprinkle with cheese and nutmeg, if desired.

Bake about 15 minutes—long enough to heat through. Makes about 12 crepes, enough for 4 to 6 people.

Piroshki

DOUGH

*4 cups whole wheat bread
   flour, finely ground*
*2 cups whole wheat pastry
   flour*
2½ teaspoons salt

*2 teaspoons active dry yeast
   (1 packet, ¼ oz, 7g)*
½ cup warm water

1 teaspoon honey or sugar
2 cups buttermilk

more water as needed

This makes 20 each of 2 fillings. The piroshki are about 4″ across, with maybe 3 tablespoons of filling in each one. The dough makes a crust that, while not crispy like piecrust, is nevertheless not thickly bready, and doesn't toughen even if it sits awhile.

વ

Mix the flours and salt in a large bowl, making a well in the center. Dissolve the yeast in the warm water. Mix the sweetener into the buttermilk and pour it into the well in the flour. Stir the liquid in the well to make a batter consistency; then add the yeast and mix the whole together to form the dough. It should be very soft; so while you knead, use water on your hands to keep the dough from sticking, adding water to it in this way until you have a supple, well-kneaded ball. With the buttermilk and the pastry flour, the kneading time will be less than usual. Keep at it until the dough is smooth and elastic, though, or it will not have enough strength to perform its required feats.

Let the kneaded dough rise in a warm place, protected from drafts. If it is kept at 80°F, the dough will be ready in about 1½ hours. (You can let it rise slightly cooler and longer, but this dough will not tolerate a really long rise.) When a ½″ hole made with your wet fingertip does not fill in, deflate the dough. (Don't wait until your fingerpoke makes the dough sigh.) After deflating, let rise again as before. At the same temperature, the second rise will take about half as long.

Deflate the dough and round it into two or three balls, keeping them covered while you work. Roll very thin and cut into 5″ squares, using plenty of pastry flour on the board. If you're not the speediest worker, chill the dough that you aren't actually working with and do this part in stages. The easiest way by far to do the rolling is to use a pasta machine, if you have one; end with the next-to-thinnest setting.

Fill the squares as shown, or any way that strikes your fancy. If you have a ravioli cutter, you can cut and seal the edges nicely with that. Use about 3 tablespoons of filling for each. Put them on greased cookie sheets and bake in a preheated 375° oven for as long as it takes to brown the crust nicely—about 10 minutes. Since the filling is already cooked and contains no egg, you don't need to worry about cooking it. Nevertheless, the filling should be warm when you put it in so that the crust browns nicely.

FILLINGS

Any zesty mixture of vegetables, cut small and nicely cooked, is a candidate. The following combinations have worked well for us, either as they are or with white or any harmonious kind of bean in place of part of the potato.

ARTICHOKE FILLING

4 shallots, chopped
1 tablespoon oil or butter
1 garlic clove, minced

1 cup cooked mashed
 artichoke hearts and
 leaf scrapings
 (about 2 large or 4
 small artichokes)
2 cups mashed or diced
 cooked potato
1 cup fresh tender peas

1½ teaspoons salt
pepper to taste

ða

Sauté the shallots in oil or butter, stirring constantly until soft. Add the garlic about halfway. Stir in the other vegetables, and cook gently until the peas are hot through. Season to taste.

MUSHROOM FILLING

Substitute 1 cup sautéed mushrooms for artichoke hearts.

ASPARAGUS OR GREEN BEAN FILLING

1 bunch scallions
1 tablespoon olive oil

2 cups cooked diced
 asparagus
 (or green beans)
2 cups cooked mashed or
 diced potato
¼ cup chopped parsley or
 coriander leaves
 and/or ¼ cup grated
 Gruyère cheese

1¼ teaspoons salt
pepper to taste

ða

Sauté the scallions in the oil until soft. Add the other vegetables and heat until the parsley is wilted, if used. Add the cheese when the vegetables are hot. Season to taste.

SPINACH FILLING

1 small onion, chopped
1 tablespoon oil
¼ cup each chopped
 bell pepper, green and
 red, and celery
(1 green chili, with seeds
 removed, very finely minced
 or ½ teaspoon chili powder)

1 cup cooked, finely
 chopped spinach
2½ cups cooked potato
 (mashed or boiled)

½ cup grated cheddar cheese
1¼ teaspoons salt
pepper

ða

Sauté the onion in the oil, stirring. Add the green pepper, then the red pepper and celery. Add the chili, if desired. Cook until they are crispy-tender. Add the other vegetables and stir. When they are warm, stir in the cheese and salt and pepper.

Spanakopita 🍲

FILLING

2 or 3 bunches spinach
½ teaspoon salt
3 cups low-fat cottage cheese
3 eggs

DOUGH

2½ cups whole wheat
   flour (fine-ground is best)
1 teaspoon salt
1 cup warm water

½ cup melted butter

When Specially Honored Friends are offered whatever they want for supper, they almost always ask for Sultana's Spanakopita. There is a knack to making it, but it's a knack you'll be glad to have developed—and even before you've quite got it the results will be most acceptable.

You will need a pizza pan and a 4-foot piece of ¾" or 1" dowel to roll out the dough. If you have neither a pita pan nor a pizza pan, don't be daunted. Use pie plates or tins: one recipe will make two 9" or 10" pie-sized pitas. Divide the dough into *four* balls instead of two in the instructions below; and since your pitas will be smaller, you can use a rolling pin instead of the dowel to make the dough paper-thin.

🍃

Wash and dry the spinach and chop it fine. Sprinkle with salt and squeeze or wring to wilt it. Add the cottage cheese and eggs. Mix very well and set aside.

Sift the flour and save the bran for tomorrow morning's porridge. Mix flour, salt, and water, and knead briefly until you have a soft dough.

Divide dough into two balls, one larger than the other. Pat the larger ball flat and roll it into an 8" circle, using your dowel or rolling pin.

Now, beginning with the edge closest to you, roll the dough over the dowel as shown. Use the sifted flour as needed to keep dough from sticking. Start with your hands in the center and move them forward and backward, working outward toward the ends of the dowel. When your hands reach the edge of the dough, unroll it gently so that it is flat again. Turn the crust (larger now, but lopsided) a ⅛ turn, and repeat this rolling operation until the dough is very round, paper-thin, even, and 3 inches bigger all around than your pan. The tricky part is to do all this without making holes in the dough.

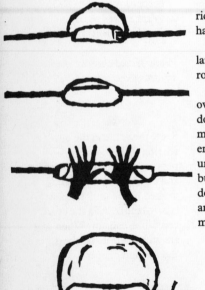

Grease your pan. Preheat oven to 400°F.

Place the dowel with the dough wrapped around it on one edge of the pan, and unroll the dough over the pan. Gently fold the excess edge of the crust in toward the center, so that it won't break while you're preparing the second crust.

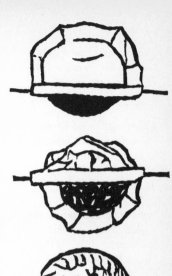

Now roll the smaller ball similarly, until it is slightly smaller than the other. Set it aside carefully.

Unfold the edges of the dough in the pan and spread with a tablespoonful or two of the melted butter. Put in the filling and drizzle again with a little butter. Place the second piece of dough over the top, leaving it loose with plenty of wrinkles. Pour half the remaining butter over the edges and fold the under-crust edge around the upper-crust edge as shown.

Drizzle the last of the butter over the top, particularly around the edges. Be sure to poke holes all over the top crust with a fork or a sharp paring knife.

Bake the pita on the bottom rack of the oven for 45 minutes, until just brown. Cover it with a towel and let it stand for 10 minutes before serving. Cut in wedges.

Serves 6 properly, though many of us could easily eat three pieces each.

Chard Pita 🍥

We're very fond of chard, which grows abundantly in our gardens. With a few changes, the Spanakopita recipe adapts very nicely. The crust is the same; here is the filling:

❧

Sauté green onions in oil in a large pan until soft. Mix with the chard. Combine all ingredients and mix well. Prepare crust and then fill and bake just as you would Spanakopita.

1 bunch green onions, chopped
1 tablespoon oil
4 quarts chopped chard leaves
3 cups low-fat cottage cheese
3 eggs
1 teaspoon salt
pinch pepper
¼ cup grated Parmesan or other sharp cheese

Pizza

2 teaspoons active dry yeast
    (1 packet, ¼ oz, or 7g)
1⅔ cups warm water
    (110°F)

4 cups whole wheat flour
¼ teaspoon black pepper
2 teaspoons salt

3 cups Tomato Sauce
    (page 248)
½ pound grated mozzarella,
    jack, Swiss, or other
    cheese
¼ cup Parmesan cheese

GARNISHES

pepper rings
sliced mushrooms
sliced olives
onion
crumbled bits of Soy Pâté,
    tofu, or Neat Balls

This recipe is a prototype, and you can vary it as you see fit. It makes two rather thin pizzas; if you like yours thicker, either halve the sauce and make only one, or double the dough and make two. The thicker version will take somewhat longer to bake. Be sure to let it rise after rolling out before you bake it. If you use sliced mushrooms on top, rubbing them with a *little* olive oil first makes a delectable difference.

❧

Dissolve yeast in the warm water and set aside. Mix the flour, pepper, and salt together, making a well in the center. Add the yeast liquid and mix together. The dough should be quite soft. Knead until silky and elastic. (Double dough will take double kneading, by the way.)

Cover and set in a warm, draft-free place to rise. You can adjust the rising times to suit you (see page 52); if you keep the dough in a warm spot, it will be ready to deflate in about an hour and a half. Carefully press the air from the dough and let it rise again. The second rise should take half the amount of time the first one did.

Preheat the oven to 375°F.

Press the twice-risen dough flat and divide in two. Form two balls and let them rest, covered, while you warm your sauce and gather cheeses and garnishes. Grease your pizza pans and dust them with cornmeal. Roll the dough into circles just a little bigger than your pizza pans (this takes some patience if the dough is good). Roll until the dough tenses up, then wait, then roll again. Take consolation from the fact that really elastic dough will rise better in the oven. Avoid forcing it though, that might crush and tear the structure of the dough.

Transfer the rolled-out dough to the pans. (If you have time, let it rest now another 15 to 20 minutes in its warm place; the bread will be lighter.) Spread the sauce on, add the garnishes, and pop the pizza in the oven. When the bread is delicately brown—about 10 to 15 minutes, depending on the oven—spread the cheeses and return to the oven until bubbly.

If you need only one pizza today, make the second completely except for the cheese; bake just until the bread is beginning to brown. Sprinkle with cheese, cool, and wrap in plastic and freeze to warm up when needed.

Use any size piece of bread dough, or else a slice of bread, a Pocket Bread, or an English Muffin. Arrange with thick slices of raw, red-ripe tomatoes, peppers, mushrooms, etc. Sprinkle with oregano, a little basil, and grated cheese. If you use bread dough, of course, the little pizza has to be baked; but with the other choices, just slip the pizza under the broiler until the cheese is melted.

A Pretty Corny Pizza

If you detect the hand of Analee the Summer Squash Queen —inventrix of Crookneck Chiffon Pie and other early-September wonders—you're right on the money. This one goes over very well with kids and other smart eaters.

❧

Cut squash in large chunks and steam until tender. Puree; you should have 2 cups. Mix honey, eggs, and oil with the puree. Combine the cornmeal, salt, and baking powder. Mix the dry ingredients and wet, stirring until smooth. Turn into a greased 12″ × 18″ baking pan or a large pizza pan (mixture should be about ¾″ deep) and bake 12 to 15 minutes, just until corn bread begins to pull in from the sides of the pan.

While corn bread is baking, sauté onion in olive oil along with chili powder, oregano, cumin, and coriander. Spread onion mixture across top of corn bread, then scatter tomato atop that. Sprinkle with basil, then cheese. Return to oven for 10 minutes.

Serves 6 generously.

CRUST

1¾ pounds summer squash
1 tablespoon honey
2 eggs, beaten
2 tablespoons oil

2¼ cups cornmeal
1 teaspoon salt
2 teaspoons baking powder

TOPPING

1 large onion, chopped
2 tablespoons olive oil
1 teaspoon chili powder
1 teaspoon oregano
1 teaspoon ground cumin
½ teaspoon ground
*   coriander seed*
3 large ripe tomatoes,
*   chopped*
1 teaspoon dried basil
1½ cups grated jack cheese

Good Shepherd's Pie

TOPPING

2 cups leftover mashed
potatoes
OR
3 medium potatoes,
¼ cup milk, and
½ teaspoon salt

pinch paprika

FILLING

1 onion, chopped big
1 tablespoon oil
1 pound broccoli
1 green pepper, diced
4 medium carrots, diced
½ teaspoon basil
1 bay leaf
¾ cup chopped fresh
tomatoes
or ¼ cup tomato paste
and ½ cup water

1 bunch spinach or Swiss
chard
1 teaspoon salt

Here's a happy home for leftovers. The vegetables will vary according to the season. A small amount of leftover lentil, pea, or bean soup may be stirred in with the vegetables to good advantage too.

❧

Unless you have leftover mashed potatoes, steam potato chunks or cook them in fast-boiling water until soft. Mash well, adding milk and salt. Save the potato water for breadmaking.

Cut broccoli into florets and stems. Peel and slice the stems in ¼″ rounds. Wash spinach thoroughly and cut into bite-size pieces.

Preheat oven to 350°F.

Sauté onion in oil. Add broccoli, green pepper, and carrots, then the basil and bay leaf. Stir well and add tomatoes. Bring to a boil, cover, turn heat to low, and simmer for 15 minutes or until vegetables are just tender. Stir in spinach. Add salt.

Put vegetables into a 9″ × 13″ baking dish. Spread potatoes over top and shake paprika over all. Bake for 10 or 15 minutes, until the potatoes are piping hot.

Serves 4 to 6.

Potato Carrot Kugel

A kugel is a pudding, and it comes in many forms. This delicious version is almost a meal in itself: serve with a green vegetable and salad and you're there.

❧

Preheat oven to 300°F.

Sauté onion in oil until well done, and add garlic. Add stock, carrots, and potatoes and cook for 3 minutes. Remove from heat and stir in eggs.

Mix together the flour, wheat germ, baking powder, and seasonings and add to vegetables. Pour into a greased baking dish and bake for 1 hour.

Serves 4 to 6.

1 onion, chopped
2 tablespoons oil
1 clove garlic, pressed
  or minced
³/₄ cup vegetable stock
  or water
1 cup grated carrots
  or 2 cups winter squash
3 cups grated
  potatoes
2 beaten eggs

¹/₄ cup whole wheat
  flour
¹/₄ cup wheat germ
1 teaspoon baking
  powder
pinch pepper
1¹/₂ teaspoons salt

Potato Poppers

So easy and so much loved, especially by the younger set.

❧

Preheat oven to 350°F.

Sauté onion and celery in oil. Combine all ingredients and form into 1½″ balls. Place on greased baking sheet and bake on the top rack of oven for about 20 minutes, until delicately browned.

Makes 12 balls.

¹/₂ onion, diced
1 celery stalk, diced
¹/₂ tablespoon oil
1¹/₄ cups mashed potato
1 cup cooked brown rice
¹/₄ cup tomato paste
¹/₂ teaspoon salt
¹/₂ cup whole-grain bread
  crumbs
¹/₄ cup grated Parmesan
  cheese

Cabbage Rolls Normande

FILLING

1 medium onion, chopped
  fine
1 tablespoon oil
1 clove garlic, minced
1 large stalk celery, diced
1 medium carrot, diced
1 teaspoon ground
  coriander seed
3 cups cooked brown rice
2 tablespoons shoyu
½ cup chopped toasted
  filberts or almonds

SAUCE

3 tablespoons whole wheat
  flour
2 cups apple juice
1 cup vegetable stock
  or water
¼ cup fresh lemon juice
zest of 1 lemon
½ teaspoon salt
½ cup raisins

12–14 large cabbage leaves
  (1 large cabbage)

Cabbage rolls are a traditional Eastern European favorite, but this version is an original (and mighty good) presentation. Vary the filling by using kasha instead of rice.

&

Make filling first: Sauté onion in oil until soft, then add garlic, celery, carrot, and coriander. Sauté briefly, then add ¼ cup water, bring to a boil and cover. Cook over low heat for 3 minutes, then stir in rice, shoyu, and nuts.

To make sauce, toast flour a minute or two in a skillet over low heat, stirring constantly, until it's just beginning to brown. Slowly add apple juice and stock or water, bring to a boil, and simmer until sauce thickens. Stir in lemon juice, peel, salt, and raisins.

Wash cabbage leaves carefully and steam them in a large pot over a steamer basket for no more than 3 minutes. With a small, sharp knife, remove the most inflexible central stem from each leaf (don't cut too high up into the leaf, though).

Preheat oven to 350°F.

Place about ¼ cup of filling on each leaf (less if the leaf is small) and roll the leaf around it into a fat little packet. Place the rolls in a 9″ × 13″ baking dish, pour sauce over them, and place in the oven. Bake covered for 30 minutes, and uncovered for another 10 or 15.

Makes about 12 to 14 rolls: serves 4 hungry eaters, 6 restrained ones.

Stuffed Chard Leaves 🍃

This dish is one of our very favorites.

☙

Preheat oven to 350°F.

Sauté onion in oil. Mix all ingredients except chard.

Wash and dry chard leaves and remove stems, including the fat part of the rib if it extends rigidly up into the leaf (select leaves that are not too "ribby"). Place 2 tablespoons or more of filling on the underside of the leaf, a third of the way from the bottom. Fold over the sides of the leaf and roll up into a square packet. Place seam-side down in a greased casserole. Cover and bake for about 30 minutes. Alternatively, steam the rolls in a steamer basket over boiling water until the leaves are tender, about 20 minutes. Bake any extra filling and serve with stuffed leaves.

Serves 6 to 8.

VARIATION
Stuff chard with Bulgar Wheat Pilaf (page 284) and serve with Sunshine Sauce (page 245).

1 onion, chopped
1 tablespoon oil
2½ cups cooked brown rice
1½ cups low-fat
    cottage cheese
1 egg, beaten
½ cup chopped parsley
¾ cup raisins
1 teaspoon dill weed
¾ teaspoon salt

16 large leaves Swiss chard

Simple Cheesy Bread Pudding 🍃

This is a standby for us, very useful when there is stale bread around. A flexible recipe which you can adjust as you like to suit the rest of the menu and the mood of the bread that wants using. (Sweet or fruity breads do better with a more dessert treatment, like the one on page 314.)

☙

Use part of the butter to grease an 8″ × 8″ pan and put the bread cubes into it. Mix the milk, egg, and cheese and pour them over the bread. Dot with the remaining butter. Bake in a moderate oven, about 350°F, until the custard is set and the top nicely brown.

Let it cool before you eat; it is incredibly hot when it comes out of the oven.

FANCIES
Use cheddar cheese and top with toasted sesame seeds.
Rye bread, especially sourdough, is particularly good with Swiss cheese. Add a sautéed onion and ½ cup chopped celery for a delicious casserole.

1 tablespoon butter
4 cups of cubed light bread
    (4–8 slices)
2 cups warm milk
1 egg, slightly beaten.
⅓–½ cup grated sharp
    cheese

Quiche 🍵

3 eggs, slightly beaten
2 cups warm milk
½ teaspoon salt
pinch each pepper
  and nutmeg
¾ cup grated Swiss cheese
1 teaspoon butter

piecrust (either Whole
  Wheat Piecrust, page
  324, or one of the
  lighter versions on
  the next page.)

TIMBALE
Omit crust; bake at 325°F,
set in a pan of very hot
water.

Quiche is not for every night, or even every *other* night, but recognizing what a beloved dish it is, we offer this relatively prudent version. It calls for half the cheese that's normally used, and low-fat milk in place of cream. It is shy one egg, too, and a mere teaspoon of butter replaces the usual generous dots on top (with *no* butter, a bothersome "skin" forms over the surface.) Use the Lighter Whole Wheat Piecrust recipe on the next page and enjoy thoroughly.

Quiches are favored for other reasons than their palatability. They are dependable, not tricky; they can wait; and they can be served hot, cold, or in between. The simplest version, made from just the ingredients listed, is perhaps the most delicate. Use a fine Gruyère cheese and you have a dish that can stand proudly anywhere the American Heart Association hasn't penetrated.

For a more complete meal, add a cup of nicely cooked, *well-drained* vegetables: spinach, asparagus, sautéed mushrooms, even zucchini. The recipe gives proportions for an 8″ pie shell, or 9″ with vegetables. Larger shells are possible: 10″, for example, or the deeper special quiche pans. To adapt the recipe, measure the capacity of your pan with water beforehand. Keep the 2:3 ratio of liquid to egg—it is the minimum for being sure the quiche will set up. As long as there are enough eggs to set the milk, you can increase the vegetables to two or more cups. Larger, especially deeper, quiches will take longer to bake. If the crust seems to be in danger of browning too much, cover it with a strip of aluminum foil.

🍃

Preheat oven to 350°F. Combine eggs, milk, salt, and pepper. (Use white pepper, or omit, with plain quiche.) Spread the cheese evenly in the bottom of the pie shell and pour the milk mixture over it. Sprinkle the top with nutmeg and dot with butter. Place pie plate on a cookie sheet and bake for half an hour, or until set. Remove when the outside is set and the middle couple of inches still jiggles if you tap the pan—quiche must stand for 10 or 15 minutes before it is cut, and in that time the center will set. Try not to overbake, as the texture will be less smooth.

Serves 6.

Lighter Whole Wheat Piecrust

Not the tender, flaky, buttery version for sure, but plenty good for all that.

৯

Stir dry ingredients together. Mix in oil and enough of the water to make the dough form a ball. Roll flat between sheets of waxed paper and lift into pan. Make decorative edge. Bake at 400°F for 10 minutes, or until slightly browned and crisp. Makes one 9" shell.

1 cup whole wheat pastry
flour
½ teaspoon salt
3 tablespoons oil
¼ cup water

Oat-Nut Crust

Preheat oven to 400°F.

Blend oats and walnuts in blender or food processor until the mixture is floury, with only a few visible oat pieces. Turn into bowl and mix in water and salt (try just 2 tablespoons of water at first, and add the third only if needed to hold dough together). Press into 9" or 10" pie tin and bake just 10 minutes.

2 cups rolled oats
½ cup chopped walnuts
3 tablespoons water
½ teaspoon salt

Analee's Crookneck Chiffon Pie 🥧

Analee is legend for her success at using beautifully what might otherwise be considered a surfeit of summer squashes.

৯

Preheat oven to 350°F.

Press bread crumbs into a liberally buttered 9" pie plate. Steam squash until barely tender and puree, making it very smooth. You should have 3 cups.

Sauté onion in oil. For a very smooth filling, puree the onion, eggs, cottage cheese, cornmeal, salt, and Swiss cheese and combine with the squash. Add dill weed. Pour into lined pie plate and decorate with tomato and/or pepper slices. Bake 40 to 45 minutes, until set. Let stand at least 10 minutes before cutting.

Serves 6.

2 cups whole-grain bread
crumbs
6 cups crookneck squash
or yellow zucchini,
in chunks
½ cup chopped onion
1 tablespoon oil
2 large eggs, beaten
½ cup cottage cheese
2 tablespoons cornmeal
½ teaspoon salt
⅓ cup Swiss cheese
1 tablespoon dill weed
tomato slices, pepper slices
for garnishing

Nori Maki Sushi

1 cup short-grain brown rice
2 cups water

4 sheets dried nori

½ teaspoon salt
2–4 tablespoons rice
    vinegar
2 teaspoons honey

FILLING INGREDIENTS
(choose three for each roll)

grated raw carrot or jicama
cooked chopped spinach
toasted sesame seeds
strips of scallion, bell
    pepper, celery, omelette,
    lightly steamed asparagus,
    carrot or green bean
pickled umeboshi plum
    (use just a bit)
avocado
chopped watercress
mushrooms (see below)

CONDIMENTS

Shoyu, sweet-and-hot
    mustard,
    pickled ginger

A perfectly vegetarian sushi, as good as the best. The outside wrapper *nori*, is made from seaweed. It has best flavor when freshly toasted and eaten soon after, but even so, sushi makes fine lunchbox fare.

If you want to include mushrooms, shitakes are traditional, but normal ones work too, sautéed and cut in strips. If you do come upon some dried shitakes, soak several in water, then simmer in 2 teaspoons each shoyu and sherry. Chop fine or cut into strips.

❧

Cook rice uncovered in boiling water for five minutes, then cover, and reduce heat to low. Simmer for 45 minutes.

While the rice is cooking, select and prepare your choice of fillings. You'll be making four rolls—it's fun to vary the fillings in each. Combine about three of the suggested ingredients in each—or whatever seems good to you.

Unless the nori sheets you have are pre-toasted, wave each one over a flame (a gas burner is ideal), holding it with tongs or fingertips, so that each sheet changes color and texture slightly, becoming lighter and coarser.

Dissolve salt in rice vinegar in a small saucepan and add honey; heat gently to liquefy. When the rice is cooked, turn it out onto a large platter or baking dish with sides. Pour the vinegar mixture over it, stirring as you do, and fanning the steam away—a folded newspaper works nicely. When the rice has cooled to room temperature, it is ready.

For rolling the sushi, a traditional bamboo mat is great, but not essential: a big cloth napkin works fine—just a little bigger than the nori sheets. Place the mat or cloth flat in front of you and put the first sheet of nori on it. Moisten your fingers with water or vinegar and spread one-fourth of the seasoned rice on the mat, covering it except for an inch or two at the top, which you'll use to seal the roll.

The rice should be not quite ½″ thick. Across the middle, parallel to the top, form an indentation and place the filling materials there, forming a thin line from one end to the other. For example: a strip of omelette, a line of chopped watercress, and strips of red bell pepper. Aim for beauty, and harmony too.

Grasping the nearest side of the mat, roll it up and away from you toward the top, pressing the whole thing together tightly and pushing the filling ingredients into place if necessary. Dampen the remaining "flap" of nori and seal the roll by presing the flap along the length of the roll. Place the roll on a cutting board and slice it with a very sharp knife into 1″ segments. Arrange cut-side up, and serve.

Makes about 6 servings.

Chillaquillas

Here is a traditional Mexican way to dispose of leftover tortillas—not that it isn't good enough to send us to the store for new ones, but less fresh tortillas hold up better in the cooking. If you don't have tasty, *ripe* tomatoes, use canned ones.

❧

Tear the tortillas into 2″ pieces. In a big, heavy skillet, sauté the onion, garlic, chili powder, and cumin lightly in the oil; then stir in the tortilla pieces, coating them with oil and spices.

Turn the tortillas out of the pan into a bowl (don't worry about where the onions and spices go) and add the herbs, salt, and tomatoes to the pan. Bring to a boil, stirring, and simmer about 5 minutes.

Stir the tortillas, sauce, buttermilk, cheese, and chilis together, reserving a little cheese to sprinkle on top. (If you aren't used to chilis, see page 236 for tips.) Cover and cook over low heat until the mixture is bubbly and the cheese melted.

The dish needs to sit for about 20 minutes before serving—ideally, in a low (325°F) oven, covered. If your skillet and lid aren't ovenware, turn the mixture out into a casserole first.

Serves 4.

1 dozen corn tortillas

1 bunch green onions, chopped
2 cloves garlic, minced
1½ teaspoons chili powder
½ teaspoon ground cumin
1 tablespoon oil

½ teaspoon oregano
1 teaspoon basil
¾ teaspoon salt
2 cups tomatoes, chopped

2½ cups buttermilk
¾ cup grated cheddar
(⅓ cup chopped green chilis or green peppers)

Fiesta

When summer's tomato crop is at its peak—and at other times of year for a change of pace—we put together an impromptu Mexican feast and let friends create the tostadas, tacos or burritos of their dreams. This meal is delicious, pretty, and easy. It is also perfect for potlucking. For dessert, serve papaya halves with lime wedges, or a giant, luscious fruit salad.

Tortillas are available in supermarkets now, in the deep freeze if nowhere else. But any town that has a sizeable Mexican community will have a source of fresh, locally-made tortillas, and they will taste *much* better: ask at a Mexican restaurant how you can get some. We like the corn variety best; the flour ones are nearly always made from white flour and contain lard. For a good flour tortilla, make our Chapatis (page 84) without pressing on them while they cook.

Tortillas are often deep-fried for tacos and chips. An alternative that is at least as authentic and plenty delicious is to heat them on a griddle or directly over a burner flame, turning them once or twice with deft fingers (or tongs) as they begin to brown. If you want the tenderness that fat adds, rub a dot of butter or oil onto both sides of the tortilla with the palms of your hands before warming it as described above. To heat a lot of tortillas for serving soft, wrap them in a damp towel and put them in a covered casserole. Warm in 325°F oven for 15 minutes, until hot through.

To make TORTILLA CHIPS, tear the tortillas into smallish triangles, spread them on cookie sheets, and bake for 30 minutes at 325°F. If you rub each tortilla first with a tiny bit of butter—¼ teaspoon to a side—the flavor steps up; cut down the baking time to 20 minutes. Either way, they will be delicious even though unsalty.

POSSIBLE OFFERINGS:

Hot tortillas
Refritos (page 307) or
    Chili con Elote (page 308)
Shredded lettuce
Steamed vegetables:
    green beans and corn
    broccoli and cauliflower
    zucchini, scallions,
        and peppers
Mexican-style Tomato Sauce
    (page 248)
    or Salsa (page 221 and 236)
Mock Sour Cream (page 240)
Avocado Dip (page 132)
Grated jack and cheddar
    cheeses
Tomato wedges
Olives
Grilled Peppers (page 137)
    or chiles
Chopped raw scallions
    or red onions
Fruit punch

TACO

crisp corn tortilla
    (folded in half while hot)
filled with:
    Refritos
    cheese
    shredded lettuce
    Salsa

ᔍ

TOSTADA

crisp corn tortilla flat
    on plate topped with:
    Refritos or Chili
    shredded lettuce
    cheese
    Salsa
    Avocado dip
    tomato wedges
    Mock Sour Cream

QUESADILLA

soft tortilla folded in half
    over slices of grilled pepper
    or chili
    chopped scallion
    jack cheese
heated on griddle to melt cheese
(serve with Salsa)

ᔍ

ENTOMATADA

soft tortilla dipped in hot
    Tomato Sauce
topped with
    shredded lettuce
    grated cheese
    Salsa
    (any other vegetables)
    fried egg, sunny side up

ᔍ

BURRITO

soft tortilla folded around
    Refritos and cheese

Grains & Beans

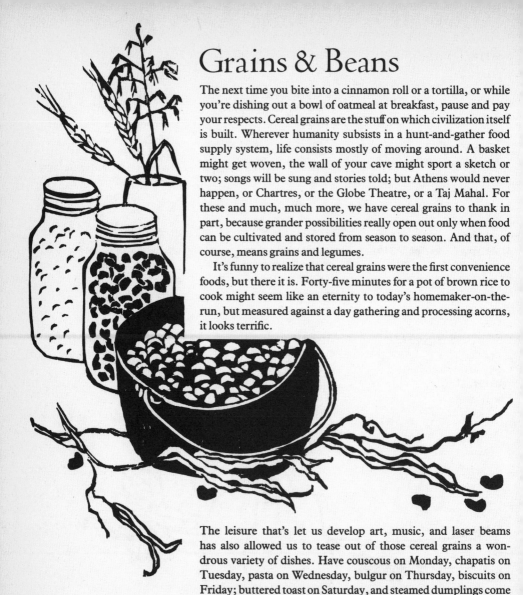

The next time you bite into a cinnamon roll or a tortilla, or while you're dishing out a bowl of oatmeal at breakfast, pause and pay your respects. Cereal grains are the stuff on which civilization itself is built. Wherever humanity subsists in a hunt-and-gather food supply system, life consists mostly of moving around. A basket might get woven, the wall of your cave might sport a sketch or two; songs will be sung and stories told; but Athens would never happen, or Chartres, or the Globe Theatre, or a Taj Mahal. For these and much, much more, we have cereal grains to thank in part, because grander possibilities really open out only when food can be cultivated and stored from season to season. And that, of course, means grains and legumes.

It's funny to realize that cereal grains were the first convenience foods, but there it is. Forty-five minutes for a pot of brown rice to cook might seem like an eternity to today's homemaker-on-the-run, but measured against a day gathering and processing acorns, it looks terrific.

The leisure that's let us develop art, music, and laser beams has also allowed us to tease out of those cereal grains a wondrous variety of dishes. Have couscous on Monday, chapatis on Tuesday, pasta on Wednesday, bulgur on Thursday, biscuits on Friday; buttered toast on Saturday, and steamed dumplings come Sunday: all these from one grain—wheat—alone. The list from rice would be much longer.

The marvelous thing about being a vegetarian today is that you have access to the traditional grain dishes of just about every ethnic cuisine. This makes for endless variety, and the great fun of slipping into another culture—another world—for the time it takes to prepare and eat those dishes.

It also makes for superb nourishment, for whole grains turn out to contain nearly everything we need for glowing health: vitamins, minerals, complex carbohydrates, and good-quality protein, present in just the right percentage. What more could you ask of a food?

Speed? Well, some whole-grain foods actually *are* convenience foods. Kasha, bulgur, and couscous cook in just 15 minutes. Whole-grain pastas take a little longer, and even brown rice, once put on to simmer, cooks itself while you do other things. Once cooked, it can be kept for days and reheated quickly. A good way to reheat is to put cooked rice in a heat-proof covered glass dish. Place that on a steamer rack in a much larger pan that has an inch or so of water in the bottom. Heat gently—the grain won't dry out. (The microwave does a good job, too.)

STORING GRAINS AND BEANS

Store whole grains in a cool, dry place, protected from bugs and mice, and they will keep for years. After grains are cracked or ground into flour, though, their freshness begins to wane, so keep flour and the like in the refrigerator if you won't be using them within a couple of weeks.

Beans are also an ancient foodstuff, denser in many nutrients. They keep a long time (store them like grains), but after a year or so you'll find they won't be so tasty and will take longer to cook.

Grains

To cook grain use a heavy pot with a tight lid. Bring the water to a boil; stir in the grain (and salt). Bring to a boil again, briefly, then cover the pot and turn the heat as low as you can, simmering very gently until the water is absorbed and grain is tender. See next page for suggested times.

Cooking Times & Proportion for Grains & Beans

Grain (1 cup dry measure)	Water	Cooking time	Yield
Barley (whole)	3 cups	1 hour 15 minutes	3½ cups
Brown rice	2 cups	1 hour	3 cups
Buckwheat (kasha)	2 cups	15 minutes	2½ cups
Bulgur wheat	2 cups	15–20 minutes	2½ cups
Cracked wheat	2 cups	25 minutes	2⅓ cups
Millet	3 cups	45 minutes	3½ cups
Coarse cornmeal (polenta)	4 cups	25 minutes	3 cups
Wild rice	3 cups	1 hour or more	4 cups
Whole wheat berries	3 cups	2 hours	2⅔ cups
Quinoa	2 cups	15 minutes	2½ cups
Black beans	4 cups	1½ hours	2 cups
Black-eyed peas	3 cups	1 hour	2 cups
Garbanzos (chickpeas)	4 cups	3 hours	2 cups
Great northern beans	3½ cups	2 hours	2 cups
Kidney beans	3 cups	1½ hours	2 cups
Lentils and split peas	3 cups	45 minutes	2¼ cups
Limas	2 cups	1½ hours	1¼ cups
Baby limas	2 cups	1½ hours	1¾ cups
Pinto beans	3 cups	2½ hours	2 cups
Red beans	3 cups	3 hours	2 cups
Small white beans (navy, etc.)	3 cups	2½ hours	2 cups
Soybeans	4 cups	3 hours or more	2 cups
Soy grits	2 cups	15 minutes	2 cups

Barley

Normal barley, like rice and oats (and unlike wheat and rye), does not grow "naked"; its indigestible hull clings tenaciously to the grain. To remove the hull, the grain is milled. In the case of *pearl barley*, the milling is repeated over and over until the germ as well as the chaff is gone. *Scotch* or *pot barley* has been milled fewer times and so is more nutritious. Sometimes you will find a special hull-less variety that grows naked like wheat and needs no milling to render it deliciously edible.

Hull-less barley is often sold as "barley for sprouting." But beware: some suppliers sell normal unmilled barley—not hull-less at all—"for sprouting", and unless you have a grain mill, barley with its chaff is not very useful. Keep asking for the real thing: demand creates supply.

If you can't get it hull-less, buy the other kind and mill it yourself. Here's how: crack the grain to the coarseness you want, and just before you cook it, flood it with water in a deep pan, letting the grain settle in the bottom and the hulls float off. To save the "fines" (flour) which would otherwise be lost along with the chaff in washing, sift the milled grain with a fine sieve before you wash it. Then you can make these great crackers:

Barley Crackers 🍥

Using a lecithin spray or the greasing formula on page 53, grease a *flat* 12″ × 18″ cookie sheet or the back of one with sides. (The crackers will stick otherwise.) If you want them especially thin, use the same amount of batter on *two* sheets.

Sift the flour, salt, and soda. Stir in the buttermilk. Spread the batter on the cookie sheet(s) as if it were frosting on a cake, making it quite even.

Bake at about 300°F until *very* delicately brown. About halfway through the baking—some 10 minutes along—score the dough in squares or rectangles or whatever you like, so the crackers will break apart easily when they are done.

1 cup barley fines (or flour)
½ teaspoon salt
½ teaspoon baking soda

1 cup buttermilk

Spinach and Barley Dumplings

*1 cup barley, finely
    cracked
1 to 1½ pounds spinach
    (1 cup cooked)
(chopped leaves from
    1 bunch coriander)
1 egg or 2 whites, beaten
½ teaspoon salt
barley flour as needed*

*good broth, simmering 3"
    deep in a big shallow pan
    with a tight lid*

Delicious floating in any tomato soup, lovely bathed in Cheddy
Sauce or Tomato Pepper Sauce.

In a large, heavy skillet, toast the barley until it is just barely
golden and becoming fragrant. Keep stirring so the toasting is
even. (If necessary to get rid of chaff, wash now—see previous
page.) Add water to cover and bring to a boil. Cover tightly and
remove from heat.

Cook the spinach and drain dry. Chop, adding coriander leaves
if you like. Mix in the barley. Allow to cool to lukewarm, then
add the egg and salt.

Add just enough barley flour to make the mixture capable of
being formed into balls, and make balls about as big as a walnut,
rolling them in more barley flour. When you have about 10, drop
them in the broth. Cover the pan and form the rest.

It's a help if the pan has a glass lid, because you want to keep
the dumplings simmering or they won't cook, but you don't want
them to boil hard or they may fall apart. Peeking is required if
you can't see through the lid. The dumplings cook quickly. Allow
about eight minutes, then use a slotted spoon to remove them to
the sauce or soup you'll be serving them in and cook the second
half.

Makes 18, which will serve 4 to 6.

WITHOUT EGG: By adding a little extra barley flour when you
mix the dough, you can make these dumplings without the egg.
Make the mixture pretty stiff and allow extra cooking time. This
is tricky, but not impossible.

Buckwheat

It looks and cooks like grain, but buckwheat grows like fruit on a pretty, hardy plant with heart-shaped leaves and white flowers that bees love. It has nearly perfect amino acid balance and is rich in calcium and riboflavin and low in fat and sodium. Because the plant is disease-resistant, it is one comercial grain almost always grown without pesticides. Most of the buckwheat on our grocery shelves is grown in the U.S.

Partly for its hardiness, but also for its heartiness, this "grain" is a staple in Russia and the Balkans. The seeds are usually toasted before cooking; if so, you have kasha. Roasting brings out the robust flavor; it is milder raw. Buckwheat flour, of course, is for pancakes. We keep the grain on hand and grind it in the blender when we want flour: it keeps fresher that way, and there's no problem grinding it because the grains are both soft and brittle.

Rinse the buckwheat grains in cold water and drain well before you cook. If you want to toast the grain before cooking, either toast and then rinse or follow the traditional cooking method: Mix a cup or so of rinsed groats with a beaten egg and then heat dry, stirring in a heavy skillet. Add water—about 1½ cups per cup of grain—and bring to a boil. Cover, and steam over very gentle heat about 15 minutes. (Iron pans will give a dark gray cast to the cooked grain.) Serve kasha with any of the winter vegetables, especially cabbage and sweet squash; mix it with sautéed onion, garlic, and whole wheat bow tie noodles to make KASHA VARNITCHKES.

Buckwheat pancakes, page 95, Blini, page 258

Bulgur Wheat

Quick-cooking bulgur wheat, with its nutty flavor and persistent fluffiness, is one of the most useful grains for pilaf and grain salads like Tabouli. When time is short, bulgur also fills in admirably for any of the longer-cooking grains in "serve over" dishes (serve over rice, serve over noodles, serve over mashed potatoes. . .).

Bulgur groats come in small, medium, and large. We like the largest size for nearly everything we make. Since it is precooked, bulgur needs only a short time on the stove; in fact, if you want it chewy, just cover with boiling water and let stand until the water is absorbed. Cooking it like rice is a little faster: use 1½ cups water to 1 cup bulgur.

Here is a very simple basic pilaf that you can vary freehandedly:

Bulgur Wheat Pilaf

1 small carrot
1 medium stalk celery
    or Florence fennel
½ green pepper
2 green onions
(¼ cup chopped mushrooms)
(1 cup tiny peas)
1 tablespoon oil
1 bay leaf
1 cup bulgur wheat
1¾ cups boiling water
½ teaspoon salt

Dice carrot, celery, pepper, and onion. Heat oil in a heavy pot and add all the vegetables and the bay leaf. Stir over medium heat for several minutes, then stir in the bulgur. Add the boiling water and salt. Reduce heat, cover, and keep over very low heat for 15 minutes.

Makes about 4 cups, to serve 4 to 6.

Uppuma

This flavorful dish was our first exposure to South Indian cuisine, and it remains one of our favorites. Uppuma ("*oop*ma") is popular in India for high tea, but it is very satisfying and suitable for breakfast, lunch, or dinner.

❧

Toast the grain in a big, heavy-bottomed pan, stirring until the grain is fragrant and just beginning to brown. The toasting ensures that the uppuma will be flaky rather than gummy. Remove from heat.

In the same pot, emptied, or in another heavy and sizeable one, heat the oil very hot and add the mustard seeds. Cover the pan and let them pop. As soon as the sound of wild popping slows down a bit, remove from heat, uncover, and add the cashews, stirring quickly until they are golden. Add the onion, ginger, and chili in succession, giving the onion a bit of a head start. Sauté until tender.

Add the water and salt and bring to a boil. Add the grain, stirring as you do to mix evenly. Cover tightly and allow to cook over very low heat until the grain is tender. (How long depends on the grain, but 10 minutes is about par.) When the water is all gone, the grain should be tender and flaky. If the grain isn't done when the water has evaporated, stir in a quarter cup more boiling water and cover again, keeping over lowest heat for 5 more minutes. If the grain is tender but gummy, or if the water is not gone, turn up the heat and stir vigorously with a fork while the excess water evaporates.

Chop the coriander leaves and mix them and the lemon juice into the grain just before serving. Serves 4.

❧

Like most beloved dishes, this one admits a lot of variation. To simplify, for example, you can omit the nuts and/or the coriander leaves. Try also cooking a cupful or so of finely chopped vegetables along with the grain: potato, carrot, green beans, or peas. Sometimes a few tablespoons of fresh grated coconut is stirred in just before serving.

1 cup finely cracked wheat or rice or barley

1 tablespoon oil
1/2 teaspoon black mustard seeds
5 cashew nuts
1 small onion, minced
1/2 tablespoon minced ginger
1/2 green chili, seeded and minced, or
1/4 green pepper, minced

1 1/2 cups boiling water
1/2 teaspoon salt, to taste

leaves of 1/2 bunch coriander
3/4 teaspoon lemon juice

Corn

Almost everybody likes the warm color and sunny flavor of corn. Cornmeal mush is good at breakfast, and Corn Bread is the quick bread we make most often. At lunchtime we like coarse cornmeal cooked like rice and served with Refritos.

If you have noticed a slight bitterness in the things you make from cornmeal, here's the cause: because of plant breeding, corn contains so much polyunsaturated oil that it goes rancid soon after it is ground. For really sweet, sweet corn bread and polenta, grinding your own is the surest way; if you're not set up to do that, buy the freshest you can and keep it airtight in the refrigerator. Freezing of course postpones rancidity, but it does destroy vitamin E.

੨੦

POLENTA

Corn is a native American, but Italians have made it their own as polenta: cornmeal mush (page 280) cooked long and slow. Usually, it's spread out half an inch thick, then topped in delicious ways—fresh tomatoes with basil; farmer's or Parmesan cheese, with a sprinkling of fresh rosemary; smoky sautéed mushrooms with marinated sun-dried tomatoes and grilled mozzarella. Reheat, slice, and serve. Round polenta slices are pretty stacked with pesto and tomato sauce, to cut like a cake; or used in casseroles, as on the facing page.

Spoonbread 🥄

1 cup coarse cornmeal
(polenta)
1 cup cold water
2 cups boiling water
1 cup skim milk powder
1 cup cold water or whole
milk
3 eggs, beaten
1¼ teaspoons salt
(1 tablespoon butter)

Put the cornmeal and 1 cup of cold water in a heavy saucepan. Bring to a boil, stirring in 2 cups of boiling water as the mixture thickens. Stir as needed to prevent the corn from sticking as it simmers for about 20 minutes. When very thick, set aside.

Preheat oven to 400°F. Butter a deep 2-quart casserole dish.

Blend smooth the milk powder and cold water or milk. Combine with eggs and salt. Mix in about one cup of the cooked cornmeal, then combine all together, adding butter if wanted. Pour into the prepared baking dish.

Bake uncovered for 30 minutes, or until golden brown on top. Spoon out hot, alongside vegetables or for breakfast.

Makes 6 servings.

Helen's Polenta with Eggplant

Place polenta in top of a double boiler with 4 cups of boiling water and ½ teaspoon of the salt. Bring to a boil, reduce heat to low, and cook for 30 to 40 minutes, until mush is quite thick. Pack into round, straight-sided containers that are, ideally, the same diameter as the eggplants. Refrigerate.

Meanwhile, sauté onion, pepper, and garlic clove in oil until tender. Crush garlic with a fork. Then add tomatoes, parsley, basil, and remaining 1 teaspoon of salt. Bring to a boil and simmer, stirring often, for 15 minutes, breaking up tomatoes as you stir.

When polenta is chilled, slice it in ½" rounds. Do the same with the eggplants. Oil a 9" × 13" baking dish and overlap alternating slices of eggplant and polenta in a pretty, fish-scale design (if the eggplant is too large to do this, simply layer it lasagna-style). Pour tomato sauce over the whole works and sprinkle cheese on top. Cover the dish and bake in a 350° oven for 45 minutes, or until eggplant tests done with a fork.

Serves 6.

*1 cup raw polenta
  (coarse-ground cornmeal)*
1½ teaspoons salt

1 large onion, chopped fine
1 green pepper, chopped fine
1 whole clove garlic
1 tablespoon olive oil
3 cups chopped tomatoes
¼ cup chopped parsley
1 teaspoon dried basil
*2 medium (or 1 large)
  eggplants (1½ pounds)*
*¾ cup grated jack or
  mozzarella cheese*

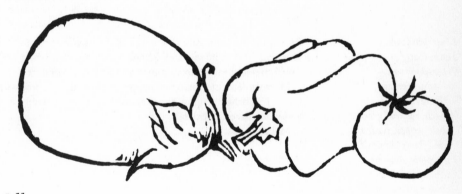

Millet

While millet is perfectly good food, it has not, so far as we know, inspired any deeply beloved ethnic dish. You can use millet where you want a mild-flavored grain accompaniment to something spicy, or for a light, rather nice breakfast cereal. Prepare millet soon before you mean to eat it, as it tends to solidify as it cools.

Quinoa

Quinoa ("*keen*wa"), sacred staple of the ancient Incas, still grows on the high slopes of the Andes—but also, nowadays, on the high slopes of the Colorado Rockies. New-age entrepreneurs are cultivating it for the small but rapidly growing American market. Quinoa appeals to natural foods enthusiasts for its good nutrition (its balance of essential amino acids is close to ideal) and to gourmets for its unique texture and delicious flavor.

Always rinse quinoa well before cooking to remove a bitter surface coating that is its natural protection against insects.

Quinoa cooks in just fifteen minutes, and it's so delicate, so light and fluffy, that you can hardly believe it is a whole food. The flavor is appealing, and not quite like anything else, either. It bears some resemblance to couscous, and can be used in much the same way. It shines in dishes where you'd normally use bulgur wheat or millet.

Confetti Quinoa

1 cup raw quinoa
2 cups water
¼ teaspoon salt
½ medium onion, finely chopped
¼ each, red and green bell pepper, seeded and finely chopped
1 teaspoon olive oil
2 tablespoons chopped toasted almonds or ¼ cup sliced water chestnuts
2 tablespoons chopped fresh coriander leaves

Rinse quinoa thoroughly in a fine sieve. Bring two cups of water to a boil, then add salt and quinoa and bring to a boil again. Cover, reduce heat to a low simmer, and cook for 15 minutes.

Meanwhile, sauté onion and pepper in olive oil. Combine with grain. Just before serving, stir in almonds or water chestnuts and coriander leaves. Check salt.

Makes 3 cups.

Rice

To half the world, "rice" means "food," and several of the great cuisines on the planet are built around the subtle delicacy of this nourishing grain. The more familiar it gets, the better we enjoy it. No other dinner grain bears repetition so endearingly.

Rice is not native to this hemisphere, but it grows well in the southern states and in California. Not long ago, supermarkets just carried "rice." Now we can count varieties: long, short, and medium grains; sweet "glutinous" rice, used for making *mochi;* perfumey Indian basmati; the new texmati and warmly ruddy wehani—and, of course, wild rice, which is another story altogether.

Brown rice, whether long, short, or medium, should look clean and uniform. Our friend Meera wouldn't consider preparing rice without picking out the discolored grains and unhulled "paddy." In this country we take for granted that the cleaning has been done for us, but sometime you may find you've bought poor-quality brown rice full of green, broken, and even moldy grains. These are far from pleasant to eat; if you don't want to pick them out, please take it back, and insist on better stuff.

We present here some recipes that reflect the enthusiasm of rice-appreciating cuisines from the four corners of the world—including our own.

The basic formula for cooking brown rice is simple enough: boil 1 cup rice in 1¾ cups water for 5 minutes; reduce heat and cover, allowing about 45 minutes in all. That's it, essentially, but certain factors can make a difference. You should use a heavy pan, and if it is *really* heavy and has a tight-fitting lid, you may need even less water—especially if the rice you are cooking is this year's rather than last's. For some reason, a larger quantity of rice also seems to need less water. If you like your rice a bit on the chewier side, cutting back the water somewhat will do it. One final tip: one friend of ours found that she couldn't cook rice on her gas stove until she spread and subdued the flame with a "flame tamer."

Spanish Rice

3 cups cooked brown rice

1 onion, chopped
4 stalks celery
1 large green pepper
2 cloves garlic
1 tablespoon oil
1 teaspoon chili powder
1 teaspoon cumin

1 cup chopped tomatoes
1 teaspoon salt
1/2 teaspoon oregano
1/4 teaspoon pepper

Rice should be warm.

Sauté onion, celery, pepper, and garlic in oil. Add chili powder and cumin. When fragrant, add tomatoes, salt, oregano, and pepper. When tomatoes are cooked through, stir in the rice.

VARIATIONS: For a rich, cheeselike taste, include 1/3 cup cornmeal with the rice when you first cook it. Then, when making the Spanish Rice, increase the tomato a little.

Top the rice dish with grated jack and/or cheddar cheese, and put in the oven long enough to melt the cheese.

Teresa's Spanish Rice

1 small onion
2 teaspoons oil
1 clove garlic

1 teaspoon cumin
1 teaspoon paprika
1/2 red bell pepper

1/2 teaspoon oregano
1 cup raw brown rice
1/2 teaspoon salt
2 cups water

A flavorful and very different version.

Chop onion and sauté in oil with garlic clove. When onion is translucent, add cumin, paprika, and red bell pepper and cook a moment more, until spices are fragrant. Mash garlic clove with a fork. Add oregano, rice, salt, and water. Bring to a boil, then reduce heat and simmer on lowest flame for about an hour, until done.

Pilaf Avgolemono 🍶

Avgolemono sauce is another fine offering from our Greek friend Sultana. It goes well on vegetables too, but here it is on rice, for a delicious, rich-tasting grain dish that's one of our favorites.

🍃

Make a cream sauce (see page 242) with butter and flour, milk, stock, and salt. Remove from heat and allow to cool to lukewarm.

Beat egg with lemon juice and slowly add to the sauce, stirring constantly. Return pan to the stove and continue cooking and stirring until the sauce thickens. Stir in half the cheese and pour sauce over grain. Top with remaining cheese.

Makes about 4 cups, to serve 4 to 6.

2 tablespoons butter
2 tablespoons whole wheat flour
1/2 cup milk
1/2 cup hot stock, or water
1/2 teaspoon salt

1 egg
juice of 1/2 lemon
1/3 cup Parmesan cheese
4 cups hot, cooked brown rice

Green Rice Casserole 🍶

Preheat oven to 350°F. Chop scallions and sauté with garlic in oil until soft; crush the garlic with a fork. Combine with remaining ingredients in a greased 2-quart casserole. (Be sure to reduce the amount of salt if you use rice that's already salted.) Bake about 45 minutes.

Serves 4 to 6.

1 small bunch scallions
1 small clove garlic
1 tablespoon oil
2 1/2 cups cooked brown rice
1/3 cup chopped parsley
1/2 cup grated Swiss cheese
2 eggs, beaten
2 cups milk
1 teaspoon salt
(1/2 teaspoon dill weed)

Sarah's Super Curried Rice

This dish is so simple that you can halve the recipe easily for smaller amounts. A very satisfying way to use up leftover rice.

🍃

Cook rice in water with salt. Meantime, chop and sauté the onion in the butter, adding the curry powder when the onion is soft and cooking them together for a minute to remove the raw taste of the spices. Combine rice, onion, raisins, and peas. Heat, stirring—or bake, covered—until hot through. Garnish with toasted cashews on special occasions.

Serves 6.

2 cups brown basmati (or long-grain) rice
4 cups boiling water
3/4 teaspoon salt
2 large onions
1 1/2 tablespoons butter
1 tablespoon curry powder
2/3 cup raisins
2/3 cup golden raisins
2/3 cup peas

Wild Rice

1 cup wild rice
1/3 cup brown rice
1 carrot
1 large stalk celery
6 green onions
1 garlic clove
2 tablespoons oil
5 cups boiling water
1 teaspoon marjoram
1/4 teaspoon thyme
pinch rosemary
1 teaspoon salt
dash pepper
1/3 cup toasted almonds

Wild rice, along with corn, is a native American. It is unarguably nutritious, and so delicious and special that even its outrageous price doesn't stop us from making this fine dish on special occasions.

❧

Rinse grain well.

Chop carrot and celery in 1/4" cubes. Chop green onions and sauté them with garlic in oil. Crush garlic clove with a fork. Add water and bring to a boil. Stir in the vegetables, rice, herbs, salt, and pepper. Bring to a boil, cover, reduce heat, and cook gently for an hour or more, until the rice is tender. Chop the almonds and add them about 20 minutes before serving.

Makes about 5 cups.

Beans

Beans are eminently nutritious, admirably ecological, low on the food chain, available everywhere, wonderfully versatile, dependably delicious, and very, very cheap. In fact, if any food (besides grains) could claim to have all the virtues, it'd have to be beans.

But. There is that annoying little problem, impossible to ignore: eating beans does cause intestinal gas in many people, especially those who are not accustomed to them.

Decades of research at the USDA have unearthed a probable set of contributing factors. Scientists have identified two sugars, with the splendidly disreputable-sounding names "raffinose" and "stachyose," which our digestive system can't break down. Bacteria that live in our intestines can and do break them down, however, producing gas as a by-product. Whether there is so much gas that it is uncomfortable, and whether it has odor, is determined by other things.

A lot of people, however, do eat beans without physical or social discomfort. How to join their enviable number? Here are some suggestions that seem to work for us. Another, more radical approach is outlined in Preparing Beans on the next page.

ᔡ When you eat beans, keep the meal light. Eating beans with a lot of fat, or eating a lot of beans at once, or eating a lot of anything when you eat beans—these three are sure to bring trouble.

ᔡ Morning (bizarrely enough) is the best time to eat beans because when you are active, your digestive processes work better. Nighttime is worst. Eating them at breakfast is an acquired skill for adults; children can take to it easily.

ᔡ Getting plenty of exercise is a good way to improve your digestion in general.

ᔡ Some beans are less gas-producing and some more. This varies from person to person, but in general, adzuki beans are considered the most digestible, with "unbean" legumes like mung beans, split peas, and lentils close behind.

ᔡ Thorough cooking helps. So does sprouting.

ᔡ Folk wisdom suggests some additions: garlic, cumin, ground coriander, and certain other spices or a little vinegar added near the end of the cooking time.

ᔡ Fermented soy foods like tempeh and miso are more easily digestible than the plain cooked beans. Tofu is not fermented, but since it contains only a fragment of the soybean, with most of the fiber removed, it doesn't cause problems for most people.

ᔡ Beans are a rich source of fiber, and when you aren't used to them, high-fiber foods will cause gas. But most people find that such troubles diminish as the body accustoms itself to high-fiber foods. Give yourself time by eating small amounts at first.

Preparing Beans

The old-fashioned procedure of sorting through beans before cooking them makes an enormous difference in how they taste. Since they come to us directly from the field, without any kind of processing at all, it isn't surprising to find perhaps a couple of rocks, a few dirt clods, and a couple of moldy or otherwise disreputable individual beans in any given cup or two. An easy way to find the offenders is to spread the beans out on the far end of a big, shallow baking pan, using your fingers methodically to flip the good ones toward you and lift the bad ones out.

After sorting, rinse beans well to remove dirt and dust. You can soak them, if you like, for several hours; it reduces cooking time about 15 minutes for quick-cooking beans and as much as half an hour for slow-cooking ones. Soybeans tend to ferment, so soak them in the refrigerator in hot weather.

SCIENTIFIC SOAKING

A more drastic soaking procedure has been developed by USDA scientists to address the flatulence problem. They claim that their method removes 90 percent of the sugars that cause intestinal gas. If you want to try it, here's how: Boil the beans for 10 minutes in 5 to 10 times their weight in water. (Beans weigh about half as much as water, so that'd be 5 to 10 cups of water for a scant 2 cups of beans.) Allow them to cool and soak for 24 hours at room temperature in the same water. Discard the soak-water, rinse the beans, and cook. This method does not affect protein content significantly, but there is considerable loss of minerals and vitamins.*

*Alfred C. Olson, et al., "Nutrient composition of and digestive response to whole and extracted dry beans," *Agricultural and Food Chemistry* (Jan.-Feb. 1982), pp. 26–32.

Cook beans in two or more times their measure of water, simmering until tender. Add salt toward the end of cooking time—added at the beginning, salt toughens the beans and makes them take longer to cook. (Our rule of thumb is ½ teaspoon of salt per cup of raw beans.) A good heavy pot helps prevent scorching. Beans cook fastest if the water is simmering all the time.

The easiest way to cook beans is in an electric slow cooker, because you can leave it to its own devices and the beans will cook perfectly overnight or while you are at work. The clay pot lets the beans keep their color and shape beautifully. Soybeans seem to cook only if the water is really at a slow boil; for some crocks, this means on "high" the whole time. Putting a thick folded towel on top of the lid helps conserve heat.

When thinking beans, maybe the most helpful thing to keep in mind is that these are natural super-foods and having a small quantity often is much better and easier than trying to center a meal around them once in a while. Add a few to soups or casseroles, or have bean spread sandwiches, or use a handful in salad; nearly all the problems people have with beans disappear when they are consumed in small quantities. Several friends with small households tell us they cook a pot of beans, then freeze the unused portion in ice cube trays. The little squares are easy to store and easy to thaw for use here and there.

Who's Who

ADZUKI (also *azuki* or *aduki*) beans are considered the most digestible of all. Their flavor is not what Western bean-fans are used to, but they are especially delicious served with rice or millet. Flavorful enough to stand on their own, but try adding a little shoyu, some green pepper, and ginger.

BLACK-EYED PEAS gained a lot of attention recently when everyone was looking for a good natural source of selenium—but Southerners needed no incentive. In the South, these quick-cooking, easily digested legumes have long been a favorite, and just tomato and a little onion are all that's required for embellishment. Serve with rice or Corn Bread, page 81) or add them to vegetable soups. (See Black-eyed Peas Virginia Style, page 309)

KIDNEY BEANS cooked gently and chilled, are wonderful in salads because of their bright color and light flavor. Most kidneys, though, find their way into chili dishes, and there they are the stars of the show. With a sautéed onion, garlic, oregano, and chili powder, you're in business. Kidneys, incidentally, cook quickest of the big beans: unless they are very old, you can boil them up in a little over an hour. (See Chili con Elote, page 308; Refritos, page 307; Refrito Spread, page 114; Tennessee Cornpone, page 309; Tamale Pie, page 307; Mexican Salad Bowl, page 135)

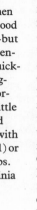

BLACK BEANS have long been the staple food in parts of Latin America, and they figure large in Japanese and Chinese cuisines as well. Super-nutritious Black Beans and Rice may be one of the most delicious of all classic bean-grain combinations. Black Bean Chili is one of the best-known dishes at Greens, the famous gourmet vegetarian restaurant of San Francisco; but if you don't want chili, season black beans with onions and plenty of garlic and add lemon just before serving. (Black Bean Soup, page 166; Refritos, page 307)

GARBANZOS (also known as chick-peas or ceci) are versatile, mildly nutty-flavored beans that keep their baby-chick shape and beige color when cooked, making them ideal for salads. Mashed, they make wonderful spreads; in vegetable and grain dishes they play a variety of parts, usually supporting roles rather than starring ones. (See Garbanzo Spread, page 114; Ceci Salad, page 134)

LENTILS take as little as half an hour to cook. They make delicious, saucy soup and stew, and they welcome flavorings of many sorts: from onion and garlic, explore tomato, potato, and eggplant; head east with green pepper, ginger, and shoyu; or try a little curry powder and yogurt for an Indian dal mixture that's surprising and soothing. Lentils can cook along with rice to make a tasty high-protein combination. Don't cook lentils in an iron pot—they turn black. (See Greek Lentil Soup, page 167; Lentil Loaf, page 306)

RED LENTILS are bright coral color when raw, but cook quickly to a soft yellowish-beige, rather like yellow split peas but more delicate.

LIMAS are two. Baby limas cook quickly but otherwise act pretty much like any white bean. Large limas or "butter beans," however, are truly one of the great beans of all time. All by themselves they make a delicious soupy sauce, to serve alongside vegetables and bulgur or rice—or to make into BUTTER BEAN SOUP with plenty of celery and sautéed green onion and maybe a dash of dill weed or parsley—one satisfying soup.

MUNG beans are familiar to everyone as Chinese bean sprouts. Cooked as beans, they are delicious and very digestible. In Indian cooking they are called *moong dal* or green gram. *Urid dal* or black gram is a close relative. (Sprouts, page 120; Kichadi, page 305)

PINTOS, if there were a bean popularity contest, might win hands down. For chili they are classic, and Refritos are pintos most pinto-y. Good in soups, too. They take a long time to cook, but they don't smoosh. (See Refritos, page 307; Refrito Spread, page 114; Tamale Pie, page 307; Tennessee Cornpone, page 309)

SPLIT PEAS are two, too: green and yellow. Green split peas are comfortably familiar, even to People Who Never Eat Beans. Digestible, tasty, and pretty, split peas make soup in half an hour or a little more, and though there are fancier versions, the very best may be the simplest: just a little sautéed onion and a bay leaf, salt, and pepper . . . well, celery, carrots, and potato are good additions, and maybe a handful of parsley. (See Hearty Pea Soup, page 167; and Split Pea Spreads, page 115)

YELLOW SPLIT PEAS have a very different flavor, much warmer, better at supporting chords than at playing the melody. We use them often, cooking them along with rice (2 rice to 1 pea) to make DAL RICE; to add heft to broth and stock, to make soups heartier, or to warm and round greens dishes. (See Golden Broth, page 151; Rasam, page 150.)

WHITE BEANS—small navy beans, great northern, even baby limas—make fine additions to soups and stews. When cooked with plenty of water, they provide a smooth, saucy broth. One of the best of all stewy soups is GREEK BEANS: cook white beans along with cut-up carrot, celery, onion, and oregano, then add a dash of olive oil, salt, and paprika.

SOYBEANS are power-packed nutritionally, with more of nearly everything than the other beans—except flavor. But their very lack of personality enables them to become many things: tofu, tempeh, miso, shoyu, TVP, and other commercial products; in the kitchen, cooked and mashed soybeans make a base for tasty spreads, disappear into bread, or thicken soup. (Pine Nut Pinewheels, page 67, Soy Bread, page 72; Spreads, page 113 and 115)

Most of the enthusiasm about soy has centered around its abundant and very high quality (complete) protein. But science marches on: we now know that for most of the people who will be reading this book, getting too much protein is more likely to be a concern than getting too little. One serving of tofu may provide a quarter of your daily protein needs—rather a lot, if you will be eating other protein foods that day.

Furthermore, soy is the one bean that has a high enough fat content that you need to watch it: about 38 percent in plain soybeans, compared to less than 5 percent for most other beans. Half the calories in tofu come from fat.

TEMPEH

A bright note on the soy foods scene is tempeh ("*tem*pay"), which, unlike tofu, uses the whole bean and so contains all its nutrients. Often prepared from a mixture of grain and soybeans, tempeh can have a lighter fat and protein profile than straight soybeans too. Until recently, it was hard to find really fresh tempeh, and freshness is essential for good flavor; so if you tried it and didn't like it, give it another chance. Tempeh is like fresh cheese or yogurt: a culture makes it happen, and there's a time when it's at its best; after that things go downhill. Tempeh's culture shows white at first, then black; so if you see many black spots, don't buy. At home a few black spots are okay, but the flavor won't be so mild as if you'd eaten it a day earlier.

When you prepare a tempeh dish, remember that the culture will grow very fast in a warm environment. Plan to cook it fast at a high temperature or marinate it before using. Usually tempeh is fried—it is a perfect meat substitute for new vegetarians—but since we don't ever recommend frying, our recipes offer other fast-cooking techniques that really work.

We have mentioned earlier that tempeh is more easily digestible than plain soybeans because of the fermenting culture. Commercial tempeh is produced under very carefully controlled conditions, but in its native Indonesia tempeh is made at home as we make yogurt, and the cultures (to say nothing of the flavors) are much more varied and complex. Some samples of tempeh that have been tested have contained the vitamin B-12, and you may see the claim that tempeh is a vegetarian source of B-12. *Sometimes* it may be; but the organism that makes tempeh (*Rhizopus oligosporus*) does not make vitamin B-12. If the vitamin is present, it means that bacteria have been at work too, either by accident or design. Read the label to see if B-12 is present.

For much more about this fine food, including directions for making your own, we recommend the superb *Book of Tempeh* by William Shurtleff and Akiko Aoyagi (New York: Harper and Row, 1985).

Tofu is not a fermented food like tempeh, but it is a form of bean that many people find quick to prepare, pleasant to eat, and easy to digest. Because of its high fat and protein content, and because it is not a whole food, we don't use tofu as often these days as we used to. But it is so versatile and popular that it has an important role in a transitional diet, when you're trying to edge out less desirable foods like meat, cheese, and eggs. An important consideration when you're buying tofu: although tofu is often touted as an excellent source of calcium, it is so *only* if the coagulant used is calcium sulfate. The label will tell you.

TOFU

MISO *and* SHOYU *are fermented soybean condiments that find many uses in a vegetarian whole foods kitchen. For more about miso, see page 164; shoyu, page 234.*

Tempeh à la King

2 cups vegetable broth
8 ounces tempeh

1 medium onion, minced
2 tablespoons olive oil
½ cup chopped red bell
    pepper, or
    ¼ cup drained canned
    pimientos
1 cup sliced fresh
    mushrooms

3 tablespoons whole
    wheat flour

(1 teaspoon light miso)
2 tablespoons sherry
freshly ground black pepper
¼ cup blanched slivered
    almonds

Bring broth to a boil. Cut tempeh in small cubes and simmer in broth for about 10 minutes. Drain, reserving liquid, and set aside.

Sauté onion in oil until clear, then add bell pepper and mushrooms and continue to sauté over low heat, stirring often, until mushrooms are tender. (If you use pimientos, add them after mushrooms are cooked.)

Stir flour into sautéed vegetables and continue to cook and stir a minute or two. Meanwhile, add water to the reserved vegetable stock to bring it back up to 2 cups liquid and stir gradually into sautéed vegetable–flour mixture. Bring to a boil, reduce heat, and simmer for 5 minutes. Stir together miso and sherry and add to sauce along with pepper and cubed tempeh. Simmer briefly, adding almonds just before serving. Serve over brown rice or on triangles of whole-grain toast.

Makes 4 servings.

Tempeh Cacciatore

1 medium onion, slivered
½ cup chopped green
    bell pepper
2 tablespoons olive oil
1 clove garlic, minced
1 cup sliced fresh mushrooms
2½ cups tomatoes,
    peeled and chopped
⅓ cup red wine
1 bay leaf
½ teaspoon oregano
1 teaspoon basil
8 ounces tempeh, cubed
2 tablespoons shoyu

Sauté onion and pepper in 1 tablespoon olive oil over low heat until onion is translucent; then stir in garlic and mushrooms and cook another 5 minutes or so. Add tomatoes, wine, bay leaf, oregano, and basil and bring to a boil. Reduce heat and simmer for 10 minutes.

Meanwhile, in another small skillet or wok, sauté tempeh in remaining 1 tablespoon oil, stirring frequently, until it browns slightly. Add to sauce along with shoyu and simmer over low heat to marry the flavors (best if it can simmer at least half an hour). Serve on a bed of whole-grain spaghetti or brown rice.

Makes 4 servings.

Tempeh à l'Orange

This is about as haute as a soybean's gonna get. And *good.*

&

Cut tempeh in ½" chunks and sauté in 2 tablespoons oil for about 5 minutes. Drain on paper towels. (Tempeh will soak up all the oil you give it, so save half the oil to sauté the second side.)

Chop onion coarse. Slice celery stalks once lengthwise, then cut across in ½" slices. Sauté onion and celery in remaining oil until celery is tender. Stir in flour and keep stirring over medium heat just a minute or so; then add boiling water gradually.

Cook, stirring, while mixture thickens. Add orange juice, salt, honey, orange zest, pepper, parsley, and wine. Stir, bring to a boil, and simmer 4 or 5 minutes. Add tempeh chunks and simmer a few minutes longer to let flavors be absorbed.

Serves 4, over brown rice, quinoa, or bulgur wheat.

8 ounces tempeh
3–4 tablespoons oil

1 large onion
2 stalks celery
3 tablespoons whole wheat flour
2 cups boiling water

½ cup orange juice
1¼ teaspoons salt
1½ teaspoons honey
zest of 1 orange
dash black pepper
¼ cup chopped fresh parsley
½ cup white wine (or more orange juice)

Swedish Bean Balls

1½ cups cooked,
   well-drained beans
   (kidney, pinto, or red)
1 cup chopped onion
1 bay leaf
2 tablespoons oil

1 teaspoon lemon zest
1½ teaspoons lemon juice
1 slice whole wheat
   bread, soaked in
   milk or water
1 egg, beaten
¼ teaspoon thyme
dash nutmeg (and
   cardamom)
¾ teaspoon salt (divided)

(¼ cup dry whole wheat
   bread crumbs or cooked
   brown rice, if needed)

⅓ cup whole wheat flour
¼ teaspoon black pepper
2 cups milk
1 cup water

Preheat oven to 350°F.

Mash beans with potato masher, processor, or meat grinder. Sauté onion and bay leaf in oil in a large skillet until the onion is golden. Remove about ¼ cup of the sautéed onion with a slotted spoon and add it to the beans along with lemon peel and lemon juice. Squeeze all the liquid out of the bread (save it for the gravy) and work the bread into the mashed beans along with egg, thyme, spices, and ¼ teaspoon of the salt. (Omit salt if beans were already salted.)

If you have time, chill the mixture; it's easier to shape the balls when cold. If it seems too loose, add the dry bread crumbs or rice to stiffen it. Form 1½" balls and place on greased baking sheet. Bake 20 minutes, until balls are dry and firm.

Meanwhile, make the gravy. Stir flour into reserved sautéed onions and cook, stirring, until flour starts to brown. Add remaining ½ teaspoon salt, pepper, and milk and water. Cook over medium-high flame, stirring frequently, until mixture begins to boil and thickens. Reduce heat to low and simmer another 7 or 8 minutes, stirring frequently.

Remove bean balls from baking sheet and place in the skillet, spooning gravy over them. Cover and let stand for 10 minutes before serving; they need time to soak up some gravy. Serve with mashed potatoes or ribbon noodles.

Makes 12 balls, to serve 4.

Walnut Oatmeal Burgers 🍲

An oatmeal-walnut "burger" that makes a satisfying sub for the nonvegetarian sort in several dishes, including the Cuban favorite Picadillo below. So that you can try the burgers as such and enjoy Picadillo too, here's a double recipe of the basic mixture. Both recipes are quite flexible. Using the smaller amount of walnuts and eggs makes for a less rich but still excellent result.

🍂

Grind walnuts in blender and combine with oats, eggs, milk, onion, sage, salt, and pepper. Set half the mixture aside and refrigerate, to be used as suggested below. Form patties with the rest: 4 or 6, depending on the size of buns you'll be using.

Brown patties on both sides in a lightly oiled skillet, then pour the stock into the skillet and bring to a boil. Reduce heat and simmer, covered, for 25 minutes. Serve on buns with "the fixin's" or crumble and use as you would hamburger in chili beans, spaghetti sauce, etc.

Makes 4 to 6 burgers plus:

1½–3 cups walnut pieces
2 cups rolled oats
3 or 4 eggs, slightly beaten
½ cup skim milk
1 large onion, chopped fine
1 teaspoon sage
1 teaspoon salt
freshly ground black pepper
* to taste*
oil to brown patties
3 cups vegetable stock

Picadillo

This spicy mixture is traditionally served with Cuban black beans and rice, accompanied by mixed greens. It serves admirably well, too, over brown rice or whole wheat buns in the "Sloppy Joe" manner.

Form burger mixture into patties and brown on both sides as above. Dilute tomato paste in vegetable stock (if you have tomato sauce on hand, use 2 cups of that and 2 of stock). Add bay leaf and pour into the skillet. Bring to a boil, break up burgers with a fork (*picadillo* means "bits and pieces"), and reduce heat to a simmer. Cook uncovered, stirring often, for 20 minutes. Add chilis, olives, apple, and raisins, bring to a boil again, and simmer just until apples are tender.

Serves 4 generously.

½ recipe for
*   Walnut Oatmeal Burgers*
oil for sautéeing
½ cup tomato paste
3½ cups vegetable stock
1 bay leaf

½ cup cooked green chilis
*   (or a 6-ounce can)*
½ cup (1 small jar) stuffed
*   green olives, cut in two*
1 large, tart green apple,
*   peeled and chopped*
(¼ cup raisins)

Neat Balls 🪱

1 cup cooked bulgur wheat
  or brown rice
½ cup Soy Spread (page 113)
¼ cup cottage cheese and/or
  grated Swiss cheese
½ cup whole-grain bread
  crumbs
1 teaspoon shoyu

Easy, tasty, and whimsical. No one will take them for their look-alike, but in spaghetti with Tomato Sauce, or with gravy, or even just alongside vegetables, they provide a welcome bit of chew.

🍂

Preheat oven to 350°F.

Combine all ingredients and form into 1½" balls. Bake on greased cookie sheets for about 20 minutes. (Place them in top third of oven, or else turn them over after 10 minutes.)

Makes 12 to 15.

Sweet and Sour Tofu

½ cup large walnut pieces
2 blocks tofu (about
  22 ounces)
4 tablespoons shoyu
2 tablespoons sherry or saki

1 large onion
1 large green pepper
1 stalk celery
1 large or 2 small carrots
2 tablespoons oil
1 heaped cup fresh pineapple
  chunks

1½ tablespoons honey
2 tablespoons vinegar
1¼ cups vegetable stock
  or water
1½ tablespoons cornstarch

Toast walnut pieces in a dry skillet over medium heat, and set aside.

Cut tofu into 1" cubes and marinate in 2 tablespoons of the shoyu and the sherry.

Cut onion across center and down through the middle into wedge-shaped slices. Cut green pepper in pointy wedges and celery and carrots in thin diagonal slices. Stir-fry in oil until crispy-tender, adding pineapple after the first 2 or 3 minutes. Use a wok or heavy pan that has a lid—but not one made of cast iron; the acidity of this dish will cause it to discolor and taste metallic.

Combine honey, vinegar, and 1 cup of the vegetable stock, and add to vegetables along with tofu. Bring to a boil and simmer for a few minutes to heat tofu thoroughly.

Dissolve cornstarch in remaining ¼ cup stock and the remaining 2 tablespoons soy sauce. Stir into vegetables. Heat, stirring, while sauce thickens and clarifies somewhat.

Just before serving, adjust balance of sweet and sour to taste. Stir in the walnuts. Serve with brown rice.

Makes 6 servings.

Rice Lentil Polou

This recipe will have its best color if you cook it in a nonferrous pot.

½ medium onion
1 tablespoon oil
1 cup raw brown rice
1 tablespoon tomato paste
2½ cups water or
   vegetable stock
¼ teaspoon cinnamon
¼ cup raw lentils
1 teaspoon salt
½ cup raisins
(½ cup pine nuts
   or chopped almonds)

ক

Chop onion and sauté in oil until soft. Add rice and stir for several minutes. Combine tomato paste with water and cinnamon. Add this mixture, along with the rinsed lentils, to the rice. Bring to a boil, cover tightly, turn heat very low, and simmer for 30 minutes.

Preheat oven to 350°F.

Stir in salt, raisins, and nuts. The mixture should still have a little water; if not, add ¼ cup. Place in greased baking dish. Cover and bake for 20 to 30 minutes.

Serves 4 to 6.

Kichadi

A traditional dish that is served in many versions all over India. If you prefer, you can use 1 teaspoon curry powder instead of the whole spices and turmeric—Western guests may not expect to remove the cloves and sticks as they go along!

1 cup mung beans
2 medium onions
1½ tablespoons oil
1 cinnamon stick
4 cloves
1 pod cardamom
¼ teaspoon turmeric

2 cups raw brown rice
6 cups hot water
1½ teaspoons salt

ক

Soak the mung beans for half an hour.

Cut onion in paper-thin slices. Sauté in oil until golden; then, using a slotted spoon, remove the onions and set aside. Using the oil remaining in the pan, sauté the mung beans and spices for 5 minutes, stirring madly. Stir in the rice; when it begins to stick, add 5 cups of the hot water and bring to a boil. Turn to low and simmer very gently about half an hour. At that point, check to see if you think the remaining cup of water will be needed, and stir in the salt. Continue to cook for 15 minutes or longer, until rice and beans are tender. Garnish with onions.

Makes 6 cups.

Lentil Nut Loaf 🐚

1 onion, chopped fine
1 tablespoon oil
2 cups cooked, drained lentils
½ cup whole wheat bread
    crumbs
½ cup chopped toasted
    walnuts, or
    toasted sunflower seeds
½ teaspoon sage or thyme
2 tablespoons whole wheat
    flour
2 eggs, beaten
½ cup broth or water
2 teaspoons vinegar
2 teaspoons shoyu
1 tablespoon toasted
    sesame seeds

A flavorful and nourishing (if somewhat rich) loaf. This recipe is a favorite from our first edition, much simplified and improved. Quick to prepare using leftover lentils, and very well received at lunchtime with mustard or Homemade Ketchup or at supper with sauce or gravy.

🐟

Preheat oven to 350°F.

Sauté onion in oil until translucent and slightly browned.

Mix ingredients except sesame seeds and place in greased loaf pan. Sprinkle top with the seeds. Bake for 30 minutes covered, then for 10 minutes uncovered.

If you are in a hurry, you can shape patties and cook them on the griddle, with bread crumbs and/or more sesame seeds on top and bottom.

Makes one loaf, or 8 patties.

Stuffing

1 small onion, chopped
1 tablespoon oil
2 stalks celery, chopped
    (about 1 cup)
1 teaspoon basil
½ teaspoon oregano
¼ teaspoon thyme
⅛ teaspoon sage
½ teaspoon salt (adjust
    if salted stock is used)
shake of pepper

⅔ cup water or stock
4 cups whole-grain bread
    cubes
(½ cup coarsely chopped
    pecans or hazelnuts)

Use this to stuff tomatoes, green peppers, oversized zucchinis, winter squash, or just yourself and your friends.

🐟

Sauté the onion in the oil and add the celery and herbs, cooking until the celery is crispy-tender. Add the water or stock, then the bread, stirring to be sure it is evenly moistened. When hot through, add the pecans if desired.

Serve at once, or bake to make a crispy top.

Serves 4 as a hearty grain dish at lunch or dinner.

Tamale Pie

Tamale Pie is a satisfying main dish that can take a lot of variation.

If you have a double boiler, you can start the polenta cooking first, stirring it only occasionally. (In a regular pan it is likely to burn if left to itself while you prepare the filling.)

❧

Sauté onion and garlic in oil. When nearly soft, add chili powder (and cumin, if desired) and crush garlic with a fork. Continue to cook and stir until spices are fragrant. Meantime, mash beans and mix them and the tomato paste into the onion, along with the other filling ingredients. When hot, adjust seasonings and set aside.

Stir cornmeal slowly into boiling water. (If you use regular cornmeal instead of coarse it is likely to lump: stir it first into 1 cup *cold* water, then into 2 cups boiling water.) Cook and stir until thick, adding the salt and chili powder once the mixture comes to a boil.

Grease an 8″ × 8″ pan and spread two thirds of the cornmeal mixture over the bottom and sides; then pour the bean mixture into this cornmeal crust and drop and spread the remaining third of the cornmeal on the top. (Don't worry if it doesn't cover completely.) Sprinkle the top crust with grated cheddar cheese and cook in a 350° oven for half an hour.

Serves 4 generously.

FILLING
1 onion, chopped
1 clove garlic
1 tablespoon oil
2 teaspoons chili powder
(½ teaspoon cumin)
2 cups cooked pinto
   or kidney beans
1 teaspoon salt (less if beans
   were salted already)
2 tablespoons tomato paste
½ cup whole ripe olives
(½ cup fresh corn)
½ green pepper, chopped
½ cup chopped celery

CRUST
3 cups boiling water
1 cup coarsely ground
   cornmeal, or
   1½ cups regular
   cornmeal
1 teaspoon salt
½ teaspoon chili powder
¼ cup grated cheddar cheese
   (more if desired)

Refritos

Heat oil in a heavy pan. Put in the beans and heat, mashing them with a potato masher. Add pepper, and salt if the beans were not salted in cooking. Delicious served with a sprinkling of cheese on top.

Makes 4 cups.

1 tablespoon oil
   (olive is best)
4 cups cooked pinto beans
black pepper
(1 teaspoon salt)

(¼ cup or so grated jack
   cheese)

Many Bean Stew

1 onion, chopped
1 tablespoon oil
(1 clove garlic)
1½ teaspoons paprika

½ cup pinto beans
5 cups boiling water
1 bay leaf
1 teaspoon celery seed
½ cup kidney beans
½ cup limas
½ cup yellow split peas
1 teaspoon dill weed
2 teaspoons salt
¼ teaspoon pepper
2 cups cubed vegetables:
   potatoes, carrots, etc.

A good, hearty stew, adaptable to endless variations. ❧

Sauté the onion (and garlic) in oil along with paprika.

If you have a slow cooker, put all the ingredients in and simmer about 8 hours. If not, add the pintos and water, bay, and celery seed, and bring to a boil. Simmer, partially covered, about an hour. Add kidneys and limas and simmer another hour, then add remaining ingredients. Check and stir occasionally, especially toward the end, to make sure there is enough liquid to prevent burning. Simmer gently another hour, until done.

Makes about 6 cups.

Chili con Elote

1 onion, chopped
1 clove garlic
2 tablespoons oil
1 green pepper, diced
1 teaspoon chili powder
1 teaspoon cumin powder
1 cup chopped tomato, or
   2 tablespoons tomato
   paste
1 cup fresh corn
4 cups cooked kidney,
   black, or pinto beans
1½ teaspoons salt
1 teaspoon oregano

Basic and classic. The corn adds a lot, but when it isn't in season we make the dish without and it's just great.

The chili powder here is just enough for flavor without fierceness. If chili without tears isn't chili to you, use more, or add cayenne.

❧

Sauté onion and garlic clove in oil until onion is soft. Crush garlic clove. Add green pepper and spices. Sauté another 2 or 3 minutes. Add tomatoes and corn if you have it. Mash 2 cups of the beans and add to pot along with whole beans and salt and oregano. Simmer 30 minutes.

Serves 6.

Boston Baked Beans

This classic, richly-flavored version is irresistible whether you
have time to bake it or not—but the baking does marry the flavors
in an especially splendid way. ✿

Preheat oven to 325°F.

Sauté onion in oil. Mix all ingredients. Place in a greased,
shallow glass or ceramic casserole. Bake covered for 45 minutes.

Makes 6 servings (about 3½ cups).

1 onion, chopped
1½ tablespoons oil
3 cups cooked navy beans
  and liquid
⅓ cup molasses
2 to 4 tablespoons
  shoyu, to taste
1 tablespoon prepared
  mustard

Tennessee Corn Pone 🐚

A homesick friend from Knoxville described a dish his grandma
used to make. He says this one is juuust like grandma's. It's
certainly one of our favorites. ✿

Heat beans until quite hot and pour into a lightly greased 8″ × 8″
baking dish. Preheat oven to 450°F.

Mix the cornmeal, baking soda, and salt in a large bowl. Melt
the butter and combine with buttermilk and egg.

Stir the wet and dry ingredients together until smooth, and
pour them over the hot beans. Bake on the top rack of your oven
until bread is a rich golden color and the sides of the corn bread
pull away from the sides of the pan—about 30 minutes.

Serves 4 to 6.

2 cups very juicy cooked
  and seasoned beans
  (especially pinto or
  kidney)
1 cup cornmeal
1 teaspoon baking soda
½ teaspoon salt
2 tablespoons butter
2 cups buttermilk
1 egg, slightly beaten

Black-Eyed Peas Virginia Style

Sauté onion in oil, add celery and green pepper, and sauté another
2 minutes. Add tomato, beans, and salt and pepper to taste (½
teaspoon salt is about right if the beans weren't already salted.)
Cook another 5 minutes and serve.

Serves 4.

1 small onion, chopped fine
1 tablespoon oil
¼ cup chopped celery
¼ green pepper, chopped
⅔ cup tomato, chopped
2 cups black-eyed peas,
  well cooked, with liquid
salt and pepper

Dessert

A keen sweet tooth tells a monkey whether the fruit in his hand will nourish or give him stomachache. Even an amoeba will go toward sugar in solution. Something very deep in us responds to sweetness, and no category of food taps such passion. (A lot of people have told us that it was easy to give up meat, but *sugar*—!)

Well, there *is* a time and place for a child's birthday cake, for oatmeal cookies slipped into a lunchbox, or for pie or cobbler to celebrate a cache of fresh-picked blackberries. But when those special gestures start to slip in several times a week, they begin to pose a real threat to health. Annual per capita sugar consumption in this country has risen to 127 pounds. Clearly, Americans are in trouble.

So, our basic premise: keep special occasions special by reserving fancy sweets for them, and let daily desserts and snacks be mostly fruit, with all its natural goodness.

In this section we offer sweets that are real alternatives. Our cookies *are* cookies, but with a lighter touch; our pound cake *is* pound cake, but with less butter; our cheese pie is *almost* cheesecake, but with a tiny fraction of the fat—and so on. Many natural food dessert books claim that because their confections are made with unbleached flour, pure honey, natural butter, and fertilized eggs, they are "healthy." How we wish we could agree! Using natural ingredients is good; you avoid many additives. But "healthy"—well, it's still the same amounts of butter, sugar, and eggs.

A dessert concoction can delight and satisfy without astronomical amounts of fat and sugar calories; but if you want "healthy," you can't come closer than fresh, ripe fruit. Plain, cut up with yogurt, made into salad, or cooked in imaginative ways when the season is on the wane, fruit really is the ideal way to say yes to a sweet tooth. Search out local sources; you may be able to get grapes, apples, peaches, apricots, berries, ripe from the tree or vine. What a difference!

Less obvious, there's a subtle magic about the rhythm of fresh fruit. Eating plenty of what is in season means that you can welcome eagerly something you haven't had all year. Enjoy it every which way until the season is finished, so you're even a little glad to see the end of it and ready to greet like a long-lost friend the next fruit that comes along.

If you have the kind of self-control that lets you enjoy sumptuous desserts when the rare occasion demands it, but never feel tempted at other times, this section is not necessary for you. But if you don't, or your family doesn't, and you are looking for ways to decelerate the sweets roller coaster, the following recipes should prove helpful.

Innocent Sweets

This works best with large fruit ("colossal" prunes are amazingly good). Stuff with Yogurt Cheese or a mixture of cottage cheese and ricotta, blended smooth with a little honey; add pizzazz with finely grated lemon rind or minced crystallized ginger and decorate with a perfect walnut half. (Chill before serving; the cheese mixture will firm up.) A festive offering at holiday time.

STUFFED PRUNES
OR DATES

In winter, Bosc pears and Winter Nelis are often available at bargain prices. Even if they are rock-hard, bake them like yams for the sweetest, most delicious, and easiest dessert imaginable. They don't want stuffing like apples; you just stand them on their bottoms in a pan (line it with brown paper if you want to save scrubbing later) and bake at about 350°F for 45 minutes or so, until the syrupy juice has broken out and the pear is soft. We usually serve them as is, but you might want to make a gingery sauce or pass toasted nuts or feta cheese to nibble alongside.

BAKED PEARS

Make fruit pops by blending equal parts of mild yogurt and ripe berries or other sweet fruit. These can be rather horrid if the yogurt is tart and the fruit not sweet, so add some honey when needed. Freeze in popsicle molds.

FRUIT POPS

FRUITED YOGURT

A perfect combination that can be plain or fancy: just fruit with a dollop of yogurt. You can alternate layers in parfait glasses, or in small jars for bag lunches. You can even make your own fruit yogurt: just place a layer of dried or cooked fruit in the bottom of several containers, pour in the milk and starter, and culture as usual. All these ideas work best when the yogurt is mild.

Here are some easy and tasty suggestions, with approximate amounts to use for one cup of yogurt:

½ cup stewed apples and a dash of cinnamon

½ cup Fruit Tzimmes

*1 large, ripe persimmon, peeled and cut up,
    and a tablespoon of raisins*

*3 or 4 chopped dried apricots (add a little honey if
    apricots are tart) or a mixture of apricots and pineapple*

4 big dates, pitted and chopped, with a dash of cinnamon

*¼ cup chopped prunes, with a slivered slice of crystallized
    ginger*

*any amount of fresh strawberries or other sweet berries,
    or fresh ripe peaches, pears, apricots, plums . . .*

3 tablespoons raisins, with a dash of cinnamon

Desserts from Apples

Since apples grow nearly everywhere and store well, they are inexpensive and good during the cold months. For winter desserts, they take many roles. Here are a few of our favorites.

Baked Apples

Preheat oven to 350°. Core apples and place in a greased baking dish with a cover. It's good if the apples are a snug fit: if not, cut up a fifth apple in quarters and tuck it around.

Mix the wheat germ, raisins, nuts, lemon zest, cinnamon, sugar, and salt and press lightly into the apple cores. Mix the flour and apple juice and pour over the apples.

Cover and bake 40 minutes, or until the apples are very soft. Let cool slightly before serving for best flavor.

Serves 4.

VARIATION:

Substitute 2 tablespoons toasted sesame seeds for the nuts, and use 6 tablespoons of raisins instead of 4. (This is a delightful combination.)

4 large flavorful apples

1/4 cup toasted wheat germ
1/4 cup raisins
1/4 cup chopped walnuts
* or filberts*
zest of 1/2 lemon
1/8 teaspoon cinnamon
1 tablespoon brown sugar
pinch salt

1 tablespoon flour
3/4 cup apple juice

Diane's Apple Crisp

This homey, quickly-made favorite, with perhaps a little yogurt alongside, can stand proudly next to the most exotic dessert.

❧

Preheat oven to 375°F. Slice apples until you have enough to fill a greased 9" × 13" baking dish. Mix the apples in a bowl with lemon juice, cinnamon, flour, and raisins. Return them to the baking dish, adding enough water or apple juice to cover the bottom.

Mix topping in a bowl and press onto top of apples. Bake for 25 minutes, or until apples are soft.

Serves 8.

8 apples (green pippins
* are best)*
juice of 1 lemon
1 teaspoon cinnamon
2 tablespoons whole
* wheat flour*
3/4 cup raisins
water or apple juice

TOPPING

1 cup rolled oats
1/3 cup toasted wheat germ
1/2 cup whole wheat flour
1/2 teaspoon salt
2 teaspoons cinnamon
1/2 cup brown sugar
1/2 cup butter (or oil)

Appley Bread Pudding 🍎

2 cups grated apples
juice of 1 lemon

4 cups whole-grain bread,
  cubed small
1/2 cup cottage cheese
1/3 cup raisins
1/4 teaspoon cinnamon

2 cups milk
1/4 cup dried skim milk
1 egg
1/4 cup brown sugar

1 tablespoon butter

The best bread pudding we have tasted. Besides being a super way to use up stale bread, the dish is so nutritious and high in protein that it can supply all the heft that is needed with a light dinner.

Of course, bread pudding can be even simpler. If you are out of apples, or in a hurry, all you actually *have* to have is the cubed bread with the milk and egg, plus sugar and spice (and a dot or two of butter) for flavor. It bakes while you eat dinner, and is ready when you want dessert.

ᴓ

Preheat oven to 350°F. Grease an 8″ × 8″ pan.

Grate the apples and mix in the lemon juice.

Put 1/3 of the bread in the bottom of the greased pan. Cover with half the apple, half the cottage cheese, half the raisins, and a sprinkle of the cinnamon.

Blend the milk, milk powder, egg, and sugar together and pour half over the ingredients in the baking dish. Now repeat the layers of bread, apples, and liquid, ending with more bread. Pour the last of the milk mixture over the top, sprinkle with cinnamon, and dot with butter.

Let the pudding sit for 20 minutes if you can, especially if the bread is not light. Bake, covered, for 45 minutes, then let stand for at least ten minutes at room temperature before serving.

Serves 4 to 6.

Fruit Tzimmes

1 pound (3 cups) dried
  fruits: raisins, prunes,
  apricots, but not dates
  or figs
2 grated carrots
2 grated apples
1 lemon or lime, thinly sliced
1 teaspoon salt
1 tablespoon butter
water for soaking fruit

Tzimmes is a favorite fruit dessert in Jewish cookery: sweet but piquant, delicious with Blintzes or Latkes, or with yogurt, or as a kind of chutney with brown rice and vegetables.

ᴓ

Wash dried fruit and soak in water, covered, for 1 hour. Drain water and reserve. Combine all ingredients in a pot with 1/2 cup of the soaking water. Bring to a boil, then cook over very low heat for 1 or 2 hours, adding more liquid as needed.

Makes 4 cups.

Vanilla Pudding 🝑

Serve this simple, wholesome dessert with fresh peaches or berries, figs, or orange slices, garnished with chopped toasted nuts—or serve it plain. It's nearly as easy as instant pudding and a whole lot cheaper. Using honey instead of sugar gives a delightful flavor, but *some* honeys can make the pudding thin out—most frustrating.

🝑

Gently heat 1½ cups of the milk in a heavy pan. Stir in the sugar and salt.

Combine the cornstarch or arrowroot with the reserved milk. Add to the milk when it is very hot; cook and stir over low heat until thick. If you are using cornstarch, continue to cook and stir over very low heat for a few minutes more. (If you want a richer version, you can stir a beaten egg into ½ cup of the pudding, then beat that into the whole pudding while it is still very hot.) Cool somewhat and add vanilla.

Makes about 2 cups to serve 4—in theory. (Sometimes it actually serves two.) Good warm or cold.

2 cups fresh milk

¼ cup brown sugar
⅛ teaspoon salt
2 tablespoons cornstarch
　　or arrowroot
1 teaspoon vanilla

Payasam 🝑

Literally food for the gods—at least, in Indian myths—this creamy rice pudding is the required finale for a South Indian feast. To make rice meal, grind brown rice fine in blender.

🝑

Make a paste with rice meal and ½ cup of the cold milk.

Heat remaining milk and stir in rice mixture and sugar. Bring gently to a boil, stirring to prevent sticking, and continue to cook gently until mixture thickens slightly, 5 to 10 minutes, depending on how fine the rice was.

Remove pods from cardamom and discard. Crush seeds in a mortar and pestle or with two spoons. Heat butter in a small skillet; add cardamom and cashews, and when cashews are just beginning to toast, add raisins. When nuts are nicely brown and raisins puffy, add them to the thickened milk.

Cool. Payasam is quite soupy when it's "just right."
Serves 4 to 8.

¼ cup rice meal

1 quart milk
¼ cup brown sugar

3 cardamom pods
1 tablespoon butter
¼ cup cashews
¼ cup raisins

Apple Spice Ring

2½ cups grated apple,
    peeled and cored first
2 cups raisins
1½ cups boiling water
3 tablespoons oil

1 cup + 2 tablespoons honey
1½ teaspoons cinnamon
1½ teaspoons allspice
½ teaspoon cloves
1½ teaspoons salt

3 cups whole wheat pastry
    flour
1½ teaspoons baking soda
¾ cup chopped walnuts

Moist, rich, and spicy, a favorite for festive occasions. Keeps for a week in the refrigerator, if no one knows it's there.

∼

Preheat oven to 350°F.

Pour boiling water over apples and raisins. Top with oil and let stand 10 minutes. Add honey and spices (including salt), then allow to cool.

Sift together the flour and baking soda, add walnuts, and combine with the other ingredients. Pour into well-greased tube pan (or 8″ × 8″ pan or two 4″ × 8″ loaf pans).

Bake for 45 minutes to 1 hour.

CARROT FRUITCAKE

Replace apples with 1½ cups grated carrots. Use 1½ cups raisins and 2¼ cups boiling water. Cook the carrots and raisins in the water 10 minutes; then add oil, honey, salt, and spices and allow to cool. Proceed as above, beginning where the dry ingredients are sifted together.

Pound Cake 🝳

2¼ cups whole wheat
    pastry flour
1½ teaspoons baking
    powder
½ teaspoon baking soda
½ teaspoon salt

⅔ cup honey
½ cup butter
1 teaspoon vanilla

2 eggs
¾ cup buttermilk

Traditional versions of this gloriously understated dessert require a pound of butter, a pound of sugar, and a pound of eggs. Yet this one is delicious.

∼

Preheat oven to 350°F.

Ingredients should be at room temperature. Sift flour before measuring, then sift with baking powder, baking soda, and salt.

Cream honey and butter. Add vanilla.

Separate eggs. Whip egg whites until stiff. Beat yolks and add to honey and butter. Add sifted ingredients to this mixture, a third at a time, alternating with buttermilk.

Fold in egg whites and turn into a 4″ × 8″ loaf pan.

Bake 1 hour.

Banana Bread

Preheat oven to 375°F.

Mash bananas and mix them with lemon juice until smooth. Cream butter or oil and sugar together and add the banana mix, stirring well.

Sift together flour, salt, baking powder, and baking soda. Mix in wheat germ. Add to the banana mix and stir in the dates and nuts if desired.

The dough will be very stiff. Turn it into a greased 4″ × 8″ loaf pan and bake for about 45 minutes. To test for doneness, insert a knife into the loaf: if it comes out clean, the bread is done.

Makes 1 loaf.

(You can also bake banana bread in an 8″ × 8″ pan, or make 12 cupcakes. Bake these for about ½ hour.)

3 very ripe bananas
(1 cup mashed)
juice of 1 lemon
⅓ cup oil or butter
½ cup brown sugar

1½ cups whole wheat flour
½ teaspoon salt
½ teaspoon baking powder
½ teaspoon baking soda
½ cup wheat germ
(1 cup chopped dates)
(1 cup toasted nuts)

Gingerbread

This may well be the definitive gingerbread. We certainly tested enough alternative versions before we agreed upon it. (In fact, this whole chapter of recipes has been extraordinarily well tested.)

ৰ

Preheat oven to 350°F.

Mix butter and molasses. Beat in egg and add buttermilk or orange juice.

Sift together the dry ingredients and combine everything together.

Turn into a greased 9″ × 9″ square pan. Bake 40 minutes.

⅓ cup soft or melted butter
1 cup dark molasses or
⅔ cup blackstrap and
⅓ cup honey
1 egg
1 cup buttermilk or orange
juice

2½ cups whole wheat flour
1 teaspoon soda
1 teaspoon cinnamon
2 teaspoons powdered ginger
½ teaspoon salt

½ cup raisins
(1 tablespoon orange zest)
(½ teaspoon mustard
powder)

Figgy Pudding 🍮

2 tablespoons soft butter
½ cup honey

3 eggs

1 cup chopped dried figs,
 packed
1 apple, peeled and sliced
1 cup apple juice

zest of 1 lemon
1 teaspoon vanilla
1 cup raisins
1 cup finely chopped walnuts
2 cups soft whole wheat
 bread crumbs

1 cup whole wheat flour
1 teaspoon baking powder
½ teaspoon salt
¼ teaspoon baking soda
1 teaspoon cinnamon
½ teaspoon nutmeg
¼ teaspoon ground cloves

Traditional as can be, and delicious, Figgy Pudding contains lots less fat than pie, though you'd never guess it.

❧

Cream butter and honey. Separate eggs, setting whites aside. Beat egg yolks until creamy. Add to butter-honey mixture.

Use a blender or food processor to grind figs and apples with apple juice to jamlike consistency. Combine with lemon rind, vanilla, raisins, walnuts, bread crumbs, and the egg yolk mixture.

Sift flour with baking powder, salt, soda, cinnamon, nutmeg, and cloves. Beat egg whites until stiff. Combine wet ingredients with dry, then gently fold in egg whites. Turn batter out into a greased 2-quart casserole or pudding mold with a lid. You can use parchment or foil for a lid, securing it with twine, but be sure to allow room for expansion: the pudding will rise to about half again its uncooked size.

Place pudding on a rack inside a pot large enough to give 2 inches of space all around for the steam to circulate. Pour boiling water into the pot halfway up the sides of the casserole. Cover the pot and let water boil briskly a few moments, then turn heat to low. Keep an eye on the water and replenish it if the level goes down. Steam for 2½ hours or until top springs back when touched.

To unmold, turn out carefully onto a plate. Splash with brandy and ignite, if you like, and serve with a scoop of vanilla ice cream or with the topping below.

Serves 12.

Yogurt Cheese Topping 🍮

1½ cups yogurt cheese
2 tablespoons honey
lemon juice to taste
zest of 1 lemon, minced

This topping is adaptable to many roles, and can be made entirely successfully with low-fat or even skim-milk yogurt. If you have good oranges or tangerines, they can sub for the lemon—try that on strawberries!

❧

Gently stir cheese smooth with a fork and add the other ingredients, adjusting the sweetness to taste.

Spicy Pattern Cookies

These are quite austere when freshly baked, so if you want to eat them right away, plan on at least a little frosting. But they improve in airtight storage so that two weeks later, they are fine even without decoration.

ᨒ

Preheat oven to 350°.

Cream butter and sugar and beat in the molasses. Sift the flour, setting aside any bran that remains behind to add later. Sift again with the soda, salt, and spices, then stir in wheat germ and reserved bran. Mix dry ingredients into molasses mixture, adding enough of the water to make a workable dough.

Roll dough out about ¼″ thick (or thinner if you prefer) and cut into shapes. Transfer to greased cookie sheets and bake for about 10 minutes, until just barely beginning to brown. Makes 4 dozen 2″ cookies.

Decorate by pressing in currants, filbert halves, etc., before baking or with a simple powdered sugar frosting after the cookies have cooled. (If you are working with children and want to tint decorative frostings with food coloring, remember that artificial food colors shouldn't be ingested in anything but truly minute quantities.)

¼ cup butter
¼ cup brown sugar

½ cup dark molasses

3 cups whole wheat flour
1 teaspoon baking soda
½ teaspoon salt
1 teaspoon ginger
½ teaspoon cinnamon
¼ teaspoon cloves

½ cup wheat germ

about ½ cup water

Anise Seed Cookies 🍪

Light, delicate cookies, softly crisp.

ᨒ

Sift together flour, baking powder, and salt. Cream butter and sugar. Beat in egg, lemon peel, anise seeds, vanilla, and water. Gradually add dry ingredients to liquid, mixing well. Divide in half and roll into logs 1½″ in diameter. Wrap each in waxed paper and refrigerate several hours or overnight.

Preheat oven to 375°F. Cut dough into slices about ¼″ thick. Dip in powdered sugar if desired and bake on greased cookie sheet for 10 to 12 minutes.

Makes 3 to 4 dozen.

1½ cups whole wheat flour
1½ teaspoons baking
powder
½ teaspoon salt
3 tablespoons butter
  (room temperature)
½ cup brown sugar
1 egg, slightly beaten
1 teaspoon grated lemon peel
1½ teaspoons anise seeds
1 teaspoon vanilla
3 tablespoons water
(powdered sugar)

Oatmeal School Cookies 🍪

½ cup butter (¼ pound)
¾ cup brown sugar, packed
1 lightly beaten egg
1½ teaspoons vanilla
½ teaspoon salt

1 cup whole wheat flour
¾ teaspoon baking powder
½ cup toasted wheat germ
¾ cup rolled oats
¾ cup raisins
¾ cup chopped walnuts or
    toasted sunflower seeds

When we make cookies, it is almost always these. They are *Cookies*: utterly satisfying. One would wish they could be maybe a little lower in fat and sugar, but there, that's *Cookies* for you—don't make a habit of 'em.

❧

Preheat oven to 375°F. Cream butter and sugar until fluffy. Add egg, vanilla, and salt, and beat well.

Stir flour, baking powder, wheat germ, and rolled oats together with a fork. Blend well with other ingredients, adding a tablespoon or more of water if necessary to hold the mixture together.

Place by tablespoonful on greased cookie sheets. Flatten them slightly. Bake for 10 to 12 minutes.

Makes 24.

Graham Cookies 🍪

2 cups whole wheat flour
½ cup wheat bran
½ cup wheat germ
1 teaspoon baking powder
½ teaspoon baking soda
¼ teaspoon salt

½ cup butter
½ cup brown sugar

½ cup milk or buttermilk

This delicious version of graham crackers is too rich to be called a cracker, but too good not to include.

❧

Stir together the dry ingredients. Cream the butter and brown sugar until fluffy. Add flour mixture alternately with milk, mixing well after each addition.

Chill dough for several hours or overnight.

Preheat oven to 350°F. Roll dough out thin, directly onto greased cookie sheets, and cut into squares or shapes. Prick with fork and bake 10 to 12 minutes, until brown.

Makes about 4 dozen 2½″ cookies.

Raisin Bars

This recipe is a gift from master whole-foods baker Manuel Freedman. It has no sugar or honey, and needs none! The taste is reminiscent of an old favorite, those giant flat cookies with smooshed raisins inside.

ᕗ

Preheat oven to 325°F.

Blend the flour, oats, salt, and oil with fingers until evenly mixed. Add raisins, nuts, and water, and mix them in, pressing together with the fingers. (Use larger amount of water only if absolutely necessary to make it all hold together.) Press down very well into a greased 8″ × 8″ pan and cut into squares with a spatula before baking.

Bake ½ hour. Makes 16 two-inch bars.

1 cup whole wheat pastry flour
1 cup rolled oats
½ teaspoon salt
¼ cup oil
1¼ cups finely chopped or ground raisins
1 cup chopped walnuts
⅓ to ½ cup water

Sunshine Bars

Well, here they are, "health food bars"—but much tastier than the ones you can buy.

ᕗ

Preheat oven to 350°F.

Heat orange juice to a boil. Put dried apricots in pan, bring to a boil again, and turn off heat. Cover pan and let apricots absorb juice until tender enough to cut with a sharp knife, but not really soft.

Meanwhile, mix honey and oil. Stir oats, flour, wheat germ, cinnamon, and salt together.

Drain apricots and add the juice to the honey-oil mixture. Chop apricots coarsely and stir into dry ingredients along with raisins and almond meal. Combine wet and dry ingredients and press mixture into an oiled 9″ × 13″ baking dish. Bake about 30 minutes. Keep an eye on them! Cookies made with honey brown quickly.

Allow to cool completely before cutting.

Makes about 2 dozen large squares.

1 cup orange juice
1 cup dried apricots, loosely packed

½ cup honey
½ cup oil

1½ cups rolled oats
1 cup whole wheat flour
½ cup wheat germ
1 teaspoon cinnamon
½ teaspoon salt

1 cup raisins, partly cut up
⅔ cup toasted almond meal

Honey-Peanut Butter Cookies 🐚

1 cup natural peanut butter
  (crunchy is best)
1 cup honey
1 egg, beaten
1½ teaspoons vanilla

½ teaspoon salt
½ teaspoon baking soda
2 cups whole wheat flour,
  preferably pastry flour

These cookies, and the following almond version, are natural-foods alternatives to the very rich and sugary standard editions. The flavor is different: the honey really sings out. It also makes the cookies softer rather than crispy, and (sad truth) prone to burn if not watched carefully while they bake. They're worth it: these are *very* good cookies indeed.

🍂

Preheat oven to 350°F.

Cream peanut butter and honey together. Stir in egg and vanilla. Sift together salt, soda, and flour, and stir into peanut butter mixture.

Drop by teaspoonfuls onto oiled cookie sheets. Mash each cookie slightly with the back of a fork, wetting the fork frequently to prevent sticking. Bake for 10 or 12 minutes, until they just begin to turn golden brown on the rims. Keep a close eye on them! Cookies made from honey pass very quickly from golden brown to black.

Makes 3 or 4 dozen. Very good keepers.

HONEY—ALMOND COOKIES

The Adult Version: light, flavorful, pretty.

🍂

Substitute smooth, toasted almond butter for peanut butter, and almond extract for vanilla.

To form the cookies, roll the dough into balls about walnut-size. Press a blanched almond down in the center of each one.

Another way to use these recipes is REFRIGERATOR COOKIES: form the dough into a cylinder, and refrigerate, slicing off what you need to bake in smaller batches. Or make pinwheels: Work ¼ to ½ cup chocolate or carob powder into half the dough; then roll both halves out thin on waxed paper and, using your rolling pin to lift the dough, transfer one onto the other. (It's tricky, because there's no moving 'em once they're together!) Roll up tightly and refrigerate overnight. Cut into thin cookies with a sharp knife or strong thread (dental floss works very nicely).

Bake as above.

Summer Fruit Mold

Molded salads are a traditional favorite for summer, but many people write them off when they become vegetarians because they don't want to use gelatin. Agar, made from seaweed, puts molded salads back on the map. The following recipe is simple, pretty, and adaptable to any number of fruits—and dressy enough for the fanciest wedding buffet. (Look for white grape juice at the supermarket if you don't want to pay a fortune for the gourmet kinds.)

2½ tablespoons agar flakes
2 cups white grape juice
2 tablespoons lime juice
  (1 big lime)
1 cup fresh raspberries or
  blackberries
1 cup sliced fresh peaches

🍃

Dissolve agar in grape juice and add lime juice. Let sit a few minutes, stir, and heat to just shy of boiling. Reduce heat and simmer for 3 minutes, stirring frequently. Pour into 4 warm wine glasses and allow to cool for just 15 minutes. Gently stir in berries and peaches, and refrigerate until ready to serve. (It will set firm in about 30 minutes.) Decorate with a sprig of mint and a few raspberries, or whatever seems pretty to you.
  Makes 4 servings.

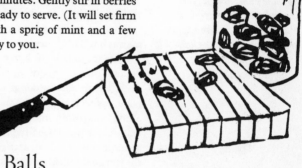

Cashew Cardamom Balls

Cashew Cardamom Balls have an oriental ambience. Sophisticated, sweet, and sinfully rich-tasting, they qualify easily as gourmet fare; but they're so easy to make that you can turn them out for lunchbox treats.

1 cup lightly toasted
  cashew pieces
cardamom seeds from
  2 to 4 pods
  (⅛ to ¼ teaspoon
  powdered)
1 cup finely chopped dates
finely grated peel of
  one orange
½ cup dried coconut, toasted
  and then powdered in
  blender

🍃

Chop cashews rather fine (the blender chops them *too* fine). Remove cardamom from pods and grind with a mortar and pestle or between two spoons. Combine cashews and cardamom in a bowl with dates and orange peel. Knead mixture with fingertips until uniform, then roll in 1″ balls and coat them with coconut.
  Makes 18.

Whole Wheat Piecrust

1½ cups whole wheat flour
½ cup wheat germ
   (or ¼ cup flour)
¾ teaspoon salt
10 tablespoons butter,
   chilled

4 to 6 tablespoons cold water

*Keep an eye on the baking
pastry; whole wheat piecrust
tends to brown easily. When
we bake pumpkin pie, for
example, we keep strips of
aluminum foil on hand to put
around the crust at the halfway point. Baking the pie on
a cookie sheet helps too.*

Whole wheat flour gives piecrust a rich flavor that makes the
white kind seem insipid. This recipe is not difficult to prepare,
and it gives a flaky, mouth-watering result, especially if you use
the wheat germ. (If there's none in the house, or if you want a less
overtly wheaty flavor, using a little extra flour works fine too.)

Use all-purpose whole wheat flour, or half bread flour and half
pastry flour. Using all pastry flour makes a tender, crumbly crust
rather than a flaky one.

૨ª

Stir together flour, wheat germ, and salt. Grate the cold butter on
a coarse grater or cut into small pieces, tossing it with the flour as
you go. Use a pastry cutter or two knives to combine the flour and
butter until it is the consistency of rolled oats. Sprinkle with the
water, using just enough to hold the dough together.

Using cupped fingers, form the dough quickly and gently. As
soon as it will hold together, make it into a ball.

Press the dough out into a thick disk. Roll to size on a lightly
floured surface, or between sheets of waxed paper, or on a pastry
cloth. Gently roll the dough over the rolling pin and onto the pie
plate, easing it loosely into the plate. If it sticks to the table, slide
a long, sharp knife underneath; if it tears, patch with extra dough
once it is in place. Gently press the dough into the plate so there
are no air pockets. Cut off the excess with a sharp knife, but make
the rim double thick to keep it from burning.

If you are making a bottom-shell-only pie, form an attractive
rim on the crust and prick the shell all over with a fork. To keep
the pastry from shrinking, and to get the flakiest crust, refrigerate
it for about 2 hours or overnight before filling.

To prebake, place in a preheated oven (400°F) for 10 to 12
minutes; cool and fill. For a partly baked shell (for quiche, for
example) bake only until the pastry is set, about 7 minutes.

If you are making a pie with a top crust or lattice, preheat the
oven to 400°F. Fill the bottom shell and put the top crust or lattice
in place, baking according to the directions in the recipe you
are using.

Makes one 10″ bottom crust or crust and lattice for one 8″ pie.

Mock Mince Pie

Simple, spicy, delicious—our favorite Thanksgiving pie.

❧

Pare and slice apples, chop raisins, and mix with apple juice.
Scrub the orange, then grate the peel and squeeze the juice. Add
peel and juice to the apple mixture and simmer together in a
covered pan until the apples are very soft. Stir in the sugar,
cinnamon, cloves, and the brandy extract if desired. This mixture
will keep for several days if you want to prepare it ahead.

Preheat oven to 450°F.

Line a 9″ pie pan with pastry and make the extra dough into a
lattice. Reheat the filling, if it has been chilled, and pour it hot
into the shell. Cover with lattice and bake for 30 minutes.

Makes one 9″ pie.

4 medium apples
½ cup raisins
⅓ cup apple juice
1 orange

¾ cup brown sugar
½ teaspoon cinnamon
½ teaspoon cloves
½ teaspoon brandy
 (or extract)
dough for a 10″ piecrust

Berry Pudding Pie 🍮

For a scrumptious summertime dessert, fill a prebaked pie shell
or crumb crust with 3 cups or so of fresh blackberries, raspberries, strawberries, blueberries, or sliced peaches. Pour Vanilla Pudding (page 315) over them while it's still warm. Sprinkle
with toasted nuts if you like, and chill.

If you have fruit too pretty to hide, fill your pie shell with
pudding and let it cool slightly. Arrange sweet berries or slices of
ripe, sweet peach, kiwi, or apricot on top. (You can prevent
sliced fruit from turning brown by dipping it in orange juice, or
by heating it briefly as described in the Blueberry Cheese Pie
recipe, on the next page.)

Yogurt Cheese Pie

graham cracker crust
(page 327)

¼ pound dried calimyrna
figs (¾ cup chopped)
⅓ cup honey

1½ teaspoons vanilla
zest of 1 lemon, finely grated
2 cups stiff yogurt cheese
(page 104)

¼ cup chopped walnuts
for topping

This delicious dessert is very like cheesecake, but a more innocent one you won't easily find. And it is easy.

❧

Chop figs and place in small saucepan with honey. Add boiling water to cover. Bring to a boil, reduce heat, and simmer, stirring occasionally, for 10 minutes. Cover and let sit until figs are fully rehydrated; boil off extra water until the remaining liquid is quite thick.

Stir stewy figs, vanilla, and lemon zest into yogurt cheese and pour into crust. Sprinkle with walnuts. Chill for a couple of hours before serving.

BLUEBERRY CHEESE PIE

2 cups berries, or a
combination of fruits

Leave out the figs and vanilla. Sweeten and flavor the yogurt cheese with honey and lemon zest, adding extra honey as needed to taste. Spread it into the crust and top it with berries or a beautiful arrangement of other prime summer fruits, such as sliced peaches, raspberries, strawberries, and blueberries.

For extra elegance, you can glaze the fruit very lightly to bring up its flavor and give it shine. Kuzu powder gives the best shine, but you can use arrowroot if you have that. (Cornstarch doesn't thicken as quickly, so the fruit may overcook.)

GLAZE
juice of 1 lemon
2 tablespoons honey
1 tablespoon kuzu powder
or arrowroot

Dissolve the kuzu powder in lemon juice and stir in the honey. Heat the fruit in a non-iron skillet, shaking or stirring gently to ensure even heat. When hot, add the mixture of lemon juice, honey, and thickener. Stir gently as before, letting the liquid coat the fruit evenly. As soon as the thickener has cooked, remove from heat. Allow to cool somewhat, then place topping on cheese filling. If you are using a combination of fruits, cook in separate batches to keep each one's color clear.

Graham Cracker Crusts 🍥

This crust holds together well, tastes good, and has no fat beyond what is in the graham crackers.

🍂

Mix ingredients very well and press into a buttered 8" or 9" pie pan or quiche pan (the kind with scalloped vertical sides and pop-out bottom). The mixture is sticky; it helps to wet your fingers.

Bake 15 minutes, until delicately brown.

1½ cups finely crushed graham crackers
3 tablespoons yogurt
1½ tablespoons honey
¼ teaspoon cinnamon

QUICK CRUST

This version is much more sinful and doesn't hold together as well as the first, but it has the advantage of not needing baking.

🍂

Mix ingredients and press into 9" pie pan.

1 cup finely crushed graham crackers
3 tablespoons warm honey
3 tablespoons melted butter
½ cup finely chopped walnuts

Peanut Butter Bars 🍥

A calorie-packed treat. Candy is what it is, and "PB Bars" probably should have been exorcised from this book long ago. But they seem to fill a need—emergency rations, if you will. They are the *only* way some among us (who want to) can gain weight; and friends testify that they are an effective last-ditch defense against chocolate truffles. Too much fat, assuredly. But not empty calories. . . .

Use peanut butter that's 100 percent peanuts, and not hydrogenated. The amount you need to use varies somewhat, depending on whether the peanut butter is off the top or bottom of the jar.

🍂

Mix wheat germ, milk, sugar, raisins, salt, and optional ingredients. Add enough peanut butter to make the mixture stiff but not crumbly.

Roll mixture into balls, or press on flat surface by hand or with a rolling pin until it's about ½" thick. Cut into 1½" squares. Cover with coconut or sesame. Store in a covered container in refrigerator.

Makes about 3 dozen bars.

2 cups crunchy peanut butter

⅓ cup toasted wheat germ
½ cup dried skim milk
⅓ cup brown sugar or honey
½ cup raisins
½ teaspoon salt

(chopped dried fruit)
(toasted chopped nuts or sunflower seeds)

¾ cup toasted unsweetened coconut flakes or
¾ cup toasted sesame seeds

The Recommended Daily Allowances

The Recommended Daily Allowances or RDAs are standards for intake of each known nutrient, revised every four or five years by the Food and Nutrition Board of the National Research Council.

The RDAs are frequently referred to but often misunderstood.[1] They are *not* minimum daily requirements which individuals should meet to avoid falling into deficiency; and although the figures appear precise—for example, "2.2 milligrams of B-6 for men, 2.0 for women"—they are estimates based on research data but derived by committees whose members may differ in how the data should be interpreted.

As the Food and Nutrition Board itself emphasizes, the RDAs are "recommendations for the average daily amounts of nutrients that *population groups* should consume over time."[2] One person may need very little vitamin C, another a lot, but the RDA for vitamin C is set high enough statistically to cover almost everyone. Public health measures, such as school lunch programs, can then be pegged to these figures with some confidence that they will be adequate for the great majority of the people for which they are intended.

As individuals, do we have an alternative between taking the RDAs literally and just "making our own decisions"? Mark Hegsted has recommended one: a "nutritious mix of foods" in which any individual's needs for particular nutrients would be roughly proportional to the calories required[3]—in other words, just what we aim at with our Food Guide.

If a person's intake of a given nutrient is consistently below the RDA, that does not necessarily mean that he or she is deficient in that nutrient. "All that can be said is that the further intake falls below the RDA, the greater is the risk of nutritional inadequacy."[4]

[1] C. W. Callaway 1985, "Nutrition," in "Contempo '85" (annual review), Journal of the American Medical Association 254(16):2338–40 (Oct. 25)

[2] Food and Nutrition Board, National Research Council, 1980, Recommended Dietary Allowances, 9th ed. (Washington, D.C.: National Academy of Sciences)

[3] D. M. Hegsted 1986, "Dietary standards: Guidelines for prevention of deficiency or prescription for total health?" Journal of Nutrition 116(3):478–481

[4] A. E. Harper 1986, "Recommended dietary allowances in perspective," Food and Nutrition News 58(2):7–9

Recommended Daily Dietary Allowances (RDA)

Food and Nutrition Board, National Research Council (Revised 1980)*

	Age years	Weight kg	Weight lbs	Height cm	Height in	Energy needs kcal	Protein g	Vit. A[a] RE[b]	Vit. A[a] IU[c]	Vit. D[d] IU	Vit. E[e] TE
Infants	0 – ½	6	13	60	24	kg×115	kg×2.2	420	1400	400	3
	½ – 1	9	20	71	28	kg×105	kg×2.0	400	2000	400	4
Children	1 – 3	13	29	90	35	1300	23	400	2000	400	5
	4 – 6	20	44	112	44	1700	30	500	2500	400	6
	7 – 10	28	62	132	52	2400	34	700	3300	400	7
Men	11 – 14	45	99	157	62	2700	45	1000	5000	400	8
	15 – 18	61	134	176	69	2800	56	1000	5000	400	10
	19 – 22	67	147	177	70	2900	56	1000	5000	400	10
	23 – 50	70	154	178	70	2700	56	1000	5000		10
	51+	70	154	178	70	2400	56	1000	5000		10
Women	11 – 14	44	97	157	62	2200	46	800	4000	400	8
	15 – 18	54	119	163	64	2100	46	800	4000	400	8
	19 – 22	58	128	163	64	2100	44	800	4000	400	8
	23 – 50	58	128	163	64	2000	44	800	4000		8
	51+	58	128	163	64	1800	44	800	4000		8
Pregnant[f]						+300	+30	+200	+1000	400	+2
Lactating[h]						+500	+20	+400	+1000	400	+3

ESTIMATED SAFE & ADEQUATE DAILY DIETARY INTAKES OF SELECTED VITAMINS & MINERALS

Because there is less information on which to base allowances, these figures are not given in the main table of the RDA and are provided here in the form of ranges of recommended intakes.

	Age years	Vit. K µg	Biotin µg	Pantothenic Acid mg	Sodium mg	Potassium mg	Chloride mg
Infants	0 – 0.5	12	35	2	115 – 350	350 – 925	275 – 700
	0.5 – 1	10 – 20	50	3	250 – 750	425 – 1275	400 – 1200
Children	1 – 3	15 – 30	65	3	325 – 975	550 – 1650	500 – 1500
and	4 – 6	20 – 40	85	3 – 4	450 – 1350	775 – 2325	700 – 2100
Adolescents	7 – 10	30 – 60	120	4 – 5	600 – 1800	1000 – 3000	925 – 2775
	11+	50 – 100	100 – 200	4 – 7	900 – 2700	1525 – 4575	1400 – 4200
Adults		70 – 140	100 – 200	4 – 7	1100 – 3300	1875 – 5625	1700 – 5100

* *Allowances are intended to provide for individual variations among most normal persons as they live in the U.S. under usual environmental stresses. Diets should be based on a variety of common foods in order to provide other nutrients for which human requirements have been less well defined.*

[a] *Assumed to be as retinal in milk during first 6 months of life. All later intakes are assumed to be half as retinol and half as beta-carotene when calculated from international units; as retinol equivalents, three fourths are as retinol and one fourth as beta-carotene.*

[b] *Retinol equivalents. One retinol equivalent = 1 µg of retinol of 6 µg of beta-carotene.*

[c] *International units. One international unit of vitamin A activity is equivalent to 0.3 µg of retinol (0.344 µg of retinyl acetate) and 0.6 µg of beta-carotene.*

[d] *As cholecalciferol. 10 µg cholecalciferol = 400 IU vitamin D.*

[e] *D-alpha-tocopherol equivalents. 1 mg d-alpha-tocopherol = 1 mg d-alpha-tocopherol equivalent.*

Vit. C mg	Folacin[f] μg	Niacin[g] mg	Riboflavin mg	Thiamin mg	Vit. B-6 mg	Vit. B-12 μg	Calcium mg	Phosphorus mg	Iodine μg	Iron mg	Magnesium mg	Zinc mg
35	50	6	0.4	0.3	0.3	0.5[h]	360	240	40	10	50	3
35	50	8	0.6	0.5	0.6	1.5	540	360	50	15	70	5
45	100	9	0.8	0.7	0.9	2.0	800	800	70	15	150	10
45	200	11	1.0	0.9	1.3	2.5	800	800	90	10	200	10
45	300	16	1.4	1.2	1.6	3.0	800	800	120	10	250	10
50	400	18	1.6	1.4	1.8	3.0	1200	1200	150	18	350	15
60	400	18	1.7	1.4	2.0	3.0	1200	1200	150	18	400	15
60	400	19	1.7	1.5	2.2	3.0	800	800	150	10	350	15
60	400	18	1.6	1.4	2.2	3.0	800	800	150	10	350	15
60	400	16	1.4	1.2	2.2	3.0	800	800	150	10	350	15
50	400	16	1.3	1.1	1.8	3.0	1200	1200	150	18	300	15
60	400	14	1.3	1.1	2.0	3.0	1200	1200	150	18	300	15
60	400	14	1.3	1.1	2.0	3.0	800	800	150	18	300	15
60	400	13	1.2	1.0	2.0	3.0	800	800	150	18	300	15
60	400	13	1.2	1.0	2.0	3.0	800	800	150	10	300	15
+20	800	+2	+0.3	+0.4	+0.6	+1.0	+400	+400	+25	[i]	+150	+5
+40	600	+5	+0.5	+0.5	+0.5	+1.0	+400	+400	+50	[i]	+150	+10

NOTE: *Since the toxic levels for many trace elements may be only several times usual intakes, the upper levels for the trace elements given on this page should not be habitually exceeded.*

Copper mg	Manganese mg	Fluoride mg	Chromium mg	Selenium mg	Molybdenum mg
0.5 – 0.7	0.5 – 0.7	0.1 – 0.5	0.01 – 0.04	0.01 – 0.04	0.03 – 0.06
0.7 – 1.0	0.7 – 1.0	0.2 – 1.0	0.02 – 0.06	0.02 – 0.06	0.04 – 0.08
1.0 – 1.5	1.0 – 1.5	0.5 – 1.5	0.02 – 0.08	0.02 – 0.08	0.05 – 0.1
1.5 – 2.0	1.5 – 2.0	1.0 – 2.5	0.03 – 0.12	0.03 – 0.12	0.06 – 0.15
2.0 – 2.5	2.0 – 3.0	1.5 – 2.5	0.05 – 0.2	0.05 – 0.2	0.1 – 0.3
2.0 – 3.0	2.5 – 5.0	1.5 – 2.5	0.05 – 0.2	0.05 – 0.2	0.15 – 0.5
2.0 – 3.0	2.5 – 5.0	1.5 – 4.0	0.05 – 0.2	0.05 – 0.2	0.15 – 0.5

[f] *The folacin allowances refer to dietary sources as determined by* Lactobacillus casei *assay after treatment with enzymes ("conjugases") to make polyglutamyl forms of the vitamin available to the test organism.*

[g] *1* NE *(niacin equivalent) = 1 mg of niacin or 60 mg of dietary tryptophan.*

[h] *The* RDA *for vitamin B-12 in infants is based on average concentration of the vitamin in human milk. The allowances after weaning are based on energy intake (as recommended by the American Academy of Pediatrics) and consideration of other factors such as intestinal absorption.*

[i] *The increased requirement during pregnancy cannot be met by the iron content of habitual American diets nor by the existing iron stores of many women; therefore the use of 30–60 mg of supplemental iron is recommended. Iron needs during lactation are not substantially different from those of pregnant women, but continued supplementation of the mother 2–3 months after parturition is advisable in order to replenish storers depleted by pregnancy.*

[331]

The Micronutrient Universe: Vitamins

	Rich Sources	Function in Body	Helpful Factors	Harmful Factors
Vitamin A	Green and yellow vegetables, fruits, whole milk	Health of skin and mucous membranes, formation of bones and teeth, night vision		
Vitamin D	Egg yolk, sunlight, vitamin D fortified milk	Regulates metabolism of calcium and phosphorus	Exposure to sunlight produces vitamin D in our skin	Living in a dark environment or in mos kinds of artificial light
Vitamin E	Vegetable oils, nuts and seeds, whole grains	Antioxidant—protects tissues against "free radicals"	Selenium enhances the antioxidant effects of vitamin E	Air pollution, ionizing radiation. Need increa with increased intake polyunsaturated fats.
Vitamin K	Green vegetables, cauliflower	Necessary for blood clotting		Loss of gut bacteria through prolonged antibiotic treatment
Vitamin C	Citrus fruit, berries, melon, green vegetables, tomatoes, potatoes	Hydrogen transport, collagen formation, wound healing, antioxidant	Better preserved in acid foods and beverages	Easily destroyed by he alkalis, oxygen. Infection, smoking, a stress decrease amoun body
Thiamin (B-1)	Yeast, whole grains, legumes	Conversion of carbohydrates, protein, and fat to energy		Easily destroyed in food handling, leachir heat and alkalis, and refining of grains
Riboflavin (B-2)	Milk, yeast, green vegetables, legumes	Metabolism of fats, carbohydrates, protein, enzyme component	Protect milk and other sources from light	Easily destroyed by light, or lost by leachir need is increased by or contraceptives
Niacin	Legumes, whole grains, green vegetables, milk, coffee	Essential for turning carbohydrates, fats, and protein into energy	The amino acid tryptophan is converted to niacin; alkalis help release otherwise unavailable niacin in corn; very stable to heat	Leaching losses if cooking water is discarded
Pyridoxine (B-6)	Whole grains, legumes, carrots, eggs, bananas	Protein metabolism; making red blood cells and nerve tissue	Need is proportional to protein intake	Need is increased by carbon monoxide exposure, oral contraceptive use, and excess protein

[332]

Deficiency Symptoms	Notes on Toxicity	Notes	
Night blindness, blindness, stunted growth	Only from supplements. Headache, vomiting, peeling of skin, diarrhea, blurred vision, loss of hair	Provitamin A intake from vegetables asociated with reduced cancer risks. Vegetarians usually get large amounts in normal diet. Vegetable provitamin is safe; animal form (in pills) highly toxic in excess.	**Vitamin A**
Rickets (bone deformation due to lack of mineralization); growth failure in children, osteomalacia (adult rickets)	Depositing of calcium in blood vessels and kidneys	This vitamin/hormone is responsible for more cases of serious poisoning due to overdose than any other supplement. The body can regulate its own production; exposure to sunlight alone can never cause toxic buildup. Some researchers feel RDA should be expressed as quantity of ultraviolet light exposure.	**Vitamin D**
Very rare—red blood cell fragility leading to anemia	Excess bleeding in some people; formation of blood clots in others. Not very toxic	Very difficult to produce vitamin E deficiency symptoms in adults, but premature infants definitely need extra amounts. Be wary of claims that vitamin E slows aging, heals scars, or cures heart disease.	**Vitamin E**
Blood doesn't clot—hemorrhage		Name comes from German word for "clotting factor." About one-half our vitamin K need is produced in the intestines by microorganisms. Plenty of vitamin K in normal intake of fresh vegetables.	**Vitamin K**
Scurvy, spongy and bleeding gums, restlessness, joint pain, poor wound healing	Urinary stones in some people, acid stomach from pills	**Vegetarians usually have high vitamin C intake from vegetables and fruit. Guinea pigs, fruit-bats, and several primates, including humans, need a dietary source; all other animals and even insects make their own.**	**Vitamin C**
Mild: reduced stamina, depression, irritability. Severe: beriberi, weight loss, mental breakdown		Deficiency was little known before widespread refining of grains. One of four nutrients added back to white flour in enrichment formula. Alcoholics often deficient. Fever increases metabolic rate and need for thiamin.	**Thiamin (B-1)**
Irritated, watery, bloodshot eyes, scaly rash on face, cracking at corners of mouth, purple tongue		People who avoid milk need alternate sources of riboflavin. Deficiency is not life-threatening, but probably not rare even in U.S. Along with physical symptoms, depression and hypochondria can result.	**Riboflavin (B-2)**
Mild: irritability, insomnia, sore tongue. Severe: diarrhea, dementia, dermatitis, death	"Niacin flush" (hot, prickly skin occurring directly after niacin dose), upset stomach, diarrhea, abnormal liver function	See Goldberger story on page 336. "Niacin flush" is caused by dilating blood vessels in face; this same ability to open up small blood vessels makes niacin a useful drug against angina, when blood supply to heart is constricted.	**Niacin**
Mild: anemia, sore mouth. Severe: dizziness, nausea, confusion, anemia, convulsions	Neurological damage and abnormalities	Considered low in average U.S. diets. Low B-6 in tissues is associated with heart and blood vessel disease. Major B-6 losses in processing are not replaced in "enrichment." Several medical uses.	**Pyridoxine (B-6)**

	Rich Sources	Function in Body	Helpful Factors	Harmful Factors
Folacin	Dark green vegetables, legumes, nuts, fresh oranges, whole wheat	DNA, RNA synthesis	Raw salads	Destroyed by lengthy cooking, holding at high temperatures, and long storage
Cobalamine (B-12)	Milk, eggs	DNA, RNA synthesis	Need is proportional to protein intake	Malabsorption in certain disease states, such as pernicious anemia
Pantothenic acid	Whole grains, legumes	Needed in cell conversions of food to energy	Widely distributed in whole foods	Removed in refining of foods

Minerals

	Rich Sources	Function in Body	Helpful Factors	Harmful Factors
Calcium	Dairy products: milk, yogurt. Leafy greens: broccoli, kale.	Bone and tooth formation, coagulation of blood, muscle contraction	Lactose; vitamin D and sunlight; keeping phosphorus intake low to moderate	Phytic acid, oxalic acid, excess dietary protein
Phosphorus	Milk, cheese, nuts, cereals, legumes	Bone and tooth structure, part of body's "energy coin" used in all energy-releasing reactions		
Magnesium	Nuts, legumes, whole grains, dark leafy greens, milk	Bone and tooth structure, nerve conduction, muscle relaxation, bowel function	Normal zinc intake	
Iron	Legumes, whole grains, potatoes, egg yolk, cocoa, green vegetables, dried fruits	Oxygen transport; part of hemoglobin, myoglobin, cellular enzymes	Absorption improved by vitamin C, cooking in iron pots, iron deficiency	Phytic acid
Iodine	Sea vegetables; plant foods in general, but highly variable depending on soil	Regulates energy metabolism, is part of thyroid hormone, involved in cellular oxidation and growth	Phytic acid, black tea, coffee	
Zinc	Eggs, nuts, cereals; wheat germ is especially rich	Essential for more than 100 enzymes involved in growth, sexual maturation, wound healing, ability to taste, protein synthesis, immunity	Normal copper intake	Phytic acid, excess copper intake

Deficiency Symptoms	Notes on Toxicity	Notes	
lor; sore, red tongue; cking at corners of uth; diarrhea; galoblastic anemia		Works with B-12 and can substitute for it partially. Tends to be richly present in the vegetarian diet, to the extent that it can mask anemia of B-12 deficiency. Oral contraceptives lower stores.	**Folacin**
re, glossy tongue; estive disorders; vous system damage		People who avoid all animal products need alternate sources of vitamin B-12. Humans require miniscule amount, and the body conserves B-12 very well; so deficiency, while serious, takes many years to develop.	**Cobalamine (B-12)**
tigue, sleep turbances, nausea, paired coordination	·	Name signifies "found everywhere"; isolated deficiencies found only in experimental situations. Few rich sources; evenly distributed in whole foods.	**Pantothenic acid**
unted growth, rickets, eomalacia	Calcium deposits in soft tissues, urinary stones in susceptible people	May protect against hypertension. Action often complemented by that of magnesium, as in muscle contraction and relaxation. Most "hard water" is rich in dissolved calcium salts.	**Calcium**
akness, osteomalacia ult rickets), decreased rt function, neuro-ical problems		Too much in standard U.S. diets, from soft drinks and meat. Lecithin, a phosporus-containing fat, once touted as a health food, is broken down in digestion, none is needed in the diet.	**Phosphorus**
owth failure, avioral disturbances, mor, weakness, zures	Diarrhea	May protect against heart disease. Action often complemented by that of calcium, as in muscle contraction and relaxation. Most "hard water" is rich in dissolved magnesium salts.	**Magnesium**
emia, pallor, akness, reduced mune function; yet blood iron *protects* inst certain types of ection	Hemochromatosis, iron deposits in soft tissues	Lost from body whenever blood is lost. Excess (from supplements) can cause constipation. Black tea with meals reduces iron absorption by some 60 percent, coffee reduces it 40 percent. Meat iron is very well absorbed, yet anemia is less prevalent among established vegetarians compared to general population.	**Iron**
iter, cretinism irth defect)	Depression of thyroid activity, hyperthyroidism in susceptible individuals	Iodization of salt virtually eliminated goiter in the U.S. Iodine is now added to bakery products and other processed foods, so today toxicity is a more likely problem than deficiency.	**Iodine**
riasis-type rash, wth retardation, slow und healing, delayed perty, abnormal taste, s of taste, abnormal se of smell	Most cases of zinc poisoning result from putting fruit drinks in galvanized steel containers such as buckets	Vegetarians get less zinc than omnivores, and nonmeat zinc is less available to the body. For balance, best to use *foods* for extra zinc rather than supplements: excess zinc interferes with absorption of magnesium and alters the blood's zinc-to-copper ratio, which affects how the body handles cholesterol.	**Zinc**

	Rich Sources	Function in Body	Helpful Factors	Harmful Factors
Copper	Nuts, legumes, whole grains, drinking water	Aids in body's use of iron in hemoglobin synthesis, part of many enzymes in protein fibers and skin pigments	Normal zinc intake	Calcium decreases absorption, requireme increased by excessive zinc
Manganese	Nuts, whole grains, legumes, tea, fruits, non-leafy vegetables	Glucose utilization, enzyme activator, role in synthesis of cholesterol and polysaccharides	Minimal refining	Refining of grains
Fluoride	Naturally or artificially fluoridated water, some kinds of black tea	Included in teeth and bones, effective against dental caries, may reduce osteoporosis		
Chromium	Brewer's yeast, whole grains	Part of "GTF" complex which maintains normal glucose tolerance	Minimal refining	High intake of refined sugar and refined flour products
Selenium	Protein-rich plant foods; however, amount in plants is highly variable depending on soils	Cellular antioxidant, essential constituent of red blood cell enzymes, decreases the toxicity of heavy metals, may inhibit cancer initiation	Wide variety of foods to make up for soil lack in any one area	
Molybdenum	Whole grains and legumes (varies greatly with soils)	Enzyme constituent		Refining of grains
Potassium	Most fruits, starchy root vegetables, dark leafy green vegetables	Main electrolyte inside all body cells	Virtually all fruits and vegetables contain good amounts	Thiazide diuretics increase the loss of potassium in urine
Sodium	Salt: plenty of sodium in food without adding any	Main electrolyte outside all body cells, in the fluid bathing body tissues		Heavy exercise or labo in very hot weather car lead to excess sodium l in sweat

[336]

Symptoms	Notes on Toxicity	Notes	
Pallor, infants' anemia, Manke's kinky hair syndrome	Wilson's disease (neurologic problems and liver damage), vomiting	Copper deficiency is unknown outside of starvation, unusual diseases, or experimental laboratories. Intake in this country may be excessive due to the widespread use of copper pipes in plumbing.	**Copper**
Impaired growth, weakness in animals; not well defined in humans.	Generalized disease of nervous system. Least toxic of trace elements.	Manganese-deficient plants do not grow well, so natural deficiency in humans is highly unlikely unless most foods in the diet are overrefined.	**Manganese**
Higher frequency of tooth decay and possibly osteoporosis	Mottling of teeth, increased bone density, neurological disturbances.	Not yet shown to be essential, though helpful in reducing cavities. People who live where water is low in fluoride should seek alternate sources.	**Fluoride**
Impaired glucose metabolism	Low order of toxicity	Can help prevent the loss of blood sugar control that accompanies aging. Best absorbed from natural sources. Hexavalent (Cr^{++++++}) form found in industrial wastes is highly toxic, the trivalent form (Cr^{+++}) is one of the least toxic of ions and an essential nutrient.	**Chromium**
Heart muscle damage; general muscle pain; associated with Keshan disease (heart muscle disease affecting children), hemolytic anemia	Agricultural wastes endanger wildlife with toxicity in U.S.; in humans toxicity results in hair and nail loss, garlic breath, vomiting, labored breathing	Adequate selenium intake from foods is associated with lower cancer risk. Plants need no selenium but pick it up if present in soil. Acts in concert with vitamin E as an antioxidant. Enhances immunity and protects cell membranes and DNA from oxidation and heavy metals, which may explain cancer protection.	**Selenium**
	Gout-like syndrome reported; high intake results in loss of copper	Needed for making uric acid, a protein waste product. Gout, involving excess uric acid, has been associated with high molybdenum intake. Excess wastes copper.	**Molybdenum**
Lassitude, muscle weakness, polyuria	Muscular weakness, arrhythmia, heart failure	Protects against hypertension. Risky to take pills without medical supervision: chronic toxicity is very dangerous to health. Amounts in foods are safe.	**Potassium**
Muscle weakness, cramps, confusion, apathy, anorexia, low blood pressure	High blood pressure, edema, heart failure	Associated with hypertension (high blood pressure), though not in all. Even very high blood pressure can be brought down by strenuous salt restriction; milder restriction helps blood pressure medications work better. Processed foods and fast foods generally contain large amounts of sodium.	**Sodium**

E

SOURCES: *R. S. Goodhart & M. E. Shils, eds., Modern Nutrition in Health and Disease, 6th ed. (Philadelphia: Lea & Febiger, 1980); J. Weininger & G. M. Briggs, Nutrition Update, vol. 1 (N.Y.: Wiley, 1983), vol. 2 (Wiley, 1985);*

W. R. Faulkner, "Trace elements in laboratory medicine," Laboratory Management July 1981:21–35; "Trace elements in human nutrition," Dairy Council Digest 53(1):1–6 (Jan.-Feb. 1982)

Index

This symbol marks recipes that require dairy products.

Leeks, 200
Leftovers
in Good Shepherd's Pie, **268**
refreshing of leftover bread loaves, 86
tortillas, 275
Legumes, 14, 40, 43, 278
flatulence associated with, 43, 292–93
See also Beans
Lemon Butter, **249**
uses for, 179, 183
Lemon juice, 127, 229
Lemon-Parsley Dressing, **130**
Lentil Nut Loaf, **306**
Lentils, 296–97
cooking of, 280, 296
and flatulence, 293
flavorings for, 296
red, 297
sprouts from, 120, 125
uses for, 296
RECIPES
Greek Lentil Soup, **167**
Lentil Nut Loaf, **306**
Rice Lentil Polou, **305**
Lettuce, 124, 125
Light and Bright Cereal, **87**
Lighter Whole-Wheat Piecrust, **273**
Light Rye Bread, **71**
Lima beans, 280, 297
RECIPES
Butter Bean Soup, **297**
Hearty Pea Soup, **167**
Lipoxidase, 106
Longevity, 99
Low fat, diet achieving, 28
Lunch, 109–21
Fruited Yogurt for, 312
homemade carry-out suggestions for, 110–11, 139, 143, 222
menus, 17

Macaroni, Sandy's, **258**
Magnesium, 334
in fresh fruit, 44
in nuts and seeds, 43
RDA for, 330
Maloshyam, 15, **220**
Manhattan Corn Chowder, **161**
Margarine, 249
alternatives for, 90, 93
RECIPE
Yeast Butter, 249
Margarita's Salsa, **236**
Marinades, 128
Masala Dosas, **97**
Masala, garam, 233
Masala Potatoes, **97**

Mashed Potatoes, 204–5
Mayonnaise, 111
Homemade Mayonnaise, **240**
Tofu Mayonnaise, 111, **241**
McGill University, 210
Meat, 32
substitutes for, 194, 298, 299
Men, RDA for, 330
Menus, 17–21, 277
Metabolism, 45-46
Metals, heavy
and sea vegetables, 210
Metchnikoff, Elie, 99
Mexican foods, 276–77
flavoring blends for, 231, 232
RECIPES
Burrito, **277**
Chillaquillas, **275**
Entomatada, **277**
Mexican Salad Bowl, **135**
Mexican-style Tomato Sauce, **248**
Quesadilla, **277**
Tacos, **277**
Tortilla Chips, **276**
Tostada, 221, **277**
Mexican Salad Bowl, **135**
Mexican-style Tomato Sauce, **248**
Microorganisms, intestinal, 292
Microwave ovens, 86, 110, 171, 279
Middle Eastern Vegetables, **227**
Milk
alternative for, 36, 105
blood cholesterol levels reduced by, 100
in breads, 65
compared with soymilk, 105, 108
cultured, 99–100, 104
nutrients in, 105
scalded, 65
Milk, powdered, 101–104
Milk, soy. *See* Soymilk
Millet, 287
adzuki beans served with, 296
in breads, 51
for breakfast, 287
cooking time for, 280
cooking tips for, 287
Mills, home. *See* Grinders, home
Mills, roller, 357–58
Mince Pie, Mock, **325**
Minerals, 334–337
in potatoes, 205
in raw leafy greens, 124
loss on refining flour, 24
released by fermentation in breadmaking, 47
Minestrone, **153**
Mint Chutney, **237**
Mint Chutney/Raita, **239**

Minty Dressing, Bright, **132**
Miso, 100, 164–65, 299
bacteria in, 164
as a coffee sustitute, 165
digestibility of, 293
gravy made from, 165
salt in, 164
Miso Soup, **164–65**
noodles in, 251
Misto, 136
Mock Mince Pie, **325**
Mock Rarebit, **119**
Mock Sour Cream, **240**
uses, 152, 178, 182, 223, 242, 277
Moderation, 25
Molded salads
Summer Fruit Mold, **323**
Tomato Aspic, **142**
Molds
on peanuts, 91
on soybean sprouts, 121
Moong Dal, **297**
MSG, 232, 234
kombu as a sustitute for, 148, 211
Muffins, quick
Apple Bran Muffins, **80**
Cinnamuffins, **80**
Lynne's Muffins, **81**
Poppyseed Muffins, **79**
Muffins, yeast
English, **74–75**
Everyone's, **78**
Puffs, **77**
Mung beans, 293, 297
sprouts from, 120, 121, 204
RECIPES
Chinese Peppers and Sprouts, **204**
Kichadi, **305**
Mushroom Filling, **263**
Mushrooms
cleaning of, 199
RECIPES
Gravy, **249**
Mushroom Filling, **263**
Mushrooms Petaluma, **228**
Spinach and Mushroom Salad, **135**
Stroganoff Sauce, **244**
Mustard Sauce, Sweet and Sour, **242**
Mustard seeds
sprouts from, 120
See also Black mustard seeds

Nasturtiums, 124
National Research Council
on RDA for protein, 329
on pesticides, 223
Navy Bean and Cashew Salad, **135**

LAUREL'S KITCHEN RECIPES
*was designed and packaged by Laurel and her friends
for publication by Ten Speed Press. The text type is
Plantin with titles in Centaur and Arrighi. The production was managed by Terry; Bob did the pasteup;
Victor did the beautiful woodcut on the cover and title
page; the rest were done by Laurel who otherwise, as
usual, informed the whole operation. For all who
contributed to* THE NEW LAUREL'S KITCHEN
and LAUREL'S KITCHEN RECIPES, *the books are
a labor of love. We hope this new, smaller
edition will prove handy and useful
in your kitchen.*